Easy-Walking Europe

Tips and Suggested Tours for the (Somewhat) Mobility Impaired

2020

Compact Edition

by Elizabeth Bingham

World Prospect Press
Waverly, Iowa

Publisher's Note

This book is designed to help prepare travelers for their trips abroad. Its purpose is to educate and entertain. It is sold with the understanding that the publisher and author are not giving legal or financial advice. The author and World Prospect Press shall have neither liability nor responsibility to any person or entity with respect to any loss or damage caused, or alleged to be caused, directly or indirectly, by the information contained in this book.

If you do not wish to be bound by the above, you may return this book with sales receipt to the publisher for a full refund.

Copyright ©2020 by Elizabeth R. Bingham

Compact Edition
3rd Printing

All rights reserved. No part of this book may be reproduced or transmitted in any form or by any means, electronic or mechanical, including photocopying, recording or by any information storage and retrieval system, without written permission from the author, except for the inclusion of brief quotations in a review.

World Prospect Press
Waverly, IA, USA
www.worldprospect.com
mail@worldprospect.com

Table of Contents

Introduction	6
Who this book is for	8
Physical challenges of Europe	9
How to minimize the challenges	12
Packaged tours	16
General tips	19
Getting your trip off the ground	22
Suggested tours	35
Edinburgh	37
Possible plan	37
Arrival	40
Easy transportation options	41
Other in-city transportation	42
Sightseeing passes	43
Day trips	44
Lodging	53
Other base cities	56
Dublin	57
Possible plan	57
Arrival	60
Easy transportation options	61
Other in-city transportation	63
Sightseeing passes	65
Day trips	66
Lodging	73
Other base cities	80
London	81
Possible plan	81
Arrival	86
Easy transportation options	87
Other in-city transportation	92
Sightseeing passes	96

Day trips	99
Lodging	106
Other base cities	115
Amsterdam	**116**
Possible plan	116
Arrival	120
Easy transportation options	121
Other in-city transportation	124
Sightseeing passes	127
Day trips	128
Lodging	134
Other base cities	143
Paris	**144**
Possible plan	144
Arrival	148
Easy transportation options	148
Other in-city transportation	153
Sightseeing passes	155
Day trips	155
Lodging	167
Other base cities	177
Madrid	**178**
Possible plan	178
Arrival	180
Easy transportation options	182
Other in-city transportation	185
Sightseeing passes	187
Day trips	189
Lodging	196
Other base cities	207
Rome	**208**
Possible plan	208
Arrival	212
Easy transportation options	213
Other in-city transportation	220
Sightseeing passes	221
Day trips	223
Lodging	233
Other base cities	244

Vienna ... 245
    Possible plan ... 246
    Arrival ... 249
    Easy transportation options ... 251
    Other in-city transportation ... 256
    Sightseeing passes ... 257
    Day trips ... 260
    Lodging ... 267
    Other base cities ... 274

Munich ... 275
    Possible plan ... 275
    Arrival ... 278
    Easy transportation options ... 279
    Other in-city transportation ... 282
    Sightseeing passes ... 284
    Day trips ... 286
    Lodging ... 299
    Other base cities ... 307

Acknowledgments ... 308

Italian Survival Guide ... 310

French Survival Guide ... 312

German Survival Guide ... 314

Italian Dictionary with Phrases for Travelers ... 316

French Twist ... 318

German Shepherd ... 320

Excerpt, *German Shepherd* ... 322

Excerpt, *French Twist* ... 330

Introduction

In July 2017, my mother and I went on a guided tour of England. It was luxurious travel, compared to what I was used to. We were driven around on a comfortable motor coach. Our luggage was delivered to our rooms and picked up again in the morning. We had delicious three-course dinners more nights than not, often conveniently located in our nice hotels.

And yet, the tour was exhausting for my mother. With city walking tours and guided country estate tours and lengthy museum wanders, it was physically demanding for someone not used to being physically active and suffering the common aches and pains of the passing years.

But my mom had a good time regardless of those drawbacks, a good enough time that she soon decided that she wanted to travel to Scotland and investigate the home of her ancestors. And I wanted to go, too, but I was determined to make the trip as physically easy for her as I could, so she could enjoy the new sights and activities but, I hoped, not end up tired and sore by the end of the day.

And that's how this approach to travel started for me. With the goal of making European travel more manageable and enjoyable for my mom.

When others heard about my plans, they said, "Oh, I would love to do that!" and "Oh, my gosh! I need to know that for my parents!" and "You need to write a book about that!" And I realized that lots and lots of people with somewhat limited mobility (and their children) could use a guide to help them plan their European trips. And thus this book was born.

Disclaimer

The material covered in this book is highly changeable. Bus routes change. Addresses change (Web and real-world). Prices change. Tour offerings change. Opening times change. And often these changes occur suddenly and unexpectedly. While every effort was made to confirm that the information in these pages was correct at the time of final edits, there will certainly be changes by the time you read this.

If you use this book as inspiration for your own trip, any changes are probably not a problem. If you want to loosely follow what I suggest, that's also probably not a problem. But if you want to follow suggested itineraries exactly as written, you really need to double check information before relying on it. I'm sorry details aren't more permanent than they are, but there you have it. Life changes, and all we can do is try to keep up.

Who this book is for

This book is for my mother. Or, rather, it's for people *like* my mother, who are fully mobile, but not as mobile as they used to be or would like to be. Many people—like my mom—still get around fine but can't walk as far or as fast as they used to, and stairs can take a while.

Those are the challenges this book is designed to help with. It assumes that travelers can walk and manage stairs—just in moderation and in their own time. People who fall into this category are sometimes called "slow walkers," and they should find much to help them here.

Individuals with more extensive mobility limitations, say, those who need walkers or are wheelchair-bound, would benefit from more specific guidance than this book can supply. There are resources to provide this additional information, such as the following:

The Society for Accessible Travel and Hospitality, www.sath.org/
Sage Traveling, www.sagetraveling.com/
Wheelchair Travel, wheelchairtravel.org/europe/
Smarter Travel, www.smartertravel.com/disabled-travel/
Gimp On the Go, www.gimponthego.com/

These resources are just a start. Most of them list *other* resources you can check out, and an Internet search on the terms "accessible travel Europe" (or similar) should lead to even more helpful links.

Physical challenges of Europe

Traveling anywhere can be difficult at times, but Europe has a lot of physical challenges to throw at us that the average American probably isn't used to.

Topography

First off, a lot of the most beautiful, most picturesque places to visit are hilly. All those lovely Tuscan villages? Hills. Ancient Edinburgh? Hills. The Rhine River Valley? Hills. Rome? Hills, hills, hills. Fortunately, not every town and city is hilly, and even in hilly destinations, we can minimize the climbing, but it *is* something to keep in mind if you're not in condition to scamper up and down inclines throughout the day.

Construction

European towns, cities, and buildings were not built to be handicapped accessible, and retrofitting buildings is expensive and often impractical. Thus, Old World construction is another challenge.

Handicap accessibility just didn't enter the picture during the Middle Ages and most of the time since (or before). Consequently, European construction, however charming, can be a nightmare for people with physical limitations. Be prepared for crooked and uneven pavements, streets, floors in buildings, and stairs both indoors and out. Rounded cobblestones, in addition to being literal stumbling blocks, can also be dangerously slippery when wet. There are also examples galore of narrow hallways and doors, awkward and cramped bathrooms and bedrooms, and, very often, no elevators in multi-story buildings.

Unlike in the United States, where you can often drive right up to a building and park nearby, much of what we want to see in Europe is in the oldest part of a city, which tends to be narrow, twisty, crowded, and often pedestrian-only. Even if you drive and park in a designated area for the city center, you will still likely have to walk a great deal to see the sights. Often even taxis are not allowed into parts of many Old Cities, which may not be disastrous for your touring, but if you're hauling luggage to an Old City hotel, you'll feel the inconvenience

And if you take a city walking tour? Be prepared to hoof it for a couple of hours, sometimes on cobblestones, possibly up and down hills and stairs.

Public transportation

Lastly, European transportation can also be tiring and difficult. Public transport—trains, buses, subways, trams—is a wonderful option for traveling like a local, but make no mistake—it's also work to use it. If your idea of transportation involves walking to the garage, driving your car to work or the mall, parking, and then walking a short distance into the building, you might not appreciate how physically demanding public transportation can be.

Taking any public transportation requires getting *to* that transportation—to the bus stop, to the train station, to the subway platform. All those usually require considerable walking, which is no problem if you are fit and mobile, but can quickly take its toll if you are not. Subway systems, in particular, can be hidden sources of exhaustion. Rarely does one walk down a flight of stairs and find a train platform right there.

Rather, there are usually several flights to descend—often on stairs—and long subterranean walks before you get to stand on the platform until the train arrives. Then you jostle on board with the rest of the crowd, very likely having to stand for the trip, grabbing a bar or strap if one is within reach, swaying and lurching with every turn and variation of speed, trying not to stumble or fall, and suffering through the heat and underground smells, if it is summer.

When you reach your stop, you have to shove your way through the crowd to the door and hustle off before the next group of riders starts pushing its way on. Then you face further long walks through tunnels, various marches up flights of stairs (sometimes with escalators and probably some handicapped elevator access), before you can reemerge at street level and then walk to wherever your next stage is. Think I'm exaggerating? The Visit London Web site actually warns of how physically difficult it can be to use the Underground system, and London is hardly alone in this.

It is hard, grubby work to ride public transportation, and if you have luggage with you, that doubles the difficulty.

Private transportation

What about renting a car, then? That can be a fabulous option for getting around, under certain circumstances, but there are still cautions to keep in mind. In Great Britain, of course, cars drive on the left side of the road, and every time you'd normally turn to the right (into a roundabout, for example), you need to turn left. Fortunately, Continental Europe drives on the right side of the road, as we Americans are used to. Hopefully you know how to drive a manual transmission car, because the vast majority of European cars have a stick shift.

Additionally, if you've never driven in Europe before, you may not be prepared for the stress of it. Other drivers can be very aggressive, traffic can be dense and fast-moving, route markings can be confusing, road signs are not always easily visible or understandable, minor roads can be frighteningly narrow, city parking can be confounding, elusive, and expensive, and drunken driving laws are very strict.

There are cases where driving a private car makes a lot of sense (getting and staying off the beaten path), but it's not for everyone in every situation.

How to minimize the challenges

So, how can you visit Europe without expending most of your energy on those challenges—hills, non-accessible construction and infrastructure, long walks, tiring public transportation, and stressful car driving and parking?

The obvious, overriding answer to minimizing the physical challenges of visiting Europe is to research, research, research! With the Internet, we have so much information at our fingertips that you can usually research your options—often in great detail—ahead of time from the comfort of your home computer. As a starting point, you have the advice and example tours of this book. For now, let's look at dealing with those previously listed challenges one at a time.

Topography and construction—Minimizing impacts

There is no changing the hills of Italy or Scotland, and we really wouldn't want to, because they lend so much character and charm to those places (and many others) and are a large part of why we visit those countries. But there's no denying that hills can be a problem if you have some limited mobility. Given that you can't change the hills, the best you can do is to try to avoid climbing up or down them. What does that mean?

This is where preparation is vital—we can't avoid all the uneven and narrow constructions in Europe but we can at least base in an easier-to-manage hotel in a convenient neighborhood so the physical demands of negotiating the Old World are just a minor part of the day, not a constant travail.

Look for a hotel in a flat location near the main transportation points you plan to use. You want to be able to walk around your home base area with as little discomfort as possible. You are likely to shop around there, visit restaurants, and come and go from your local transportation. I've made suggestions for each city covered in this book for promising areas to stay, as well as some specific lodging possibilities to consider in each city.

Public transportation—Alternatives

Hey, I am all for public transportation and ride it when I visit a city, but there's no denying that considerable effort is usually involved. If you prefer not to walk sometimes long distances above or below ground, not to have to crowd on to buses or train cars, not to have to climb and descend many (often many, many!) steps, you need to consider alternative ways of getting around a city.

The easiest solution is to ride taxis wherever you want to go, but that is an expensive option. A more affordable mode of transportation is a designated tourist bus. Most tourist cities have fleets of hop-on/hop-off buses (sometimes several companies), which provide a good balance between convenience and cost. The buses follow set routes near the major sights of the city, stopping to let riders off and on near those sights.

Buses follow a frequent schedule, and during the tourist season, you can count on them to come by several times an hour. (You may need to wait for more than one bus during the busiest times. This can also be the case with public transportation, however.) This still requires you to board a bus, but you'll do it with other tourists, not impatient locals. You buy a ticket for usually one or two days, and that allows you to get on and off the buses as many times as you'd like during that time period. Or maybe you'd like to ride the bus loop around a few times just looking at things and listening to the commentary. That's fine, too.

It's possible that you can find a local bus that does much the same thing, one that swings by major landmarks of the city. You could also ride that around, probably at considerably less expense, but also less convenience, as the bus is more likely to be crowded, will not include commentary, and probably won't have an upper observation deck, as most hop-on/hop-off buses do. You will probably have a fairly short time limit on your single-use bus ticket, too. However, if your goal is to keep costs down, the right local bus *can* get you to the places you want to go, and most cities have reasonably priced day tickets for public transportation use. (And, to be honest, not all hop-on/hop-off buses get strong enough ratings that I would want to use them. In those cases, I might use public transportation, but probably just above ground—buses and trams.)

Private transportation—Alternatives

Cars are largely worthless for seeing sights *in* a city, but they can be very convenient for day trips or moving from town to town. If you're willing to hassle with the parking and the often stressful driving, it is certainly handy to drive where you want to, when you want to, with as much luggage as you care to pack in. If you *don't* want to hassle with the parking and the stressful driving and the expense of having a car, you do have other options.

For day trips, most cities have companies that specialize in bus trips to the most popular and interesting sights within a day's drive (or sometimes 2, 3, or more days). You can line up one or several of these, possibly for less than the price of car rental, fuel, insurance, and parking fees. If you have a larger group or want to see things on your own, it's also possible to arrange private tours out into the countryside or to other cities, usually in a minivan or a minibus. These options allow you easy point-to-point transportation (you can even arrange pickup at your hotel), a knowledgeable local guide, and efficient use of your time compared to taking public transportation or trying to drive yourself around.

Experiencing the day with like-minded tourists on a group tour can add to the fun. Some of these tours include entrance fees into the sights and some don't, so pay attention to that if you are comparing them. A day trip that does *not* include entrance fees may, in fact, be more desirable, because it gives you the option of, say, paying to take the castle tour (lots of walking, probably lots of stairs) *or* instead taking a short walk around the grounds or shopping in the village and then having a nice cup of coffee before your group gathers to continue. (*You* get to make the call.)

I have taken bus day trips and found them to be an effective and enjoyable way to get out into the countryside, but I recommend not booking them for more than two consecutive days. Even with someone else doing the driving, being on the go for the whole day is tiring. Two days in a row are fine. More than that can be wearisome. Schedule an open day in your base city to recharge your batteries before heading out on more day trips. And while I love the intimacy and efficiency of small-group minibuses, do be aware that their seats can be uncomfortably narrow for wider Americans (and there are many of us). If there is a single seat on one side of the aisle (as opposed to two seats together), it's easier to manipulate the seatbelt and to buckle in than when shoved in against another seat.

As for driving between cities, as you will see later in this book, I suggest minimizing city-to-city transportation for simplicity and ease. You may choose to base entirely in one city and then radiate out using established day trips. This avoids having to pack and move between hotels and minimizes having to haul luggage (which acquired the name of "luggage" for a reason).

If you want to extend your trip to more than one city base, then I would use the train or a city-to-city bus to travel between them, but with some considerations. 1) Plan on taking plenty of time to do it. If you are rushed to make a tight schedule, your change of location and lodging will be that much more difficult. 2) If hauling your own luggage to the train or bus station will sap your strength more than you'd care for, this is a good time to line up a cab. Yes, there is additional expense, but conserving your energy so you can enjoy your trip makes sense, especially when the trip itself surely cost a lot.

You may, of course, choose to drive yourself from city to city, and there is certainly nothing wrong with that, as long as you realize the challenges as well as the advantages of doing so.

What about flying? If you are planning to travel a considerable distance between cities, flying may be a desirable option, or even the only reasonable one. Just be aware that European flights are every bit as unpleasant as American ones but have the advantage of usually being short.

There are usually some sort of shuttle services to transport you to and from the airport. If you arrange a private shuttle, the driver can pick you and your luggage up at the hotel and deposit you at the right part of the airport for your flight. If you line up private transport from the hotel (or a hotel desk worker does it for you), make sure you have the name of the company, in case your ride doesn't show up at the expected time and you need to investigate.

You can certainly find bus, train, or subway options for getting to the airport, as well, if you want to travel more like a local, but you are adding to your workload for the day if you choose those modes of transportation. That may be just fine, but be aware of the tradeoffs.

Conversely, you could use a taxi to take you to the airport (and pick you up at the other end), but you will usually pay considerably more for that convenience. You may decide that it's well worth it, however, to make the drudgery part of travel less burdensome.

However you get to the airport, make sure you know what you are getting into with your flight. European flights tend to have very strict luggage limits (by size and weight), and if you like to take a lot with you, you will certainly pay for at least one checked bag and very possibly more. You want to be clear on all restrictions *before* you book your flight, because it can cost more to pay for extra luggage at check-in than it does when you buy your ticket.

Packaged tours

Not everyone wants to go on their own to Europe, making their own arrangements and traveling independently. There are many pre-arranged, packaged tour options for seeing the Old World with less work on your part, but be prepared to pay more for the convenience.

Group bus tours

One option, if you have the funds and want to make your trip-planning as easy as possible, is to look for a guided tour that specializes in low physical requirements. If your knees, hips, feet, lung capacity, or whatever keep you from walking with ease for some distance, for an hour or more at a time, you want tours that are marked "easy" on physical activity. Most group tours, even ones noted as "moderate" on the difficulty scale, will still involve a lot of walking. City tours. Castle tours. Getting to group dinners. All require considerable walking.

It's easy to overestimate your walking ability in the United States, because we do so little of it. If you typically walk to your car, drive to work or the shopping center, get through the grocery store or your work day, walk back to your car, drive home and then walk into your house (You know the routine!), you may think that you're all set for "moderate" walking in Europe.

Not necessarily, though. Many, many Americans discover their less-than-adequate fitness level or physical ability only when they are pained or fatigued by group tour walking. If you are *at all* concerned about your fitness level, erring on the side of caution will help ensure that you have an overall enjoyable trip. If it turns out that you can handle more than the group activities, you will almost certainly have opportunities to venture off on your own.

There are numerous travel companies that offer slower-paced tours to Europe. Search on combinations such as "slow walker Europe tours" or "gentle walking tours Europe" or "accessible Europe tours" or "senior tours Europe" to find the latest offerings. Some will be specifically designed for slow walkers; other are "slow" in the sense of staying based in one area and taking life at a slower pace to enjoy it, to suck the marrow out of it (as with the "slow food" movement). Find one that meets your particular needs and interests.

Slow Travel Tours (slowtraveltours.com/) offers examples of enjoy-the-slow-pace-of-life tours, while Stride Travel (www. stridetravel.com/senior-tours-in-europe.html) offers lists of tours graded by physical difficulty. AARP-affiliated Grand European Travel (www.getours.com/aarp) helps travelers select tours based on pace as well as destination, with physical intensity ranging from "leisurely" through "comfortable" to "active."

For example, on the Grand European Travel site, you can choose the country you are interested in, filter by pace (as well as by duration, price, travel style and more) and see what is offered. (Be aware that "pace," in this case, refers to how often you move from hotel to hotel, which can have a big effect on your energy level, and also indicates amount of free time, so you can determine how much additional running around you want to do versus resting up.)

At the time of this writing, selecting "Great Britain" as a destination and filtering by a "leisurely" pace yielded seven possible tours. (Make sure you click the "Apply Filter" buttons to get the results you want.)

Regardless of how you get to the tours, look trip itineraries over carefully, because tour company definitions of "leisurely" or "easy" may not be the same as yours.

River cruises

River cruises are now a popular way of visiting Europe. You can travel through a country (or through multiple countries) taking your hotel and restaurant with you. The countryside flows by your window, and you make regular stops in cities to see their sights and experience their culture.

Many travel search sites lead to river cruise options, including those sites listed above. Some main European river cruise lines (among others) are:

Viking (www.vikingrivercruises.com)
Avalon Waterways (www.avalonwaterways.com)
AMA Waterways (www.amawaterways.com)
Scenic (www.scenicusa.com/)
Tauck (www.tauck.com)

The book *River Cruising in Europe* (a Berlitz Cruise Guide) includes much information about the routes, ports of call, tour companies, and even the individual ships on European river cruises. The author, cruise ship authority Douglas Ward, rates and reviews the river cruise lines and their various ships.

Again, it is important to look tour information over carefully, particularly the parts about the on-land excursions. Are the land activities based on lots of walking? Do you have to hike from the river to the Old City, or is there a bus to take your group? Make sure you are clear on what you are signing up for before you select a trip. But, that being said, there are many options today for comfortably seeing Europe largely from the deck of a river ship.

General tips

- First and foremost, plan ahead. Spontaneity has its place, but if you want to snag the most comfortable, convenient options (especially with hotels and prebooked tours), you need to get in early, especially during high tourist season. If you are more than *somewhat* mobility impaired, then it's even more important that you do your research and plan ahead.
- Be willing to compromise. You may need to give up a quaint and charming hotel in favor of a modern one with easy accessibility. The area around the train station may not be the romantic quarter you were hoping for, but if it is the hub of city and regional transportation (as is often the case), that weighs heavily in its favor.
- Lower the bar. There's nothing wrong with planning your visit around what's easiest to get to. If you want to see or do particular things despite their difficulty, make sure that the rest of that day is easy, so you have a chance to recuperate. There are no extra tourist points for making things hard.
- Slow down in general and take breaks. If you push, push, push yourself all the time (even at a slower speed), you'll have a harder time enjoying what you do. That's a good point for *all* visitors, but especially those with physical challenges. Down time is important. It's always good to have time to catch your breath when traveling. This can be time in a coffee shop, in your hotel room, in a park, sitting on a tour bus. Most of us benefit from recharging our batteries a bit during the day, but that's especially so when we have physical limitations.
- This is, again, true for all travelers, but travel as lightly as you can. Large suitcases are less of a problem if you stay based in one or two hotels, but even then, hauling them from the airport to the hotel and back is never fun. If you plan to travel with your luggage on trains and

buses, you will be grateful for every unnecessary pound you left at home.

- If you take the train, look into ordering tickets online ahead of time. You can usually save considerably on train fare if you book early. You will also know exactly where your reserved seat is and can save yourself wandering through the train cars looking for open seats. By ordering in advance, you can also secure yourself a place on popular trains, where seats can sell out.

- Consider packing a collapsible walking stick or hiking pole for additional support and stability on the inevitable stairs and inclines (and cobblestones!). A $25 investment could save your knees and help you get through the day more easily. Just make sure that the smallest-size pole will fit in your checked luggage, to make sure you'll be able to transport it easily. Of course, if you use it to get on the plane itself, a flight attendant will probably find a home for it during the flight, but check with your airline's rules before relying on that.

- If standing (say, during a city tour or while waiting for the bus) exhausts or pains you, you may want to pack a collapsible 3-legged stool in your day bag. Some collapse up to only 15 inches long and weigh less than 2 pounds (while supporting hundreds of pounds). A company called Walkstool, for example, offers various collapsible models with telescoping legs. Check the sitting height before buying, to make sure it's not a camping chair that you essentially squat in and may struggle to stand up from. (For comparison, a standard dining chair seat is around 18 inches from the floor.) Also look at maximum supportable weight, of course. You probably can't use a collapsible stool everywhere, such as when touring a palace, but one could ward off pain and exhaustion outside, at least, if standing in place is a problem for you.

- You may already be a packing cube convert, or perhaps you've never even heard of them, but they can be a traveler's best friend. Packing cubes aren't actually cube-shaped, but they are squared-off zippered bags of various sizes helpful for organizing items in your luggage. Some people use them to compress their clothes into a carry-on and avoid checking bags entirely, but they are also helpful for organizing a checked bag.

There's a good chance that your hotel room (small European rooms, after all) will not have a dresser or even shelves and you will have to live out of your suitcase during your stay. Packing cubes can serve rather like dresser drawers, keeping all your shirts together, your pants together, socks and underwear, etc. If kneeling next to your suitcase is a problem, you can snag the bags you want and use them at bed level. Using packing cubes really does work well to keep items compartmentalized and prevent them from getting all mixed up in your suitcase, and they could save your knees some wear and tear, as well.

Recapping the points of the previous sections, weigh these tips, as well:

- Consider basing in a single city, or just a couple, and take day trips offered by sightseeing companies to see things outside of the city (limiting day trips to two consecutive days and then taking a break).
- Select a hotel that is accessible, with flat entrances (or limited stairs) and an elevator.
- Locate in a convenient, accessible location. You want easy access to transportation, restaurants, and shops without having to scale hills or lots of stairs.
- Consider hop-on/hop-off buses or other riding sightseeing tours to take you around to the sights.
- If you fly between cities in Europe, look very closely at luggage restrictions before buying a ticket. You are likely to need an extra baggage allowance, which you will probably have to pay for.

Getting your trip off the ground

You may be an old hand at traveling overseas (in which case you can skip this section), but if you're new to international travel, especially independent travel (making your own arrangements), you may feel a little overwhelmed by trying to figure it out. Here is a step-by-step guide to help you through the process.

I've included timing guidelines, to give you an idea of a comfortable planning schedule, but realize that the lead-times listed below are elastic. I've planned trips from almost two years in advance to as little as two months, and both extremes worked out fine. You may also choose to take these steps in a different order, which is also fine, of course. The order here is just one way to make sure you do what you need to at an appropriate time. Your own schedule may work out quite differently.

1. (*9 months to 1+ year in advance*) Decide where you want to go. This is an obvious step, but it's often surprisingly difficult to do. If you are at a loss of where to go, consider a few things: Does your family come from a country that sounds appealing to explore? (Ireland seems to get a lot of traffic in this way.) Are you limited to a certain time of year when you can travel? (Northern Europe is a lot harder to enjoy in the cold winter, and Mediterranean countries can be unpleasantly hot in the summer.)

   Do you have a hobby you want to explore, possibly using it as a theme? (Beer in Germany. Whisky in Scotland. Food and cooking in France or Italy. Gardens in England. Emmigration in Ireland. War sites across any number of countries.) Are you comfortable in a counry that speaks a different language, or do you want to stay where people speak English in the streets?

2. (*6 months to 1+ year in advance*) When can you go, and for how long? This will depend on finances, vacation time, and myriad other details in your life. It's nice to be able to spread out the cost of airfare

(usually the largest single expense) over a two-week trip or more, but if that's not possible, I can assure you that even a week's trip (2 days' flights, 5-6 days in the country) can be enjoyable, rewarding, and totally worth the effort.

Once you know when you can go, research the weather in your intended destination and make sure the season and destination are a good match. If you find yourself heading to a place in the off-off season, know that not everything will be open or may have limited opening times, that you are likely to hit more unpleasant weather (usually wet and cold), but crowds are likely to be lighter, prices lower, and hotel rooms more available. If you are on a limited budget, Vienna in February might be just the ticket for you, for example. Just be aware of what to expect so you don't get too many unpleasant surprises.

3. *(6-9 months in advance)* Look for airfare. Airfare prices can change considerably from one week to the next. You'll probably want to start monitoring sites weeks or even months before you really need to buy a ticket, so you can get a feel for what is an acceptable price or, with luck, a good price.

There are numerous airfare and travel sites online that will comb through airfare offerings and display them for you. I usually use kayak.com, but expedia.com, orbitz.com, priceline.com and others are worth looking into. If you are new to these airfare search sites, be aware that they usually have a predictor somewhere that tells you whether they expect prices to increase or decrease in the near future, and you can sign up for notification of fare decreases for routes you are interested in.

When you start looking seriously at booking a flight, make sure you pay attention to departure time, arrival time, and how long any layovers are. You don't want an eight-hour layover if you can avoid it, but don't cut things too close, in case your first flight has a delay. A couple of hours may sound like a long time between flights, but much of that time is taken up getting off of one plane, through the airport, and finding your new gate and boarding again. If you have a direct, non-stop option for a flight, it's worth paying a little more *not* to have to switch planes.

If you can be a little flexible with your travel dates, choose the flexible date option on your search. (It is usually an option around the travel calendar, "exact day" or, say, "+/- 1 day" or "+/- 3 days.") You can often save hundreds of dollars if you can shift your travel dates by a day or two.

Make sure that the prices you look at include one carry-on bag and one checked bag. Airlines have started listing bare-bones fares that often do not include a checked bag, which is unrealistic for most of us (and deceptive on their part, I think). Some prices don't even include a carry-on bag! You can click a little bag icon to add a checked bag (or a carry-on) or select an optional seat upgrade (from "economy" to "main cabin," for example) and get a more accurate price for tickets that include a reasonable luggage allowance.

Once you have a good idea of which flights you think you are interested in, you could (if you wanted) go directly to the airline's Web site. It might be easier to find a combination of flights that works best for you there. You can also look over luggage allowances and any restrictions listed on the airline's site, so you know from the start what you'll be dealing with. After looking things over, you may choose to book on the phone through an airline agent, if you are more comfortable with that. You can confirm luggage allowances and choose seats with an agent, too.

Be aware that however you choose your flights—through an aggregator such as Kayak or directly on the airline's Web site or with a representative on the phone—you may not end up with the "perfect" flight times you select. It is common for airlines to shift the times of flights, often in ways that completely negate the careful thought you put into your selection. They will notify you of any major change, but there's nothing you can do about it.

I suppose this might be a roundabout way of recommending that you not get too hung up on finding the "perfect" combination of flights, at least if you have to pay more to get that combination to begin with. I've done that multiple times (paid more for a more desirable flight time), then had the flight changed to a time I could have chosen for less money from the start. It's frustrating, but there's nothing we customers can do about a change except live with it.

I like to buy my tickets 6-9 months in advance (if I think I see a good price), but I have done so in as little as 2 months. The closer you cut it, though, the more likely it is that you will pay a premium.

4. (*When you buy your plane ticket*) At this point, it's a good idea to look into trip insurance. While trip insurance is not required, it can provide great peace of mind to know that you won't be out a huge chunk of change if something unexpected pops up and you can't go on your trip as planned. (Or, even worse, if you have a medical emergency while out of the country.)

You should figure out the largest amount of money you are committed to on your trip (prepaid, non-refundable expenses) and get quotes for how much trip coverage for that amount would cost from different companies. I have been very satisfied using Allianz trip insurance (www.allianztravelinsurance.com), but any reputable company will do. Travelex, John Hancock, and IMG are all recommended, as well. Insuremytrip.com will give you information from various plans and different companies to compare.

For full coverage during your trip, you may need to **buy insurance within a week or two** of making your first major payments, so **do not delay** on this, if you plan to purchase a plan. Also, make sure you read the fine print closely to confirm that you will be covered for what you need and want to have covered. Pre-existing conditions are an important issue.

If you have questions, call the customer service number for clarification. I've always found the company reps to be extremely helpful and pleasant, but if they're not, that may help you decide to use a different company. You may, of course, choose to skip trip insurance (I did for years and years and never had a problem), but if you have relatives who could easily end up in the hospital or your own health is iffy, I would want it.

5. (*6-9 months in advance*) Plot out the days you will be at your destination. A rough version is fine, but knowing what days you have to work with is useful. Don't plan much that first day in Europe—give

yourself time to get to your hotel, check in, and see something of the town, but don't overdo it. Ideally, you won't pre-pay for any expensive activity the first day in Europe, because if your flight is delayed a day (it has happened to me more than once), you generally forfeit that payment. Remember that your first two trip days blend into one because of the overseas flight through the night, and the last day of your trip will be taken up by your return home.

6. (*6-9 months in advance*) If you don't already have these travel research materials, get at least one traditional guide book for the city/country you want to visit (depending on how far afield you want to go), a city map for checking out locations of major sights and possible hotels, and, if you plan to take day trips into the countryside, also get a country map, as well. (One may be included with your city map.)

7. (*4-9 months in advance*) Once you have nailed down your travel dates with your airfare purchase, line up your hotel. In this book, I suggest specific hotels in specific areas of cities, but you can certainly search for your own. My go-to lodging site is tripadvisor.com, but that often leads me to expedia.com, booking.com or other sites, all of which are perfectly acceptable. Remember that you are looking for a convenient location and an easily accessible hotel. I like to have breakfast included, if possible, but you may need to pay extra for the convenience of an in-hotel breakfast, and often it's more expensive than it seems to be worth. (There are usually plenty of other breakfast options around, from local cafés to grocery stores.)

You can often get a better price if you choose the non-cancellable option for a room, but I prefer the flexibility of being able to cancel a hotel if my plans change or I find a hotel (or a deal) that I like better, even though the cancellable option generally costs a little more.

I especially like that flexibility because different hotels and B&Bs open up their reservation schedules at different times. Some will let you reserve rooms more than a year in advance (but it depends on time of year, when they open up the next year's booking schedule). For other hotels, you can't reserve until a couple of months out. I sometimes grab something early that meets my needs, then keep an eye on when my top choice becomes available. No-cancellation-fee reservations make it possible to switch without penalty. However, there's no problem sticking with your first choice, if you don't like going through the reservation/cancellation process any more than is necessary.

If you want a specific hotel but it doesn't show up on one of the aggregator sites for your dates, try going directly to the hotel's Web site. They often open their own reservations before they share with the aggregator sites, and they can also hold back a number of rooms to book directly, even if the aggregator sites say none are available.

Bear in mind that *if you plan to base in one hotel for more than a few days* (recommended), it can be harder to get a room because of availability for an extended time. *Start looking early* in that case, and get at least a provisional reservation in as soon as you can. Also, if you are hoping to stay in a crazy-popular tourist spot with limited lodging, such as on the Isle of Skye in Scotland, you may need to book a full year in advance to get what you want.

If you reserve a room directly with a European hotel, they may charge your credit card immediately even if the reservation is fully cancellable. However, your credit card company may decline to put this charge through, because it is coming from another country and, as far as the credit card company knows, it could be fraudulent. They will contact you to verify that you approve of the purchase. Even better, you can head off a verification call from the start. *If you know you will be using a card for an overseas charge, such as reserving a hotel room, you can notify the credit card company in advance to avoid the verification delay.*

8. (*4-9 months in advance*) Once you're thinking about booking overseas reservations, you may want to check your credit cards and see what (if any) fee they charge for foreign transactions. Credit card companies typically charge a 3% conversion fee, but that amount can vary, and some cards may be used abroad for a 0% fee. If you will be charging a lot to your credit card (and a lengthy hotel reservation can add up to a lot), it may be worth tracking down a card that has no fee. My credit union provides a VISA card with a 1% fee, which I'm satisfied with.

9. (*4-9 months in advance*) If you're planning to rent a car, you can look into that now, too. (Travel search sites such as www.expedia.com and

www.kayak.com will give you many options to look over.) Most reservations are fully cancellable with no penalty, so it doesn't hurt to book early.

If you can't drive a manual transmission car (stick shift), then you will definitely want to reserve early, because supplies of automatic transmission cars are often limited. (And check that filter option—"Automatic transmission," possibly under a heading of "Car Options"—to narrow your search to appropriate cars.)

Look over your own insurance coverage (auto insurance and whatever the credit card you use includes) before you decide whether you want to pay for insurance through the rental company, because it's usually quite expensive. It *is* easy to line up, however, and then you know you are sufficiently insured. In the end, you need to decide on one kind of coverage or the other—your credit card's coverage or coverage through the rental agency. They don't double up.

10. (*4-6 months in advance*) Make sure your passport is valid for at least 6 months past your expected return date. This is a **requirement**, not a recommendation. If your passport expires before that 6-month cushion, apply for a replacement. And if you *don't* have a passport, apply for one immediately. It can take a couple of months to get your passport (although usually not that long). If your time is short and you're worried about getting your passport in time, you may choose to expedite your application for a fee. Go to the U.S. Department of State Web site at travel.state.gov for information about applying for or renewing a passport.

11. (*4-6 months in advance*) You should have a stretch of time in your preparations when you get to relax. Look into your travel books and see what you most want to see and do. As you jot down ideas for each day of your trip, keep in mind that not every sight is open every day, and opening hours can vary considerably. You don't want to turn up at the Louvre to spend your Tuesday there only to discover that it's closed Tuesdays. Also, keep in mind that insanely popular spots (such as the Palace of Versailles on a summer weekend) will be somewhat less crowded during the week, if that's something you can be flexible about.

12. (*3-9 months in advance*) Check into any sightseeing tours you think you might want to take. See how far in advance the company starts taking registrations (this can vary by time of year, if they open up the whole next year's schedule at once), and consider when you want to make your arrangements. Sightseeing day trips during peak tourist season can fill up months in advance, so try to beat the crowd if you're visiting at a busy time.

    Are there any other activities you want to be on top of? Performances? Wine tastings? Cooking classes? If you check into them in advance, you'll have a better chance of getting into the activity while there's still space. Look over cancellation policies, if your plans might change. You'll also want to make sure you know how you'll get to and from the activity, although you can likely figure that out when you're in the country. (That's me being over-prepared, researching those details in advance. Not a bad strategy, I'll note, but also not the only path to success.)

13. (*3-6 months in advance*) If you will be visiting a non-English-speaking country, use this time to learn some of the basics of the national language. You don't have to become fluent, but knowing how to cover the bare minimum can go a long way in making you feel more confident and easing transactions when you are there. (You'll make a better impression, too.) Hello, goodbye, yes, no, please, thank you, excuse me, and numbers up to 10 should be considered mandatory. Even that little bit is better than nothing. (And I happen to know of short books for Italy, France, Germany and Austria that are designed for just this purpose! Check out my Survival Guides and see whether you think you would benefit from them. See the back pages of this book for descriptions.)

14. (*1-3 months in advance*) If there are "must see" sights in the places you are visiting, check into those as early as you can. The most popular tourist destinations in cities often recommend or even require pre-booking. So, if a walk through the Anne Frank House is vital to your visit to Amsterdam, know that tickets go on sale two months in advance, they're only available online, and, yes, they sell out. Most major cities have a couple or several sights that are so popular that they re-

quire prebooking. Don't find yourself shut out of a longed-for visit because you were not aware of that.

15. (*1-3 months in advance*) If you plan to use a city sightseeing pass (a flat-fee pass for entrance into numerous top sights over a chosen number of days), look options over carefully. Some passes include transportation and some don't. Some require supplemental fees and some don't. Some allow access to as many covered sights as you can fit in, while others require that you pre-select a certain limited number of sights. These passes often include entry (usually fast-track entry) to the most popular sights in the city, but if a sight requires prebooking, that generally applies to pass holders, as well, which can get a little sticky. Entrance is covered with the pass, but you need to book it ahead of time, possibly before you have even thought about *acquiring* that pass.

In order to book your spot at these entrance-controlled sights ahead of time, when there are still plenty of available slots, you need to buy your sightseeing pass first. (If you don't care whether or when you get to those particular sights, you don't need to worry about this. You can afford to wait and see what happens when you are there.) After deciding which pass (if any) you want, you order it online (usually for less money than on-site in the city). Going through the order process, you will probably be offered a choice of having an electronic delivery to your mobile phone, or picking up a prepaid pass when you arrive in the city.

If you need your pass for free entry to a sight that prebooks, you will probably need a valid individual pass number to enter during the booking process. I have learned from painful (and somewhat pricey) experience that ordering passes for pickup does *not* result in a specific pass number that can be used for booking entrances. (I had thought that my confirmation email would include the necessary number. It didn't.)

I discovered after much dismayed digging around on a Web site that the "mobile" pass (which I did not want to use on my phone, and that's why I had avoided it) is actually an *emailed* pass, one that customers can either download onto their cell phones *or* (and this is the crucial bit) can print out and use as a paper pass. (Or both!) The emailed passes had the crucial individual numbers I needed to book my group at popular tours at the times we wanted.

If you, too, want to use a sightseeing pass and prebook tour times, you will probably need to choose the "mobile" pass option, whether you intend to use your cell phone to display the pass or not.

16. (*1-2 months in advance*) Decide how you will keep in touch with the world at home when you are abroad. Almost all hotels now provide WiFi, as well as restaurants and other public places, so it's easy to stay in touch via the Internet. Your U.S. cell phone company might offer a reasonable international plan (although many are prohibitively expensive—ask lots of questions), or you could get a local SIM card and a prepaid plan while you are in Europe. (You'll need an unlocked GSM phone to do that. Some people choose to buy a cheap phone in Europe to use there.)

    If you use your U.S. smart phone for just WiFi when abroad, make sure you have it in airplane mode so you don't rack up huge roaming fees in Europe. Too many people have returned home to unexpected cell phone bills of thousands of dollars.

17. (*1-2 months in advance*) Consider whether you will want to wait until your arrival to get local currency from an ATM or whether you want to order pounds or euros ahead of time through a U.S. bank. If you plan to order foreign currency before you go (many people prefer to have some useable money in hand when they arrive in Europe), give yourself time for its delivery. Fees for ordering foreign currency in the U.S. are higher than when you extract the foreign currency from a foreign ATM, but the payoff is cash in hand from the start.

    This is also a good time to consider how you want to keep your cash, credit/debit cards, and passport safe when you are touring. Many people choose secure cross-body bags, often fancy travel models with slash-proof sides, a steel cable in the strap, and locking clasps. A money belt is the safest bet for theft-proofing your items, and I've taken to keeping large sums of cash and my back-up cards and passport in one. (It's not at all uncomfortable, as I had thought it would be. Just a little inconvenient to get at. But I guess that's the point.) Of course, the most important safety tip is to be aware of your surroundings, attentive to your bags, and not get distracted in crowds (especially at popular tourist sights and on public transportation).

As a side note, be aware that using a credit card for charges is more secure than using a debit card, because a credit card does not give an unauthorized user direct access to your bank account. Try to limit debit card use to ATM withdrawals.

18. (*1-2 months in advance*) As your trip nears, you need to plan what you are taking. Keep things as simple as you can, realizing that it's fine to re-wear clothes as long as they aren't smelly or visibly dirty. And there *are* laundry facilities available in Europe, if it comes to that. Check into your airline's size and weight restrictions for personal items, for carry-ons, and for checked baggage. You might get away with pushing the limits a bit, or you could be hit with additional fees—you decide whether you're willing to risk it. For most of Europe, you'll want to include a small umbrella or other rain gear for much of the year. You also probably want to take a lightweight, reusable shopping bag with you, because free bags are not automatically supplied everywhere in Europe. Be prepared to fill your own bag, too. (It's like a trip to Aldi's in the U.S.)

19. (*1 week in advance*) Within a week or so of your trip, contact your bank (for debit cards) and your credit card companies to notify them of your upcoming travels. They will want to know where you'll be for what dates, so they do not shut down card activity in an unexpected location. Include any foreign country where you'll be making a connection, as well, in case you want to buy something at the airport during a layover. MasterCard and VISA are your best bets for acceptable credit cards.

Even with forewarning, there are often problems with using your plastic the first few days abroad. Not all cards work at all ATMs all the time. Have a way to contact your bank (or someone who can contact your bank for you) if your debit cards don't work.

And make sure you take back-ups, such as multiple debit cards, other people who can tide you over if you have problems, and probably a supply of American cash, in case you really get in a bind. When you're talking with your bank, raise your cash withdrawal daily limit (if

Getting your trip off the ground 33

desired) for your time away. You will be better off withdrawing large amounts of cash at a time to minimize fees and avoid the inconvenience of having to visit an ATM frequently. And realize that you will be withdrawing monies from your *checking* account, not your savings account (not allowed), so make sure you have enough cash to easily cover what you think you might want to use.

You need to know your PINs as numbers, not as letters, because European number pads don't include the alphabet. Also, make sure you have the contact numbers for your credit card companies, in case your cards are lost or stolen. At this time, I also make copies of my passport, to leave one at home and to trade a copy with my travel partner.

When using a foreign ATM, you should abide by the same safeguards as when using one in the U.S.—shield your PIN entry from any prying eyes or hidden cameras, and check before use that the card slot seems to be normal and not "funny" at all, with nothing loose around the opening. You don't want your card information to be "skimmed" at the machine and used fraudulently. ATMs at banks are generally considered safest, especially machines in secured entry areas that limit access. Using an ATM during banking hours is also considered a safeguard, as thieves are more likely to insert skimming devices (and the devices are less likely to be discovered) when fewer people are around, at night and especially on weekends.

20. (*1-3 days in advance*) As your departure date nears, double check that you have your passport, your flight information, copies of any reservations you made or tickets you bought (e.g., hotels, tours, land transportation, dinners, entertainments), your debit and credit cards, your U.S. health insurance card, trip insurance information (if you bought it), money, your driver's license (if you will be renting a car), and emergency contact numbers.

21. (*1-3 days in advance*) When you pack for your trip, try to fit clothes for a day or two into your carry-on bag, along with your toiletries and any medications, in case your checked luggage doesn't arrive with you. Make sure that anything sharp is in your checked bag, not your carry-on. (You can take medical needles in your carry-on. Most airlines also

allow an additional medical bag, if needed. Check with representatives to confirm this.) Look over the TSA checklist to make sure you comply with their latest requirements: www.tsa.gov/travel/travel-tips/travel-checklist.

The most important carry-on restriction for most of us is that we have to limit our carry-on liquids, gels, creams, pastes, and aerosols (not including medications) to travel-size containers of no more than 3.4 ounces, and all the containers have to fit into a clear 1-quart bag.

You might also want to check out the Dept. of State's traveler's checklist, to make sure you're not overlooking anything important: travel.state.gov/content/travel/en/international-travel/before-you-go/travelers-checklist.html.

22. (*1-3 days in advance*) Confirm that your flight information has not changed, and check how much time your airline suggests you allow for check-in at your departure. Do not wait until the last minute to catch your plane, or you could find that your seat has been given to someone else. For overseas flights, you should generally allow at least three hours to check in and get through security with ample time to spare. You can usually check in online the night before your flight, but you still want to get to the airport in plenty of time to check your bag and get through security.

23. (*Departure day*) Time to go! Remind yourself that *nothing* is perfect. Your trip will not be perfect. Things will go wrong. And that's OK. Try not to let the hiccups upset you too much. The more things go wrong, the better story you'll have to tell later. And expect that the first day abroad—after flying through the night and maybe struggling to get to your hotel—is likely to be tough. Things get much better after that, and you'll probably have a wonderful trip in the end. Enjoy!

Suggested tours

The following sections provide travel information about various cities in Europe—good areas to base in, hotels in those areas, transportation options, day trip options—almost everything you need to plan your own trip abroad. (Just add a couple of guide books for specific information about sights.) I have not been able to include every city worth visiting but have aimed to include major cities that can serve as hubs for excursions out into the country and to other cities.

Information about various options is provided—contact information, costs, itineraries—all of which is useful, but also changeable. Use this information as a starting point, but then *double check* specifics before relying on them. Maybe that day trip to the Highlands *used* to run every day, but now it doesn't. Details were correct at the time of writing this book, but certainly some information will have changed by the time you *use* it. If you find inaccuracies, feel free to let me know at bingham@worldprospect.com so I can update them.

The chapters about the hub cities are organized in the following way. First, there's a short introduction to the city, and then I put the cart before the horse and include a detailed (*very* detailed) possible itinerary that probably won't make complete sense at that point. Why do I do that? So you know from the start what you may be working toward. So you don't have to wade through thirty pages of listings to find the part that is probably most interesting to you. So you can easily locate it to refer to, when making your own decisions later. Don't feel you have to follow the suggested itinerary exactly (or at all). Use it as a starting point, an example of something that works, and adjust it to best suit your own interests and needs.

Once you have an idea of how a visit can be pieced together, the next sections offer information you can use to make your own choices: arrival and transportation into the city, transportation *within* the city, day trips, lodging, and other base cities in the country. I recommend again that you supplement this book with at least one traditional guide book, to help you decide what *you* want to see in each place (which may not be what *I* want to see!).

After you have planned your trip and traveled to Europe, I would love to hear from you. If you have successful experiences or tips for others, I would be grateful to learn about those, possibly to use in future printings of this book. As the U.S. population ages, more and more people will appreciate knowing how they can travel abroad despite physical limitations. You can be part of making their trips successful. I can be reached most easily at bingham@worldprospect.com or on Facebook under Elizabeth Bingham, Author.

Cities covered in the remaining chapters in this book are Edinburgh, Dublin, London, Amsterdam, Paris, Madrid, Rome, Vienna, and Munich. Now, happy planning, and then *bon voyage*!

Edinburgh

Overview

Edinburgh ("ed-in-burr-uh" or, locally, "ed-in-bruh") is the capital of Scotland. It's located just 40-some miles east of Glasgow, so it's possible to visit the country's largest city (Glasgow) while staying based in historic and beautiful Edinburgh. Edinburgh is ancient, with evidence of human habitation as long ago as 8500 BC. Since then, its seven major hills (like Rome) have attracted generations of defensive buildings, such as the current Edinburgh Castle.

Scotland is famous for many things—kilts, bagpipes, haggis, and, of course, whisky (no "e" here, for what Americans call Scotch). But that's not all. Scotland is also famously rainy and cool, so plan accordingly. Fortunately, Edinburgh is on the drier *east* side of the country, so it only gets about half the rain of Glasgow, but that's still 191 days a year with rain, on average.

Scotland, as part of the United Kingdom, uses the British pound sterling for its currency. English bank notes are universally accepted in Scotland. Scottish bank notes, however, are frequently *not* accepted in England, even though they are supposed to be. As a tourist, you probably want to use up any Scottish notes before English ones, if you plan to use leftover currency anywhere other than in Scotland.

Possible plan for Edinburgh (What I'd do)

If I were traveling to Edinburgh with my mother, this is what I would plan for us to do. Obviously, you may prefer to do something different, but you may find this itinerary handy as a starting point, changing it as much as you'd like. **Please double check any details before relying on them, as specifics may have changed since I wrote these pages.**

This section will make more sense as you work your way through the chapter. Having a city map at hand will help to visualize this itinerary and other tourist options. This plan assumes lodging around Waverley Station in New Town.

Once you have a pretty good idea of what you want to do, check out ticket sales online, because online booking is almost always less expensive than buying a ticket on-site. Of course, when buying online, you save money but might give up flexibility, so it's not always the best choice, but it's certainly worth looking into. As for day trips, you probably don't want to plan for more than two consecutive out-of-town excursions at a time, to avoid bus fatigue.

Day 1—Depart U.S.

Day 2—Arrive Edinburgh. Visit ATM for British pounds, if needed. Take Airlink bus 100 to Waverley Bridge. Check into the hotel. Rest as needed.

>   **Comfort upgrade:** If exhausted after the flight and your budget can handle it, take a cab into the city. It will be easier to find and board than the bus or the tram and will deliver you directly to your hotel. Cost split among multiple riders can be as economical as public transportation.
>
>   Visit sights within walking distance of the hotel. If lodging in New Town (e.g., Motel One—Princes), stroll around New Town, visit the Scottish National Gallery (free entry) and/or walk up Calton Hill. Stop for tea or coffee. Wrap up the day by visiting the Guildford Arms pub around the corner from the hotel (or different pub, if lodging elsewhere).

Day 3—Go to Waverley Bridge and buy a Royal Edinburgh ticket for the hop-on/hop-off (HOHO) buses and fast-track access to three main sights. (Check before buying to make sure Holyrood House is open for visiting. If not, the company may substitute a different experience.)

>   Assuming a 48-hour Royal Edinburgh ticket, here is a plan for the first day:
>
>   Take the green tour ("Edinburgh Tour"). Stop at Holyroodhouse, fast-track entry. Ride the green bus up the Royal Mile to Lawnmarket. Fast-track entry to Edinburgh Castle. (If you instead choose to buy a separate castle ticket, that must be done at least 1.5 hours in advance for a timed slot.)
>
>   Break for a late lunch. (Café in the castle? The Hub, save 10% with HOHO ticket? The Witchery, expensive but an experience? Amber Restaurant at the Whisky Experience?) Get back on the green bus. If not too tired, get off at Charlotte Square to visit

Georgian House (2019 admission £8). Take green bus back to Waverley Bridge when done.

Or, if feeling up to it after visiting the castle, walk downhill on the Royal Mile. Free sights on the way are: St. Giles Cathedral, Museum of Childhood, Museum of Edinburgh, The People's Story Museum. Get on the red "City Sightingseeing" bus at Canongate or Holyroodhouse and ride to Waverley Bridge.

Relax the rest of the day. (Pub time??) Energetic group members can ride any of the three buses to Holyroodhouse and walk up to Arthur's Seat. Be aware of when the HOHO buses stop running for the day, if you plan on riding one back to the hotel area.

Day 4—Use the 2nd day of the 48-hour HOHO bus ticket to explore Edinburgh further.

Take the blue bus ("Majestic Tour") to the Ocean Terminal stop for fast-track entry to the Royal Yacht Britannia. (Garden enthusiasts may want to stop at the Royal Botanic Garden on the way—free entry to garden, doesn't open until 10.)

After touring the yacht, take the blue bus to the Canongate stop. Lunch break on the Royal Mile around Canongate. (Tollbooth Tavern? Café Vivo? Oink?)

Take the green line ("Edinburgh Tour") at Canongate and ride to the Chambers Street stop. Visit the National Museum of Scotland (free entry). Open until 5 p.m.

If you haven't been on the red tour yet, you can get on here and ride around for the overview. (There's some overlap with other tours.) If you want to take the walk down the Royal Mile suggested for the previous day, you can take the green bus to Lawnmarket and walk down the Royal Mile, then get back on the red bus at Canongate or Holyroodhouse and ride to Waverley Bridge. (The green bus and the red bus both stop by the National Museum of Scotland and return to Waverley Bridge, but they travel in opposite directions.)

Relax the rest of the day. Energetic group members may choose to take a Mercat ghost tour (2 hours) or visit the Real

Mary King's Close for an evening tour (prebooking recommended). (Or both! Mary King's Close tours run all day. Ride the green bus from the National Museum of Scotland to Lawnmarket and then walk down the Royal Mile to the tour start, around St. Giles Cathedral—or walk from the Museum of Scotland to the tour start.) Both tours explore Edinburgh's hidden underground world.

Day 5—Loch Ness/Highlands day trip (Order of day trips depends on dates/availability)

Day 6—Stirling Castle/Loch Lomond/Distillery day trip

Day 7—Free day in Edinburgh

Day 8—Rosslyn Chapel/Hadrian's Wall day trip

Day 9—St. Andrew's/Fishing Villages of Fife day trip

Day 10—Final day in Edinburgh. Perhaps the 3 Bridges half-day tour. Final sightseeing. Final shopping. Final night out. (Scottish Dinner at The Café Royal on Register Street by Motel One? Roast Dinner or group Set Menu at Ghillie Dhu, at the west end of Princes Street?)

Day 11—Return to U.S.

Arrival

You will probably fly into the Edinburgh airport (EDI), eight miles west of the city. However, if you find a fantastic flight into Glasgow, it might be worth the hassle of the train ride to save a bundle. To get from the airport to the city, you have your choice of bus, tram, or taxi. All depart from outside the Arrivals hall. Exit through the main doors.

Every ten minutes, Airlink bus 100 runs from the airport to Waverley Bridge by the train station (and back), a 30-minute ride that stops at Haymarket, West End, and Princes Street on the way. Cost for a one-way ticket is £4.50 (in 2019, £7.50 round-trip).

Edinburgh Trams are a little more frequent, every 6-8 minutes, and take you into Edinburgh's city center in 30-33 minutes, including stops at Haymarket, Princes Street, and St. Andrew's Square and ending at York Place in New Town rather than Waverley Station. One-way cost for an adult is £6.00.

Taxis are also available for a 20-30 minute ride into the city at a cost of around £20. (Ask about price before committing.) City "Black Cabs" can seat 5-6 people with modest luggage and are wheelchair accessible. You can prebook cabs on the airport Web site, but it's not necessary.

Airport information, including transportation options, is available at www.edinburghairport.com.

Easy transportation option

Once in the city, your probable transportation choices are bus, taxi, and tram. Much of the city is walkable, but hilly and uneven. Think cobblestones and stairs. Even if you are transported around town, you'll still need to walk to and between some sights.

The easiest way to get around to the sights in Edinburgh is to ride a hop-on/hop-off (HOHO) tourist bus. Edinburgh Bus Tours (edinburghtour.com) offers four guided bus tours to take you around the city, and they all come highly recommended. You purchase a 24- or 48-hour ticket and then may hop on and hop off the buses as much as you'd like in that time. (If you want the bus to make a stop, press the red button as you approach the stop, or the bus might sail right by.) You may choose to take the whole tour to get an overview and then, on the second time around, hop off to see sights up close.

Buses run year-round, though hours of operation and frequency of buses vary by season. The main hub of these tours is on Waverley Bridge, next to the train station, but you can catch the HOHO buses all over central Edinburgh. (Check the Web site above for the latest prices and tour routes.)

1) The Edinburgh Tour is an hour-long, live-guided tour around the city, with the highlights of Edinburgh Castle, Holyrood Palace, and the Royal Mile. A 24-hour ticket costs £16 for an adult, £15 for a senior (60+), £8 for a child (5-15), and £39 for a family (2 adults and up to 3 children). Buses have easy access.
2) The Majestic Tour is also a one-hour tour (with recorded commentary) but heads to parts farther north. Highlights include The Royal Yacht Britannia, the Royal Botanic Garden Edinburgh, and the Scottish Parliament. Costs for a 24-hour ticket are the same as for The Edinburgh Tour. Buses have easy access.
3) The Edinburgh City Sightseeing Tour again offers a tour about one hour long (with recorded commentary). Highlights include Dynamic Earth, the National Museum of Scotland, and Greyfriars Bobby. A

24-hour ticket costs the same as for the previous two tours, and again the buses have easy access.

4) The Royal Edinburgh ticket combines the first three tours with 48 hours of access and includes tickets and fast-track admission to Edinburgh Castle, the Palace of Holyrood House, and The Royal Yacht Britannia. You can mix and match different buses and different routes over two days. Cost is £57 for adults, £50 for seniors, and £31 for children.

5) The 3 Bridges Tour goes farther afield and includes both a bus tour and a boat cruise to fully appreciate the bridges over the Firth of Forth. The tour lasts at least three hours and costs £25 for adults, £23 for seniors/students, £12 for a child, and £59 for a family. Buses have easy access, but the boat may be difficult for wheelchair users, who are advised to check with the boat company in advance (phone: 0131 331 3030 or www.forthtours.com) so the company can provide a ramp for wheelchair access. (They note that no wheelchair-accessible toilet is available on board.)

Other in-city transportation

City **buses** are an economical if less convenient option for getting around the city. Lothian buses cost £1.70 for a single ticket or £4 for a day ticket that allows unlimited travel on all Lothian buses and Edinburgh Trams. (Choose your best ticket option here: www.lothianbuses.com/tickets/.) You can buy single tickets from the driver on the bus (must have correct change), and you can buy day tickets either on the bus, online, or from a vending machine at a tram stop. See lothianbuses.co.uk for timetables, maps, and more ticket specifics. An online Journey Planner can help you determine the best route to sights.

Edinburgh's single **tram** line runs from the airport to York Place in the New Town. It is integrated with the Lothian bus system. Single tickets cost £1.70 and day tickets can be used on them. You can buy tickets at vending machines at the tram stops. More information is available at edinburghtrams.com.

Taxis are the most personalized—and most expensive—option for getting around the city. If the "taxi" light is on, the cab is available. The black cabs can be flagged down on the street, hired at a taxi rank outside major sights, or ordered by phone (for a small extra fee). All taxis can accommodate wheelchairs. Fees are high, and people usually don't tip on short trips. You can round up to the nearest 50 pence if you desire to tip.

If you want an estimated cost, an online fare calculator is available at www.taxifarefinder.com. A sample afternoon ride from Princes Street to Edinburgh Castle, for example, would take about 9 minutes, is 1.3 km and would cost £7.45. Cost in heavy traffic for the same ride could be as high as £18.75.

Should you want to phone for a cab, here are some options: City Cabs (0131-228-1211), Central Taxis (0131-229-2468), and Capital Cars (0131-777-7777).

Sightseeing passes

The **Edinburgh City Pass** (www.edinburghcity pass.com/) offers free entry to 22 attractions over 1, 2, or 3 consecutive calendar days. The pass includes round-trip tram transport from the airport. The Edinburgh City Pass covers the Edinburgh Dungeon, Georgian House, Scott Monument, Edinburgh Zoo, City Bus Tour, Forth Boat Tours, the National Mining Museum Scotland and more, but *not* the Palace of Holyrood House, Edinburgh Castle, or the Royal Yacht Britannia. Passes can be purchased online or in Edinburgh at the VisitScotland iCentre on Princes Street. They are activitied when used at the first attraction. Prices are as follows:

- 1-day pass—adult (17+ years) £45; child (5-16) £20
- 2-day pass—adult, £55; child £26
- 3-day pass—adult £65; child £30

The **Historic Scotland Explorer's Pass** (previously known as the Edinburgh Pass) (www.historicenvironment.scot/visit-a-place/explorer-passes/) covers entry into 70 historical sights around Scotland (40 in winter) at no additional cost, including Edinburgh and Stirling Castles, but not the Palace of Holyroodhouse. A few sights require prebooking. Choose a pass for 5 or 14 days, for sale online or at the first sight you visit. Prices are as follows:

- 5-day pass, adult (ages 16-59) £35
- 5-day pass, student (with valid ID)/senior (60+) £28
- 5-day pass, child (5-15) £21
- 5-day pass, family (2 adults and up to 6 children ages 5-15) £70
- 14-day pass, adult £45

- 14-day pass, student/senior £36
- 14-day pass, child £27
- 14-day pass, family £90

There are also regional passes available if you don't want a pass that covers all of Scotland: Islands Explorer Pass, Orkney Explorer Pass, Scottish Borders Explorer Pass, and Dumfries and Galloway Explorer Pass.

Day trips

It's possible to see much of Scotland without having to leave the comfort of your base hotel at night, because Edinburgh has plenty of tourist companies that specialize in day trips. As always, use the information here as a guide, but check each company's Web site for tour details and the most current price and schedule information. **Tour details—even which tours are offered—routinely change from season to season.** Whichever tours you decide on, look over cancellation policies, if your plans aren't completely firm.

Browsing through Web sites will also help you decide which company's tours seem a good fit for you. Be aware that some specific tours have special requirements—closed shoes for distillery tours, for example—so you'll want to look descriptions over closely before you show up at the departure point. And make sure you show up early so you are not considered a no-show and your seat sold to someone else!

Also take into account where the tours depart from. The first two companies listed—Heart of Scotland Tours and Rabbie's Tours—depart from New Town at Waterloo Place near the train station. Gray Line says they pick up at your hotel. The last four —Timberbush Tours, The Hairy Coo, Highland Experience Tours, and Haggis Adventures—all depart from the Royal Mile or just off it. If you want to save your walking energy for the tour itself but you select a tour with a departure point that is not very close to your hotel, you may want to invest in a taxi ride to get there. Hopefully, you'll have a good sense of Edinburgh and its hills before you need to make that decision.

If you take a multi-day tour, you will likely be restricted to one small bag and will need to store the lion's share of your luggage. Your hotel may do that for you, or you can check into storing your luggage at the train or bus station.

Heart of Scotland Tours

Heart of Scotland Tours (www.heartofscotlandtours.co.uk) has earned TripAdvisor's Certificate of Excellence every year since 2013. They specialize in small guided tours (max. 16) on their "wee red buses" (Mercedes mini-coaches). Cost covers transportation and services of a tour leader. Meals, refreshments, entry fees, and gratuities are not included. The company will also arrange private tours, if desired. Heart of Scotland Tours all leave from Waterloo Place, just north of Waverley train station at the end of Princes Street. Their main day trips are as follows:

Tour 1—Loch Ness and the Highlands—Tour highlights include the Trossachs National Park, Glen Coe, Ben Nevis viewpoint, Fort Augustus, Loch Ness (opt. cruise), Cairngorms National Park, and Highland Perthshire. Daily, 12 hours. Adults £45–£59.

Tour 2—Stirling Castle, Highland Lochs and Whisky—Tour highlights include Loch Lomond nature walk and Highland viewpoint, Stirling Castle, Highland cows (April to October), Duke's Pass scenic drive in the Highlands, Glengoyne Distillery and whisky tasting. 10 hours. Daily. Adults £36–£47.

Tour 3—Rosslyn Chapel, the Borders and Hadrian's Wall—Tour highlights include Rosslyn Chapel (featured in the DaVinci Code), Scotland/England border, Melrose Abbey, and Hadrian's Wall. Daily except Sun, 10.5 hours. Adults £39–£54.

Tour 4—The Best of Scotland in a Day—Tour highlights include Dunkeld Cathedral, Blair Castle, Queen's View (famous Highland viewpoint), scenic drive through Highland Perthshire, The Hermitage woodland and waterfall walk, Highland cows. Daily except Thur/Sat, 9.75 hours. Adults £45–£49.

Tour 5—The Viking Coast and Alnwick Castle—Tour highlights include Northumberland coast, Holy Island, and Alnwick Castle (featured in Harry Potter and Downton Abbey). Tue/Thu/Sat/Sun, 9 hours. Adults £39–£45.

Heart of Scotland Tours **also offers** overnight trips of 2 days to Inverness and the Highlands; 3 days to the Isle of Skye and the Highlands; and 5 days of the Grand Tour of Scotland. See their Web site for details. Note luggage restrictions and lodging costs on overnight trips.

Rabbie's Tours

Rabbie's Tours (www.rabbies.com/en/scotland-tours) also has TripAdvisor's Certificate of Excellence and specializes in small-group tours of 16 people or fewer. Cost covers transportation and services of a tour leader. Meals, refreshments, entry fees and gratuities are not included. Rabbie's Tours all leave from Waterloo Place, just north of Waverley train station at the end of Princes Street. Their main day trips are as follows:

Rosslyn Chapel and the Scottish Borders—Tour highlights include Scott's View at the Scottish Borders, William Wallace Statue, Melrose Abbey, Tweed Valley, Rosslyn Chapel (featured in The DaVinci Code). Daily, 9:45 a.m.-4:30 p.m. £29–£45.

St. Andrews & the Fishing Villages of Fife—Tour highlights include the Forth Bridges, Anstruther fishing village, St. Andrews Cathedral, St. Andrews Old Town, The Old Course (golf club), the historic village of Falkland. Daily, 9:30 a.m.-6 p.m. £34–£52.

Loch Lomond and Whisky Distillery Half-Day—Tour highlights include a visit to Loch Lomond and the Trossachs National Park, views and strolling opportunities in Balloch Country Park, a tour of Glengoyne Distillery. Daily, 1:45 p.m.-6:45 p.m. £19–£26.

Alnwick Castle, the Northumberland Coast & the Borders—Tour highlights include Kelso (ruined abbey and town), the Borders, Alnwick Castle (seen in Harry Potter and Downton Abbey), Northumberland coastline, River Tweed, East Lothian plains. Daily, 8:45 a.m.-6:15 p.m. £36–£49.

Loch Lomond National Park, Kelpies & Stirling Castle—Tour highlights include Stirling Castle, the Trossachs, Loch Lomond, Rob Roy country, and the Kelpies (giant horse statues). Daily, 9:15 a.m.-6:13 p.m. £36–£52.

Hadrian's Wall, Roman Britain & the Scottish Borders—Tour highlights include the Borders, the market town of Jedburgh, Hadrian's Wall, Steel Rigg (UNESCO World Heritage site). Daily, 8:15 a.m.-7 p.m. £39–£59.

Highland Lochs, Glens & Whisky—Tour highlights include Dunkeld village and cathedral, the Hermitage, Pitlochry, Queen's View, Loch Tay and Kenmore, and Dewar's Aberfeldy Distillery. Daily, 9 a.m.-6:30 p.m. £39 – £59.

West Highlands, Lochs & Castles—Tour highlights include Kilchurn Castle, Inveraray, Doune Castle, Loch Awe, and the village of Luss on Loch Lomond. Daily, 8:15 a.m.-6:30 p.m. £39–£59.

Outlander Adventure—Tour highlights include Culross village, Doune Castle, Linlithgow Palace, Blackness Castle, and Midhope Castle. Daily, 9:15 a.m.-6:30 p.m. £42–£55.

Loch Ness, Glencoe & the Highlands—Tour highlights include Rannoch Moor, Glencoe, the Great Glen, Fort Augustus, Loch Ness (opt. cruise), Grampian Mountains, Highland Perthshire. Daily, 8 a.m.-8 p.m. £43–£66.

A Taste of Scotland's Craft Beer and Whisky—Tour highlights include a visit to Kingsbarns Distillery, the university town of St. Andrews with its many pubs, Lindores Abbey Distillery, Innis & Gunn Brewery. Tue/Thur/Fri. 9 a.m.-6:30 p.m. £31-£45.

Discover Malt Whisky—Tour highlights include a visit to Glengoyne Distillery, Loch Lomond National Park, and Deanston Distillery. Daily, 9:30 a.m.-6:15 p.m. £34-£48.

Rabbie's Tours **also offers** overnight trips of 2 days to Loch Ness, Inverness & the Highlands; 3 days to the Isle of Skye; 3 days to the Speyside Whisky Trail; 3 days to the Lake District (England); 3 days to the Isle of Arran; 4 days to the Isle of Skye & West Highlands; 4 days to Mull, the Isle of Iona & West Highlands; 4 days on the Outlander Trail; 5 days to Skye and the far north; 4 days on a Scottish castle experience; and many more. Look closely at costs, inclusions/exclusions, lodging options, and luggage restrictions.

Timberbush Tours

Timberbush Tours (www.timberbush-tours.co.uk) has earned TripAdvisor's Certificate of Excellence every year since 2011. They run a fleet of 7- to-47-seat air-conditioned buses, with tours departing from Lawnmarket on the Royal Mile. Costs include transportation with a tour guide, but not meals, entrance fees, or gratuities. Timberbush Tours also offers bespoke (custom) tours to meet your needs and interests. Their day trips are as follows:

Loch Ness, Glencoe & the Highlands—Tour highlights include stopping in Kilmahog for refreshments and Highland cattle, Rob Roy country,

Glencoe, the Fort Williams area for lunch, the Great Glen, views of Ben Nevis, Loch Ness, optional boat ride and exploration of Urquhart Castle ruins, passing through Inverness and the Grampian Mountains, evening refreshment stop in Pitlochry. Daily, 8 a.m.-8:30 p.m. Adults from £49.

Rosslyn Chapel, Scottish Borders & Glenkinchie Distillery—Tour highlights include Rosslyn Chapel (of DaVinci Code fame) (opt. entrance), the Scottish Borders, Melrose Abbey (opt. entrance), Scott's View, Glenkinchie Distillery (opt. entrance). Not Sun/Wed, 9:15 a.m.-5:45 p.m. Adults from £39.

Loch Lomond, the Trossachs & Stirling Castle—Tour highlights include a stop at Loch Lomond, optional cruise or stroll through the village of Luss, Trossachs National Park, lunch stop in Rob Roy country, Stirling Castle (opt. entrance). Daily, 9:15 a.m.-6:30 p.m. Adults from £39.

West Highland Lochs, Mountains & Castles—Tour highlights include visiting Doune Castle (featured in "Outlander" and "Monty Python and the Holy Grail"), lunch in the Highlands, Inveraray on the banks of Loch Fyne, optional visit to Inveraray Castle (Duke of Argyll, chief of the Clan Campbell), Loch Lomond, the village of Luss. Daily, 9:15 a.m.-7 p.m. Adults from £45.

The Outlander, Palaces & Jacobites Experience—Tour highlights include Midhope ("Lallybroch") Castle, Blackness Castle (opt.), Linlithgow, Linlithgow Palace ("Wentworth Prison") (opt.), Callendar House, village of Culross in Fife, Tuilyies Standing Stones, Hopetoun House ("Duke of Sandringham's" house). Daily, 8:30-6 p.m. Adults from £42. A **Winter Outlander & Jacobites Experience** also available.

St. Andrews & the Fishing Villages of Fife—Tour highlights include a photo stop in Aberdour, a stop in the town of Anstruther, travel through several fishing villages in East Neuk of Fife, approx. three hours in St. Andrews (opt. St. Andrews Castle and St. Andrews Cathedral entrances), stop in Falkland, stop in South Queensferry. Daily, 9 a.m.-5:45 p.m. Adults from £45.

Holy Island, Alnwick Castle & the Kingdom of Northumbria—Tour highlights include Holy Island with the village of Lindisfarne (opt. priory visit), market town of Alnwick (opt. Alnwick castle and gardens visit—Harry Potter film site), border town of Coldstream, Flodden Field battle site (if time). Daily, 8:45-6:15 p.m. Adults from £40.

The Ultimate Whisky Experience—Tour highlights include visits to Dewar's and Deanston distilleries, views across Loch Lubnaig, village of Aberfeldy on the Scottish Whisky Trail. Tue/Thur/Fri/Sat, 8:45 a.m.-6:30 p.m. Adults from £38.

Blair Atholl and the Central Highlands—Tour highlights include the town of Blair Atholl, Blair Castle, Falls of Dochart, Queen's View, Loch Lubnaig, town of Callander, "Gateway to the Highlands." Tue/Sun, 8:30 a.m.-6:30 p.m. Adults from £38.

Timberbush Tours **also offers** 2-day tours to Eilean Donan, Loch Ness & the North West Highlands and Loch Ness, Inverness & the Highlands; a 3-day tour to Isle of Skye, the Highlands & Loch Ness; and a 5-day tour to Orkney, Ullapool, and the Northern Highlands. Look closely at costs, inclusions/exclusions, lodging options, and luggage restrictions.

Gray Line Scotland

Gray Line tours (graylinetours.com) is a large international company that offers free hotel pickup, toilets onboard larger coaches, several city center drop-off points, and free WiFi. The company's Scottish line has TripAdvisor's Certificate of Excellence. Costs include transportation with tour guide. Meals, entrance fees, and gratuities are not included. Tours depart April-October. Their main day trips are as follows:

Loch Ness and the Highlands of Scotland—Tour highlights include Glen Coe, Loch Ness (opt. cruise), Fort William, Forth Road and rail bridges. Daily, 12 hours. From £50.

Loch Lomond, the Highlands & Stirling Castle—Tour highlights include Glasgow, Loch Lomond (opt. cruise), travel through the Trossachs, Stirling Castle visit. Daily, 9.5 hours. From £40.

Doune Castle, Loch Lomond & the Western Highlands—Tour highlights include Doune Castle (from Monty Python and Outlander), photo stops at Loch Awe and Kichurn Castle, Inverary town and Castle, village of Luss on the shores of Loch Lomond. Sat, 10 hours. From £32.

Loch, Castle & Distillery Experience—Tour highlights include view of the Kelpies (giant horse statues), Stirling Castle visit, Glengoyne Distillery, Loch Lomond. Tue/Thur, 9 hours. From £40.

The Hairy Coo

The Hairy Coo (www.thehairycoo.com) is a small local company that specializes in just a few small-group tours. It has earned TripAdvisor's Certificate of Excellence. The company is also happy to arrange private, personalized tours from a few hours long to up to 14 days. Tours do not include entry fees, food, drink, or gratuities. Tours depart from the Royal Mile, on Lawnmarket. Hairy Coo day trips include the following:

Loch Ness, Glencoe, Highlands & Whisky Tour—Tour highlights include Deanston Whisky Distillery, Loch Lomond and Trossachs National Park, Rannoch Moor, Glencoe, Fort Augustus, Loch Ness cruise (opt.), Commando Memorial, Cairngorms National Park, and Pitlochry Highland village. Daily, 8 a.m.-8:30 p.m. Adults £42–£55.

FREE Scottish Highlands Tour (Tips Only)—Tour highlights include Forth Bridge, Wallace Monument, Lake of Menteith, Aberfoyle Highland village, Glen of Trossachs/Duke's Pass, Loch Katrine, Doune Castle, Highland cows. Mon/Wed/Fri, 8:45 a.m.-6 p.m. (Different schedule in winter.) No set cost (£45 value).

Stirling Castle, Loch Lomond and Whisky Tour—Tour highlights include Kelpies (huge horse sculptures), Stirling Castle, hairy cows, Loch Lomond and the Trossachs National Park, Deanston Distillery *or* Doune Castle. Tue/Thu/Sat/Sun, 8:30 a.m.-6:30 p.m. Different schedule in winter. Adults £39–£45.

Hairy Coo Tours **also leads** a 2-day tour of Loch Ness, Glencoe, Glenfinnan Viaduct, and St. Andrews; a 3-day tour of the Isle of Skye, Inverness & the Highlands; and a 5-day tour of Isle of Skye, Oben, St. Andrews, and Northwest Highlands. Look closely at costs, inclusions/exclusions, lodging options, and luggage restrictions.

Highland Experience Tours

Highland Experience Tours (www.highlandexperience.com) offers small-group tours that get a gold award for green tourism. Bus sizes range from 16-32 passengers. Tours depart from Parliament Square near St. Giles Cathedral on the Royal Mile. Prices do not include entrance fees, food, drinks, or gratuities. Day trips include the following:

Loch Ness, Glen Coe & the Highlands—Tour highlights include the Cairngorm Mountains, Inverness, Loch Ness (opt. cruise), Ben Nevis (the

UK's highest mountain), and Glen Coe. Daily, 8 a.m.-8 p.m. Adults from £45.

Loch Ness Discovery, Small Group—Tour highlights include Glen Coe, Ben Nevis, Loch Ness (opt. cruise), Cairngorm Mountains, and Pitlochry Highland town. Daily, 8 a.m.-8 p.m. Adults from £50.

Stirling Castle, Loch Lomond & Whisky—Tour highlights include Stirling Castle or town, Loch Lomond and the Trossachs National Park, Glengoyne Distillery. Daily, 9 a.m.-6:45 p.m. Adults from £36.

Rosslyn Chapel, Stirling Castle & Dumferline Abbey—Tour highlights include Forth Railway Bridge, Dumferline Abbey, Stirling Castle, Bannockburn, and Rosslyn Chapel (featured in The DaVinci Code). Tue (& Fri/Sat in summer), 9 a.m.-5:30 p.m. Adults from £36.

St. Andrews, Falkland & Fishing Villages—Tour highlights include the Forth Railway Bridge, fishing villages of East Neuk in the Kingdom of Fife, St. Andrews town, cathedral and golf club, Falkland village and optional palace visit, East Neuk. Sun/Thur, 9:30 a.m.-6 p.m. Adults from £36.

Oban, Lochs & Inveraray—Tour highlights include Loch Lomond, Loch Awe, Kilchurn Castle, seaside town of Oban, Inveraray seaside town. Fri/Sat/Sun, summer only. 8 a.m.-7:30 p.m. Adults from £45.

Alnwick Castle & the Borders—Tour highlights include the Borders, Melrose Abbey, Alnwick Castle (featured in Harry Potter and Downton Abbey), coastal town North Berwick, and the east coast of Scotland. Mon/Wed/Sat, summer only, 9 a.m.-7 p.m. Adults from £42.

Highland Experience Tours **also offers** two day trips in Spanish and numerous 2-to-9-day excursions. Look closely at costs, inclusions/exclusions, lodging options, and luggage restrictions.

Haggis Adventures

Geared to the younger traveler, Haggis Adventures (www.haggisadventures.com) started as a backpacking company and remains youth-oriented. (Their motto is #StayWild.) They have TripAdvisor's Certificate of Excellence and offer numerous 1-day and multi-day tours. Costs cover transportation, tour guide, and WiFi. Most tours start from their office halfway down the Royal Mile on High Street (a bit south of Waverley Station).

Day trips include the following (Prices in dollars fluctuate with the exchange rate.):

Loch Ness Hunter Tour—Highlights include Loch Ness, Fort Augustus, Glencoe. Optional cruise. Picnic lunch included. Daily, 8 a.m.-8 p.m. Adult prices from $75.

Lochs, Castles and the Kelpies—Highlights include Stirling Castle, Balmaha village, Loch Lomond and the Trossachs National Park, and the Kelpies (30-meter high steel sculptures). Wed/Fri/Sat (fewer days in off-season), 8:45 a.m.-5:30 p.m. Adult price from $64.

Whisky, Warriors & Waterfalls—Highlights include Famous Grouse Experience (whisky sampling), William Wallace monument, Hermitage Forest stroll, and Dunkeld Cathedral. Tue/Thu/Sat (fewer days in off-season), 8:45 a.m.-5:30 p.m. Adult prices from $71.

Castles & Broomsticks—Highlights include Alnwick Castle (seen in Harry Potter and Downton Abbey), the seaside village of Bamburgh, Bamburgh Castle, the town of Coldstream, the Borders region, and the River Tweed. Fri/Sun, summer only, 8:15 a.m.-5:30 p.m. Adult prices from $71.

Outlander Trail—Highlights include Duone Castle (Castle Leoch), Culross, Falkland, Midhope Castle (Lallybroch), Dysart Harbour (port of Le Havre). Mon/Tues/Thu/Sun, less in off-season, Apr.-Sept. only, 8:45 a.m.-5:30 p.m. Adult prices from $77.

The St. Andrews and the V&A Museum—Highlights include the Victoria and Albert Museum in Dundee, British Golf Museum (opt.), St. Andrews Castle and Cathedral, stop in the quaint fishing village of Anstruther, views of the Forth Bridge. Sat, summers only, 8:15 a.m.-5:30 p.m. Adult prices from $74.

Highland Games Tour—(Limited dates) Clan gathering, piping competitions, Highland dancing, caber tossing, hammer throwing, Highland dress and scenery. Times vary according to location. Adult price from $122. May-Sept. only.

Haggis Tours **also offers** multiple overnight trips. Look closely at costs, inclusions/exclusions, lodging options, and luggage restrictions. Note: Lodging is generally in a shared hostel dorm.

Lodging

Hotels on this list are based on location and general accessibility. Those closest to transportation hubs (Waverley Station, Waverley Bridge, Waterloo Place) and in flatter areas are listed first. That means that hotels in New Town are given priority.

Some hotels at the foot of Old Town are also close to those transportation sites and are included, but they may require walking on an incline. Listed hotels vary greatly in price, and listed price ranges can vary significantly by time of year, so use price ranges for comparison among hotels rather than as actual price indicators. Regardless of season, you should find something within your budget, if you start looking early enough.

This is by no means a comprehensive list of suitable hotels. You may find a wonderful deal on what looks to you like a good choice. By all means—grab it! Same with charming B&Bs, which aren't covered here because they tend to have a limited number of available rooms and generally don't have elevators. If you can nab one in a convenient location that gets good reviews, has a great breakfast, decent accessibility, and a workable price, do it! You may prefer to find your own hotel near or on the Royal Mile for that medieval flavor, and that's fine, as long as you know what you're getting into. Just be aware that walking anywhere in the Old Town will require more effort than in the New Town.

Remember that airport shuttles, city buses, and the hop-on/hop-off (HOHO) buses stop at Waverley Bridge and elsewhere around Waverley Station; Heart of Scotland tour buses and Rabbie's tour buses leave from Waterloo Place; and Timberbush Tours, Hairy Coo, Highland Experience, and Haggis Adventure tour buses all leave from the Royal Mile.

Hotel price ranges are based on late 2019 TripAdvisor averages. Your own quotes may be higher or lower.

Balmoral Hotel—1 Princes St. (at Waverley Station) (www.roccofortehotels.com/hotels-and-resorts/the-balmoral-hotel). Edinburgh's flagship hotel. Has TripAdvisor's Certificate of Excellence. Location: between Waverley Bridge and Waterloo Place. Pros: luxury, style, accessible rooms, free WiFi, refrigerator in room, award-winning restaurant, air conditioning, offers afternoon tea, room service, bar, business center, fitness center, spa, pool, airport shuttle. Cons: price, rooms can be smaller than expected, only double rooms, no price break for singles, expensive breakfast. (TripAdvisor price range for standard room: $199-$885.)

Distances: Waterloo Place (.1 miles), Waverley Station (.1 miles), Royal Mile (.3 miles), Edinburgh Castle (.5 miles)

Motel One, Princes—10-15 Princes St. (across from Waverley Station) (www.motelone.com/en/hotels/edinburgh/hotel-edinburgh-princes). Has TripAdvisor's Certificate of Excellence. Location: between Waverley Bridge and Waterloo Place. Pros: modern rooms, accessible throughout, air conditioning, free WiFi, bar, excellent continental breakfast available. Cons: only double rooms (but price break for 1 adult). (TripAdvisor price range for standard room: $86-$143.)

Distances: Waterloo Place (.1 miles), Waverley Station (.1 miles), Royal Mile (.3 miles), Edinburgh Castle (.5 miles)

Hotel Indigo—20 Princes St. (www.ihg.com/hotelindigo/hotels/us/en/edinburgh/ediin/hoteldetail). Has TripAdvisor's Certificate of Excellence. Location: across Princes Street from Waverley Station. Pros: free WiFi, air conditioning, restaurant, room service, bar, accessible bedrooms, great full breakfast available (part of some room rates), fitness center. Cons: only double rooms (no price break for singles), small/slow lift. (TripAdvisor price range for standard room: $111-$335.)

Distances: Waterloo Place (.1 miles), Waverley Station (.1 miles), Royal Mile (.3 miles), Edinburgh Castle (.5 miles)

Old Waverley Hotel—43 Princes St. (www.oldwaverley.co.uk). *Only consider if you are OK with stairs.* Location: close to Waverley Bridge, across from Jenners Dept. Store. Pros: free WiFi, breakfast available (included in some room prices), single, twin, and triple rooms available, air conditioning, restaurant, room service, offers afternoon tea. Cons: worn rooms, some weak water pressure, 27 steps to reach reception level (lift above that). (TripAdvisor price range for standard room: $92-$260.)

Distances: Waterloo Place (.2 miles), Waverley Station (.2 miles), Royal Mile (.2 miles), Edinburgh Castle (.4 miles)

Motel One, Royal—18 Market St. (on the Old Town side of Waverley Station) (www.motelone.com/en/hotels/edinburgh/hotel-edinburgh-royal). Has TripAdvisor's Certificate of Excellence. Location: at the foot of Old City, right at Waverley Bridge. Pros: modern rooms, accessible throughout (but may require looking for ramps and power lifts), free Wi-Fi, bar, good continental breakfast available, air conditioning. Cons: single rooms same price as double for one, some rooms difficult to get to, cheap rooms may have no natural light. (TripAdvisor price range for standard room: $97-$164.)

Distances: Waverley Station (.1 miles), Royal Mile (.1 miles), Edinburgh Castle (.4 miles)

Apex Waterloo Hotel—23-27 Waterloo Place (www.apexhotels.co.uk/apex-waterloo-lace-hotel). Has TripAdvisor's Certificate of Excellence. Location: between Waverley Station and Calton Hill at Waterloo

Place. Pros: air conditioning, free WiFi, restaurant, room service, bar, large rooms, triple and family rooms available, accessible rooms available, fitness center, spa, pool. Cons: no single rooms, many consider breakfast overpriced. (TripAdvisor price range for standard room: $113-$316.)

Distances: Waterloo Place (0.0 miles), Waverley Station (.2 miles), Calton Hill (.2 miles), Royal Mile (.4 miles), Edinburgh Castle (.6 miles)

The Scotsman Hotel—20 North Bridge (scotsmanhotel.co.uk). Has TripAdvisor's Certificate of Excellence. Location: south of Waverley Station at foot of Old Town. Pros: many spacious rooms, free WiFi, whisky sample in room, good breakfast, bar, room service. Cons: only double rooms, old lift is small and slow, new lift can be "temperamental." (TripAdvisor price range for standard room: $168-$455.)

Distances: Waterloo Place (.2 miles), Waverley Station (.1 miles), Royal Mile (.2 miles), Edinburgh Castle (.5 miles)

Barcelo Carlton Hotel (Hilton)—19 North Bridge (www3.hilton.com/en/hotels/united-kingdom/hilton-edinburgh-carlton-EDICAHI/index.html). Location: south of Waverley Station on the north side of Old Town. Pros: free WiFi, bar, restaurant, room service, excellent breakfast available (sometimes included in room rate), accessible rooms, air conditioning, telephone, many spacious rooms, triple and quad rooms available, pool. Cons: slightly uphill from the train station, no single rooms, sound insulation. (TripAdvisor price range for standard room: $137-$375.)

Distances: Waterloo Place (.2 miles), Waverley Station (.1 miles), Royal Mile (.3 miles), Edinburgh Castle (.5 miles)

Additional hotels, not quite as conveniently located:

Ibis Styles—19 St. Andrew Square (www.ibis.com/gb/hotel-9058-ibis-styles-edinburgh-centre-st-andrew-square/index.shtml). TripAdvisor's Certificate of Excellence. Location: on St. Andrews Square in New Town. Pros: air conditioning, reduced-mobility rooms available, some rooms with balcony, restaurant, bar, free WiFi, good breakfast available (included in some rates). Cons: only double/twin rooms. (TripAdvisor price range for standard room: $90-$286.)

Distances: Waterloo Place (.3 miles), Waverley Station (.3 miles), Royal Mile (.4 miles), Edinburgh Castle (.5 miles)

The Principal Edinburgh George St.—19-21 George St. (the-principal-edinburgh.edinburgh-hotel.org/en/). Location: close to train station in New Town. Pros: free WiFi, restaurant, bar, room service, breakfast available (included in some room rates), family rooms available, accessible, air conditioning. Cons: no single rooms (but single price break on double room). (TripAdvisor price range for standard room: $157-$424.)

Distances: Waterloo Place (.3 miles), Waverley Station (.3 miles), Royal Mile (.3 miles), Edinburgh Castle (.4 miles)

Le Monde Hotel—16 George St. (lemondehotel.co.uk/). Location: close to train station in New Town. Pros: free WiFi, 2 restaurants, 3 bars, nightclub, boutique style, air conditioning, room service. Cons: nightclub and street noise at night, only double rooms. (TripAdvisor price range for standard room: $138-$318.)

Distances: Waterloo Place (.3 miles), Waverley Station (.3 miles), Royal Mile (.3 miles), Edinburgh Castle (.4 miles)

The Hub by Premier Inn Edinburgh City Centre—Rose Street, South Lane. (www.premierinn.com/gb/en/hotels/scotland/lothian/edinburgh/hub-edinburgh-rose-street.html). Location: on Rose Street in New Town, the next major street north from Princes Street. Pros: value, accessible rooms, restaurant, lounge, breakfast available, WiFi. Cons: farther from transportation, rooms rather small, stripped-down modern. (TripAdvisor price range for standard room: $39-$153.)

Distances: Waverley Station (.9 miles), Edinburgh Castle (.9 miles)

Other base cities in Scotland

You can base yourself in Glasgow and Inverness, as well, if you prefer to experience different parts of the country in greater depth than a day trip allows. Both cities offer hop-on/hop-off tours and excursions into the countryside. Bear in mind the principles of easy-walking hotel selection—easy access to the buildings, ideally in a relatively flat area, and proximity to transportation hubs—if you want to limit walking and climbing and save your energy for seeing the sights.

Dublin

Overview

Dublin is the capital and largest city of The Republic of Ireland (not to be confused with Northern Ireland, which is part of the United Kingdom and has Belfast as its capital). The city is located on the east coast of the island nation, at the mouth of the River Liffey. Dublin was first settled by Celtic-speaking people in the 7th century and was then expanded by Viking and later Norman invaders. Fortunately, central Dublin is relatively flat, so hills are not a problem.

Ireland is famous for its whiskey and its Guinness, its music, its potato famine and subsequent waves of emigration, its silver-tongued gift of the gab, leprechauns, and 20th-century political turmoil.

The famously green island owes its verdant growth to lots of rain, up to 225 days with rain a year, so whenever you visit, make sure you are prepared for a wet welcome. Fortunately, Dublin is in the driest part of the country and only receives about half the rain of the west coast (but that's still about 151 days with rain annually). Historically, Ireland's climate has been quite cool in summer and mild in winter, but recently it has had some summer hot spells (into the upper 80s and even 90s Fahrenheit), so you won't necessarily need nothing but sweaters in the summer.

Possible plan for Dublin (What I'd do)

If I were traveling to Dublin with my mother, this is what I would plan for us to do. Obviously, you may prefer to do something different, but you may find this itinerary handy as a starting point, changing it as much as you would like. **Please double check any details before relying on them, as specifics may have changed since I wrote these pages.** This section will make more sense as you work your way through the chapter. Having a city map at hand will help to visualize this itinerary and other options. This plan assumes lodging around O'Connell Street.

Once you have a pretty good idea of what you want to do, check out ticket sales online, because online booking is almost always less expensive than buying a ticket on-site. Of course, when buying online, you save money but might give up flexibility, so it's not always the best choice, but it's certainly worth looking into. As for day trips, you probably don't want to plan for more than two consecutive out-of-town excursions at a time, to avoid bus fatigue.

If you have no idea where you want to go in Dublin, it might be useful to know that guide books highly recommend 1) the Book of Kells (and Old Library), 2) the National Museum—Archeology, and 3) Kilmainham Gaol (all covered in this itinerary), but beyond that, it's a matter of personal preference. For many people, the top sight in Dublin is the Guinness Storehouse, but for others, that's way too touristy, so it's a personal choice.

Day 1—Depart U.S.

Day 2—Arrive Dublin.

    Visit ATM for euros, if needed. Buy Airlink bus ticket online ahead of time. (Or Aircoach Dublin.) Take Airlink bus 747 (or 757) or Aircoach bus to appropriate central Dublin stop. (Example: take 747 Airlink bus to Cathal Brugha St/O'Connell St stop and walk around corner to the Holiday Inn Express on O'Connell Street.)

    Check into hotel. Rest as needed, if room is available. Visit a tourist information office for city maps and other city information you may want. (Locations: 25 Suffolk St. and 14 Upper O'Connell St.) Any reservations, tickets, or passes still needing to be lined up?

    Visit sights within walking distance of hotel (self-guided walking tour). (If lodging north of the river, see St. Mary's Pro Cathedral, stroll down O'Connell Street, see the Spire and the General Post Office. Cross the river.) Go to Temple Bar for tea or coffee or something stronger. Wander around neighborhood. Locate a grocery store. Wrap up the day by visiting a pub to eat and drink, probably near hotel.

Day 3—Get an introduction to Dublin's sights. Walk to General Post Office on O'Connell Street (or ride HOHO bus there, if staying south of the river). Take tour.

    Validate a 72-hour HOHO or other ticket (if not done already)—ask driver about a voucher for any city walking tour included, but realize that the tours involve much walking without breaks). Ride HOHO bus to Kilmainham Gaol for tour. (Must book ahead online—up to 60 days in advance. If you have special needs, e.g., wheelchair, contact directly at kilmainhamgaol@opw.ie.) Finish HOHO route. If more than one HOHO route is available, consider another round to hear commentary of other sights.

Day 4—Use the 2nd day of a HOHO bus ticket to explore Dublin further.

Ride HOHO bus to Trinity College. Visit Book of Kells when it opens (if it's on display—it was planned to be unavailable until early March 2020 for conservation), then possibly Trinity College guided walking tour. (A combo ticket costs very little more than the Kells ticket alone, but combo tickets can only be purchased at the gate from "Authenticity Tours." Timed Book of Kells tickets can be ordered online at www.tcd.ie/visitors/book-of-kells/tickets-information/, but they don't include the guided walking tour. You can "upgrade" your online ticket to a combo ticket at a reduced cost, but only in person.)

Take a break at a café or restaurant along the south side of Trinity College. Walk to the National Museum—Archeology (free entry). If still going strong, consider visiting the National Gallery or the Natural History Museum, both nearby and with free entry. Merrion Square is nearby, with its famous Oscar Wilde statue and iconic Georgian houses ringing the square. Take a short stroll.

Walk to nearest HOHO stop. Ride the rest of the HOHO route back to the hotel and rest up to go out for the evening. Night tour bus (if included in HOHO ticket).

Day 5—3rd day of HOHO pass in Dublin.

Ride HOHO bus to Famine Statues and Jeanie Johnston Tall Ship and Famine Museum. (Book tour slot in advance. Confirm ship will be docked during visit date.) Walk back to EPIC—The Irish Immigration Museum. Break for lunch or snack.

Ride HOHO bus to Pearse Lyon Distillery (if included in HOHO pass). Ride HOHO bus back to hotel area. (Make sure to know when final buses run, so as not to miss one.)

Day 6—Day trip—Belfast (with the Titanic Experience) (Day trip order may be adjusted or different tours substituted, of course, depending on interest and availability.)

Day 7—Day trip—Wicklow Mountains & Glendalough Tour

Day 8—DublinRide city bus to St. Stephen's Green. (Buy ticket at station or on bus or buy a Leap Visitor Card.) Tour Little Museum of

Dublin. Stroll to Chester Beatty Library (behind Dublin Castle) (free)—the Silk Road Café is recommended for a light lunch. Open time to shop, explore, rest. Possibly check out St. Patrick's Cathedral.

Day 9—Day trip—Newgrange & Hill of Tara Tour

Day 10—Final day in Dublin. Half-day tour to Malahide Castle (or fit in any final Dublin sights that were skipped or missed before). Final shopping. Final night out. Dinner and theatre? (Celtic Nights dinner and dance show next to O'Connell Bridge?)

Day 11—Return to U.S. Use Airlink return ticket, if purchased ahead of time.

Arrival

You will probably fly into the Dublin Airport (DUB), about 5½ miles north of the city (www.dublinairport.com). To get from the airport to the city, you have your choice of bus or taxi. To find a taxi at the airport, follow the Taxi signs to the taxi ranks. Fares into the city typically cost around €30 (or more, in heavy traffic). You are entitled to a printed receipt of your fare from the taxi meter.

To take an airport express bus, exit outside of Arrivals on ground level and look for one of these options:

Airlink Express—Will take you directly to central Dublin (dodublin.ie/airport-transfers/airlink-express). Stops on route **#747** (departs every 10 minutes) include Point Village & 3Arena, North Wall Quay (Central Bank), The Convention Centre Dublin, Irish Financial Services Centre (IFSC), Common Street & Connelly Car Park, Talbot Street & Talbot Place, The Central Bus Station (Busáras), Connolly Rail Station, Gardiner Street & Railway Street, Cathal Brugha Street & O'Connell Street, O'Connell Street & Abbey Street, College Green & Trinity College & Temple Bar, Christ Church Cathedral, High Street, Ushers Quay and Heuston Rail Station.

Stops on route **#757** (departs every 30 minutes) include North Wall Quay (Central Bank), The Convention Centre Dublin, Irish Financial Services Centre (IFSC), Custom House Quay, Eden Quay & O'Connell Bridge, Hawkins Street & Temple Bar, Westland Row, Merrion Square, St. Stephen's Green, Earlsfort Terrace, Adelaide Road, Camden (Charlotte Way) and Harcourt Street.

Tickets may be purchased online, at the Bus and Travel Information Desk in Terminal 1, at vending machines outside Terminals 1 and 2

Arrivals at the Airlink stops, and from Airlink promoters wearing green jackets/t-shirts. Cost is €7 (€6 online) for a single adult trip and €12 (€11 online) for an adult round trip. Covered by the Leap Visitor Card. A map showing where to find the Airlink pickup at the airport is located here: dodublin. ie/airport-transfers/airlink-express/airport-to-city-centre.

Aircoach Dublin—Aircoach Dublin can also be found outside the Arrivals areas at the airport. Route 700 runs from both Terminal 1 and Terminal 2 to O'Connell Street (25 minutes) and Trinity College/Grafton Street (30 minutes). Buses run every 15 minutes most of the day and night, dropping to every 30 minutes from around midnight to around 3:30 a.m. You can book tickets online (www.aircoach.ie/route-700-dublinairport-dublin-city-centre) or from Aircoach staff members at the Aircoach departure stands or from the coach driver. Online cost is €6 for an adult one-way ticket, €11.50 round-trip, and €1.50 for a child one-way ticket, €3 round-trip. Prices are slightly higher when purchased on the bus. There's a 15% discount at the Aircoach desks in the airport terminals with presentation of a valid Dublin Pass purchase receipt.

Easy transportation options

Once in the city, your probable transportation choices are bus, taxi, and tram. Much of the city is walkable, if you prefer to get around under your own steam. The easiest way to get to the sights, though, is to ride a hop-on/hop-off (HOHO) tourist bus. Dublin has at least two HOHO bus companies, listed below. You purchase a 24-, 48-, or 72-hour (or 1-day, 2-day, or 3-day) ticket and then may hop on and hop off the buses (of the line you paid for) as much as you'd like in that time. You may choose to take the whole tour to get an overview and then, on the second time around, hop off to see sights up close. Buses run year-round, though hours of operation and frequency of buses vary by season. Prices are listed below, but check each company's Web site for the latest costs and schedules.

City Sightseeing Dublin

City Sightseeing Dublin runs one hop-on/hop-off (HOHO) route with more than 25 stops, starting at 37 College Green (west of Trinity College). Audio guides on buses, with a live guide every other bus. The route takes 120 minutes for the whole loop and runs from 9 a.m. to 6 p.m. Buses leave about every 20 minutes. The route and ticket information are viewable at city-sightseeing.com/en/50/dublin/60/hop-on-hop-off-dublin.

Tickets may be purchased online or at/on the bus. Mobile or paper vouchers are supposed to be accepted (but the Web site also says that paper vouchers are required). Up to 2 children ages 4-12 travel free with every paying adult. Prices are as follows:

- 24-hour HOHO bus access + guided walking tour (10:30 a.m.)—adult online €19.80 (€22 on street); child (4-12) on-line €9 (€10 on street); student (with student card) online €16.20 (€18 on street); family (2 adults and up to 4 children aged 4-12) online €39.60 (€44 on street)
- 48-hour HOHO bus access + guided walking tour (10:30 a.m.)—adult online €25.20 (€28 on street); child (4-12) on-line €9 (€10 on street); student (with student card) online €20.70 (€23 on street); family (2 adults and up to 4 children aged 4-12) online €50.40 (€55 on street)

Big Bus Dublin

Big Bus Tours is new to Dublin but offers two routes with over 30 stops, as well as a night tour (www.bigbustours.com/en/dublin/dublin-bus-tours/). Most buses (85%) are wheelchair accessible. The blue route (2 hours) includes a live guide, and buses run approximately every 30 minutes. The route starts at O'Connell Street, swings by the National Gallery and to Stephen's Green, College Green by Trinity College, then down Dame Street to Dublin Castle, St. Patrick's Cathedral, Guinness Storehouse, Kilmainham Gaol, Teeling Whiskey Distillery, Glasneven Cemetery, and more. The first bus from O'Connell Street is at 9:30 a.m.; the last is 3 p.m.

The red route (1 hour 45 minutes) also starts at O'Connell Street, with the first bus departing at 8:45 a.m., last bus at 6 p.m. Buses run every 20-30 minutes. Where the blue route swings far north of the river, the red route stays close to the city center, running along the north side of the river. Many stops are common to both routes, making transfer between the routes easy.

The night tour bus is a 1-hour live-guided panoramic tour that departs from O'Connell Street at 7 p.m., 8 p.m., and 9:30 p.m.

Tickets may be purchased at the bus stop or for a discount online. Online purchases can be validated in the following 6 months. All HOHO tickets include a free walking tour with Yellow Umbrella. Tickets options are as follows:

- Classic Ticket—1 day HOHO access, walking tour. Adult €19.80 (€22 on street); child (5-15) €9 (€10 on street); family (2 adults + 2 children) €48.60 (€54 on street)
- Premium Ticket—2 days HOHO access, walking tour, night tour. Adult €23.80 (€28 on street); child (5-15) €8.50 (€10 on street); family (2 adults + 2 children) €56.10 (€66 on street)
- Deluxe Ticket—3 days HOHO access, walking tour, night tour, Pearse Lyons Distillery Entry. Adult €29.60 (€37 on street); child (5-15) €8 (on street €10); family (2 adults + 2 children) €67.20 (€84 on street)
- Classic Ticket + Guinness Storehouse—1 day HOHO access, walking tour, Guinness Storehouse. Adult €42.30 (€47 on street)

Other HOHO buses

Dublin CityScape (www.cityscapetours.ie) appears to shut down in the off season. When running, it offers HOHO tours of Dublin, claiming to have the best value for the money, but, at least recently, has drawn quite bad reviews. As such, I will list the company, but cannot recommend it.

DoDublin (dodublin.ie) used to offer attractive hop-on/hop-off tickets on its green buses, with the 72-hour card also including Airlink and city bus access during that time. As of this writing, however (late 2019), DoDublin cards have been discontinued. It is worth searching on them before making your plans, though, because they offered desirable packages and were highly rated.

Other in-city transportation

City buses are an economical if less convenient option for getting around Dublin. Dublin Bus trip costs depend on how many stages you'll be crossing. A Route Planner and Fare Calculator are both available on the bus Web site: www.dublinbus.ie. A city-center map with public transportation marked and a Destination Finder is at www.dublinbus.ie/Global/Core_routes_interactive_map_March 2018.pdf.

If you will use the **buses** only occasionally, you can pay for individual trips (from €2.10 to €3.30 for adults, depending on distance), or slightly lower (€1.50 to €2.15) with a Leap Card (general transit card—see below).

LUAS is the **light rail** system of Dublin (www.luas.ie). It has two lines, red and green. The Web site provides a link to a journey planner (also shows bus options). The red line runs from Connelly and Heuston train stations, and the green line runs north/south down O'Connell Street, around Trinity College, and to St. Stephen's Green. Ticket prices vary according to peak or off-peak hours, adult or reduced fare, and number of zones entered, but a single ride at full price is €2.10-€3.30 for an adult and €1-€1.20 for a child. Leap Cards (see below) cover rides on the light rail system.

The **DART (Dublin Area Rapid Transit)** system (www.irishrail.ie/about-us/services/dart-commuter) offers commuter trains that connect Dublin to its suburbs. As a tourist, you are unlikely to use this system, but it is covered by Leap Cards.

The **Leap Card** (about.leapcard.ie/Dublin) is a discount public transport card that you buy for a refundable fee of €5 at tourist information offices, newsstands, markets—wherever you see the leap frog logo. You load credit on the card and top off as necessary, using the card for reduced fare (up to 31% less) on Dublin's public buses, LUAS, and DART routes.

The **Leap Visitor Card** (about.leapcard.ie/leap-visitor-card) is an attractive option for tourists staying in Dublin, allowing unlimited travel on Airlink, Dublin Bus, LUAS, DART, and Commuter Rail. Prices are 1 day/24 hours (€10), 3 days/72 hours (€19.50), and 7 days/168 hours (€40). Your chosen time period starts from the first time you use the card.

The Leap Visitor Card can be purchased at the airport (including at the Bus & Travel Information Desk in Terminal 1) or in the city (including at Dublin Bus, 59 Upper O'Connell St.; Discover Ireland Centre, 14 Upper O'Connell St.; and Dublin Centre, 25 Suffolk St.) You can top up Leap Visitor Cards, too, at any Leap Card Payzone outlet (about.leapcard.ie/about/where-to-buy).

Taxis are the most personalized—and most expensive—option for getting around the city. Taxis have yellow and blue roof signs. You can hail them on the street, find one at a taxi stand (usually outside major tourist sights), or call to order one (or use an app).

Typical cab fees from Dublin Airport to Temple Bar (central Dublin) are around €25.64 (up to €55 in heavy traffic); a center-city run from the General Post Office to Dublin Castle costs around €7.66. Fares can vary greatly depending on traffic. For example, the trip from the General Post Office to Dublin Castle just listed ranges from €5.33 to €17.86, depending on traffic. You can use a taxi fare finder to get estimated taxi costs: www.taxifarefinder.com or transportforireland.ie/taxi/taxi-fare-estimator/).

Taxi companies in Dublin include the following:

City Cabs, Phone: 01 872 7272
Metro Cabs, Phone: 01 668 3333
National Radio Cabs, Phone: 01 677 2222
Pony Cabs, Phone: 01 661 2233
Taxi 7, Phone: 01 460 0000
Xpert Digi Taxis, Phone: 01 667 0777

General Dublin taxi information can be found here: www.dublin.info/taxi/.

And what about Uber? Yes, this service is available in Dublin: uber.com/cities/dublin/, but will just bring you a taxi cab. Service from the airport can be requested at www.uber.com/airports/dub/. *Be aware that UberBLACK is a premium (expensive) option.*

Sightseeing—The Dublin Pass

The Dublin Pass (www.dublinpass.com) is a 1-, 2-, 3-, or 5-calendar-day sightseeing pass that allows free, fast-track entry to more than 30 tourist attractions in Dublin. (When entry is limited to guided tours, you must wait for the first available tour.)

Covered attractions include the following popular sights (prices listed are normal 2019 adult entry costs): Guinness Storehouse (€18.50-€23), Jameson's Distillery (€22), Dublin Castle (€8), EPIC The Irish Emigration Museum (€16.50), Christ Church Cathedral (€7), Teelings Whiskey Distillery Tour (€15), GPO Witness History Exhibition (€14), St. Patrick's Cathedral (€8), Dublinia (€10). The pass also includes the Dublin Zoo, National Wax Museum Plus, Malahide Castle, and more. (It does not, however, include the Book of Kells.)

The Dublin Pass includes 24 hours on the City Sightseeing HOHO buses. (Using the pass for the first time activates it.) Passes can be ordered online and picked up at a tourist information office. Prices are as follows (online sales can result in up to a 20% reduction in some prices):

- 1-day pass—adult €62, child (5-15) €33
- 2-day pass—adult €83, child (5-15) €43 (sale prices €79 and €41)
- 3-day pass—adult €102, child (5-15) €55 (sale prices €92 and €49)
- 5-day pass—adult €128, child (5-15) €74 (sale prices €102 and €59).

Usage is limited to a certain "purse value" per pass. The "purse value" is based on what attractions would normally cost, and limits are as follows for tickets: 1-day pass, adult limit €129, child limit €60; 2-day pass, adult limit €175, child limit €81; 3-day pass, adult limit €232, child limit €104; 5-day pass, adult limit €303, child limit €150.

Online advice is that the Dublin Pass is a good deal if you plan to visit the expensive attractions (particularly the Guinness Storehouse and the two distillery tours) and use the HOHO bus tour, but otherwise probably not. Cost it out and see whether it makes sense for you. Keep in mind that you can also avoid most lines with the pass, saving time.

And if you opt to use a ticket that is longer than the 24-hour HOHO bus access that comes with it, you may want to look into a Leap Visitor Card for cost-effective transportation. The Dublin Pass descriptions for the various attractions tell which city buses to take to reach each sight. (Or there is also the city bus route finder online, see above.)

Day trips

It's possible to see much of Ireland without having to leave the comfort of your base hotel at night, because the entire island is only a little larger than South Carolina, and Dublin has plenty of tourist companies that specialize in day trips.

As always, use the information here as a guide, but check each company's Web site for tour details and the most current price and schedule information. **Tour details—even which tours are offered—routinely change from season to season.** Whichever tours you decide on, look over cancellation policies, if your plans aren't completely firm.

Browsing through Web sites will also help you decide which company's tours seem a good fit for you. Be aware that some specific tours have special requirements or recommendations—good shoes and warm clothing for Neolithic tombs, for example—so you'll want to look descriptions over closely before you show up at the departure point. And make sure you show up early for a tour so you are not considered a no-show and your seat sold to someone else!

Tour companies differ on which entry fees they include in their prices, so check those specifics (and confirm online), if your selection comes down to price.

Also take into account where the tours depart from, in Dublin mostly from O'Connell Street or around Trinity College. You may, in fact, decide on tours according to which ones depart from near your hotel.

If you want to save your walking energy for the tour itself but you select a tour with a departure point that is not close to your hotel, you may want to invest in a taxi ride to get there. Hopefully, you'll have a good sense of Dublin and its layout before you need to make that decision.

If you take a multi-day tour with one of these companies, you will likely be restricted to one small bag and will need to store the lion's share of your luggage. Your hotel may do that for you (many offer baggage storage), or you can check into storing your luggage at the train or bus station. BagBNB at Connolly Rail Station costs €5/bag per day but requires an online reservation. Wild Rover Tours (see below) advertises luggage storage at its office beside O'Connell Bridge in addition to its bus trips (€6/bag for 24 hours, €25/bag for 7 days, €3/bag for 4 hours). Tourist Office Dublin stores luggage in their office on College Green (across from Trinity College) (€6/bag for 24 hours). Other luggage storage options can be found by searching on "Dublin luggage storage."

Rabbie's Tours

Rabbie's Tours (www.rabbies.com/en/ireland-tours/from-dublin) offers small-group tours on air-conditioned, 16-seat minibuses. The company is a TripAdvisor Traveler's Choice award winner (the highest honor the company offers). Costs cover transportation and guide, but not entry fees. Tours depart from Nassau St., by Trinity College. Their day trips are as follows:

Glendalough, Powerscourts & the Wicklow Mountains—Tour highlights include the ancient monastic city of Glendalough, Wicklow Mountains, Powerscourt House and Gardens, Avoca historic village ("Ballykissangel"), Sally Gap mountain pass, Lough Tay, Enniskerry Village. Not daily, 9:15 a.m.-7 p.m. Adults €46-€69.

Boyne Valley, Celtic Ireland & Trim Castle—Tour highlights include Fourknocks tomb, Drogheda town, Monasterboice High Crosses, Bective Abbey, Trim Castle (Europe's largest Norman castle), not daily, 9:15 a.m.-6:30 p.m. Adults €46-€49.

Connemara, Galway & the Far West—Tour highlights include Cong Village and Abbey, Lough Corrib, Connemara National Park, Galway City. Not daily, 8 a.m.-8 p.m. Adults €62-€85.

The Blarney Stone & Rock of Cashel—Tour highlights include Rock of Cashel castle and religious complex, the Golden Vale, Blarney Castle, Stone and gardens. Not daily, 8 a.m.-8 p.m. Adults €62-€79.

Rabbie's Tours **also offers** 2-to-11-day tours of Ireland.

Paddywagon Tours

Paddywagon Tours (www.paddywagontours.com/) claims to be Ireland's "leading tour outfitter," in business since 1998. The company has received Trip Advisor's Certificate of Excellence Award. Most tours are on large buses, with some small-group (16-passenger) tours available. Tour pickups are at Lower Gardiner St., O'Connell St., *and* the Molly Malone Statue on Suffolk St. All buses have free WiFi. Paddywagon tours also offers custom tour planning. Their day trips are as follows:

Cliffs of Moher Day Tour—Tour highlights include Ireland's Wild Atlantic Way, the Burren landscape, Doolin Village, the fishing Village of Kinvara, the Cliffs of Moher, Atlantic Edge Exhibition (entry included), and Bunratty Castle. Tour available in Spanish. Includes free Dublin walking tour. Daily, pickup 7:30-8 a.m. (depending on location), return 8 p.m. From €40.

Cliffs of Moher Day Tour (Small Group)—Tour highlights include King John's Castle in Limerick, Wild Atlantic Way, Doolin Village, Cliffs of Moher, Atlantic Edge Exhibition (entry included). Daily, includes hotel pickup and drop-off, 7-7:30 a.m., return 7:30 p.m. From €85.

Giant's Causeway Day Tour—Tour highlights include Giant's Causeway, Carrick-a-Rede Rope Bridge, Dark Hedges ("King's Road" in *Game of Thrones*), Dunluce Castle, White Park Bay, Ballintoy (*Game of Thrones* set), the Antrim Coast, and Belfast. Tour available in Spanish. Daily, depart 7:15-7:30 a.m., return 8:30. From €60.

Giant's Causeway Day Tour (Small Group)—Tour highlights include Giant's Causeway, Belfast (either Titanic Experience or Black Taxi Tour, price included). Hotel pickup and drop-off. Daily, depart 7-7:30 a.m., return 7:30. From €85.

Blarney Day Tour—Tour highlights include Rock of Cashel (entry included), Cork City, Blarney Castle and Gardens (entry included). Daily, 8 a.m.-8 p.m. From €50.

Kilkenny and Wicklow Tour—Tour highlights include the St. Kevin's monastic city of Glendalough, Wicklow Gap, medieval Irish capital Kilkenny. Daily, depart 9-9:15 a.m., return 6 p.m. From €50.

Belfast Day Tour (Including the Titanic Experience)—Tour highlights include Monasterboice ruins, Belfast (opt. Black Taxi Tour), The Titanic Experience (entry included). Daily, depart 9-9:15 a.m., return 6:30. From €50.

Connemara and Galway Day Tour—Tour highlights include Cong, Cong Abbey, Lough Corrib (2nd largest lake in Ireland), Connemara Wilderness, The Deserted Valley, Galway. Mon/Wed/Fri/Sat/Sun (in high season), depart 8-8:15 a.m., return 8:30. From €35.

Kerry Day Tour—Tour highlights include Adare village, Killarney National Park, Killarney town, Torc Waterfall, Muckross House and Gardens, Killorglin (on the "Ring of Kerry"), Dingle Bay, Inch Beach, Wild Atlantic Way. Sat/Sun, depart 6:20-6:30 a.m., return 9 p.m. From €65.

Half Day tour to Glendalough/Wicklow—Tour highlights include Glendalough with its ruined Monastic City and two lakes, Wicklow mountains. Daily, departs 8-8:15 a.m. and 1:30-1:45 p.m. From €22.

Paddywagon Tours **also offers** day trips in Spanish and numerous 2- to-9-day tours.

Wild Rover Tours

Wild Rover Tours (wildrovertours.com/) has TripAdvisor's Traveler's Choice Award and offers one-day (and multi-day) tours in air-conditioned 53-seat coaches that all have complimentary WiFi. Tours include almost all entry fees and each has a dedicated guide. Different tours have different pickup and drop-off points, often starting at Dame Street and/or O'Connell Street and often ending at O'Connell Street or Bachelor's Walk. Detailed tour schedules are available on the Web site. Save 10% when booking a second tour at the same time as the first, as well as other specials on within-Dublin options. Wild Rover Tours offers luggage storage services at their Bachelor's Walk office. Their day trips are as follows:

Giants Causeway, Belfast City & Carrick-A-Rede Rope Bridge Day Tour—Tour highlights include Belfast (black taxi tour *or* Titanic Experience), Dunluce Castle, Antrim Coastal Drive, Giant's Causeway, Carrick-a-Rede Rope Bridge. Includes all admissions. Daily, depart 7-7:10 a.m., return 8:30 p.m. Adult €75, Students €65, Children €55.

Cliffs of Moher, Atlantic Edge Ocean Walk & Galway City Day Tour—Tour highlights include Cliffs of Moher, the Atlantic Edge, Wild Atlantic Way, Burren National Park, Galway City (30-minute guided tour). Includes all admissions. Daily, depart 7-7:10 a.m., return 8 p.m. Adults €55, students €45, children €40.

Kilkenny, Wicklow Mountains, Glendalough Day Tour—Tour highlights include the medieval monastic settlement Glendalough (30-minute guided tour), Village of Annamoe, sheep dog demonstration on working sheep farm, Wicklow Mountains, Wicklow Gap, Kilkenny (45-minute walking tour). Includes all admissions. Daily, depart 8:10-8:30 a.m., return 6:15 p.m. Adults €37, students €32, children €30.

Game of Thrones Tour—Tour highlights include Carrickfergus Castle, Magheramorne Quarry (Castle Black), The Glens of Atrim Coastal Route, Ballycastle, Larrybane Quarry (Renly Baratheon's camp), Ballintoy (Pyke), House of Greyjoy, Dunluce Castle, King's Road. Includes all admissions and GOT costumes. Limited days available. 6:45 a.m.-8:30 p.m. Adults €55. (No children.)

Wild Rover Tours **also offers** 2-day tours and private tours.

Irish Day Tours

Irish Day Tours (www.irishdaytours.ie/) offers seven day tours on their fleet of coaches that seat 9 to 64 passengers. They have received TripAdvisor's Certificate of Excellence 2013-2018, as well as TripAdvisor's exclusive Traveler's Choice award. Many buses have free WiFi. Offices are on College Green and O'Connell Street (opposite the Spire). Most tours meet at the Molly Malone Statue on Suffolk Street. Repeat/multiple bookings get a €5 discount. Irish Day Tours also offers private tours or will arrange custom tours. Their offerings overlap with Extreme Ireland Adventures (www.extremeireland.ie) and Day Tours (daytours.ie). Their day trips are as follows:

Cliffs of Moher Tour—Tour highlights include the Atlantic Ocean Cliffs of Moher, the village of Doolin, Burren National Park, and Galway City. Daily, all day, depart 6:50 a.m. Adults from €50, seniors/students from €45, children €25.

Cliffs of Moher Premium Tour—Tour highlights include the Cliffs of Moher, a boat tour beneath the Cliffs of Moher (depending on season), 10th-12th century Caherconnell Fort in the Burren region, sheep dog demonstration, Doolin Village. Includes price of boat ride and sheepdog demonstration. Daily, 7:15 a.m.-8 p.m. Adults €69, students/seniors €65, children €35.

Wild Connemara Tour—Tour highlights include Kylemore Abbey, Killary Harbour Cruise (or sheep farm visit), Galway City. Daily, 6:30 a.m.-7 p.m. Adults from €55, students/seniors from €50, children from €27.50.

Titanic & Belfast Day Trip—Tour highlights include the Belfast Peace Wall, Republican Museum, HMS Caroline, Titanic Experience. Daily, 8 a.m.-7 p.m. Adults €65, students/seniors €60, children €32.50.

Blarney Castle & Cork Tour—Tour highlights include the Blarney Stone and Castle, the Rock of Cashel, Cahir Castle. Daily, 6:50 a.m.-7 p.m.. Adults €60, students/seniors €55, children €30.

Celtic Boyne Valley Tour, Ireland's Ancient East—Tour highlights include the Hill of Tara, Boyne Valley, Trim Castle, Hill of Uisneach, Loughcrew Passage Tomb. Daily, 8 a.m.-6 p.m. Adults €45, students/seniors €40, children €22.50.

Gray Line Tours

Gray Line Tours (www.grayline.com/things-to-do/ireland/dublin/) is "the largest provider of sightseeing tours on the planet," according to their Web site, touring on large buses and offering easy cancellation of reservations. They have TripAdvisor's Certificate of Excellence. Day tours start at O'Connell Street. (Prices listed in dollars will fluctuate based on the current exchange rate.) Their day trips are as follows:

Wicklow Mountains & Glendalough Tour—Tour highlights include the ancient monastic city of Glendalough, Wicklow Mountains National Park, Glencree German Cemetery, Tay "Guinness" Lake, Avoca village ("Ballykissangel"), lunch in famous Fitzgerald's Pub (for €10). Daily, 9:15 a.m.-6:15 p.m. Adult $39.42, children $29.86.

Newgrange & Hill of Tara Tour—Tour highlights include the Hill of Tara, Newgrange Neolithic burial chambers (guided tour), fishing village of Howth. Entry to Newgrange and on-board WiFi included. Mon/Tue/Fri/Sat (Apr-Oct), 9 a.m.-6 p.m. Adults $44.20, students/seniors $41.81, children $32.25.

Cliffs of Moher Fully Guided Day Trip—Tour highlights include non-stop coach shuttle service to and from the Cliffs of Moher, Visitor Centre, Doolin Village, WiFi on board. Daily, 10 a.m.-8 p.m. Adults $53.75, children $35.83.

Giant's Causeway Fully Guided Experience—Tour highlights include the Giant's Causeway, Carrick-a-Rede Rope Bridge, The Dark Hedges, Dunluce Castle. WiFi on board. Daily, 8:55 a.m.-7 p.m. Adults $77.64, children $47.78.

Malahide Castle & Northern Coastal Tour (AM and PM tours)—Tour highlights include Malahide Castle, gardens and grounds (entry and guided tour included), views of Dublin Bay, fishing village of Howth. Daily, depart 9:30 a.m. and 2 p.m., return 1:30 p.m. and 6 p.m. Adults $31.05, students/seniors $28.66, children $17.91.

Howth Village Walking Tour & Malahide Castle Tour—Tour includes 2-hour guided walking tour in Howth (piers, Balscadden Road, abbey and village), admission and guided tour to Malahide Castle, gardens and grounds. Views of Dublin Bay. Daily, 9:30 a.m.-6 p.m. Adults $59.72, students/seniors $57.33, children $29.86.

DoDublin Tours

DoDublin Tours (dodublin.ie/day-tours) discontinued its Hop-On, Hop-Off buses after 2019, so do not assume the following options are still available in 2020. (Check the Web site!) Save 10% when ordering online, but be aware that online ticket vouchers *must be printed out* to be used. Tours depart from Dublin Bus Head Office, 59 Upper O'Connell St. A shuttle bus from select city center hotels is available. Cost covers transportation, services of a tour leader, and some entry fees. Their day trips are as follows:

Coast & Castle Tour—Malahide Castle and Howth. Tours the coast north of Dublin. Highlights include a guided tour of Malahide Castle (entry included), castle grounds, Avoca clothing shop, Howth Harbor. Includes free Dublin city loop, Little Museum entry, and Dublin walking tour. Daily (Fri/Sat in off season), 11 a.m.-4 p.m. Adult price €25, children €12 (online €22.50/€10.80).

Wicklow Wonders—Glendalough & Powerscourt Gardens Tour. Highlights include Glendalough lakes and monastic city, Powerscourt gardens (entry included), Wicklow and Dublin Mountains. Includes free

Dublin city loop, Little Museum entry, and Dublin walking tour. Daily (Fri/Sat in off season), 10:30 a.m.-5 p.m. Adult price €27, children €12 (online €24.30/ €10.80).

Lodging

Hotels on this list are based on location, good reviews, and general accessibility, including access to easy transportation options. This section is a good starting point to narrow down your search, but then check online to make sure that information is still accurate, both on TripAdvisor and on the hotel's own Web site.

This is by no means a comprehensive list of suitable hotels in Dublin. You may find a wonderful deal on what looks to you like a good choice. By all means—grab it! Same with charming B&Bs, which aren't covered here because they tend to have a limited number of available rooms and generally don't have elevators. If you can nab one in a convenient location that gets good reviews, has a great breakfast, and a workable price, do it!

Airport shuttles, city buses, and hop-on/hop-off (HOHO) buses stop throughout central Dublin. For day trips, tours generally depart from around O'Connell Street (north of the river) and the Molly Malone Statue or College Green (by Trinity College, south of the river).

- Rabbie's Tours leave from Nassau Street by Trinity College.
- Paddywagon Tours offer multiple pickup locations, from Lower Gardiner Street, O'Connell Street, *and* the Molly Malone statue. (Take your pick!)
- Wild Rover Tours leave from Dame Street *and* the Gresham Hotel on O'Connell Street (south *and* north of the river!).
- Irish Day Tours leave from the Molly Malone Statue.
- Gray Line Tours leave from Upper O'Connell Street at the City Sightseeing shop *or* Lower O'Connell Street at the Dublin Visitor Centre *or* Grafton Street at the Dublin Visitor Centre (look closely when booking).

The area north of the River Liffey is traditionally working-class, even gritty in places, while the area south of the river is more genteel, fashionable, and generally more expensive. The Temple Bar area is conveniently located but can get loud from the crowds and boisterous nightlife. If you plan to spend lots of time exploring your neighborhood and enjoying what it has to offer, you probably want to lodge south of the river. If you use your hotel more as a base for launching out to other areas, then you would probably appreciate the easy transportation options and somewhat lower prices north of the river.

In addition to hotels and B&Bs, Dublin has a lot of hostels that include private rooms, if you don't mind bare-bones lodging and are interested in keeping your budget low. (One hostel is included below as a starting point.) Look possibilities over carefully so you don't inadvertently book yourself into a top bunk in a large mixed-sex dorm room, up three flights of stairs. See what you can learn about the physical situation of the building—lots of stairs? Close to sightseeing buses? Hostels aren't for evryone, but if you're interested, you can find good deals and ready company.

Hotel price ranges in this section are based on late 2019 TripAdvisor averages. Your own quotes may be higher or lower.

Around O'Connell Street (north of the river)

Arlington Hotel O'Connell Bridge—23-25 Bachelor's Walk. (www.arlington.ie) TripAdvisor Certificate of Excellence. Location: next to River Liffey near O'Connell St., close to Airlink 747 shuttle bus stop (O'Connell St., Abbey St.), close to hop-on/hop-off bus stop (Bachelor's Walk). Pros: Free WiFi, excellent breakfast buffet, Irish dinner and dancing show available, live music, bar, restaurant, room service, family rooms and triples available, ATM on-site, good elevators, wheelchair access, accessible rooms. Cons: no price break for singles, no air conditioning, some noise, *Georgian wing has no elevator access*—be specific when reserving. (TripAdvisor price range for standard room: $109-$288.)

Distances: Ha'Penny Bridge (.1 miles), General Post Office (.1 miles), The Spire (.2 miles), Temple Bar (.2 miles), Trinity College (.2 miles)

Jury's Inn Dublin Parnell Street—Parnell St./Moore St. Plaza (www.jurysinns.com/hotels/dublin/parnell-street). TripAdvisor's Certificate of Excellence. Location: west of O'Connell St., near hop-on/hop-off stop, near Airlink 747 shuttle bus stop (Cathal Brugha, O'Connell St.) Pros: free WiFi, very good breakfast buffet, air conditioning, restaurant, room service, coffee bar, family rooms, bar/lounge, wheelchair access, accessible rooms. Cons: only slight reduction for singles. (TripAdvisor price range for standard room: $114-$347.)

Distances: Dublin bus head office (.1 miles), The Spire (.2 miles), Temple Bar (.4 miles), Trinity College (.5 miles), Dublin Tourism Center (.6 miles)

Holiday Inn Express—28-32 Upper O'Connell St. (www.ihg.com/holidayinnexpress/hotels/us/en/dublin/dblct/hoteldetail). TripAdvisor's Certificate of Excellence. Location: Upper O'Connell St., near hop-on/hop-off stop, near Airlink 747 shuttle bus stop (Cathal Brugha, O'Connell St.). Pros: new and modern, air conditioning, free WiFi, very good continental breakfast included, café, bar/lounge, wheelchair access, twin/family rooms. Cons: no single rooms, no single price break. (TripAdvisor price range for standard room: $118-$320.)

Distances: Dublin bus head office (.1 miles), St. Mary's Pro Cathedral (.1 miles), The Spire (.2 miles), Temple Bar (.5 miles), Trinity College (.5 miles), Dublin Tourism Center (.6 miles)

Hotel Riu Place The Gresham Dublin—23 Upper O'Connell St. (www.riu.com/en/hotel/ireland/dublin/hotel-riu-plaza-the-gresham-dublin/). Location: Upper O'Connell St., near hop-on/hop-off stop, near Airlink 747 shuttle bus stop (Cathal Brugha, O'Connell St.). Pros: free WiFi, parking, very good breakfast buffet included, restaurant, room service, bar/lounge, rooms for disabled, suites available, air conditioning, fitness center, family rooms, larger-than-average rooms. Cons: no single rooms, no price break for singles. (TripAdvisor price range for standard room: $182-$373.)

Distances: Dublin Bus Head Office (.1 miles), St. Mary's Pro Cathedral (.1 miles), General Post Office (.2 miles), The Spire (.1 miles), Temple Bar (.4 miles), Trinity College (.5 miles), Dublin Tourism Center (.6 miles)

Academy Plaza Hotel—10-14 Findlater Place (www.academyplazahotel.ie/en/). TripAdvisor's Certificate of Excellence. Location: just east of O'Connell St., near hop-on/hop-off stop, near Airlink 747 shuttle bus stop (Cathal Brugha, O'Connell St.), 5 minutes from Connolly Train Station. Pros: free WiFi, good buffet breakfast, air conditioning, restaurant, room service, bar/lounge, singles/twins/triples/quads available, fitness center, wheelchair access, Airlink bus stops outside hotel, beauty salon. Cons: single room no cheaper than larger double. (TripAdvisor price range for standard room: $93-$265.)

Distances: St. Mary's Pro Cathedral (.1 miles), Dublin Bus Head Office (.1 miles), The Spire (.2 miles), Temple Bar (.5 miles), Trinity College (.6 miles), Dublin Tourism Center (.6 miles)

Wynn's Hotel—35-39 Lower Abbey St. (www.wynnshotel.ie). TripAdvisor's Certificate of Excellence. Location: just east of O'Connell St. on Abbey St., near hop-on/hop-off stop, close to Airlink 747 shuttle bus stop (O'Connell St., Abbey St.), on LUAS red line Abbey Street stop. Pros: free WiFi, hot breakfast included, restaurant, room service, suites, bar/lounge, fitness center. Cons: no air conditioning, can be noisy, not handicapped accessible. (TripAdvisor price range for standard room: $166-$1,052.)

Kingfisher Townhouse—166 Parnell St. (kingfisherdublin.com/). TripAdvisor's Certificate of Excellence. Location: west of O'Connell St., near hop-on/hop-off stop, near Airlink 747 shuttle bus stop (Cathal Brugha, O'Connell St.) Pros: free WiFi, restaurant, very good full Irish/English breakfast, twins and triples available, also offers apartments. Cons: no elevator (upper floors accessible by stairs only), no single rooms, no price break for singles. (TripAdvisor price range for standard room: $116-$200.)

Distances: Dublin Bus head office (.1 miles), Henry Street (.2 miles), The Spire (.2 miles), Temple Bar (.4 miles), Trinity College (.5 miles), Dublin Tourism Center (.6 miles)

Anchor House Dublin—49 Lower Gardiner St. (anchorhousedublin.com/). Location: between Connolly Train Station and O'Connell Street, near Airlink 747 shuttle bus (Talbot St, Talbot Place), near Airlink 757 stop (Custom House Quay). Pros: free WiFi, good breakfast buffet, single/twin/triple rooms also available, free breakfast when booking on Web site, accessible facilities. Cons: can be noisy, no air conditioning, few rooms available. (TripAdvisor price range for standard room: $127-$214.)

Distances: Connolly Train Station (.2 miles), St. Mary's Pro Cathedral (.2 miles), The Spire (.2 miles), Trinity College (.4 miles), Temple Bar (.5 miles), Dublin Tourism Center (.6 miles)

North Star Hotel—Amiens Street (www.northstarhotel.ie). Location: near Connolly Train Station, near Airlink 747 shuttle bus stop (Talbot Street, Talbot Place). Pros: free WiFi, good breakfast, air conditioning, restaurant, room service, suites, fitness center, sauna, bar/lounge, wheelchair access, twin/triple/quad rooms available. Cons: no price break for singles. (TripAdvisor price range for standard room: $145-$299.)

Distances: to Connolly Train Station (0.0 miles), to St. Mary's Pro Cathedral (.4 miles), to River Liffey (.3 miles), to Trinity College (.6 miles), to Temple Bar (.7 miles), to Dublin Tourism Center (.7 miles)

The Address—Amiens Street (www.theaddressatdublin1.ie). TripAdvisor's Certificate of Excellence. Location: near Connolly Train Station, near Airlink 747 shuttle bus stop (Talbot Street, Talbot Place). Pros: free Wifi, full English breakfast, air conditioning, restaurant, room service, bar, suites, fitness center, sauna, wheelchair access, baggage storage, hypoallergenic room available. Cons: no single rooms, no price break for singles, no triples. (TripAdvisor price range for standard room: $190-$325.)

Distances: Connolly Train Station (.1 miles), St. Mary's Pro Cathedral (.3 miles), The Spire (.4 miles), River Liffey (.2 miles), Trinity College (.6 miles), Dublin Tourism Center (.7 miles), Temple Bar (.7 miles).

Sky Backpackers (Hostel)—2-4 Litton Lane (www.hostelworld.com/hosteldetails.php/Sky-Backpackers/Dublin/58605). TripAdvisor's Certificate of Excellence. Location: west of O'Connell St. just north of the river, close to Airlink 747 shuttle bus stop (O'Connell St., Abbey St.), close to hop-on/hop-off bus stop (Bachelor's Walk). Pros: free WiFi, good breakfast buffet, has twin/double/triple/quad rooms in addition to dorms, price, kitchen available. Cons: limited number of rooms, non-dorm rooms sell out early, upper floors accessible by stairs only, basic rooms, no air conditioning, can be noisy. (TripAdvisor price range for standard room: $31-$239.)

Distances: Ha'Penny Bridge (.1 miles), General Post Office (.1 miles), The Spire (.2 miles), Temple Bar (.2 miles), Trinity College (.2 miles).

Trinity College/Temple Bar Area (south of the river)

The Westin Dublin—Westmoreland Street at College Green (www.thewestindublin.com/). TripAdvisor Travelers' Choice Award (top 1% of category). Location: next to Trinity College and Temple Bar, close to Airlink 747 shuttle stop (Trinity College, College Green), close to hop-on/hop-off stop (College Green, Trinity College), close to Molly Malone statue, close to Grafton Street. Pros: free WiFi, breakfast buffet, air conditioning, restaurant, room service, very good breakfast, bar/lounge, suites, fitness center, wheelchair access, disabled facilities, accessible rooms, spacious rooms, very high user satisfaction. Cons: price, no parking nearby, no single rooms, no price break for singles. (TripAdvisor price range for standard room: $292-$951.)

Distances: Trinity College (.1 miles), Molly Malone Statue (.1 miles), Dublin Tourism Center (.2 miles), Ha'Penny Bridge (.2 miles), River Liffey (.1 miles), Temple Bar (.2 miles)

Temple Bar Inn—40-47 Fleet Street (www.templebarinn.com). TripAdvisor's Certificate of Excellence. Location: between Trinity College and Temple Bar, close to Airlink 747 shuttle stop (Trinity College, College Green), close to hop-on/hop-off stop (College Green, Trinity College), close to Molly Malone statue. Pros: free WiFi, very good breakfast buffet, room service, single/twin/triple/quad rooms, wheelchair access, accessible rooms, refrigerator in room. Cons: can be noisy, no air conditioning, single rooms sell out early. (TripAdvisor price range for standard room: $138-$355.)

Distances: Trinity College (.1 miles), Ha'Penny Bridge (.1 miles), Dublin Tourism Center (.1 miles), Molly Malone Statue (.2 miles), Temple Bar (.2 miles), River Liffey (.1 miles)

Trinity City Hotel—Pearse Street (www.trinitycityhotel.com/us/home/). TripAdvisor's Certificate of Excellence. Location: next to Trinity College, near Airlink 757 shuttle bus stop (Westland Row, Pearse Rail Station), next to hop-on/hop-off stop (Pearse Street). Pros: free WiFi, parking, good breakfast, air conditioning, restaurant, room service, bar/lounge, fitness center, wheelchair access, accessible rooms, single and twin rooms available. Cons: can be noisy, no price break for single room. (TripAdvisor price range for standard room: $177-$371.)

Distances: Trinity College (.2 miles), Famine Memorial (.2 miles), Molly Malone Statue (.2 miles), Dublin Tourism Center (.3 miles), Temple Bar (.4 miles)

Dublin Citi Hotel—46-49 Dame St. (www.dublincitihotel.com). Location: Temple Bar between Dublin Castle and Trinity College, near Airlink 747 shuttle bus stop (College Green, Trinity College), near hop-on/hop-off stop (Dame Street/Temple Bar), near Molly Malone Statue. Pros: free WiFi, breakfast, restaurant, room service, bar/lounge, comedy and music nights, fitness center, twin rooms available, lift available. Cons: no air conditioning, can get noisy, no single rooms, no price break for singles, limited rooms available. (TripAdvisor price range for standard room: $122-$304.)

Distances: Temple Bar (.1 miles), Dublin Tourism Center (.1 miles), Ha'Penny Bridge (.1 miles), Dublin Castle (.2 miles), Trinity College (.2 miles)

The Clarence—6-8 Wellington Quay (theclarence.ie). TripAdvisor's Certificate of Excellence. Location: Temple Bar along River Liffey, close to Airlink 747 shuttle bus stop (Lord Edward St., Carnegie Centre), close to HOHO stops (Dame St/Temple Bar, Dame St/Dublin Castle). Pros: free WiFi, breakfast buffet, restaurant, room service, suites, bar/lounge, wheelchair access. Cons: no air conditioning. (TripAdvisor price range for standard room: $172-$413.)

Distances: Dublin Castle (.2 miles), Temple Bar (.1 miles), Trinity College (.3 miles)

Paramount Hotel Temple Bar—Essex Gate, Parliament Street. (www.paramounthotel.ie). Location: Temple Bar near Dublin Castle, close to Airlink 747 shuttle bus stop (Lord Edward St., Carnegie Centre), close to HOHO stops (Dame St/Temple Bar, Dame St/Dublin Castle). Pros:

free WiFi, good breakfast buffet, bar/lounge, room service, wheelchair access. Cons: no air conditioning, street can get noisy. (TripAdvisor price range for standard room: $120-$242.)

Distances: Dublin Castle (.1 miles), Temple Bar (.2 miles), River Liffey (.1 miles), Dublin Tourism Center (.3 miles), Trinity College (.4 miles)

A bit farther south, but still central (May require more walking):

Drury Court Hotel—28-30 Stephen St. Lower (www.drurycourthotel.ie). TripAdvisor's Certificate of Excellence. Location: between Dublin Castle and St. Stephen's Green, nearest Airlink shuttle bus stop either 747 College Green/Trinity College or Lord Edward St/Carnegie Centre or 757 St. Stephen's Green, similar distance from several hop-on/hop-off stops (such as Dame St/Temple Bar). Pros: single/twin/triple/quad/6-person rooms available, free WiFi, breakfast buffet, restaurant, room service, suites, upper floors accessible by lift. Cons: no air conditioning, single rooms book early, apartments non-refundable, steep-sided bath/shower with high step in. (TripAdvisor price range for standard room: $134-$313.)

Distances: Dublin Castle (.2 miles), Grafton Street (.2 miles), Stephen's Green Shopping Centre (.2 miles), River Liffey (.5 miles), Dublin Tourism Center (.2 miles), Temple Bar (.3 miles), Trinity College (.3 miles)

Brooks Hotel—59-63 Drury St. (www.brookshotel.ie). TripAdvisor's Certificate of Excellence. Location: between Dublin Castle and St. Stephen's Green, nearest Airlink shuttle bus stop either 747 College Green/Trinity College or Lord Edward St/Carnegie Centre or 757 St. Stephen's Green, comparable distance from several hop-on/hop-off stops (such as Dame St/Temple Bar). Pros: free WiFi, very good breakfast buffet, air conditioning, restaurant, room service, bar/lounge, wheelchair access, accessible rooms, twin rooms available, fitness center, suites, excellent reviews. Cons: no single rooms, no price break for singles. (TripAdvisor price range for standard room: $227-$395.)

Distances: Grafton Street (.1 miles), Stephen's Green Shopping Centre (.1 miles), Dublin Castle (.2 miles), Dublin Tourism Center (.2 miles), River Liffey (.3 miles), Temple Bar (.3 miles), Trinity College (.3 miles)

The Westbury—Balfe Street (www.doylecollection.com/hotels/the-westbury-hotel). TripAdvisor's Travelers' Choice Award (top 1% of category). Location: between Trinity College and St. Stephen's Green just west of Grafton St., nearest Airlink shuttle bus stop either 747 College Green/Trinity College or 757 St. Stephen's Green, near hop-on/hop-off stop (St. Stephen's Green). Pros: free WiFi, parking, very good breakfast buffet, air conditioning, restaurant, afternoon tea available, room service, spacious rooms, twins available, fitness center, bar/lounge, wheelchair access, accessible rooms, refrigerator. Cons: price, no single/triple/quad rooms. No price break for singles. (TripAdvisor price range for standard room: $335-$521.)

Distances: Grafton Street (0.0 miles), Stephen's Green Shopping Centre (.1 miles), Dublin Tourism Center (.1 miles), Molly Malone Statue (.2 miles), River Liffey (.4 miles), Trinity College (.2 miles), Dublin Castle (.3 miles), Temple Bar (.3 miles)

Buswells Hotel—Molesworth House 23-27 (www.buswells. ie). TripAdvisor's Certificate of Excellence. Location: between Trinity College/St. Stephen's Green, near Airlink 757 shuttle bus stop (St. Stephen's Green), near hop-on/hop-off stop (St. Stephen's Green and others), near national museums. Pros: free WiFi, good buffet breakfast, restaurant, room service, suites, bar/lounge, wheelchair access, accessible rooms, single and twin rooms available, free overnight parking. Cons: no air conditioning. (TripAdvisor price range for standard room: $159-$264.)

Distances: National Museum of Ireland—Archeology (.1 miles), National Gallery of Ireland (.2 miles), Trinity College (.3 miles), Dublin Tourism Center (.3 miles), Temple Bar (.5 miles)

Other base cities in Ireland (and Northern Ireland)

You can base yourself in Belfast, Galway, Killarney, and Cork, as well, if you prefer to experience different parts of the island in greater depth than a day trip allows. These cities offer hop-on/hop-off tours and excursions into the countryside. Bear in mind the principles of easy-walking hotel selection—easy access to the buildings, ideally in a relatively flat area, and proximity to transportation hubs—if you want to limit walking and climbing and save your energy for seeing the sights.

London

Overview

London is the capital and largest city of England, a world-class metropolis that stretches across a vast area of more than 600 square miles (Greater London). There is so much to do across so much of London that it can be a real challenge to visit as a tourist. Much of that challenge is due to the congested traffic and unavoidable crowding of a dense urban center. But the city is so rich in history and culture that it's well worth the effort to visit!

In the southeast of England on the Thames River, London is mostly flat, so there aren't a lot of hills to contend with. But there is a lot of old construction, so you're unlikely to avoid stairs or uneven surfaces entirely. That's what happens when the site has been inhabited since the Romans founded it around 50 A.D., at a spot where the Thames River was narrow enough to bridge.

England is famous for its rain, its royal family, its literary tradition, and the remnants of the British Empire. The climate in southeast England is mild but unpredictable, and locals know to carry an umbrella with them. (Between 11 and 15 rainy days per month is typical for London.) Summer temperatures are usually pleasant, but there have been heat waves driving temps into the mid-90s Fahrenheit. Winter is usually above freezing, but snow appears occasionally.

Possible plan for London (What I'd do)

If I were traveling to London with my mother, this is what I would plan for us to do. Obviously, you may prefer to do something different, but you may find this itinerary handy as a starting point, changing it as much as you'd like. **Please double check any details before relying on them, as specifics may have changed since I wrote these pages.** If our budget would allow it, I would include private cars for tours in the city and out. Sadly, this example tour does not stretch to that luxury. This section will make more sense as you work your way through the chapter. Having a city map at hand will help to visualize this itinerary and other options.

Once you have a pretty good idea of what you want to do, check out ticket sales online, because online booking is almost always less expensive than buying a ticket on-site. Of course, with buying online, you save money but might give up flexibility, so it's not always the best choice, but it's certainly worth looking into. As for day trips, you probably don't want more than two consecutive out-of-town excursions at a time, to avoid bus fatigue.

Day 1—Depart U.S.

Day 2—Arrive London. Find an ATM and withdraw pounds, if needed.
> If at Heathrow and taking public transportation into the city, follow signs to the Underground and, inside the Underground entrance, buy an Oyster Card from a machine. (Refundable £5 for the card, then you choose the amount you put on it. Maybe £20? Can use a credit card. You can redeem unused credit up to £10 before you leave the country.)
>
> Ride the Piccadilly line to the stop closest to your hotel, probably Gloucester Road or South Kensington, if you are staying in the Gloucester Road/South Kensington/Knightsbridge area. If staying around Victoria Station, ride the Piccadilly line to the Hammersmith stop. Exit the train there and change to a District train heading east. (You should be able to cross the platform you just got to and catch a District train on the other side, avoiding stairs.) Ride to the Victoria stop.
>
> If staying around Victoria Station, another option from Heathrow is to take a National Express direct coach from the Central Bus Station (near Terminals 2 and 3) or right outside the Arrivals level at Terminals 4 and 5.
>
> **Comfort upgrade:** If you have any trouble getting around, it makes sense to splurge here at the airport. Give yourself a break and line up a private driver instead of trekking to public transportation, if you can stretch your budget that far. Yes, it costs more, but you'll be met in the Arrivals hall by a driver and escorted to a car rather than having to locate and hike to a train platform. You will also be delivered directly to your hotel.
>
> (The example schedule below assumes lodging around Victoria Station. It could easily be modified, however, for the Gloucester Road/South Kensington area or elsewhere.)

After arriving at the hotel, check in, if possible, then rest up before heading out. If it's too early for that, leave your luggage at reception and check in later.

Investigate the neighborhood. Line up cell phone service, if needed. Scout out a local grocery store and possible pub or restaurant for dinner. Take a self-guided tour of the neighborhood. If in the Victoria Station area, possibly walk to Buckingham Palace, see a little of St. James's Park, and visit Westminster Cathedral on the way back. Take frequent breaks. Stop for lunch or tea/coffee. Rest before dinner, then go out to eat.

Day 3—Start 48-hour Original Tour HOHO (hop-on/hop-off) pass (purchased in advance). Walk to Victoria & Grosvenor Gardens (if staying near Victoria Station), exchange online voucher for ticket. Take a yellow bus T1 (with live English commentary) to the stop by St. Paul's. View the cathedral as desired (inside or out—advanced booking recommended, £17 online in late 2019), then walk south to the Millennium Bridge. Walk across the bridge and either tour the Globe Theatre (adult door price of £17 in late 2019) or visit the Tate Modern art museum (free). Consider taking a break at The Swan (restaurant) near the Globe or at the Tate Modern Café or somewhere else nearby. (There's a Starbucks between the Tate and the Globe, and Café 101 is at 101 Queen Victoria Street on the way back to the HOHO stop by St. Paul's.)

Ride the yellow line bus to the stop at Tower Hill. Get out, walk around the Tower complex, if interested and not too tired. (If choosing to tour inside the Tower of London, realize that there is significant climbing and walking involved. General advice is to allot half a day for the experience. Slower walkers should budget more time. Consider either touring on a different day or giving up the stop at St. Paul's if wanting to do this. The 2019 adult online ticket price is £24.70. More if purchasing on-site.) (A Big Bus HOHO tour would also work for this day and the next, but would require some modification because of slightly different routes and stops.)

Return to yellow-line bus and ride to the stop at Buckingham Palace Road. Walk back to hotel.

Day 4—Take the HOHO yellow bus again (T1, if it works out) to Westminster Bridge/Westminster Pier. (This will repeat most of the previous day's ride, so consider sitting in a different area of the bus than before for a different vantage point.) Take the City

Cruise Thames River Cruise to (and back from) Greenwich (included with HOHO ticket). Disembark at Greenwich.

Visit Tourist Information by the pier in Greenwich. Walk around town. Take photos. Consider touring the Cutty Sark (2019 walk-up adult ticket price, £15). Have lunch or tea in Greenwich. Cruise back to Westminster. Walk around Westminster. View the Parliament building, Big Ben, Westminster Abbey up close. Return to the Westminster stop and ride the yellow line bus back to the Buckingham Palace Road stop. Or, if feeling spry, walk from Westminster back to the hotel. Rest up, then eat out.

Day 5—Walk to Victoria Station. If needed, buy an Oyster Card now. Use Oyster Card to ride bus C1 from Victoria Station (stop R) to the Victoria and Albert Museum (stop N), a ride of approximately 20 minutes. (If you bought an Oyster Card previously, go to whichever C1 bus stop is closest to your hotel, possibly Victoria Coach Station (stop V) or Eaton Square (stop F).) Tour the V&A Museum (free entry). Break for lunch. If desired, also look in at the Natural History Museum across the street (free entry).

When done, take bus C1 from the V&A Museum (stop M) to Eaton Square (stop J)/Victoria Coach Station area (stop Y)/Victoria Station (stop S) (may choose to stop at Harrod's 2 stops along the way). Walk back to hotel. (Check the tfl route finder online for the best route back—tfl.gov.uk/plan-a-journey/. You can choose a preference of "bus only" or "routes with least walking" and also check out accessibility options. The fastest way back is to take the Tube from South Kensington to Victoria on the Circle or District Line, but that can involve a lot of walking/climbing. The trip is payable with an Oyster Card, however.)

Comfort upgrade: Cab fare from Victoria Station to the V&A ranges from £6.74 to £26.14. Check with a taxi fare finder (such as taxifarefinder.com) to get an estimate for when you want to travel. For London sights, you may need to type "London" in the search bar, followed by the location name, e.g., "London Victoria Station," if your desired location does not appear in the drop-down menu.

Relax in hotel. Shop. Eat out. West End musical??

Day 6—Day trip: Stonehenge, Bath and a Secret Place. Dinner out or pick up something on way back to hotel. *Day trips may need to be moved around, based on when they are available.*

Day 7—Walk to Victoria Coach Station. Take bus 38 (stop D) to Museum Street (stop E). Walk to British Museum. Tour the British Museum (free), with ample rests. Ride bus 38 from Museum Street (stop C) to Victoria Bus Station (stop D). Relax. Eat out. Rest up for bus trip the next day.

Comfort upgrade: Cab fare from Victoria Station to the British Museum ranges from £10.48 to £45.88.

Day 8—Day trip: Oxford and Traditional Cotswold Villages. Dinner out or pick up something on way back to hotel.

Day 9—Take bus 24 or bus 11 from near Victoria Station to Trafalgar Square/Charing Cross Station. Visit the National Gallery (free). Visit the National Portrait Gallery (free). Spring for a 2-3 course meal or indulge in afternoon tea at the Portrait Restaurant (National Portrait Gallery) for amazing views across London.

Finish any last-minute shopping. Final dinner out.

Day 10—Return home. Take the Piccadilly line (or District/Piccadilly lines) in reverse from arrival. Or take the National Express from Victoria Station. Or arrange for a private driver.

When finished with your Oyster Card, redeem at a machine for remaining credit and the deposit. (Or keep for a return trip, as the credit does not expire.)

If I had more time in London, I would include some of these:

- Museum of London (free)
- Imperial War Museum (free)
- Churchill War Rooms (adults £22 at door, less online)
- St. Paul's Cathedral (not as crowded as Westminster Abbey, adults £20 walk-up price)
- Tower of London (a leisurely visit, 2019 adult online ticket price £24.70)
- Thames cruise through Richmond to Hampton Court (although probably not Hampton Court itself, because of its sprawling size, 2019 adult round-trip ticket from Westminster to Hampton Court, £27, Thames River Boats)
- More day trips, such as Dover/Canterbury or Downton Abbey sights

Arrival

You will probably fly into Heathrow airport (LHR) when you arrive in England, about 15 miles west of central London (www. heathrow.com), or possibly Gatwick (LGW), about 28 miles south of the city (www. gatwickairport.com). Realize that after flying through the night, hiking through the terminal, wrestling with your luggage, and standing up to an hour (or more) to get through customs, you will not be in your sharpest shape for tracking down transportation into the city. Any of the options below are doable, but accept that you will probably be fatigued and may decide that paying more for convenience is worth it.

To get from **Heathrow** to the city, you have your choice of train, Tube (Underground), taxi, or coach. The fastest way to get to central London from Heathrow is to use the **Heathrow Express** train (www. heathrowexpress.com). Every 15 minutes a train runs non-stop to Paddington Station, a ride of about 15 minutes. Tickets are available online, at the station, or on the train. Fare varies according to time of trip (£5.50-£32 one-way), with savings for buying in advance and higher fees when buying on-board. Round-trip tickets are also available. It can be a bit of a hike to get to the Heathrow Express departure point at the Heathrow Central station. Once you get to Paddington Station, you can take a cab to your hotel, if you want to.

The **Underground** (blue Piccadilly line) is the most economical way to reach the city, with rides lasting 50-60 minutes. Station stops include several in Kensington/South Kensington, Knightsbridge, Mayfair, Bloomsbury, and St. Pancras/King's Cross Stations. One-way adult fare from Heathrow (Zone 6) to central London (Zone 1) is £6, or £3.10-£5.10 with an Oyster Card (see below). It can require a good bit of walking to get to the Underground station.

National Express (www.nationalexpress.com/en/destinations/london/heathrow-to-london) offers direct coach transfers to and from the airport and London Victoria Coach Station. Departure from Terminals 2 and 3 is from the Central Bus Station (a 5-minute walk from the terminal buildings), from Terminals 4 and 5 from right outside the terminal buildings at the Arrivals level. Fares vary from £6-£10 for one-way. (Ratings of this service vary greatly. Service can be inconsistent.)

Taxis are available outside each terminal. The trip to central London takes about one hour and costs £45-£70. A London black cab takes up to 5 passengers and 4 large suitcases.

You could also line up a **private driver** ahead of time, one who will meet you as you exit customs and escort you to your vehicle, for less cost than taking a black cab into the city. Find information here, including examples of fares: www.londontoolkit.com/travel/heathrow_taxi.htm. A sample fare for 2 people, 2 large cases and 2 small ones to near Victoria Station is around £52, while 4 people with 3 large cases and 2 small ones to the same area costs around £60.

From **Gatwick** airport, your transportation options are pretty much the same. The Gatwick Express train is the fastest and most comfortable option, whisking you to Victoria Station, where you could pick up a cab, if you wanted. Trains leave from the south terminal every 15 minutes, and the ride lasts about 30 minutes. You can buy tickets at Gatwick and Victoria railway stations, but they are always cheaper when purchased online. You can also buy round-trip tickets that are valid for a month. Standard one-way fare is £19.90 at the station or £17.80 online. One-way Oyster Card cost is £19.80.

National Express buses are again an option (see above for Heathrow). Prices are cheaper than rail, but transportation time can be three times as long, and buses leave only about once an hour.

Private cars and taxis are also available from Gatwick, but the London travel advice site London Toolkit advises the following regarding them: "Unless you have mobility problems or a lot of luggage a private car doesn't make much sense. The Gatwick Express Train plus a cab at its terminus in London, Victoria is going to be much faster, more comfortable and much less cost than a private car or taxi" (www.londontoolkit.com/travel/gatwick_transport.htm).

Easy transportation options

Once in the city, your probable transportation choices are bus, taxi, and Tube. The easiest way to get around to the sights, though, is to ride a hop-on/hop-off (HOHO) tourist bus. London has multiple HOHO bus companies; I've listed the two highest-rated ones below. You purchase a 24-, 48-, or 72-hour ticket and then may hop on and hop off the buses (of the line you paid for) as much as you'd like in that time.

You may choose to take the whole tour to get an overview and then, on the *second* time around, hop off to see sights up close. Buses run year-round, though hours of operation and frequency of buses vary by season. Prices are listed below, but check each company's Web site for the latest information.

Be aware that London HOHO companies seem to have spottier reviews than those of other cities, perhaps because the city is such a sprawling, crowded, traffic-jammed metropolis. Many people rave about their

London HOHO bus experiences. Others complain about poor guides, poor service, poor buses and equipment, overcrowded buses, and insufficient bus frequency. If things go well, this is a fantastic way to cover a lot of ground and get to the sights you want to see. Unfortunately, there's no guarantee that all will go smoothly. Perhaps the best we can do is hope for the good experience that the majority of users report having.

Hop-On/Hop-Off Tours

The Original Tour (www.theoriginaltour.com) has had TripAdvisor's Travelers' Choice Award (a top honor, the top 1% of a category). The Original Tour has 6 different hop-on/hop-off routes covering more than 80 stops around London (including a hotel connector route), plus a free hop-on/hop-off Thames River cruise (with the City Cruise line) and free walking tour.

Most bus routes concentrate on a certain area of London (e.g., West End), with recorded commentary. The "Original Tour" (yellow route) covers the most tourist territory, and every other bus has a live guide. Tours have overlapping stops for easy transfer from one tour route to another. There is free WiFi on board. Buses are wheelchair accessible.

Download the map of routes and list of stops here: www.theoriginaltour.com/en/map-times.

Prices are as follows:

- 24-hour adult £32.50 (age 16+), child 5-15 £15.25, family £80 (2 adults + 2 children)
- 48-hour adult £42.50, child 5-15 £20, family £104
- 72-hour adult £52.50, child 5-15 £24.50, family £129

The Original Tour also offers combination packages for entry to top tourist sights (e.g., Tower of London, London Eye, Cutty Sark, Westminster Abbey).

If you get a voucher from online, exchange it for a ticket at The Original Sightseeing Tour visitor center in Trafalgar Square or with a staff member on the street or on some buses, if you have a QR code. (Officially, you're also supposed to present the credit card you used to buy the ticket.) Electronic vouchers are accepted (but printing them to redeem for tickets is safest). All sales are final.

Big Bus London (www.bigbustours.com/en/london/london-bus-tours/) has 4 sightseeing routes covering more than 40 different stops on buses with free onboard WiFi. Transfers between routes are possible. The red tour (approximately 2 hours 20 minutes) covers central London with live guides; the other three tours use digital commentary. Tickets are for sale on the company Web site, from Big Bus staff at the stops or on the bus, or from many hotels. If you get a pre-paid voucher, you can redeem it for a ticket at any stop on three routes. Electronic vouchers are accepted (but printouts are safer).

Route map and information is here: www.bigbustours.com/en/london/london-routes-and-tour-maps/.

Prices are as follows:

- Classic Ticket, 1 day HOHO on 4 routes, walking tours, one-way cruise—adult £35.10 online (£39 on street), child £26.10 online (£29 on street), family £107
- Premium Ticket, same as Deluxe Ticket but for 2 days HOHO—adult £40.50 online (£49 on street), child £31.50 online (£35 on street), family £125
- Deluxe Ticket, 3 day HOHO on 4 routes, 90-minute walking tour, round-trip river cruise (Westminster to Greenwich with City Cruises)—adult £45 online (£50 on street), child £36 online (£40 on street), family £140

Offers combo tickets and packages to major London attractions (e.g., Classic Ticket + entrance to Tower of London or Premium Ticket + St. Paul's Cathedral). Tickets can be cancelled at least 24 hours in advance. Buses are wheelchair accessible.

Non-stop bus tour London

If you'd like a two-hour big-bus overview of London that's non-stop (not HOHO), Megabus (uk.megabus.com/products/londonbus-tour) is highly rated. Open-top double-decker buses leave daily on the hour, 10-5, from the London Eye (also in the past from the Tower of London and Park Lane—east of Hyde Park. Check departure points when booking.). It's possible to book wheelchair space (call ahead). Price varies, £5-£11.

Private tours

If you want to avoid the crowds and the sometimes unpredictable schedules of the HOHO sightseeing buses, you could consider lining up a private tour of London. These are costlier options, but they get rave reviews, and divided over multiple riders, the cost becomes much more affordable.

Frankly, this sounds like a wonderful way to get a city overview, if it can fit into your budget. (Bespoke/customizable tours are also possible.)

London Tours by Taxi—(londontoursbytaxi.com/) TripAdvisor's Certificate of Excellence 2013-1019. Adrian Rouse is a licensed London taxi driver with over 25 years experience and is also a qualified City of London Guide. His Mercedes black cab is air conditioned and wheelchair accessible, seating up to 6 people. Prices are per cab, not per person. He offers a variety of tours:

- London Highlights tour (£135 for 2 hours, £180 for 3 hours, £240 for 4 hours)
- VIP Day Tour (pickup at hotel after breakfast, delivery to hotel or theater afterwards, 8 hours, £400)
- Royal London (£135 for 2 hours, £180 for 3 hours, £240 for 4 hours)
- London by Night (Oct.–March only, £190, 3 hours)
- Shopping Trip (£220 for 4 hours, £350 for 7-8 hours)
- Hidden and Secret London (£135 for 2 hours, £180 for 3 hours, £240 for 4 hours)
- Celebration (special occasions, such as wedding proposals) (£135 for 2 hours, £180 for 3 hours, £240 for 4 hours)
- London in the Movies (£180, 3 hours)
- Oxford (£425, 9-10 hours)
- Cotswolds/Oxfordshire (£470, 9-10 hours)
- Windsor and Hampton Court (£410, 9-10 hours)
- Stonehenge and Bath (or Glastonbury) (£525, 10 hours)

Black Cab Heritage Tours—(blackcabheritagetours.com) Has TripAdvisor's Certificate of Excellence. Traditional black cabs are driven by London cabbies/accredited guides. Prices are per cab, and they seat up to 5-6 people (depending on model). All cabs are wheelchair accessible and have air conditioning. Courtesy drinks are provided. Tours are as follows:

- Roman and Medieval London Tour (from £220, 3 hours)
- Beatlemania! Magical Mystery Tour (from £245, 3.5 hours)
- Downton Abbey London Movie Location Tour (from £250, 3 hours)

- Downton Abbey Countryside Day Excursion (from £395, 8 hours)
- Jack the Ripper Tour (from £220, 3 hours)
- Classic Westminster Tour (from £170, 2 hours)
- 007 in London—Licensed to Thrill Spy MysteriesTour (from £270, 4 hours)
- Harry Potter in London Movie Site Locations Tour (from £220, 3 hours)
- Harry Potter in Oxford Day Excursion (from £445, 8 hours)
- Light Up London Night Tour (from £125, 1.5+ hours)
- Black Cab Heritage London Tours (from £220, 3+ hours)
- Bath and Lacock Village Day Excursion (from £485, 10 hours)
- The Windsor Day Excursion (from £395, 6 hours)
- Bath and Stonehenge Day Excursion (from £475, 10 hours)

London Black Taxi Tours—(www.londonblacktaxitours.com/) Has TripAdvisor's Certificate of Excellence 2011-2019. Founder Michael Churchill is a native Londoner and 30-year licensed cab driver, as well as a qualified tour guide. Prices are per taxi and not per person. Tours are in his London black cab and have the following themes:

- The City and Central London (£220, 4 hours)
- Whistle Stop London Daytime Tour (£140, 2 hours)

London Cab Tours—(www.londoncabtours.co.uk/) Has TripAdvisor's Certificate of Excellence. Graham Greenglass is a licensed black cab driver, City of London Tour Guide, London Taxi Tour Guide, and more. He offers the following tours (prices per cab, up to 5 people):

- London Highlights Tour (£190, 3 hours)
- London Highlights and More Tour (£280, 5 hours)
- London Big Day Out (£380, 7 hours)
- Beatles and More London Rock'n Roll Tour (£240, 4 hours)
- London Horror Tour: A Way of Death (£190, 3 hours)
- Harry Potter in London Tour (£215, 3.5 hours)
- Heathrow to Hotel + London Tour (£270, 3 hours)

- Hampton Court Palace + Royal London Tour (£380, 7-8 hours)
- Windsor Castle + Royal London Tour (£380, 7-8 hours)
- English Countryside Tour (£380, 7 hours)
- Windsor Castle + Eton + Runnymede (£380, 7-8 hours)
- Stonehenge + Magna Carta Tour (£495, 9 hours)
- Bath and Lacock Village Tour (£490, 9 hours)
- Stratford-upon-Avon + Oxford Tour (£550, 10 hours)
- Oxford Tour (£380, 7 hours)

Small Car Big City—(smallcarbigcity.com) Has TripAdvisor's Certificate of Excellence. Private tours of London in classic Mini Coopers. Limited to 3 passengers. Tours offered include the following:

- Landmarks of London (£189, 1.5 hour)
- Best Bits of London (£399, 4 hours)
- Panoramic London Tour (£245, 2 hours)
- Live Like a Local (£659, 8 hours, includes coffee, lunch)

London Cabbie Tours—(londoncabbietours.com/) Has TripAdvisor's Certificate of Excellence. Steve is a fully licensed London cabbie and Green Badge Guide who takes groups around the city in his cow-painted cab. He offers tours with these themes (and more):

- Classic London Tour
- Royal London
- Roman Tour
- Rock Tour
- Haunted London and Ghostly Pubs
- Girls in the City (e.g., "hen parties")

Rates are by ride (up to 5 passengers), £150 for 2 hours, £180 for 3 hours, £220 for 4 hours, and £400 for 8 hours.

Other in-city transportation

You have many options for getting around London beyond sightseeing buses or private tours. London offers a rich buffet of public transportation modes—subway, bus, tram, river bus. Check out the VisitLondon .com site to get the latest information: www.visitlondon.com/traveller-information/getting-around-london. Journey planning is available at tfl.gov.uk/plan-a-journey/.

The first thing you need to know about public transportation is that you will probably want an **Oyster Card** to ride it. An Oyster Card is a pre-paid transit card that you can use to ride the bus, Tube, tram, Docklands Light Railway (DLR), MBNA Thames Clippers (river buses), London Overground, and most National Rail services in the metropolitan area. Not only do you get the convenience of a pre-paid card, but the Oyster Card provides discounts on the transportation.

Oyster Cards come in two forms—a Visitor Oyster Card and a regular Oyster Card. A Visitor Oyster Card is one you order in advance and have shipped to you, which makes it a bit of a pain for American travelers, but I've done this, and as long as you order in plenty of time, it's nice to have your transit cards in hand before flying to London. Visitor Oyster Cards cost £5 plus whatever amount of credit you have loaded on it. The £5 cost is not refundable (unlike the regular Oyster Card), but the Visitor Card offers numerous discounts at restaurants and on entertainment.

You can get a regular Oyster Card in London by paying a refundable £5 deposit and then loading up the amount of credit you want. (Cards are most easily purchased at Underground stations, including at Heathrow Airport, from ticket machines.) To use your card, tap it on the yellow card reader when entering transportation, then (on the Tube) tap again when exiting.

Both types of Oyster Cards give discounts on transportation and have capped fees for each day and for the week. You can top up your card credit at machines located in Underground stations. At the end of your stay you can either retain your card for future visits (cards and credits do not expire) or redeem the card at a machine for the £5 deposit (non-visitor cards only), as well as any credit on the card up to £10 (both types of cards). Oyster Cards are *the* way to go if you will be using public transportation. Now let's get an introduction to the transportation itself.

London is justifiably famous for its **Underground** (the world's first underground railway), also known as the Tube. And it is true that the Tube can efficiently transport you to the far reaches of the metro area. As in other cities, though, riding the underground train system, however extensive and efficient, does require a good bit of walking, sometimes up and down stairs (although usually escalators are available—often looong ones), to get to the appropriate train platforms. Riding the Underground is doable for slow walkers, but be prepared to take plenty of time to do it, and realize that it may take its toll physically. The accessibility warning on the Visit London Web site is strong enough that I will quote it verbatim:

> Access to most Tube stations is via numerous steps. The London metro system can become very crowded at peak times and, therefore, difficult for those with mobility problems.
>
> Many deep-level Tube stations have escalators to platforms. But nearly all the stations with escalators or lifts also have stairs between street level and the ticket hall and/or between the escalator/lift and the platforms. The down-loadable Tube map on our free London travel maps page indicates which Tube stations are step-free.
>
> When boarding Tube trains, be aware that there is generally a step of up to 8 inches (20cm), either up or down, between the platform and the train. If this is problematic, travel in the first carriage, so the driver can see you more clearly, and allow enough time for you to get on or off. (from www.visit london.com/traveller-information/getting-around-london/london-tube)

Tube fares vary according to how far you ride, time of day, and how you pay. (Oyster cards are as cheap as it gets.) A regular one-way fare in Zone 1 (central London) costs £4.90. With an Oyster card, it is £2.80. In 2019, the daily cap for Zones 1-2 was £7, Zones 1-3 £8.20, Zones 1-4 £10.10, Zones 1-5 £12, and Zones 1-6 £12.80. Weekly caps also exist. For example, the 7-day cap for travel in Zones 1-3 is £41.20.

Buses are another economical option for getting around the city, with the possibility of sightseeing on the way. London's red double-decker buses are iconic. The vast bus network runs around the clock, although buses are less frequent very late at night. A single bus fare of £1.50 is good for one hour, but here's the catch—you can't pay cash for the ride. You have to use some sort of "contactless" payment—probably using some sort of Oyster Card (see above). Just touch your Oyster Card to the yellow card-reader pad as you board. Use the same card all the time, and cards cannot be shared on a ride, because your travel expenses are capped at £4.50/day for unlimited bus and tram travel. (Caps are higher when riding the Underground; see above.)

If you plan to ride just buses and trams (no Underground), you may want a one-day bus and tram pass for £5. These passes are good until 4:29 a.m. the next day.

London buses are wheelchair accessible. (Wheelchair users ride for free.)

If you want the driver to stop at the next stop, push a red stop button (on metal posts throughout the bus). Plan your bus route at /tfl.gov.uk/maps/bus.

What about **river buses**? Rides along the Thames are a legitimate form of transportation with a great view of central London. MBNA Thames Clippers operate frequent bus service from almost all London piers. Popular stops include Westminster Pier (Houses of Parliament, Big Ben, Westminster Abbey), London Eye Pier, Bankside Pier (Globe Theatre, Tate Modern), London Bridge Pier (HMS Belfast, Borough Market), Tower Millennium Pier (London Tower, Tower Bridge), North Greenwich Pier, and Greenwich Pier.

Fares vary according to the zones you travel in and how you pay. (Oyster Cards get a discount.) If you travel through all zones, the standard fare is £19.30 and the Oyster Card (either kind) fare is £9. (Note that daily caps for Oyster Cards do not apply to river buses.) All river buses have step-free access, and many have wheelchair access. Most piers are wheelchair accessible. No commentary is provided.

River bus routes can be found online at www.thamesclipper.com. Look under the Routes, Timetables & Prices heading for a route map.

Tourist-oriented **Thames River cruises** are another transportation possibility. **City Cruises** offers a hop-on/hop-off cruise that might be just the ticket for seeing central London sights. Cruises run daily from 10 a.m. to 6 p.m., year-round, leaving every 30-40 minutes from Westminster, the London Eye, Tower of London, and Greenwich. Lunch, afternoon tea, dinner and themed cruises (e.g., Elvis, murder mystery) are also available. Cruises have live commentary in English and recorded commentary in other languages. Most boats are wheelchair accessible and have restrooms appropriate for disabled users.

A 24-hour adult Red Rover ticket costs £19.50 (no Oyster Card option), a 24-hour child (5-15) ticket is £12.75, and a 24-hour family ticket (2 adults, 3 children) is £39. Tickets can be bought at any City Cruises pier or online at www.citycruises.com. (City Cruise hop-on/hop-off services are *included* in the London Pass—see below—and with most HOHO tours.)

Circular Cruise Westminster (www.circularcruise.london) is another river cruise option offering hop-on/hop-off flexibility but on a shorter stretch of river. (Ratings seem to come in a bit lower than they are for City Cruises.) Boats run from 9 a.m. to 5 p.m. with stops at Westminster Pier, Embankment Pier, Festival Pier, Bankside Pier, and St. Katharine's Pier (Tower of London). Commentary in English is live by the captain.

Adult single £10.75 or round-trip £16, senior single £7.25 or round-trip £11, child single £7 or round-trip £10.75, and family single £28.50 or round-trip £36.90. (Return trips to Westminster are non-stop.) You can use your Oyster Card at a ticket office to purchase a discounted ticket. A 50% cruise discount is available if you order a Tower of London ticket at the same time online. (See Circular Cruise site.)

Finally, if you are looking for convenience more than economy, you can't find a better solution than traveling around the city in a **taxi**, using London's famous black cabs (or other options). Black cabs are the only ones that can be hailed on the street. If their yellow TAXI light is on, they are available. Cabs are also found in taxi ranks outside Tube and train stations or prominent sights. You can also book a cab on the phone, but there is an additional fee to do so. Black cabs are wheelchair accessible.

Cab fares are metered, with a minimum fee of £3.

To get an idea of cab expenses, you can use a fare finder such as www.taxifarefinder.com/main.php?city=London. The estimated cab fare from South Kensington to the British Museum in Bloomsbury, a trip just under 5 km (about 3 miles) ranges from £11.25 (light traffic) to £57.42 (heavy traffic). Fares from South Kensington to the Tower of London (8.7 km, about 5½ miles) range from £17.77 (light traffic) to £82.87 (heavy traffic). And that's just one way, of course.

Your hotel will certainly have recommendations for a cab company, and will probably call one for you, if you would like. A few numbers for booking a cab are:

- Computer Cab, 0207 908 0207
- Dial-A-Cab, 020 7253 5000
- Radio Taxis, 020 7272 0272
- One-Number Taxi, 0871 871 8710

You may find slightly lower fares on minicabs or with private drivers, but for your own safety, make sure they are licensed. For guidance on this, see www.visitlondon.com/traveller-information/getting-around-london/taxis or tfl.gov.uk/modes/taxis-and-minicabs/?cid=pp001.

Sightseeing—The London Pass

London is loaded with world-class museums that offer free entry (e.g., British Museum, Victoria and Albert Museum, Tate Modern, National Gallery, and many more), but some of the most popular sights (e.g., Tower of London, Westminster Abbey, Windsor Castle) are definitely not free (and also not cheap). If you want to see a lot of *those* sights, the London Pass can save you lots of money.

The London Pass (www.londonpass.com) provides free access to over 80 attractions, tours, and museums, as well as fast-track entry to many sights and additional special offers. It covers a free 1-day HOHO bus tour and a free Thames River cruise. Available for time frames of 1, 2, 3, 6, or 10 consecutive days, the London Pass is activated the first time you use it. (Try to start use early in the morning, to maximize calendar-day coverage.)

The London Pass is limited to a "purse value" of gate prices you will be avoiding. Adult purse value maximums are as follows: 1 day (£175), 2 days (£275), 3 days (£350), 6 days (£605), and 10 days (£905).

A London Pass can also be combined with an Oyster Travelcard (standard reloadable Oyster Card) to maximize savings. (London Pass activation is separate from Oyster Card activation, so you could use your Oyster Card to ride the Underground from Heathrow to central London, if you ordered your pass and card in advance.)

Fast-track privileges apply at these attractions: Tower Bridge Exhibition, St. Paul's Cathedral, Hampton Court Palace, London Zoo, London Bridge Experience, and Kew Gardens.

London Pass 2019 prices were as follows (Children are 5-15 years old. No discounts for groups, students, or seniors. Note that children under 11 can ride for free with an adult who has an Oyster Card.):

- 1 day—adult £75 (with travel £90), child £55 (with travel £64.30)
- 2 days—adult £99 (with travel £119), child £75 (with travel £93.60)
- 3 days—adult £125 (with travel £155), child £89 (with travel £116.90)
- 6 days—adult £169 (with travel £214), child £125 (with travel £157.10)
- 10 days—adult £199 (with travel £254), child £149 (with travel £204)

You can buy a London Pass online (to have shipped to you, to pick up in the central London office, or have delivered immediately to your Smart phone—although no travel option for Smart phones), at retail partners in London, or at London airports. NOTE: If you want the travel option, you must order online or at the London Pass Redemption Centre at 11a Charing Cross Road. (Standard worldwide shipping in 2019 was estimated at 15 days for a cost of £7.95, with express shipping to the U.S. and to Canada estimated at 4 days and with a cost of £20.)

Before you decide whether you want a London Pass for sightseeing, consider how very many excellent London museums, parks, and other sights are completely free to visit. An advantage of visiting a free sight (rather than one you've paid £20 pounds for) is that you can leave whenever you want without feeling that you've wasted your entry fee. If you know you can handle a half day exploring the Tower of London, by all means, pay for entry and enjoy every minute of it! But if you think you're better suited for shorter visits, you can probably piece together enough free sights to more than fill your sightseeing time in London.

The following London sights are free of charge:

- British Museum
- Natural History Museum
- National Gallery
- Science Museum
- Victoria and Albert Museum
- Tate Modern
- Museum of London
- Imperial War Museum
- National Maritime Museum
- V&A Museum of Childhood
- Sir John Sloane's Museum
- Wallace Collection
- National Portrait Gallery
- Tate Britain
- Royal Air Force Museum
- Wellcome Collection
- British Library

You can also see the outside of many ticketed sights for free: the Tower of London, St. Paul's Cathedral, Westminster Abbey, the London Eye. Iconic department stores are also free (to enter and browse in, if not to shop); check out Harrod's or Selfridge's. You may also prefer to save your time and money for London experiences rather than sights, such as a West End show or afternoon tea at Claridge's (or elsewhere, if you don't want to spend £70!). Experience the city however it makes sense for you, and don't feel you have to run yourself ragged seeing all the top sights. London will be there for you to come back to some day.

Day trips

It's possible to see much of southeastern England without having to leave the comfort of your base hotel at night, because London has plenty of tourist companies that specialize in day trips.

As always, use the information here as a guide, but check each company's Web site for tour details and the most current price and schedule information. **Tour details—even which tours are offered—routinely change from season to season.** Whichever tours you decide on, look over cancellation policies, if your plans aren't completely firm.

Browsing through Web sites will also help you decide which company's tours seem a good fit for you. Be aware that some specific tours might have special requirements or recommendations, so you'll want to look descriptions over closely before you show up at the departure point.

Tour companies differ on which entry fees they include in their prices, so check those specifics (and confirm online), if your selection comes down to price.

Also take into account where the tours depart from. London tours included below leave from the London Eye (The English Bus), Victoria Station (The English Bus, Rabbie's Tours, Day Tours London, Premium Tours), from near the V&A (England Experience), and from the Gloucester Road Underground Station (Day Tours London). You may, in fact, decide on tours according to which ones depart from near your hotel. Wherever you leave from, make sure you show up early for any tour so you are not considered a no-show and your seat sold to someone else!

Be aware that many tourists advise *not* including Windsor Castle in a multiple-stop day trip, because that leaves too little time to see things and it's much better to get there on your own via public transportation and spend a good half day (rather than a rushed hour).

If you want to save your walking energy for the tour itself but you select a tour with a departure point that is not close to your hotel, you may want to invest in a taxi ride to get there.

If you take a multi-day tour with one of these companies, you will likely be restricted to one small bag and will need to store the lion's share of your luggage. Your hotel may do that for you (many offer baggage storage), or you can check into storing your luggage at the train or bus station.

London offers "left luggage" storage across the city, including these train stations: Charing Cross (main concourse), Euston (Platform 16-18), King's Cross (main concourse), Liverpool Street (Platform 10), Paddington (Platform 12), St. Pancras International (main concourse), Victoria (Platform 8), Waterloo (Exit 6, South Bank). For more information see www.visitlondon.com/traveller-information/essentialinformation/baggage-left-luggage.

Storing luggage for several days or a week can get very expensive. Visitors are advised to use a self-storage rental, in that case. Companies that offer luggage rentals in several locations include Safestore, ABC Selfstore, and Access Self Storage. See www.toptiplondon.com/practical-tips/left-luggage for more information.

The English Bus

The English Bus (theenglishbus.com) has TripAdvisor's Certificate of Excellence. Specially built small luxury vehicles (16 passengers, air conditioning, USB ports) with panoramic windows and a glass roof take scenic back roads to numerous destinations from London.

Stonehenge, Bath & a Secret Place—Tour highlights include guided commentary on the way out of London, Stonehenge with audio guide and Visitor Centre access (entry fee not included—adults £19 in 2019), guided commentary on back roads through rural countryside and villages, independent lunch in Bath, optional guided walking tour of Bath (included), a secret place (guide's choice) on the return trip to London. Daily (possibly less in off-season), depart 8:45 from the London Eye or 9:10 from around Victoria Station, return 8:15-8:30 p.m. with some flexibility on drop-off points. From £94.

The Cotswolds, Oxford and Stratford Upon Avon—Tour highlights include guided commentary on bus ride, an hour's free time in Stratford followed by a walking tour (optional entrance to Shakespeare's birthplace, not covered), driving tour of the Cotswolds, free time in a Cotswolds market town, free time in Oxford followed by an hour-long walking tour, then more free time. Sun/Wed, depart London Eye 8:45 and Victoria Station 9:10, return to various drop-off points 8:15-8:30 p.m. From £89.

A Cotswolds Village, Bath and Stonehenge—Tour highlights include guided commentary on bus ride, Castle Combe ("prettiest village in England"), panoramic driving tour of Bath, free time and optional walking tour in Bath, Stonehenge with audio-guide and Visitor Centre access (entry fee not included, adult £19 in 2019). Mon, depart London Eye 8:45 and Victoria Station 9:10, return 8:15-8:30 to various drop-off points. From £94.

Canterbury, Dover Cliffs & Castle, Rochester & Kent Villages—Tour highlights include the Prime Meridian in Greenwich, the city of Rochester, back roads to the English Channel at the white cliffs of Dover, Dover Castle (optional entry not included—adult £20.90 in 2019), drive through scenic Kent, village of Chilham, free time in Canterbury, optional entry into the cathedral (not included—adult £12.50 in 2019), Tue/Fri, depart London Eye 8:45, return to London Eye around 8:15-8:30 p.m. From £89.

Warner Bros. Studio Tour London—The Making of Harry Potter & Oxford—Tour highlights include a 90-minute guided walking tour of Oxford (included) plus free time, entry to the 15-century Divinity School (included), then 3½ hours at the Warner Bros. Studio and the Making of Harry Potter tour (entry included). Tour operated by partner company, "International Friends." Thu, depart 7:20 a.m. outside the British Museum, depart 7:30 from the Marble Arch, depart 7:45 from Kensington, return 7 p.m. to Victoria Station. From £139.

Other day tours are Winter Solstice Sunrise at Stonehenge (Dec. 22, from £94); and Belgium—A Day in Beautiful Bruges (soon-to-be-added, from £104). **Multi-day tours** are Edinburgh and Scottish Highlands by Train (from £289); and Paris by Eurostar or Coach (from £319).

England Experience

England Experience (englandexperience.com) has TripAdvisor's Certificate of Excellence and provides small-group tours on air-conditioned buses (most tours with 16 passengers or fewer). Tours leave from Caffé Nero, 126 Brompton Rd, Knightsbridge (near the V&A Museum).

Stonehenge, Bath, Lacock and Avebury—Tour highlights include Stonehenge (entry included), the Georgian city of Bath with walking tour (included), Avebury's Neolithic Stone Circle, Lacock National Trust rural village ("Harry Potter" and "Downton Abbey" filming site). Daily, 8:15 a.m.-8 p.m. Adults from £73, concessions from £70.

Canterbury, Dover and Leeds Castle—Tour highlights include guided storytelling on the ride to Canterbury, walking tour of Canterbury, tour of Canterbury Cathedral (not included, adults £12.50 in 2019), the White

Cliffs of Dover, Leeds Castle (optional tour, not included, adults £26 in 2019). Mon/Thu/Sun, 8:30 a.m.-7 p.m. Adults from £59, concessions from £56.

Oxford and Cotswold Villages—Tour highlights include the city of Oxford, Bourton-on-the-Water ("Venice of the Cotswolds"), Coln Valley, hidden Cotswolds villages such as Moreton-in-Marsh and Stow-in-the-Wold. Tue/Sat, 8:30 a.m.-9 p.m. Adults from £65, concessions from £62.

Windsor, Runnymede, and Kew Gardens—Tour highlights include a visit to Runnymede (where Magna Carta was signed), the Ankerwyke (2,500-year-old yew), Windsor, with an optional tour of Windsor Castle (adults £22.50 in 2019, not included), UNESCO World Heritage Site Kew Gardens with tree-top walk. Wed/Fri, 8:30 a.m.-7 p.m. Adults from £65, concessions from £62.

England Experience **also offers** a 2-day tour to Stonehenge, Bath, Cotswolds and Oxford; 5-day tours called South West Experience and England and Wales Experience; an 8-day tour of England, Wales, Skye & the Scottish Highlands; a 9-day tour of the Best of England and Wales; and a 12-day tour of the Ultimate UK Experience.

Rabbie's Tours

Rabbie's Tours (www.rabbies.com/en/england-tours/from-london) has TripAdvisor's Certificate of Excellence. It specializes in small-group tours (16 passengers) in air-conditioned Mercedes minibuses.

Shakespeare's Stratford-upon-Avon—Tour highlights include ample free time to explore half-timbered Stratford (Shakespeare's birthplace, school, River Avon, Royal Shakespeare Theatre), Ann Hathaway's cottage, and Holy Trinity Church (Shakespeare's grave). Sun/Mon/Wed/Fri, depart 9:15 a.m. Victoria Station, return 9:15 p.m. Adults from £55-£75, concessions £42-£62.

Oxford & Traditional Cotswold Villages—Tour highlights include a bus ride through "Vicar of Dibley" country of "Outstanding Natural Beauty," Oxford University, the Great Hall of Christ Church College, Bampton (the village of "Downton"), Burford market town, afternoon tea (optional), village of Bibury ("prettiest village in England"). Entry fees not included. Daily, depart 9:15 a.m. Victoria Station, return 7 p.m. Adults £49-£72, concessions £46-£69.

Bath, Avebury & Lacock Village—Tour highlights include exploration time in Bath, Lacock Village and Abbey (popular film site, including for "Harry Potter"), and the largest prehistoric stone circle in the world at Avebury. Entry fees not included. Tue/Thu/Sat (can be less in off-season), depart 9:15 a.m. from Victoria Station, return 7:30 p.m. Adults £49-£65, concessions £46-£64.

Bombay Sapphire Gin & Winchester—Tour highlights include visiting the city of Winchester, historic Norman cathedral, Laverstoke Distillery for Bombay Sapphire Gin, Runnymede (site of Magna Carta signing). Mon/Thu/Fri, depart 9:15 a.m. from Victoria Station, return 7 p.m. Adults £62, concessions £59.

Rabbie's Tours also offers **multi-day tours** into the countryside. They have a two-day tour to the Cotswolds, Bath & Oxford (£89-£129). Three-day tours include Leeds Castle, White Cliffs & Flavours of Kent (£129-£189); Shakespeare's England, Warwick Castle & the Cotswolds (£139-£199); Stonehenge, Glastonbury, Bath & the South West Coast (£139-£199); and The Lake District Explorer (£189-£245). They also offer 3 five-day tours and 1 eight-day tour.

London Country Tours

London Country Tours (londoncountrytours.co.uk) specializes in private tours of the English countryside. (More expensive for singles or couples, but they get rave reviews.) A small, hand-picked team of guides chauffeur groups of 1-8 around in air-conditioned cars. (Cost out the per-person price for a tour, because it may not be bad for a larger group.)

You can develop a custom tour with the company, but popular destinations (among many) include Bletchley Park (home of top-secret WWII code breakers) and Woburn Abbey and Gardens; Windsor Castle, Eton, and Hampton Court; Harry Potter tours; Stonehenge; and the Cotswolds.

Pricing is by length of tour and number of people, from £425 for many destinations requiring 5-10 hours (including those listed above) for 1-4 people, to £450 to the same destinations for 5-8 people. Wheelchair use can be arranged. Pickup in western and central London is included; pickup elsewhere can be arranged for an additional fee. (Also available for private tours *within* London, 7 hours, £395-£425.)

Day Tours London

Day Tours London (www.daytourslondon.com/) has TripAdvisor's Certificate of Excellence. They provide small group tours (maximum 28 passengers) that leave from multiple departure points in London. The main departure point is the Gloucester Road Underground station in South Kensington, but also Victoria Station (and previously Paddington Station). Day Tours London promotes their tours as "leisurely," with "enough time to enjoy and explore the sites."

Oxford, Stratford-Upon-Avon & Cotswolds—Tour highlights include 90 minutes to explore Stratford-Upon-Avon, drive through the Cotswolds, photo stop in Bibury, at least 2 hours in Oxford with guided walking tour. Depart 7:40 a.m. from Victoria Station/7:45 Gloucester Road. Return to Hammersmith Station around 6:30 p.m. Adults from £60, seniors from £52.

Stonehenge, Bath & English Countryside—Tour highlights include a guided bus tour through the English countryside to Stonehenge, entry to Stonehenge and Visitor Centre, short tour in Bath and free time to explore independently. Daily, depart 7:40 a.m. Victoria Station/7:45 a.m. opposite Gloucester Road Tube station, return to Hammersmith Station around 6:30 p.m. Adults from £64, seniors from £60.

White Cliffs of Dover, Canterbury City & Kent Coast—Tour highlights include panoramic views of the Kent countryside, the white cliffs of Dover, with enough time to take a walk along National Trust paths or an optional visit to Dover Castle (entry not included), Canterbury City short walking tour, free time to eat and drink and visit the famous cathedral (entry not included). Daily (less in off-season), depart 7:40 Victoria Station, return near Victoria Station around 6 p.m. Adults from £60, seniors from £52.

Day Tours London also offers **small-group** day trips (max. 16 people) to Cotswolds/Oxford (£79) and to Stonehenge/Bath/Lacock (£99—includes Stonehenge admission), as well as **half-day shuttle tours to Stonehenge** (£52).

Premium Tours

Premium Tours (www.premiumtours.co.uk/category/out-of-london-tours-uk-britain-england) has a TripAdvisor Certificate of Excellence. They offer professionally guided tours on double-decker air-conditioned coaches with free WiFi (usually). (Know the trade-offs of a full itinerary—some tours can feel rushed, according to customers.)

England in One Day: Stonehenge, Bath, Stratford & the Cotswolds—Tour highlights include Stonehenge (entry and audio headset included), Bath and the Cotswolds, Stratford-Upon-Avon, private tour of Shakespeare's school (with champagne and scone). Days vary by season, depart/return Victoria Station 7:45 a.m.-8:30 p.m. Adults from £108, children (3-16) from £98, senior/student from £105.

Lunch in the Cotswolds—Tour highlights include a 2-course lunch in the 17th-century Swan Hotel in Bibury (the "prettiest village in England") (included), photo stops at Bourton-on-the-Water, Burford, and Stow-on-the-Wold. Days vary by season, depart/return Victoria Coach Station, ending at 6:30 p.m. Adults from £95, children from £85, senior/student from £92.

Warwick Castle, Stratford, Oxford & the Cotswolds—Tour highlights include Stratford-Upon-Avon and fast-track entry into Shakespeare's birth place (included), private tour of Shakespeare's school and guildhall, Warwick Castle (entry included), walking tour of Oxford, drive through the Cotswolds. Days vary by season, depart/return Victoria Coach Station, 7:45 a.m.-7 p.m. Adults from £102, children (3-16) from £92, senior/student from £99.

Leeds Castle, Canterbury, Dover & Greenwich—Tour highlights include Leeds Castle private tour, Dover, Canterbury Cathedral (entry included), walking tour of Greenwich, Thames River cruise back to central London. Days vary by season, depart Victoria Station, return Embankment Pier at 7 p.m. Adults from £102, children from £92, senior/student from £99.

Downton Abbey: Highclere Castle—Tour highlights include Oxford walking tour, Bampton ("Downton Village"), Highclere Castle ("Downton Abbey") tour, Lady Carnavon's book. Limited availability, no refunds. Adults from £132, children from £122, senior/student from £129.

Other tours offered periodically:

- Stonehenge, Salisbury Cathedral and Georgian Bath including Pub Lunch, from £83
- Cathedrals, Castles and Gardens of England, from £125
- Spires, Shires and Shakespeare, from £145

Golden/Gray Line Tours

Golden/Gray Line Tours (www.goldentours.com/day-trips-from-london) offers large-group tours from London to popular tourist sights, but reviews are mixed. Day tours include a free lunch. Review the options at the Web site listed above.

Lodging

Lodging in central London is expensive. Plan to either lower your expectations or raise your budget while staying there. Fortunately, the city is bursting with hotels and good neighborhoods that cover a wide range of budgets, from reasonable to stratospheric. Just bear in mind that a "reasonably" priced hotel is likely to have tiny rooms and look a little worn. That's just part of the London experience.

Hotels on this list are based on location, good reviews, and general accessibility, including access to easy transportation. No place is perfect—the city is simply too big to offer an ideal neighborhood that includes everything you're looking for at a great price. But this section is a good starting point to narrow down your search. Just check online to make sure that information is still accurate, both on TripAdvisor and on the hotel's own Web site.

Central London is chock-full of old buildings, and many of them now house hotels. The dominant Georgian-style architecture typically features a set of stairs (not a full flight) leading up to the front door. I have included information about stairs if they were mentioned in a hotel's description or in reviews about them, but that's no guarantee that the hotels that *don't* list stairs here are actually stair-free. **If you are interested in a hotel and stairs are a deal-breaker, contact the hotel and ask about stairs and ways to avoid them.**

This is by no means a comprehensive list of suitable hotels in London. You may find a wonderful deal on what looks to you like a good choice in a convenient location. By all means—grab it! Same with charming B&Bs, which aren't covered here because they tend to have a limited number of available rooms and generally don't have elevators. If you can nab one in a convenient location that gets good reviews, has a great breakfast, decent accessibility, and a workable price, do it!

The Heathrow Express, you may recall, takes travelers directly to Paddington Station. The Underground transports travelers along the blue Piccadilly line. The Gatwick Express delivers travelers to Victoria Station.

For day trips, tours generally leave from around Victoria Station, Gloucester Road, Brompton Road, the London Eye, and (sometimes) Paddington Station.

- The English Bus leaves from the London Eye and Victoria Station.
- England Experience buses leave from Caffé Nero on Brompton Road in Knightsbridge.
- Rabbie's Tours buses leave near Victoria Station.
- Day Tours London buses leave from Gloucester Road and Victoria Station.
- Premium Tours leave near Victoria Station.
- Golden/Gray Line Tours leave near Victoria Station.

Hotel price ranges are based on late 2019 TripAdvisor averages. Your own quotes may be higher or lower.

Gloucester Road/South Kensington area

Located south of Hyde Park. Area hotels listed here are close to the Gloucester Road and/or South Kensington Underground stops on the blue Piccadilly, yellow Circle, and green District lines. Day Tours London buses leave from near the Gloucester Road Underground entrance. Gloucester Road is one stop from the Brompton Road area (where England Experience tours leave from) and two more stops from Victoria Station, where numerous day trips depart. The South Kensington station is near Brompton Road and two stops from Victoria Station.

The hop-on/hop-off Original Tour stops at Gloucester Road and Brompton Road on its blue line. (Riders can switch to the tourist-sights yellow route at the Hyde Park/Queen Elizabeth Gate stop.) HOHO Big Bus Tours stop at Gloucester Road and South Kensington on their blue line. (Riders can switch to the tourist-centered red route at stops for Marble Arch or Mayfair.)

Nearby sights in this area include the Victoria & Albert Museum, the Natural History Museum, the Science Museum, Royal Albert Hall, and Harrod's Department Store.

Crown Plaza London Kensington—100 Cromwell Road. TripAdvisor's Certificate of Excellence. Location: across from Gloucester Road Underground station. Pros: free WiFi, restaurant, good breakfast buffet, non-smoking, room service, suites/family/twin rooms available, air conditioning, accessible rooms, wheelchair access, bar/lounge, fitness center. Cons: some stairs between street level and entrance (but disabled stair lift available), no single rooms, no price break for singles. (TripAdvisor price range for standard room: $190-$383.)

Distances: Gloucester Tube station (0 miles), Natural History Museum (.3 miles), Science Museum (.4 miles), Hyde Park (1.1 miles), Buckingham Palace (1.9 miles)

Montana Hotel—67-69 Gloucester Road. (www.montanahotel.co.uk/) Location: close to Gloucester Road Underground station. Pros: free WiFi, good breakfast included, air conditioning, non-smoking, Indian restaurant, bar/lounge, refrigerator, single/twin/triple/quad rooms available, lift, airport shuttle (fee). Cons: lift slow and small. (TripAdvisor price range for standard room: $94-$257.)

Distances: Gloucester Tube station (.1 miles), Natural History Museum (.3 miles), Science Museum (.4 miles), V&A Museum (.5 miles), Hyde Park (1.1 miles), Buckingham Palace (1.8 miles)

Hotel London Kensington Managed by Melia—61 Gloucester Road. TripAdvisor's Certificate of Excellence. Location: close to Gloucester Road Underground station. Pros: free WiFi, breakfast buffet, air conditioning, non-smoking, restaurant, room service, lift, bar/lounge, fitness center, singles/twins/triples/suites available. Cons: complaints about air conditioning, some rooms small, weak WiFi, pillow/mattress complaints. (TripAdvisor price range for standard room: $194-$591.)

Distances: Gloucester Tube station (.1 miles), Natural History Museum (.3 miles), Science Museum (.4 miles), Royal Albert Hall (.4 miles), Hyde Park (1 mile), Buckingham Palace (1.8 miles)

Radison Blu Edwardian Vanderbuilt—68-86 Cromwell Road (www.radissonblu-edwardian.com/london-hotel-gb-sw7-5bt/gbvander). TripAdvisor's Certificate of Excellence. Location: east of the Gloucester Road Tube station. Pros: free WiFi, very good breakfast buffet, air conditioning, restaurant, non-smoking, room service, bar/lounge, single/twin/family rooms available, facilities for disabled guests, fitness center. Cons: some stairs between levels. (TripAdvisor price range for standard room: $133-$467.)

Distances: Gloucester Tube station (.1 miles), Natural History Museum (.2 miles), Science Museum (.4 miles), V&A Museum (.4 miles), Royal Albert Hall (.4 miles), Hyde Park (1 mile), Buckingham Palace (1.8 miles)

Fraser Suites Queen's Gate—39B Queen's Gate Gardens. Location: east of the Gloucester Road Tube station. Pros: free WiFi, breakfast, air conditioning, non-smoking, lift, suites/triples/quads available, kitchenettes in rooms, bar/lounge, fitness center. Cons: no singles, no price break for singles, some stairs. (TripAdvisor price range for standard room: $199-$397.)

Distances: Gloucester Tube station (.1 miles), Natural History Museum (.2 miles), Science Museum (.3 miles), V&A Museum (.4 miles), Royal Albert Hall (.4 miles), Hyde Park (1 mile), Buckingham Palace (1.7 miles)

The Bailey's Hotel London—140 Gloucester Road. TripAdvisor's Certificate of Excellence. Location: across from Gloucester Road Underground station. Pros: free WiFi, good breakfast buffet, air conditioning, non-smoking, restaurant, room service, suites, airport shuttle (fee), lift, facilities for disabled guests, fitness center, single/family rooms available, refrigerator. Cons: nothing notable. (TripAdvisor price range for standard room: $209-$486.)

Distances: Gloucester Tube station (.1 miles), Natural History Museum (.3 miles), South Kensington Tube station (.4 miles), Science Museum (.5 miles), V&A Museum (.5 miles), Royal Albert Hall (.5 miles), Hyde Park (1.2 mile), Buckingham Palace (1.9 miles)

The Harrington—1 Harrington Gardens. Location: south of Gloucester Road Underground station. Pros: free WiFi, air conditioning, non-smoking, family/quad rooms available, suites, kitchenette, self-serve laundry, private parking. Cons: can be noisy, no breakfast, no restaurant/bar/lounge, no singles, no price break for singles, no twins. (TripAdvisor price range for standard room: $165-$677.)

Distances: Gloucester Tube station (.1 miles), Natural History Museum (.3 miles), South Kensington Tube station (.4 miles), Science Museum (.5 miles), V&A Museum (.5 miles), Hyde Park (1.2 mile), Buckingham Palace (1.8 miles)

The Pelham—Starhotels Collezione—15 Cromwell Place (www.starhotelscollezione.com/en/our-hotels/the-pelham-london/). TripAdvisor's Certificate of Excellence. Location: opposite South Kensington Underground station and by bus stop. Pros: free WiFi, good breakfast buffet, air conditioning, non-smoking, restaurant, room service, bar/lounge, fitness center, twins/triples/suites available, airport shuttle (fee). Cons: price (but deals are sometimes available), no singles, no single price break. (TripAdvisor price range for standard room: $250-$526.)

Distances: S. Kensington Tube station (.1 miles), Natural History Museum (.1 miles), Gloucester Road Tube station (.4 miles), Science Museum (.2 miles), V&A Museum (.2 miles), Royal Albert Hall (.5 miles), Hyde Park (.9 miles), Buckingham Palace (1.5 miles)

Cheval Harrington Court—13 Harrington Road. TripAdvisor's Certificate of Excellence. Free WiFi, non-smoking, suites, fitness center, kitchenette, air conditioning, private parking, triple/quad/quint rooms available. Cons: price, no singles, no price break for singles. (TripAdvisor price range for standard room: $243-$589.)

Distances: S. Kensington Tube station (.1 miles), Natural History Museum (.1 miles), Gloucester Road Tube station (.3 miles), Science Museum (.3 miles), V&A Museum (.2 miles), Royal Albert Hall (.5 miles), Hyde Park (1 mile), Buckingham Palace (1.6 miles)

The Ampersand Hotel—10 Harrington Road. TripAdvisor's Certificate of Excellence. Location: west of South Kensington Underground station. Pros: free WiFi, good breakfast buffet, Mediterranean restaurant, room service, bar/lounge, air conditioning, non-smoking, fitness center, wheelchair access, airport transportation. Cons: price, only doubles/twins, no price break for singles, some doubles very small. (TripAdvisor price range for standard room: $274-$456.)

Distances: S. Kensington Tube station (.1 miles), Natural History Museum (.2 miles), Gloucester Road Tube station (.3 miles), Science Museum (.2 miles), V&A Museum (.2 miles), Royal Albert Hall (.5 miles), Hyde Park (1 mile), Buckingham Palace (1.6 miles)

Number Sixteen—16 Sumner Place (www.firmdalehotels.com/hotels/london/number-sixteen/). TripAdvisor's Certificate of Excellence. Location: southwest of South Kensington Underground station. Pros: free WiFi, good breakfast buffet, air conditioning, non-smoking, restaurant, bar/lounge, room service, suites/single/twin rooms available, airport shuttle. Cons: elevator only to second floor, price. (TripAdvisor price range for standard room: $343-$576.)

Distances: S. Kensington Tube station (.1 miles), Natural History Museum (.2 miles), Gloucester Road Tube station (.3 miles), Science Museum (.3 miles), V&A Museum (.3 miles), Hyde Park (1 mile), Buckingham Palace (1.6 miles)

Victoria Station area

Located south of Buckingham Palace near Westminster Cathedral (not to be confused with Westminster Abbey), Victoria Station is a hub for much of the transportation of interest to us. HOHO buses, day trip buses, Underground lines—abundant options run right through here. Unfortunately, what Victoria Station *doesn't* have is direct train access to Heathrow Airport. (Gatwick is well-covered with the Gatwick Express.)

To get to this area from Heathrow by using the Underground, take the Piccadilly (blue) line to Hammersmith and change to the District (green) line to Victoria. (Make sure you change at Hammersmith, not one of the later possibilities. It's easiest there, with no stairs.) Once you get to Victoria Station, there are a couple flights of stairs from the Underground platform to street level.

National Express coaches run from Heathrow Airport to Victoria Station, but reviews of this service are mixed. Being able to travel directly from Heathrow to Victoria Station (without the expense of a taxi or private driver) may make this option well worth it, though. Find information here: www.nationalexpress.com/en/destinations/london/heathrow-to-london.

Area hotels listed here are close to the Victoria Underground stop on the Victoria (light blue), Circle (yellow), and District (green) lines. Day trips with departures around Victoria Station include those by The English Bus, Rabbie's Tours, Day Tours London, Premium Tours, and Golden/Gray Line Tours. That's pretty much all the major day tour companies except England Experience, and *those* tours leave from Brompton Road, only two Underground stops to the west.

The hop-on/hop-off Original Tour starts and ends its tourist-sights-heavy yellow route on Grosvenor Gardens, by Victoria Station. HOHO Big Bus Tours stops at Victoria Station on its main tourist red route and orange route. Nearby sights in this area include Westminster Cathedral, Victoria Place Shopping Centre, and Buckingham Palace and Gardens.

The Grosvenor Hotel—101 Buckingham Palace Road (www.guoman.com/en/london/the-grosvenor.htm). TripAdvisor's Certificate of Excellence. Location: connected to Victoria Station. Pros: free WiFi, good breakfast buffet, air conditioning, non-smoking, restaurant, room service, bar/lounge, wheelchair access, lift, single/twin/family rooms available, suites, fitness center. Cons: price, some rooms small. (TripAdvisor price range for standard room: $217-$486.)

Distances: Victoria Tube Station (.1 miles), Victoria Railway Station (.1 miles), Apollo Victoria Theatre (.1 miles), Victoria Palace Theatre (.1 miles), Victoria Coach Station (.3 miles), St. James Theatre (.3 miles), Westminster Cathedral (.3 miles), Buckingham Palace (.4 miles).

The Hotel Z Victoria—5 Lower Belgrave St. TripAdvisor's Certificate of Excellence. Location: by Victoria Station. Pros: free WiFi, breakfast buffet, air conditioning, non-smoking, lift, bar/lounge, wheelchair access. Cons: small rooms, no singles/twins/triples/quads. No singles price break. (TripAdvisor price range for standard room: $98-$254.)

Distances: Victoria Tube Station (.1 miles), Victoria Railway Station (.1 miles), Apollo Victoria Theatre (.2 miles), Victoria Palace Theatre (.2

miles), Victoria Coach Station (.2 miles), St. James Theatre (.3 miles), Westminster Cathedral (.3 miles), Buckingham Palace (.5 miles)

B+B Belgravia—64-66 Ebury St. Location: 2 streets west of Victoria Station. Pros: free WiFi, very good breakfast included, non-smoking, facilities for disabled guests (ground floor units), twins/quads/family rooms/apartments available. Cons: no air conditioning, no lift, no single rooms, no price break for singles, limited number of rooms. (TripAdvisor price range for standard room: $142-$302.)

Distances: Victoria Coach Station (.1 miles), Victoria Underground Station (.2 miles), Victoria Railway Station (.2 miles), Apollo Victoria Theatre (.3 miles), Victoria Palace Theatre (.3 miles), St. James Theatre (.4 miles), Westminster Cathedral (.4 miles), Buckingham Palace (.6 miles)

The Lord Milner—111 Ebury St. Location: 2 streets west of Victoria Station. TripAdvisor's Certificate of Excellence. Pros: Internet, air conditioning, non-smoking, suites, lift, good breakfast, refrigerator, singles/twins available, facilities for guests with disabilities (units on ground floor). Cons: singles sell out early, no restaurant/bar/lounge, only 11 rooms. (TripAdvisor price range for standard room: $197-$325.)

Distances: Victoria Tube Station (.3 miles), Victoria Railway Station (.3 miles), Apollo Victoria Theatre (.3 miles), Victoria Palace Theatre (.4 miles), Victoria Coach Station (.1 miles), St. James Theatre (.5 miles), Westminster Cathedral (.5 miles), Buckingham Palace (.6 miles)

Doubletree by Hilton Hotel London-Victoria— 2 Bridge Place. TripAdvisor's Certificate of Excellence. Location: across from Victoria Station. Pros: free WiFi, air conditioning, good buffet breakfast, non-smoking, restaurant, room service, bar/lounge, fitness center, refrigerator, wheelchair access, suites, single/twin/triple rooms available. Cons: property a bit worn, no appreciable price break for singles. (TripAdvisor price range for standard room: $206-$431.)

Distances: Victoria Tube Station (.1 miles), Victoria Railway Station (.1 miles), Apollo Victoria Theatre (.1 miles), Victoria Palace Theatre (.2 miles), Victoria Coach Station (.2 miles), St. James Theatre (.3 miles), Westminster Cathedral (.2 miles), Buckingham Palace (.5 miles)

Premier Inn London Victoria Hotel—82-83 Eccleston Square, off 55 Gillingham St. (www.premierinn.com/gb/en/hotels/england/greater-london/london/london-victoria.html). TripAdvisor's Certificate of Excellence. Location: 1 street east of Victoria Station. Pros: non-smoking, free WiFi, very good buffet breakfast, air conditioning, restaurant, bar/lounge, wheelchair access, lift, family rooms available. Cons: sells out early, no singles, no twins, no price break for singles. (TripAdvisor price range for standard room: $102-$262.)

Distances: Victoria Tube Station (.2 miles), Victoria Railway Station (.2 miles), Apollo Victoria Theatre (.2 miles), Victoria Palace Theatre (.4 miles), Victoria Coach Station (.2 miles), St. James Theatre (.3 miles), Westminster Cathedral (.2 miles), Buckingham Palace (.6 miles)

Park Plaza Victoria London—239 Vauxhall Bridge Road (www.parkplaza.com/london-hotel-gb-sw1v-1eq/gbvictor? language=e). TripAdvisor's Certificate of Excellence. Location: between Victoria Station and Westminster Cathedral. Pros: free WiFi, parking, very good buffet breakfast, air conditioning, non-smoking, Italian restaurant, room service, facilies for disabled guests, lift, twin/triple rooms and apartments available, fitness center. Cons: no single rooms, no appreciable price break for singles. (TripAdvisor price range for standard room: $198-$458.)

Distances: Victoria Tube Station (.1 miles), Victoria Railway Station (.1 miles), Apollo Victoria Theatre (.1 miles), Victoria Palace Theatre (.2 miles), Victoria Coach Station (.3 miles), St. James Theatre (.3 miles), Westminster Cathedral (.1 miles), Buckingham Palace (.5 miles)

Eccleston Square Hotel—37 Eccleston Square. TripAdvisor's Certificate of Excellence. Location: south of Victoria Station. Pros: free WiFi, breakfast available, air conditioning, non-smoking, restaurant, room service, bar/lounge, wheelchair access, elevator, facilities for disabled guests. Cons: small rooms, no singles/twins/triples/quads, no single price break. (TripAdvisor price range for standard room: $205-$372.)

Distances: Victoria Tube Station (.3 miles), Victoria Railway Station (.3 miles), Apollo Victoria Theatre (.3 miles), Victoria Palace Theatre (.4 miles), Victoria Coach Station (.2 miles), Westminster Cathedral (.4 miles), Buckingham Palace (.7 miles)

The Goring—15 Beeston Place (www.thegoring.com). TripAdvisor's Traveler's Choice Award (top 1% in category). Location: between Victoria Station and Buckingham Palace Gardens. Pros: free WiFi, non-smoking, air conditioning, restaurant, wonderful breakfast, room service, bar/lounge, suites, wheelchair access, facilities for disabled guests, lift, fitness center, twins/suites available. Cons: price, no single rooms (but a slight price break for singles). (TripAdvisor price range for standard room: $471-$977.)

Distances: Victoria Tube Station (.2 miles), Victoria Railway Station (.2 miles), Apollo Victoria Theatre (.2 miles), Victoria Palace Theatre (.1 miles), St. James Theatre (.2 miles), Victoria Coach Station (.4 miles), Westminster Cathedral (.4 miles), Buckingham Palace (.3 miles)

Hotel 41—41 Buckingham Palace Road (www.41hotel.com). TripAdvisor's Travelers Choice Award (top 1% of category). Location: across from Buckingham Palace. Pros: free WiFi, parking, breakfast buffet, air conditioning, non-smoking, restaurant, room service, bar/lounge, facilities for disabled guests, lift, suites available, exceptional breakfast. Cons: price, no twin/single/family rooms, no price break for singles. (TripAdvisor price range for standard room: $410-$1,644.)

Distances: Victoria Tube Station (.2 miles), Victoria Railway Station (.2 miles), Apollo Victoria Theatre (.2 miles), Victoria Palace Theatre (.1 miles), St. James Theatre (.1 miles), Victoria Coach Station (.4 miles), Westminster Cathedral (.3 miles), Buckingham Palace (.2 miles)

The Rubens at the Palace—39 Buckingham Palace Road (www.rubenshotel.com). TripAdvisor's Certificate of Excellence. Location: across from Buckingham Palace. Pros: free WiFi, breakfast buffet, air conditioning, non-smoking, restaurant, excellent breakfast, bar/lounge, room service, suites, wheelchair access, lift, single/twin rooms and suites available. Cons: price. (TripAdvisor price range for standard room: $232-$530.)

Distances: Victoria Tube Station (.2 miles), Victoria Railway Station (.2 miles), Apollo Victoria Theatre (.2 miles), Victoria Palace Theatre (.1 miles), St. James Theatre (.1 miles), Victoria Coach Station (.4 miles), Westminster Cathedral (.3 miles), Buckingham Palace (.2 miles)

Two less highly rated but more affordable hotels:

Astors Belgravia—106-112 Ebury St. Location: 2 streets west of Victoria Station. Pros: free WiFi, breakfast included, air conditioning, non-smoking, single/twin/triple/quad rooms available, walk-in showers. Cons: no elevator, no restaurant/bar/lounge, small rooms, worn. (TripAdvisor price range for standard room: $136-$284.)

Distances: Victoria Tube Station (.3 miles), Victoria Railway Station (.3 miles), Apollo Victoria Theatre (.3 miles), Victoria Palace Theatre (.4 miles), St. James Theatre (.5 miles), Victoria Coach Station (.1 miles), Westminster Cathedral (.4 miles), Buckingham Palace (.7 miles)

Comfort Inn Buckingham Palace Road—8-12 St. George's Dr. Location: 1 street south of Victoria Station. Pros: free WiFi, breakfast buffet, non-smoking, lift, single/twin/triple/quads available. Cons: no air conditioning, small/basic/worn rooms, no restaurant/bar/lounge, stairs to front door (ramp leads to dining room). (TripAdvisor price range for standard room: $108-$385.)

Distances: Victoria Tube Station (.2 miles), Victoria Railway Station (.3 miles), Apollo Victoria Theatre (.3 miles), Victoria Palace Theatre (.4 miles), St. James Theatre (.5 miles), Victoria Coach Station (.1 miles), Westminster Cathedral (.4 miles), Buckingham Palace (.7 miles)

Other areas to base in London

Paddington Station—North of Hyde Park, the area around Paddington Station is less conveniently located than the Gloucester Road/South Kensington or Victoria Station neighborhoods. It does have a couple things in its favor, though—the Heathrow Express whisks travelers from the airport to Paddington in only 15 minutes; both HOHO companies make stops at Paddington Station (on the blue line for the Original Tour—London Street/Norfolk Square—and on the blue line for the Big Bus tours—both can transfer to central tourist routes at the Marble Arch); and the area has easy access to the Underground.

St. Pancras Station—On the north side of central London by the British Library, St. Pancras Station is on the blue Piccadilly line that runs from Heathrow. Although no day tours depart from St. Pancras, it has excellent access to many Underground lines, and visitors who don't mind using the Tube can easily reach tour departure points. The orange hop-on/hop-off Original Tour route stops at the Eurostar Arrivals area, and the Big Bus green route has a St. Pancras stop.

Russell Square—Near the British Museum in Bloomsbury, Russell Square is a great location if using public transportation. It's a little off the main drag of tourist offerings, but doable with a little effort. Again, transportation from Heathrow is fairly easy on the blue Piccadilly line. The HOHO orange Original Tour route stops nearby, at Bedford Place, British Museum, and elsewhere not too far away (depending on where one's hotel is). The Big Bus green route stops near the British Museum on Southhampton Row. No day tours leave from this area, but a Tube ride can bring you to the Gloucester Road options or, with a transfer, any of the other starting points.

Other base cities in England

You can base yourself in Bath, York, Birmingham, or Liverpool (among other cities), as well, if you prefer to experience different parts of the country in greater depth than a day trip allows. These cities offer hop-on/hop-off tours and excursions into the countryside. Bear in mind the principles of easy-walking hotel selection—easy access to the buildings, ideally in a relatively flat area, and proximity to transportation hubs—if you want to limit walking and climbing and save your energy for seeing the sights.

Amsterdam

Overview

Amsterdam is the largest city and capital of the Netherlands (although the government and royal family are based in The Hague). Amsterdam was established as a fishing village in the 1100s and grew to a world-leading port during the Golden Age in the 1600s, when the Dutch dominated world trade. Amsterdam has the oldest stock exchange in the world and is still a major center for finance and diamonds.

Much of Amsterdam, like much of the Netherlands, is below sea level. (Altitude in the city varies from 4 meters below sea level up to 2 meters above sea level.) The lowest part of the country is 6 meters below sea level. (That's more than 18 feet!) Much of the land in the country is reclaimed from the sea by a series of dikes that hold back the sea and canals that drain water. The iconic Dutch windmill functioned for centuries to pump excess water from the reclaimed land.

Today water is pumped electronically, but the canals and many of the windmills remain. Amsterdam is crisscrossed with a series of waterways (more than 60 miles of them) that form a great part of its charm. Amsterdam is also famous, of course, for its legal prostitution and soft drugs use, but those exist merely as curiosities for most tourists.

Amsterdam's climate is strongly influenced by the nearby North Sea. Winters and summers are both considered to be mild. Average summer highs are in the 70s, and average winter highs are in the 40s. Still, uncomfortable weather can creep in. The record high is 95 Fahrenheit and the record low is 3.5 below zero. Typically, 132 days a year will have some sort of precipitation.

Possible plan for Amsterdam (What I'd do)

If I were traveling to Amsterdam with my mother, this is what I would plan for us to do. Obviously, you may prefer to do something different, but you may find this itinerary handy as a starting point, changing it as much as you'd like. (And it will make more sense as you work your way through the chapter. Having a city map at hand will help, too.) **Please double check any details before relying on them, as specifics may have changed since I wrote these pages.** This plan assumes lodging near Central Station but could easily be modified for the Leidseplein/Museum Quarter areas.

Once you have a pretty good idea of what you want to do, check out ticket sales online, because online booking is almost always less expensive than buying a ticket on-site. The Anne Frank House and the Van Gogh Museum, in particular, can be hard to get tickets to—even in advance. Of course, when buying online, you save money but might give up flexibility, so it's not always the best choice, but it's certainly worth looking into. As for day trips, you probably don't want to plan for more than two consecutive day trips at a time, to avoid bus fatigue.

Day 1—Depart U.S.

Day 2—Arrive Amsterdam. Find an ATM and withdraw euros, if needed. Look for the I amsterdam visitor desk at the Holland Tourist Information center in Schiphol airport. Get tourist information and buy an Amsterdam Pass by Stromma (sights and in-city HO-HO transportation) for 5 days. (Or skip this step because you bought online ahead of time or will buy one in Amsterdam.).

To get from the airport to the city, book a Schiphol Hotel Shuttle ride *in advance* (www.schipholhotelshuttle.nl), then, at the airport, go to Platform A7 at the Schiphol Plaza to find the shuttle van. (If staying near Leidseplein/Museum Quarter, take Airport Express Bus 397 instead.)

(If not using a HOHO pass—of some sort—for transportation within Amsterdam, choose one of these options: Buy an OV chip card or a GVB multi-day card, if intending to ride public transportation around the city. The OV chip card covers the train ride into Amsterdam; the GVB multi-day card doesn't. Or buy an Amsterdam Travel Ticket, which includes travel from the airport to Central Station in 2nd class on the train or on the Amsterdam Airport Express Bus 397, which goes to the Museum District/Leidseplein, but not Central Station. It also covers public transportation in Amsterdam, as well as the return trip to the airport if it is within the chosen time period. Or buy an I amsterdam City Card for public transportation within the city *and* an extensive sightseeing pass.)

At the hotel, go to room and rest, if possible. If too early for that, leave luggage and explore the neighborhood. Take a self-guided tour. Line up cell phone service, if needed. Scout out a local grocery store and possible pub or restaurant for dinner. Stop for lunch or tea/coffee. Rest before dinner, then go out to eat.

Day 3—Start 5-day Amsterdam Pass by Stromma (or whatever is chosen). *(This day features sights open daily. Can be visited on a Monday.)* Ride HOHO bus to the Rijksmuseum stop. Visit the Rijksmuseum (entry included, but must still stand in line to get a ticket). Break for lunch. Visit the Stedelijk Museum (entry included—skip if not interested). Visit the House of Bols cocktail and gin experience (included). Catch the HOHO boat or the HOHO bus at the Rijksmuseum stop and ride back to hotel area. (Note: HOHO boats tend to fill up faster than buses. You may need a Plan B.) Relax. Go out for dinner. If up to it, take the 7 p.m. Red Light District Walking Tour or the 100 Highlights Cruise (both included with Amsterdam Pass).

Day 4—*(This day features sights open daily. Can be visited on Monday.)* Take the HOHO boat to Jordaan stop, near the Anne Frank House. Visit the Anne Frank House. (Must order tickets online. Try to order before leaving home. 80% of tickets are released 2 months in advance. 20% are released on the day. Move this day around to fit when your Anne Frank House ticket is for.)

Walk around Anne Frank neighborhood, view Westerkerk. Consider visiting the Tulip Museum (entry included). Take HOHO boat to Waterlooplein stop and walk to Museum Willet-Holthuysen (entry included). Break for coffee/lunch as desired. Ride HOHO boat to A'DAM Lookout stop. (Or stop at Central Station for a rest in the hotel first, before continuing to the A'DAM Lookout.) Visit "This is Holland" (open until late, entry included) and the A'DAM Lookout (open until late, entry included). Walk to Buiksloterweg and take the free ferry across the IJ ("eye") to Central Station. Grab take-out for supper. (Or eat across the IJ before taking the ferry.) Return to hotel.

Day 5—*(This day features sights open daily. Can be visited on a Monday.)* Take the HOHO bus to the Waterlooplein stop (near the Jewish Cultural Quarter). *If up to it,* walk first to Versetzmuseum (Dutch Resistance Museum, opens at 10, entry extra). Then visit the Jewish Cultural Quarter (opens at 11, pass includes entry to Jewish Historical Museum, Portuguese Synagogue, National Holocaust Memorial and Museum, Children's Museum). Break for coffee/lunch as desired. Ride HOHO bus to the Heineken Experience stop. Visit the Heineken Experience (entry included—must preorder tickets after getting passes). Rest. Dinner.

Day 6—(*Do not do this on a Monday, because of museum closures. Switch days as necessary.*) Walk to the Museum Ons' Lieve Heer ob Solder (Our Lord in the Attic) (opens at 10, 1 on Sunday, entry included). Buy a 48-hour GVB ticket (e.g., at Central Station). Using GVB ticket, take tram (1, 2, 5, among others) to SPUI stop. Walk to Amsterdam Museum (opens at 10, entry included). Break for lunch.

Walk to Museum of the Canals (open 10-5, closed Mondays, entry included). Consider visiting Cromhoutuis very close by (11-5, closed Mondays, entry included). Take tram (1, 2, 5) back to Central Station area. Rest. Dinner. If up to it, take the 7 p.m. Red Light District Walking Tour or the 100 Highlights Cruise (both included with Amsterdam Pass).

Day 7—(*Do not do this day on a Monday.*) Using GVB ticket, take tram 26 IJBurg to last stop to catch the 11-o'clock ferry to Amsterdam Castle Muiderslot (closed Mondays, entry included) *or* to Fortress Island Pampus (closed Mondays, entry included). (Ferry stop is the unmarked building on the shore, next to a canal leading to a marina, *not* the long walk out to the public beach.) Take ferry and tram back to Central Station.

OR take bus 22 from near Central Station to Kadijksplein. Walk to the Maritime Museum (Nederlands Scheepvaart Museum) (open 9-5, entry included). Take bus 22 back to Central Station. Lunch. Rest, if needed. Take tram 9 or 14 or HOHO boat to Waterlooplein. Walk to Rembrandt House Museum (open 10-6, entry included). Walk to nearby Gassan Diamonds for a free tour (book in advance online, tours 9-5). Return to hotel area on tram 9 or 14 or HOHO boat.

Dinner. Last evening with HOHO/Amsterdam Pass privileges: If not done yet, take the 7 p.m. Red Light District Walking Tour or the 100 Highlights Cruise (both included with Amsterdam Pass).

Day 8—Day trip: Marken, Volendam, and the Windmills

Day 9—Day trip: Delft, the Hague, and Madurodam, or Bruges. Final evening in Amsterdam

Day 10—Return to U.S. Use prebooked return Hotel Shuttle bus ride (or take train or bus 397 or other).

Arrival

You will probably fly into Schiphol airport (AMS) when you arrive in Amsterdam, about 10 miles southwest of central Amsterdam (www.schiphol.nl/en/).

To get from Schiphol to the city, you have your choice of train, bus, taxi, or private driver. Whichever mode of transportation you choose, make sure you know where you want to go. When taking the train, you will probably want to get off at Central Station, deep in central Amsteram. Depending on your lodging, though, you could need to get off at a different station, so make sure that is clear before you travel. (The lodging I discuss below is all reachable from Central Station, although the trip may require a tram or bus ride, as well.)

The Schiphol **train** station is located below the airport and can be reached by stairs, elevator, or escalator. If you plan to ride into the city (2nd class) but not use public transportation while you are there, you probably want a one-use paper ticket (2019 price €5.50). Look for a bright yellow kiosk that says "Train Tickets" (or possibly a blue-gray machine that says "Public Transport Tickets"). (NS is the abbreviation for Dutch Railways.)

If you plan to use public transportation while in Amsterdam, you can instead buy an **Amsterdam Travel Ticket** at an NS Tickets and Service counter or online, good for 1 day (€17), 2 days (€22.50), or 3 days (€28) (Note: valid by *day*, not by 24-hours) (www.ns.nl/producten/en/onbe perktreizen/p/amsterdam-travel-ticket). The Amsterdam Travel Ticket includes bus and train travel to and from Schiphol Airport within its period of validity. If you intend to buy a reloadable **OV Chip Card** for transport, you can buy and top up those cards at the yellow machines in railway stations. At the airport, look for them in the Schiphol Plaza, near the red-and-white-checkered meeting point. The card itself costs €7.50 and can be used for 5 years.

Another choice is the **Amsterdam Airport Express Bus 397** from Schiphol Plaza to Elandsgracht (west of Prinsengracht and south of the Anne Frank House—*not* Central Station), a 30-to-40-minute ride that cost €6.50 in 2019. (Can use the Amsterdam Travel Ticket for this, or buy a 1.5 hour Bus Tram Metro ticket at the red Info and Tickets minibus or on the bus from the driver or buy a bus ticket online at (www.connexxion.nl/en/our-routes/special-routes/amsterdam-airport-express.) The bus has multiple stops on the way to its end station, most usefully for us at Museumplein, Rijksmuseum, and Leidseplein before the end at the bus station on Elandsgracht.

The **Schiphol Hotel Shuttle** (www.schipholhotelshuttle.nl) is another way to reach your hotel from the airport, in an 8-seat van. A sample shuttle ride from the airport to the Double Tree Hotel by Central Station cost €18.50 one-way in late 2019. Book your ride online, then at the airport, go to Platform A7 at Schiphol Plaza (follow the sign for Taxis and Buses). (You may choose to book your return ride at the same time, for at least 3 hours before your scheduled flight departure.) Maximum 30-minute waiting period. Fees include one large piece of luggage and one piece of hand luggage per person.

As always, **taxis** probably provide the easiest (and most expensive) way to reach your hotel. Taxis are available outside the Arrivals hall. You can choose a regular taxi, a **Travel Taxi** (for groups up to 8, to share cost), or a luxury taxi. Follow signs to the taxis for a metered ride to the city. Drivers accept credit cards and will issue a printed receipt. (Do not accept unsolicited taxi rides from unofficial "taxis.") In 2019, airport taxis could typically reach Amsterdam city center for €45-€50, depending on traffic. With Travel Taxis, you can choose to share a van with travelers not in your group, but drive time will take longer because of stopping at various hotels.

As of this writing, Uber does run in Amsterdam, and prices tend to be a little lower than taxi fare.

Easy transportation options

Once in the city, your probable transportation choices are bus, tram, metro, and taxi. Trams are the most useful mode of public transportation for most tourists, particularly lines 1, 2, and 5, which all start at Central Station and then stop at Dam Square and Leidseplein. Lines 2 and 5 coninue to the Museum District. Lines 7 and 10 cross lines 1, 2, and 5 at Leidseplein and arc around the canal belt, useful for reaching, for example, the Heineken Experience. City buses can also be useful, and all forms of public transport are made fairly easy to use with the OV-chipcard or other transport passes. Check the journey finder online at maps.gvb.nl/en to see what the best travel options for a particular trip are.

The easiest way to get around to the sights mostly outside the canal belt is to ride a hop-on/hop-off (HOHO) tourist bus. Within central Amsterdam, with its many canals, a HOHO tourist boat is more effective, very atmospheric, but not fast. (Enforced down time can provide a welcome break, however.) Amsterdam has a couple of HOHO bus companies and HOHO boat companies, and they offer combo tickets that cover both modes of transportation. You purchase a 1-day, 24-hour, or 48-hour ticket and then may hop on and hop off the buses or boats (of the line you paid for) as much as you'd like in that time.

You may choose to take the whole tour to get an overview and then, on the second time around, hop off to see sights up close. Buses and boats run year-round, though hours of operation and frequency of buses/boats may vary by season. Remember that boat rides are scenic but more leisurely, and boats do not come as frequently as buses. (They also fill up faster.) Buses, however, can't get to much of central Amsterdam because of narrow streets and bridges. Prices are listed below, but check each company's Web site for the latest information.

Hop-On/Hop-Off Tours

City Sightseeing Amsterdam offers hop-on/hop-off buses and boats through the central part of the city (www.citysightseeingamsterdam.nl). You may join the tour at any stop and get on and off the vehicles as much as you like during the time frame you select—24 or 48 hours. Along with your hopping privileges, you get free wifi, a free city map, a free app to follow where buses and boats currently are, and discounts for attractions (such as 10-15% off and fast-track admission to the Heineken Experience).

Red double-decker City Sightseeing buses start around the central train station (near Lovers Boat Company), run from 9:15 a.m.-6 p.m. (10-5:15 in winter), and run every 15-20 minutes. Riding the entire loop (something like 9-11 stops, which can change from season to season) takes 70-90 minutes. Audio guide commentary in 18 languages is provided. The tours run daily except April 27 (King's Day).

Two boat lines cover opposite sides of central Amsterdam. The Green boat line starts at Central Station East and has ten stops as it loops around the east side of central Amsterdam. The Green boat line departs 10:05 a.m.-6 p.m. (10-5 in winter), every 20-25 minutes (less frequently in the off-season). The whole loop takes approximately 100-138 minutes.

The Blue boat line starts at Central Station West and winds its way through the western part of central Amsterdam with eight stops. The Blue line departs 10:15 a.m.-5:15 p.m. (10-5 in winter), every 20-25 minutes. The entire Blue loop takes approximately 60 minutes.

Most buses have easy access. Boats require two steps in and out of the vessel. Prices are as follows:

- 24-hour bus and boat combination, adults (€28), children 4-13 (€14)

- 48-hour bus and boat combination, adults (€39), children (€19.50)
- 24-hour bus only, adults (€21), children (€10.50)
- 24-hour boats only, adults (€25), children (€12.50)
- 24-hour bus and boat family ticket (1 ticket for 2 adults + 2 children between 4-13, €70)

Buy tickets online and redeem on the bus or boat at any of the stops. Smart phone booking confirmation is accepted.

Stromma NL/Amsterdam Sightseeing is another hop-on/hop-off bus and boat option (www.stromma.nl/en/amsterdam/sightseeing/). The bus line starts near Central Station and circles central Amsterdam clockwise. The boat line starts by the Rijksmuseum and travels a smaller counter-clockwise loop. There are 4 crossover stops between bus and boat. Tours include a free 3-hour walking tour.

Summer boat departures run 9:25 a.m.-6:20 p.m. from the Rijksmuseum and 9:45 a.m.-6:30 p.m. from near Anne Frank's house, with intervals between boats of approximately 25 minutes. (Hours and frequency are reduced in the off-season.) You can see a map of bus and boat routes by selecting the map option on this page: www.stromma.nl/en/amsterdam/sightseeing/combo-tours/hop-on-hop-off/. Prices are as follows:

- 24-hour HOHO bus and boat, from €25
- 48-hour HOHO bus and boat, from €35
- 24-hour HOHO, boat only, from €20.50
- 48-hour HOHO, boat only, from €29.50
- 24-hour HOHO, bus only, from €20.50
- 48-hour HOHO, bus only, from €29.50

Tickets can be purchased at Stromma shops around the city (especially near the Central Station) or online. If you buy online, take your printed voucher to a Stromma shop to exchange it for a ticket. You can find locations on their Web site.

Boats require climbing 3 steps and are not wheelchair accessible. Buses are green double-deckers.

Non-stop sightseeing tours

If you're not interested in hopping on and off and would like a guided city tour, here are some other options.

Amsterdam City Tours (www.amsterdamcitytours.com/tours/bus-tours/guided-amsterdam-city-bus-tour-boat/) offers a 1-hour canal cruise (ticket can be used any time) and a live-guided tour through Amsterdam in an air-conditioned bus. (Commentary is in three languages—English, Spanish, and German—which can get in the way of matching commentary with the sights, according to at least one reviewer.) Tour includes a photo stop at a windmill and a tour of a diamond factory. Adults €39, children 4-13 €19.

Canal Tours Amsterdam's 100 Highlights Cruise, which they claim is Amsterdam's #1 canal cruise, has TripAdvisor's Certificate of Excellence and offers an alternative boat tour. The 1-hour cruise sees 100 Amsterdam highlights, with audio guides available in 15 languages. Online price is €11.50 and up (more on-site) (www.stromma.nl/en/amsterdam/sightseeing/canal-tours/100-highlights-cruise/).

Other in-city transportation

If you want to get around Amsterdam like a local, ride a bike. (Just kidding!) It's true, locals do ride bikes everywhere (endless streams of them, it seems), but that may be too much to ask of tourists unacquainted with the city, the traffic rules, and the biking customs. So let's look at public transportation instead.

The Amsterdam transportation site includes an overview for visiting tourists, where you may want to start your investigations: en.gvb.nl/ontdek-amsterdam/tourist-guide. Basic information is covered below. (If you need to know about accessible transportation, the city Web site for that is here: en.gvb.nl/reizen/toegankelijk-ov.)

GVB (Amsterdam public transportation) **day tickets** or **multi-day tickets** may be your best option for a short stay if you don't want to use a hop-on/hop-off pass (en.gvb.nl/bezoek-amsterdam). They are good for use on Amsterdam's metros, trams and buses, but not on regional buses or the train. You can get cards from 1 hour (€3.20, buy from the conductor or driver) to up to 7 days (€8 for 24 hours-€36.50 for 7 days, buy on the tram or at the airport or metro stations at GVB vending machines, at Holland Tourist Information, and online in advance at reisproducten.gvb.nl/en/uur-en-dagkaarten).

A journey planner can help you find the best route to your destination (maps.gvb.nl/en), or you can look over transportation routes here: reisinfo.gvb.nl/en (place cursor on the stop you're interested in).

The **OV chip card** (*OV-chipkaart*) is a reloadable transport card good for traveling on Amsterdam's trams, buses, and metros. The initial price for an "anonymous" (non-long-term) card is €7.50, and then you load however much credit you want on it.

It's also possible to buy a "disposable" card for a specified, short length of time from 1 hour (a paper ticket) to 24 hours. A disposable card is generally more expensive to use than an "anonymous" reloadable card, but you don't need to worry about unused credit on it. Cards can be bought at public transportation (GVB) offices, vending machines at stations, at newsstands, and at supermarkets. (Be aware that you may need to use cash at machines, or, if the machines require a European chip and PIN, you may need to find a person to buy from.)

The reloadable OV chip cards are generally less expensive than travel cards for a specific length of time, but if you don't plan to hold on to the OV chip card for future use, you have to deal with unused credit on it. A reloadable card is good for 5 years, but you can request a refund of unused credit, if you prefer. Doing so requires visiting a public transportation office and filling out a form to mail along with your card to a specific address.

The **I amsterdam** card (see below), which covers entrance into top attractions, also includes unlimited use of the public transport system for the allotted time, 24, 48, 72, 96, or 120 hours (www.iamsterdam.com/en/i-am/i-amsterdam-city-card).

The **Amsterdam Travel Ticket** covers public transportation for 1, 2, or 3 days and includes round-trip second-class train travel from Schiphol airport to any of the Amsterdam train stations, as well as travel on the Amsterdam Airport Express Bus 397. Prices are 1 day (€17), 2 days (€22.50), 3 days (€28) (reisproducten.gvb.nl/en/toeristen/amsterdam-travel-ticket). Buy at Schiphol Airport, Holland Tourist Information, or NS ticket sales outlets.

Confused? You can look at various GVB products in one place to compare what they offer: the Amsterdam Travel Ticket, the GVB day or multi-day ticket, and the I amsterdam City Card at reisproducten.gvb.nl/en/toeristen.

It's possible to get around Amsterdam and the region on city, local, and regional **buses**. Check out the city (GVB) bus network here: maps.gvb.nl/nl/lijnen?bus&show. For specifics on how to get from Point A to Point B, go to the home page: maps. gvb.nl. (You may want to select English at the upper right.) Amsterdam buses no longer accept cash, so make sure you have some sort of ticket before you board. (See the transportation cards listed above.) Use your card when you enter and when you exit the bus.

Amsterdam's **trams** can carry you from the Central Station straight through the city to some of the main tourist areas. Leaving from two tram stations in front of Central Station—one in the east and one in the west—tram lines travel to the city center and then radiate out from there to different parts of the city. It's possible to buy a 1-hour ticket on the tram, but most locals use the transport chip card (*OV-chipkaart*) listed above. Use your ticket when you enter and again when you exit the tram. See the tram map here (select English in the upper right): maps.gvb.nl/nl/lijnen?tram&show. Again, the route planner is on the home page.

Amsterdam has four **metro** lines that terminate at Central Station and are probably the fastest way to reach outlying districts. You must have a travel card (see above) or a 1-hour card (available at GVB service desks or in vending machines) to ride the metro. Use your card to get in and out of the gated metro areas. Read more about the metro and see a metro map here: www.amsterdamtips.com/tips/amsterdam-metro.php.

Finally, if you are looking for convenience more than economy, you can't find a better solution than traveling around the city in a cab. **Taxis** may take longer than public transportation, but if you want to minimize walking and standing, they may be the best choice for you.

Taxis in Amsterdam are not allowed to stop wherever they want. If you want a taxi, your best bet is to find one in a taxi rank, which can be found all over the city. Taxi fares are not cheap, just as you would expect. For example, fares from Central Station to the Rijksmuseum range from €16.43 to €26.10, depending on traffic. The ride from Schiphol Airport to Central Station ranges from €61.98 to €70.05, according to a late 2019 search. If you want an estimated fare for a particular ride, try www.taxifarefinder.com (or search on "Amsterdam taxi fare finder").

If you want to order a taxi, you may do so online: www.amsterdamtaxi-online.com

If you prefer to contact the taxi company directly, here are some official taxi services in Amsterdam:

- Taxicentrale Amsterdam (TCA) (with online booking service), 020-777 7777
- Staxi (with online booking service), 020 705 8888
- Taxistad (with online booking service), 020-208 0000
- Taxi Direct Amsterdam (with online booking service), 020-633 3333
- BBF (TCS and Schipholtaxi) (with online booking service), 0900 900 6666

- Sustainable Taxi Services B.V. (Taxi Electric) (with online booking service), 088-100 4444
- Aemstel Taxi (with online booking service), 0900-0288

Sightseeing passes

The I amsterdam City Card (www.iamsterdam.com/en/i-am/i-amsterdam-city-card) includes free entrance to over 60 sights (including the Rijksmuseum and the Van Gogh Museum, but not the Heineken Experience), free public transportation, a free canal cruise, discounts and giveaways, a city map, and free entry to some sights beyond Amsterdam. (Limited spots for the Van Gogh Museum—must book ahead.)

The museum component and the public transportation component are separate on the card. Each is activated the first time you use that component.

With public transportation, the online City Card cost as follows in late 2019:

- 24 hours (€60)
- 48 hours (€80)
- 72 hours (€95)
- 96 hours (€105)
- 120 hours (€115)

You can order online and trade your voucher in at an I amsterdam store or information center at the airport or Central Station. You may also buy cards at I amsterdam locations and other locations throughout the city, including many hotels and museums, but ordering online may result in a discounted price.

With the **Amsterdam Pass by Stromma** (www.amsterdampass.com), you get free entry to more than 30 Amsterdam attractions (includes the Rijksmuseum and the Heineken Experience, but not the Van Gogh Museum), multi-day hop-on/hop-off Stromma bus and boat tours, and Canal Tour Amsterdam's 100 Highlights Cruise. Costs are as follows (discounts possible online):

- 1 day, adult (€66), child (€33)
- 2 days, adult (€91), child (€46)
- 3 days, adult (€112), child (€57)

- 5 days, adult (€145), child (€74)

You can buy a pass online and download it instantly to your smart phone or pick up your pass in Amsterdam (for free). (It used to be possible to have the pass shipped to you for a fee, but that option no longer appears to be available.) You can also buy a pass in Amsterdam at Stromma stations throughout the city, including Central Station, and at the I amsterdam Visitor Centre at Stationsplein 10 opposite Central Station or at Schiphol Airport at the Holland Tourist Information office (Arrivals 2) or the Connexxion Help Desk (behind Starbucks in Arrival Hall 4).

The biggest difference between the I amsterdam City Card and the Amsterdam Pass by Stromma is whether you want to travel on public transportation (buses, trams, and metro, with the I amsterdam City Card) or whether you want to use hop-on/hop-off buses and boats (with the Amsterdam Pass by Stromma). Another big difference is that the Amsterdam Pass by Stromma includes the Heineken Experience but not the Van Gogh Museum, while the I amsterdam City Card includes the Van Gogh Museum but not the Heineken Experience. While much of the sight coverage is the same, there are other difference, as well. Choose the pass that works best for you overall, and if you want to see something it doesn't include, pay out of pocket for it.

The **Museumkaart** used to be a good option for tourists (no transportation included), but now is limited only to Dutch residents (although it sounds as if some visitors work around this requirement). There is a limited tourist version of this card (available at museums), good for 5 sights within 31 days, but advice is now to go with one of the other sightseeing cards, such as the I amsterdam City Card.

Day trips

It's possible to see much of the little Netherlands (as well as some of Belgium) without having to leave the comfort of your base hotel at night, because Amsterdam has tourist companies that specialize in day trips. (And the country is so small and well connected that if you wanted to takes trains or buses around on your own, you could.)

As always, use the information here as a guide, but check each company's Web site for tour details and the most current price and schedule information. **Tour details—even which tours are offered—routinely change from season to season.** Whichever tours you decide on, look over cancellation policies, if your plans aren't completely firm.

Browsing through Web sites will also help you decide which company's tours seem a good fit for you. Be aware that some specific tours might have special requirements or recommendations, so you'll want to look descriptions over closely before you show up at the departure point.

Tour companies differ on which entry fees they include in their prices, so check those specifics (and confirm online), if your selection comes down to price.

Also take into account where the tours depart from. The Dam Guide tours and Amsterdam City Tours leave from the Central Station or near the Central Station, but Stromma.nl's large group tours leave from the A'DAM Tower across the IJ from the Central Station, their small group tours leave from the Heineken Experience (east of the Museum Quarter) and, in one case, the tour leaves from the Van Gogh Museum. You may, in fact, decide on tours according to which ones depart from near your hotel. Wherever you leave from, make sure you show up early for any tour so you are not considered a no-show and your seat sold to someone else!

If you want to save your walking energy for the tour itself but you select a tour with a departure point that is not close to your hotel, you may want to invest in a taxi ride to get there.

That Dam Guide Amsterdam

Since 2013, That Dam Guide has been providing small group tours of up to 10 people (thatdamguide.com). The company has TripAdvisor's Certificate of Excellence and gets rave reviews (rated #1 tour company in Amsterdam as of this writing). It offers an Amsterdam walking tour and an Amsterdam Red Light tour in addition to these minivan tours. They are also available for private tours. Their day trips include the following:

Amsterdam Windmill Tour—Tour highlights include a ride through the countryside, a guided walking tour through the harbor town of Monnickendam (about 1 mile), included Dutch apple pie and coffee at a historic orphanage, a family farm that farms potatoes, tulips, and dairy cows, a 400-year-old water-pumping windmill to explore inside and out, cheese tasting and wine picnic lunch (included). *Steep steps inside the windmill to the top.* Max. 8 people. Days vary, depart 9 a.m./return outside Starbucks near Central Station, 6 hours. €100.

Keukenhof Tulip Tour—Tour highlights include transportation to Keukenhof gardens (entrance extra), 3 hours of exploration in gardens, Dutch pancake lunch (extra), drive by working tulip farms, photo stop in tulip fields. Max. 8 people. Seasonal. Depart 8:30/return outside Starbucks near Central Station, 8 hours. €100.

Stromma.nl

Stromma.nl is affiliated with the international Gray Line tour company and offers not only hop-on/hop-off Amsterdam bus and boat options, not just sightseeing passes, but also large and small group day trips from Amsterdam (www.stromma.com/en-nl/amsterdam/tours-excursions/). The company has TripAdvisor's Certificate of Excellence. Large group tours are in full-size coaches. Small groups are in air-conditioned minivans.

To get to the A'DAM Tower/This is Holland site where the large group tours depart, go to the Central Station and follow the signs to "IJ-Zijde" (IJ-Side). Take the free ferry (the Buiksloterwegveer) from outside the Central Station to the Buiksloterweg, then walk to the tower next to the Eye Film Institute. Their tours include the following:

Zaanse Schans & 100 Highlights Cruise—Tour highlights include the windmill village Zaanse Schans, an operating windmill visit, traditional wooden shoe production, a dairy farm and cheese tasting, free time in the historic village. Includes 100 Highlights cruise. Depart This is Holland site, 3.5 hours. Adults from €44.50, children €22.25.

Zaanse Schans & A'DAM Lookout—Same as previous tour, but adds panoramic view from the A'DAM Tower in Amsterdam at the end of the tour instead of cruise. 3.5 hours. Adults €44.50, children €22.25.

Volendam, Edam & Windmill Village—Tour highlights include Zaanse Schans historical heritage site, the polders (reclaimed land from the sea), a stroll through medieval Edam (home of cheese making and boat building), a visit to a cheese maker to sample cheese, a short stroll through the fishing village of Volendam, a 100 Highlights canal cruise back in Amsterdam. Depart This is Holland site, 5.5 hours. Adults from €62.50, children €31.25.

Volendam, Edam, Windmills + A'DAM Lookout—Same as previous tour, but adds a panoramic view from the A'DAM Tower in Amsterdam instead of cruise at the end of the tour. Adults from €62.50, children €31.25.

Kröller-Müller Museum and National Park (small group)—Tour highlights include a drive through the Dutch landscape to the Hoge Veluwe National Park to the Kröller-Müller Museum (home to the second-largest Van Gogh collection in the world), adjoining sculpture garden, exploration of the national park with either a free bike or a scenic guided tour. Includes 1-hour 100 Highlights Cruise in Amsterdam. Depart Heineken Experience, 9 hours. Adults from €172.50, children 4-12 same.

Rotterdam, Delft & The Hague (small group)—Tour highlights include a cruise through Rotterdam's port area, historic Delft, tour of De Delftse Pauw pottery factory, visit The Hague, home of the Dutch royal family and seat of the Dutch government. Includes 100 Highlights Cruise. Depart Heineken Experience, 9 hours. Adults from €172.50, children 4-12 €172.50.

Van Gogh Returns—The Life and Work of Vincent Van Gogh (small group)—Tour highlights include a journey to Nuenen, where Van Gogh lived, the Vincentre Museum in Nuenen, 23 locations associated with Van Gogh, the Van Gogh Museum in Amsterdam. Includes 1-hour 100 Highlights canal cruise in Amsterdam. Not Monday, depart Van Gogh Museum, 9 hours. Adults from €172.50, children 4-12 same.

Keukenhof, Volendam & Windmills—Tour highlights include a bus tour through the Bulb Region, 3.5 hours at Keukenhof (the largest flower garden in the world), village of Zaanse Schans, visit windmill, view clog-making, visit cheese factory, fishing village of Volendam, ticket for 100 Highlights cruise in Amsterdam. Mid-March to mid-May, depart Heineken Experience, 9 hours. Adults from €172.50, children 4-12 same.

Camp Vught & s-Hertogenbosch—Tour highlights include a 90-minute minibus ride to s-Hertogenbogsch, a guided tour through the city center, 2 hours free time, Camp Vught National WWII Memorial, audio-guided walking tour. Includes 1-hour 100 Highlights cruise in Amsterdam. Depart Heineken Experience, Adults from €172.50, children 4-12 same.

Amsterdam City Tours (affiliated with/also known as **Tours and Tickets**)

Amsterdam City Tours provides city, local, and regional tours led by Amsterdam experts (www.amsterdamcitytours.com). The company offers bus tours (featured here), as well as boat, bike and walking tours. Amsterdam City Tours has TripAdvisor's Certificate of Excellence. Note: Central Station departures are on the BACK side of the station, along the IJ side, way on the east end. You can get there via shopping passages or the pedestrian/bike passage.

Marken, Volendam, and the Windmills—Tour highlights include Zaanse Schans windmill village, fishing villages of Marken and Volendam, visit to a working windmill (entry included), boat ride on the Ijsselmeer (included), demonstration in a cheese factory (included), demonstration from a wooden clog maker (included). Morning and afternoon departures, times vary by season, depart/return Central Station. 5.5-6 hours. Adults from €53.10, children from €29.50.

Combination City Tour + Marken Volendam and Windmills—Same as above tour, but with Amsterdam city tour added. Also see old and new parts of Amsterdam by bus, windmill visit on the Amstel, diamond factory visit (included), free time for lunch in Amsterdam. Depart 9 (summer) or 9:15 (winter)/return Central Station. 11 hours. Adults from €79, children from €39.50.

Combination Flowerfields and Keukenhof Tour + This is Holland—Tour highlights include the world's largest flower garden at Keukenhof tulip garden (fast-track admission included), "This is Holland" film with air perspectives, special effects, and a huge spherical screen (entry included). Depart/return various times from near Central Station, duration 5 hours. Seasonal. From €74.50.

Flowerfields and Keukenhof—Same as previous tour, but without "This is Holland." From €59.

Flowerfields and Keukenhof + Bulbfarm—Same as previous tour, but with a visit to a bulb farm with an explanation of the bulb industry, meeting the bulb farmer and his family. Duration 6.5 hours. From €69.

Rotterdam, Delft and the Hague including Madurodam—Tour highlights include a bus ride to Rotterdam, fast-track entry to the Euromast tower, free time in Delft for lunch, Delft Blue Pottery factory, walking tour of Delft, photo stop at The Hague, visit Madurodam (Holland in miniature). Includes all entrances. *Quite a bit of walking.* Tue/Thu/ Sun, depart/return Central Station. Adults from €89, children from €44.50.

Delft, the Hague and Madurodam—Tour highlights include a tour of old town and royal Delft, visit Delft Blue Pottery (included), 30-minute walking tour of The Hague, driving tour of The Hague, photo stop at the Peace Palace (home of International Court of Justice), fast-track admission to Madurodam miniature town. Depart/return Central Station. 9.5 hours. Adults from €59, children from €29.50.

Day Trip to Brussels—Tour highlights include a short bus tour of Brussels, guided walking tour and free time in Brussels, demonstration and chocolate tasting at Planete Chocolat. *Must bring valid ID.* Days vary by season, depart 9:30/return Central Station. 11.5 hours. Adults from €85, children from €42.50.

The Best of Holland Tour, North and South Holland incl. Madurodam—Tour highlights include the fishing villages of Volendam and Marken, an antique working windmill, demonstration by a traditional wooden clog maker, cheese tasting at cheese factory, boat trip on Ijsselmeer, historic center of Delft, Delftware factory visit, The Hague, miniature park of Madurodam. Includes admissions. Depart/return near Central Station. 11.5 hours. Adults from €99, children from €49.50.

Charm of Holland—Volendam, Marken, Edam & Windmills—Tour highlights include guided walks through the picturesque villages of Volendam, Zaanse Schans, Marken and Edam, cheese tasting, demonstration by a clog maker, antique windmills, traditional Holland bakery, lunch in a traditional fish restaurant (included), boat trip on the Ijsselmeer. A full day. Includes admissions, tours, and lunch. Days vary by season, depart 9:45/return near Central Station, 8 hours. Adults from €119, children 4-12 from €59.50.

Giethoorn and Volendam—Tour highlights include the canals and old farm houses of Giethoorn (no roads or cars), boat cruise and free time in Giethoorn to explore and eat lunch (not included), picture stop at the Houtrigdijk dike, cheese factory with tasting and Dutch bakery in Volendam fishing village. Summer only, depart/return near Central Station, 9.5 hours. Adults from €89.

Giethoorn "the Dutch Venice" & Enclosing Dike—Tour highlights include a cruise of Giethoorn canals, free time in Giethoorn for lunch (not included), bus to Houtrigdijk dike for photos. Days vary by season, depart 9:30 Central Station, 9 hours. Adults from €89, children from €44.50.

Day Trip to Bruges—Tour highlights include a guided tour through the historical city center of Bruges, then hours of free time in the "Venice of the North," famous for its chocolate and lace-making. Depart/return Central Station, 11.5 hours. Days vary by season. Adults from €95, children from €47.50.

Additional combinations of tours and sights can be found on the Amsterdam City Tour Web site.

Holland Hop-On/Hop-Off Countryside Bus Tour

If you enjoy the hop-on/hop-off concept, there is an option that tours the countryside near Amsterdam (tickets.holland.com/en/tours/hop-on-hop-off-cheese-windmills-dutch-villages/). The bus departs from the This Is Holland site (by A'DAM Tower). It includes at least 6 stops throughout the day (This is Holland, Zaanse Schans, Edam, Volendam, Henri Willig Cheese Farm, Monnickendam), guided tour at Henri Willig Cheese Farm, self-guided walking tours at all stops, audio tour through app, and buses every 45 minutes (Note: Reviews say timing of buses can vary greatly). Not available in winter. Adults (12+) €28, children 4-11 €15.

Private tours

You can also arrange private tours of Amsterdam, elsewhere in the Netherlands, and beyond. Here are some guides who specialize in this area.

- Tom's Travel Tours, tomstraveltours.com
- Tours by Locals, www.toursbylocals.com/Amsterdam-Tours
- Urban Adventures, www.urbanadventures.com/Custom-Amsterdam-Amsterdam-private-tour
- Holland Private Tours, www.hollandprivatetour.com
- Amsterdam VIP Tours, www.amsterdam-viptours.com/
- Private Day Tours Amsterdam, privatedaytoursamsterdam.com/
- Sarah's Tours, sarahstours.com

Lodging

Amsterdam is a popular destination, and lodging in the central part of the city fills up early, which drives prices up. Make sure you get your reservation in (or at least *a* reservation, one you may change later) as early as you can.

The most obviously connected neighborhood is in the old city center, easy walking distance from the Central Station, but it's by no means the only area that can make a convenient base.

Hotels on this list are based on location, good reviews, and general accessibility, including access to easy transportation. It favors modern buildings with elevators over charming old converted mansions that rely on steep stairs to reach the upper floors. (Some hotels without elevators are included here, simply because modern buildings are in short supply in desirable areas, but see whether you can reserve a room on the ground or first floor if you're not willing to climb.) This section isn't the last word on acceptable accommodation, but it makes a good starting point to narrow down your search. Just check online to make sure that information is still accurate, both on TripAdvisor and on the hotel's own Web site.

You may find a wonderful deal on what looks to you like a good choice in a convenient location. By all means—grab it! Same with charming B&Bs, which aren't covered here because they tend to have a limited number of available rooms and generally don't have elevators. If you can nab one in a favorable location that gets good reviews, has a great breakfast, decent accessibility, and a workable price, do it!

The Schiphol airport train, you may recall, takes travelers quickly to Central Station (or Zuid Station, if selected). The Amsterdam Airport Express Bus 397 takes travelers to Museumplein, Rijksmuseum, Leidseplein, and Elandsgracht. The Schiphol Hotel Shuttle can take you directly to your hotel, as can a taxi.

Keep in mind whether you will take commercial day trips and where those depart from.

- The Dam Guide tours depart from near Central Station.
- Amsterdam City Tours leave from Central Station or nearby.
- Stromma.nl's large group tours leave from the This is Holland site/A'DAM Tower (across the IJ), their small group tours leave from the Heineken Experience (east of the Museum Quarter), and the Van Gogh tour leaves from the Van Gogh Museum.

Hotel price ranges are based on late 2019 TripAdvisor averages. Your own quotes may be higher or lower.

Centraal Station area

The area around Central Station is the heart and oldest part of Amsterdam. It has been here since medieval times and is loaded with history. It can be noisy and gritty (the famed Red Light District is here) but is tremendously convenient as a tourist base. Buses, trams, boats, trains, ferries, day trips, hop-on/hop-off tours—they almost all come through somewhere around here.

About the Red Light District.... Yes, it does have legal prostitution and sex shops and sex shows and maybe more than you want to know or see about humans' baser drives, but during the day and evening (until about 10 p.m. or later), it's not that uncomfortable a location. People live here. *Families* live here. There are churches, and shopping malls, and cafés (as well as "coffee shops" that sell and allow the use of marijuana, but those are throughout the city). And hotels. There are lots of hotels. Hotels where respectable people stay. (That doesn't mean everyone is upstanding, though. Be on the alert for pickpockets, especially anywhere it's crowded.)

The quickest way to get to central Amsterdam from the airport is on the train, but there is also the hotel shuttle or a taxi or an Uber ride, if you prefer.

The hop-on/hop-off City Sightseeing buses leave from in front of Central Station near Lovers Boat Company. The Green boat line starts at Central Station East, and the Blue boat line starts at Central Station West.

The Stromma.nl hop-on/hop-off bus starts in front of Central Station, the hop-on/hop-off boat stops near Central Station West, and the 100 Highlights Cruise starts around there, also.

As for day trips, Amsterdam City Tours leave from the back of Central Station. Stromma.nl large group tours leave from across the IJ (free ferry crossing behind Central Station) from the A'DAM Tower/This is Holland site. Dam Guide Amsterdam small group tours leave from east of Central Station near the Double Tree Hotel.

Hotels in the area include the following:

Kimpton De Witt Amsterdam—Nieuwezijds Voorburgwal 5 (www.ihg.com/kimptonhotels/hotels/us/en/amsterdam/amsnl/hoteldetail). TripAdvisor's Certificate of Excellence. Location: .2 miles mostly west of Central Station. Pros: free WiFi, parking, good breakfast buffet, air conditioning, non-smoking, restaurant, room service, fitness center, refrigerator, bar/lounge, wheelchair access, facilities for disabled guests, shuttle service, single/twin rooms available, GreenLeaders Silver level, free use of bikes (if available). Cons: no triple/quad rooms. (TripAdvisor price range for standard room: $222-$450.)

Distances: Sex Museum (.1 miles), Central Station (.2 miles), Old Church (.2 miles), St. Nicholas Church (.2 miles), Dam Square (.3 miles),

Anne Frank House (.5 miles), Leidseplein (1.1 miles), Rijksmuseum (1.3 miles), Van Gogh Museum (1.4 miles), Museum Square (1.6 miles)

INK Hotel Amsterdam, MGallery by Sofitel—Nieuwezijds Voorburgwal 67 (www.ink-hotel-amsterdam.com). TripAdvisor's Traveler's Choice Award (top 1% of category) and Certificate of Excellence. Location: .2 miles north of Dam Square. Pros: very good breakfast buffet, air conditioning, free WiFi, non-smoking, restaurant, room service, bar/lounge, suites available, wheelchair access, facilities for disabled guests, refrigerator, fitness center, GreenLeaders Silver level, twins/kings available, slight price break for singles. Cons: small rooms, no single/triple/quad rooms. (TripAdvisor price range for standard room: $187-440.)

Distances: New Church (.2 miles), Dam Square (.2 miles), Sex Museum (.2 miles), Central Station (.4 miles), Anne Frank House (.4 miles), Leidseplein (.9 miles), Rijksmuseum (1.1 miles), Van Gogh Museum (1.3 miles), Museum Square (1.4 miles)

Sir Adam Hotel—Overhoeksplein 1 (www.sirhotels.com/adam). TripAdvisor's Certificate of Excellence. Location: in the A'DAM Tower north of Central Station across the IJ, reachable by free 24-hour ferry. Pros: free WiFi, good breakfast buffet, bar/lounge, room service, fitness center, wheelchair access, elevator, air conditioning, non-smoking, restaurant, room service, suites available, trendy, amazing views, GreenLeaders Silver level. Cons: no single/twin/triple/quad rooms, no price break for singles, not quite as convenient across water. (TripAdvisor price range for standard room: $166-$382.)

Distances: A'DAM Lookout (0.0 miles), Central Station (.4 miles), St. Nicholas Church (.5 miles), Dam Square (.8 miles), Anne Frank House (1 mile), Leidseplein (1.6 miles), Rijksmuseum 1.8 miles, Van Gogh Museum (2 miles), Museum Square (2.1 miles)

Art'otel Amsterdam—Prins Hendrikkade 33 (artotelamsterdam.com). TripAdvisor's Traveler's Choice award (top 1% of category) and Certificate of Excellence. Location: across from Central Station. Pros: free WiFi, very good breakfast included in some rates, pool, non-smoking, restaurant, room service, suites available, bar/lounge, fitness center, wheelchair access, facilities for disabled guests, twins available, slight price break for singles. Cons: no singles/triples/quads, multiple guests note the hotel does not live up to 5-star expectations because of service or unappealing rooms. (TripAdvisor price range for standard room: $240-$529.)

Distances: Sex Museum (.1 miles), Canal Company (.1 miles), Central Station (.1 miles), Dam Square (.4 miles), Anne Frank House (.6 miles),

Leidseplein (1.2 miles), Rijksmuseum (1.3 miles), Van Gogh Museum (1.5 miles), Museum Square (1.6 miles)

NH Collection Amsterdam Barbizon Palace—Prins Hendrikkade 59-72. TripAdvisor's Certificate of Excellence. Location: across from Central Station. Pros: free WiFi, parking, breakfast buffet, air conditioning, non-smoking, restaurant, room service, bar/lounge, airport transportation, fitness center, wheelchair access, GreenLeaders Silver level. Cons: Red Light District behind hotel, expensive breakfast. (TripAdvisor price range for standard room: $196-$439.)

Hotel Sint Nicolaas—Spuistraat 1A (www.hotelnicolaas.nl). TripAdvisor Certificate of Excellence. Location: .2 miles mostly west of Central Station. Pros: free WiFi, good breakfast included, non-smoking, refrigerator, bar/lounge, wheelchair access, facilities for guests with disabilities, single/twin/triple rooms available, parking available. Cons: no air conditioning, can be noisy with windows open. (TripAdvisor price range for standard room: $160-$472.)

Distances: Sex Museum (.1 miles), Central Station (.2 miles), St. Nicholas Church (.3 miles), Old Church (.3 miles), Dam Square (.3 miles), Anne Frank House (.5 miles), Leidseplein (1.1 miles), Rijksmuseum (1.3 miles), Van Gogh Museum (1.5 miles), Museum Square (1.6 miles)

Hotel Luxer—Warmoesstraat 11 (hotelluxer.nl). TripAdvisor Certificate of Excellence. Location: in the Red Light District, 600 feet southwest of Central Station. Pros: free WiFi, good breakfast buffet, air conditioning, non-smoking, bar/lounge, wheelchair access, facilities for disabled guests, twin/triple/quad rooms available. Cons: standard rooms very small, Red Light District/bars can be loud, no singles, no single price break. (TripAdvisor price range for standard room: $125-$339.)

Distances: Canal Company (.1 miles), St. Nicholas Church (.1 miles), Sex Museum (.1 miles), Old Church (.2 miles), Central Station (.2 miles), Dam Square (.3 miles), Anne Frank House (.7 miles), Leidseplein (1.1 miles), Rijksmuseum (1.3 miles), Van Gogh Museum (1.4 miles), Museum Square (1.6 miles)

DoubleTree by Hilton Hotel Amsterdam Centraal Station—Oosterdoksstraat 4. Location: next to Central Station. TripAdvisor's Certificate of Excellence. Pros: free WiFi, parking, very good breakfast buffet, air conditioning, non-smoking, restaurant, room service, bar/lounge, fitness center, facilities for disabled guests, twin/triple/quads rooms available, shuttle service, elevator. Cons: some rooms with no views, expensive cocktails. (TripAdvisor price range for standard room: $180-$500.)

Distances: to St. Nicholas Church (.2 miles), Amsterdam Central Station (.3 miles), Canal Company (.3 miles), Sex Museum (.4 miles), Dam Square (.6 miles), Anne Frank House (.9 miles), Leidseplein (1.3 miles), Rijksmuseum (1.4 miles), Van Gogh Museum (1.6 miles), Museum Square (1.8 miles)

A-Train Hotel—Prins Hendrikkade 23 (atrainhotel.nl). TripAdvisor's Certificate of Excellence. Location: across from Central Station. Pros: free WiFi, air conditioning, good breakfast included, non-smoking, lift, airport shuttle, facilities for guests with disabilities, single/twin/triple/quad/quint rooms available. Cons: can be hard to find cancellable room. (TripAdvisor price range for standard room: $121-$343.)

Distances: Sex Museum (.1 miles), Central Station (.2 miles), Canal Company (.2 miles), Dam Square (.4 miles), Anne Frank House (.6 miles), Leidseplein (1.2 miles), Rijksmuseum (1.4 miles), Van Gogh Museum (1.5 miles), Museum Square (1.7 miles)

Ibis Amsterdam Centre—Stationsplein 49. Location: directly next to Central Station. Pros: free WiFi, breakfast buffet, air conditioning, non-smoking, restaurant, bar/lounge, laundry services, wheelchair access, upper floors accessible by lift, Green Leaders Silver level, twins/triples available, price break for singles. Cons: small rooms, no singles, some train noise. (TripAdvisor price range for standard room: $124-$317.)

Distances: Central Station (.2 miles), Sex Museum (.2 miles), Dam Square (.5 miles), Anne Frank House (.6 miles), Leidseplein (1.3 miles), Rijksmuseum (1.4 miles), Van Gogh Museum (1.6 miles), Museum Square (1.7 miles)

Leidseplein/Museum Quarter area

Leidseplein is a busy, popular square with many shops, restaurants and an active nightlife, in addition to excellent transportation connections. It sits on the south end of Amsterdam's canal ring. The Museum Quarter is just south of the canal ring, south of Leidseplein, and is home to three major museums—the Rijksmuseum, the Van Gogh Museum, and the Stedelijk Museum. Both neighborhoods are close to the large Vondelpark.

Public transportation options in and near Leidseplein include tram lines 1, 2, and 5, with 7 and 10 around the corner, and loads of city buses. Near the Rijksmuseum, you can catch trams 2, 5 and 16 (which go to Central Station) and numerous city buses. Airport bus 397 stops at Museumplein, at the Hobbemastraat bus stop outside the Rijksmuseum, and at Leidseplein.

The hop-on/hop-off City Sightseeing tours stop at Leidseplein/Vondelpark, Museumplein/Rijksmuseum, Museum District, Leidsestraat/Prinsengracht, and Spiegelgracht/Prinsengracht (by the Rijksmuseum).

The Stromma.nl hop-on/hop-off tours stop at Leidseplein/Vondelpark, at the Rijksmuseum/Van Gogh Museum on the bus line, and the Rijksmuseum on the boat line. Stromma.nl small group bus tours leave from the Heineken Experience, which is an easy tram or bus ride from Leidseplein or the Rijksmuseum.

Hotels in these neighborhoods include the following:

Hotel Fita—Jan Luykenstraat 37 (hotel-fita.hoteleamsterdam.net/en/). TripAdvisor's Traveler's Choice Award (top 1% of category) and Certificate of Excellence. Location: west of Rijksmuseum/Van Gogh Museum. Pros: free WiFi, excellent breakfast included, non-smoking, elevator, parking, single/twin rooms available. Cons: steep steps from street to door, weak WiFi, no air conditioning, no triple/quad rooms, limited rooms available. (TripAdvisor price range for standard room: $144-$234.)

Distances: Van Gogh Museum (.1 miles), Diamond Museum Amsterdam (.1 miles), Museum Square (.2 miles), Rijksmuseum (.2 miles), Leidseplein (.3 miles), Vondelpark (.6 miles), Anne Frank House (1.1 miles), Dam Square (1.1 miles), Central Station (1.6 miles)

Hotel JL No76—Jan Luijkenstraat 76 (www.hoteljlno76.com/en). TripAdvisor Traveler's Choice Award (top 1% of category) and Certificate of Excellence. Location: west of Rijksmuseum/Van Gogh Museum. Pros: free WiFi, good breakfast buffet, air conditioning, non-smoking, restaurant, room service, bar/lounge, wheelchair access, facilities for guests with disabilities, twin/quad rooms available. Cons: no singles, no price break for singles, souterrain rooms are in basement. (TripAdvisor price range for standard room: $129-$332.)

Distances: Van Gogh Museum (.1 miles), Diamond Museum Amsterdam (.1 miles), Museum Square (.2 miles), Rijksmuseum (.2 miles), Leidseplein (.3 miles), Vondelpark (.6 miles), Dam Square (1.1 miles), Anne Frank House (1.1 miles), Central Station (1.5 miles)

Amsterdam Marriott Hotel—Stadhouderskade 12. TripAdvisor's Certificate of Excellence. Location: across the Singelgracht from Leidseplein. Pros: free Internet, parking, good breakfast buffet, air conditioning, non-smoking, restaurant, room service, bar/lounge, very good fitness center, wheelchair access, facilities for disabled guests, GreenPartner, quad rooms. Cons: no single/twin rooms, no significant price break for singles, free Internet only in public areas, expensive breakfast and parking. (TripAdvisor price range for standard room: $189-$570.)

Distances: Leidseplein (.1 miles), Van Gogh Museum (.3 miles), Rijksmuseum (.3 miles), Museum Square (.4 miles), Vondelpark (.7 miles), Anne Frank House (.9 miles), Dam Square (.9 miles), Central Station (1.4 miles)

Hotel La Boheme—Marnixstraat 415 (www.la-bohemeamsterdam.com/en/index.html). TripAdvisor's Certificate of Excellence. Location: NW of Leidseplein. Pros: free WiFi, excellent breakfast included, non-smoking, bar/lounge, single/twin/triple rooms available. Cons: *no elevator*, narrow/steep stairs, only 18 rooms. (TripAdvisor price range for standard room: $122-$261.)

Distances: Leidseplein (.1 miles), Rijksmuseum (.4 miles), Van Gogh Museum (.4 miles), Museum Square (.5 miles), Anne Frank House (.7 miles), Vondelpark (.8 miles), Dam Square (.8 miles), Central Station (1.2 miles)

Boutique Hotel View—Leidsekade 77 (www.boutiquehotelview.nl/en/). TripAdvisor's Certificate of Excellence. Location: NW of Leidseplein along Singelgracht. Pros: free WiFi, excellent breakfast buffet, non-smoking, twin/triple rooms available. Cons: no air conditioning, *no elevator*, steep/narrow stairs, no single rooms, no price break for singles, only 14 rooms. (TripAdvisor price range for standard room: $106-$198.)

Distances: Leidseplein (.2 miles), Rijksmuseum (.4 miles), Van Gogh Museum (.4 miles), Museum Square (.6 miles), Anne Frank House (.7 miles), Vondelpark (.7 miles), Dam Square (.8 miles), Central Station (1.3 miles)

American Hotel Amsterdam—Leidsekade 97 (www.amsterdamamericanhotel.com/en/). TripAdvisor's Certificate of Excellence. Location: NW of Leidseplein along Singelgracht. Pros: free WiFi, good breakfast buffet, air conditioning, non-smoking, extra-long beds, restaurant, room service, bar/lounge, wheelchair-friendly, room accessible for disabled persons, twins and suites available, refrigerator, fitness center, GreenLeaders Gold level. Cons: no singles, no price break for singles, expensive breakfast. (TripAdvisor price range for standard room: $170-$355.)

Distances: Leidseplein (.1 miles), Rijksmuseum (.3 miles), Van Gogh Museum (.4 miles), Museum Square (.5 miles), Vondelpark (.8 miles), Anne Frank House (.8 miles), Dam Square (.8 miles), Central Station (1.3 miles)

Max Brown Hotel Museum Square—Jan Luijkenstraat 40-46 (maxbrownhotels.com/museum-square-amsterdam/). TripAdvisor's Certificate of Excellence. Location: west of Rijksmuseum. Pros: free WiFi, good breakfast included, non-smoking, bar/lounge, elevator, twin/triple/quad rooms available. Cons: no single rooms, no price break for singles, small rooms, steep stairways, no lift to breakfast room in basement, no air conditioning. (TripAdvisor price range for standard room: $120-$305.)

Distances: Diamond Museum Amsterdam (.1 miles), Van Gogh Museum (.1 miles), Rijksmuseum (.1 miles), Leidseplein (.2 miles), Museum Square (.2 miles), Vondelpark (.7 miles), Dam Square (1 mile), Anne Frank House (1 mile), Central Station (1.5 miles)

Hotel Espresso—Overtoom 57 (www.hotelespresso.nl). Location: west of Leidseplein across the Singelgracht. Pros: free WiFi, parking, good breakfast buffet, air conditioning, non-smoking, family rooms available, wheelchair access, facilities for disabled access, twin/triple/quad rooms available. Cons: small rooms, no singles, no price break for singles. (TripAdvisor price range for standard room: $108-$375.)

Distances: Leidseplein (.3 miles), Van Gogh Museum (.3 miles), Rijksmusem (.4 miles), Museum Square (.4 miles), Vondelpark (.5 miles), Anne Frank House (.9 miles), Dam Square (1 mile), Central Station (1.5 miles)

Hotel Cornelisz—PC Hooftstraat 24-28 (hotelcornelisz.nl/en/hotel-cornelisz-en/). TripAdvisor's Certificate of Excellence. Location: between Vondelpark and Rijksmuseum. Pros: free WiFi, parking, good breakfast buffet, non-smoking, elevator, single/twin/triple rooms available. Cons: no air conditioning, some problems with elevator, small rooms. (TripAdvisor price range for standard room $102-$270.)

Distances: Rijksmuseum (.1 miles), Leidseplein (.2 miles), Van Gogh Museum (.2 miles), Museum Square (.3 miles), Vondelpark (.8 miles), Dam Square (.9 miles), Anne Frank House (1 miles), Central Station (1.4 miles)

Hotel Van Gogh—Van de Veldestraat 5 (www.hotelvangogh.nl/). Location: west of Rijksmueum. Pros: free WiFi, breakfast buffet, air conditioning, non-smoking, elevator, twin/triple rooms available, parking. Cons: no single/double/quad rooms, shared reception/breakfast area with a hostel. (TripAdvisor price range for standard room: $80-$244.)

Distances: Van Gogh Museum (0 miles), Diamond Museum Amsterdam (.1 miles), Museum Square (.2 miles), Rijksmuseum (.2 miles), Leidseplein (.3 miles), Vondelpark (.6 miles), Dam Square (1.1 miles), Anne Frank House (1.1 miles), Central Station (1.6 miles)

NH Amsterdam Centre—Stadhouderskade 7 (www.nhhotels.com/hotel/nh-amsterdam-centre). Location: across the Singelgracht from Leidseplein. Pros: free WiFi, air conditioning, non-smoking, restaurant, room service, bar/lounge, refrigerator, good breakfast buffet, fitness center, wheelchair access, facilities for disabled guests, single/twin/triple rooms and suites available, GreenLeaders Silver level. Cons: tiny rooms, worn, some complaints about cleanliness. (TripAdvisor price range for standard room: $143-$369.)

Distances: Leidseplein (.1 miles), Rijksmuseum (.3 miles), Van Gogh Museum (.3 miles), Museum Square (.4 miles), Vondelpark (.4 miles), Anne Frank House (.8 miles), Dam Square (.9 miles), Central Station (1.4 miles)

Other base cities in the Netherlands

The Netherlands is such a compact country that you can see most of it while based in Amsterdam, if you wish, by taking day trips via bus or train. That said, if you prefer to base in other Dutch cities, The Hague has a hop-on/hop-off tourist tram and Rotterdam has a hop-on/hop-off double-decker tourist bus that makes 6 stops throughout the city.

Paris

Overview

Paris (pronounced in French as pah-REE) is the capital of France and the subject of many a traveler's romantic day dreams. Atmospheric streets, historic neighborhoods, iconic bridges and landmarks—everyone knows *something* about the city, big or small. On the big end you have the Eiffel Tower. The Louvre art museum. Notre Dame Cathedral. Famous fashion houses. The hip and happening Left Bank. The nearby royal Palace of Versailles. And on the smaller end? Accordion players. Cancan dancers. Flea markets. Houseboats. Booksellers.

And then there's the food scene, from crêpe vendors to ubiquitous bistros to five-star restaurants. Julia Child. The Cordon Bleu. It's a gourmet's delight. And let's not forget the wine. Lots and lots of wine. And Champagne. And Cognac.

Paris really must have something for everyone, and not just in food and drink. Those who aren't interested in history can head to Disneyland. Those who don't like art can go shopping. Those who want to sit in a sidewalk café and drink wine or coffee and debate the meaning of life, write the next great novel, or watch the world go by—well, they have ample opportunity to do so.

Paris has a mild, temperate climate, strongly moderated by the Gulf Stream. Temperatures range from an average of 41 degrees Fahrenheit in winter to an average of 68 degrees in the summer, and only rarely do extremes extend much below freezing. Climate change is leading to hotter summers, though, and July 2019 produced a record-breaking high of 108.6 degrees Fahrenheit in Paris. Rain showers are frequent but generally light and quick. About half the days a year see measurable precipitation.

Possible plan for Paris (What I'd do)

If I were traveling to Paris with my mother, this is what I would plan for us to do. Obviously, you may prefer to do something different, but you may find this itinerary handy as a starting point, changing it as much as you'd like. (And it will make more sense as you work your way through the chapter. Having a city map at hand will help, too.) **Please double check any details before relying on them, as specifics may have changed since I wrote these pages.** This plan assumes lodging near the Louvre but could easily be modified for the Latin Quarter or elsewhere.

Be aware that many sights in Paris are closed on Mondays or Tuesdays. Order these daily itineraries in such a way as to avoid Monday or Tuesday for Paris sightseeing. Arriving in Paris on a Monday, Tuesday or Wednesday allows for the use of this sample itinerary without modification. If you change the order of days, keep these points in mind:

- Keep the 4 days of the Paris Museum Pass consecutive (if choosing this option).
- Keep the 2 days of HOHO bus or boat access consecutive, and also use the 2 days of transportation during the validity period of the Paris Museum Pass, so they overlap.
- Do not plan to visit Paris sights (whether included on this itinerary or not) without checking to see whether they are closed any days during the week.
- Days 3 and 4 of this itinerary can be flipped to avoid Monday/Tuesday closures on those days.

Also be aware that visiting Paris requires *walking*. We can minimize the walking, but only to a certain extent. Expect to rely on leg power for much of the day and night. Probably the most practical plan for making Paris workable for those with walking difficulties is to deliberately take things slowly. Plan to rest when it's possible—at cafés, on benches, on buses or boats. Build rest time into your day. Anywhere you can take a load off, *do*. As for day trips, you probably don't want to plan for more than two consecutive out-of-town excursions at a time, to avoid bus fatigue.

If this itinerary looks too full for you, cut back on it. If the Museum Pass no longer looks like a financially attractive option because of that, don't get it. (But the fast-track access is worth something on its own, so if individual entry tickets get anywhere close to the cost of a Museum Pass, it's worth getting the pass to avoid the ticket lines.)

Day 1—Depart U.S.

Day 2—Arrive Paris. Find an ATM and withdraw euros, if needed. Look for tourist information office at the airport. Get tourist information and buy a 4-day Paris Museum Pass. (*Do not validate yet.*)

To get from the airport to the city, book a shuttle ride *in advance*, then, at the airport, find the shuttle pickup area. (Depending on where you're staying, you may prefer to ride the RER train or take an airport shuttle bus.)

At the hotel, go to room and rest, if possible. If too early for that, leave luggage and explore the neighborhood. Take a self-guided walking tour. Line up cell phone service, if needed. Scout out a local grocery store and possible bistro for dinner. Stop for lunch or tea/coffee. Get a feel for Paris. Rest before dinner, then go out to eat. (Or eat in.)

Day 3—(*Do not plan this day for a Monday.*) Start 4-day Paris Museum Pass. Go to the Big Bus stop at Louvre-Pont des Artes to catch the HOHO bus (or other bus line/bus stop). Exchange prepurchased online voucher for a 2-day HOHO ticket. Ride to the Ile de la Cité-Notre Dame stop. (OR go to the nearest Batobus stop and buy a 2-day HOHO shuttle boat pass. Ride to the Notre Dame stop.) (If staying in the Latin Quarter, just walk to Notre Dame.)

View fire-damaged Notre Dame Cathedral from the outside. Visit the Crypt in front of the cathedral (entry included with Museum Pass). (*Crypt closed Mondays.*) Lunch on the island (e.g., at Sur le Pouce, 7 rue d'Arcole) or in the Latin Quarter. Visit the Conciergerie (entry included). Consider visiting Ste.-Chapelle church (entry included, but requires 1 level up and then down on narrow stone spiral staircases). Take the HOHO bus around the rest of its route (or take the Batobus shuttle from the Notre Dame stop or the Hotel de Ville stop). Return to hotel. Relax in room. Dinner out or pick up food at a grocery store or take-out stand.

Day 4—(*Do not plan this day for a Tuesday.*) Pick up supplies for a picnic lunch. Ride the HOHO bus or HOHO Batobus to the Eiffel Tower stop. Use a pre-ordered, fast-access, timed ticket to go up the Eiffel Tower. (Buying tickets on-site is very time-consuming and may only get you to the second level of three.) After the Eiffel Tower visit, take the Bateaux Parisiens boat tour on the river next to the Eiffel Tower (ride included on Big Bus HOHO ticket). (Skip boat cruise if traveling via Batobus.)

Cross the river to the Trocadéro for best views of the Eiffel Tower. Eat lunch at the top of the hill in the courtyard between the two sides (*weather permitting*). Ride the HOHO bus from the Trocadéro to the Champs-Elysées stop by the Arc de Triomphe. *If fit*, use fast-access entry (included on Museum Pass) and then climb to the top of the arch. (*Climb is difficult.* Wheelchair access by elevator is available to the middle level, but to reach the top requires climbing the last 46 steps.) If not up to climbing, take the underpass, walk around the bottom of the arch, and watch traffic from street level (free). When done, take the HOHO bus to the Place de la Concorde stop and visit the Orangerie (if time—open daily except Tuesday until 6, but check the last HOHO bus times) (entry included with Museum Pass).

If taking the Batobus, skip the Arc de Triomphe and ride the Batobus to the Champs-Elysées station to visit l'Orangerie OR, to include the Arc, walk or take a city bus (probably 22) from the Trocadéro to the Arc de Triomphe (Place Charles de Gaulle). (You can buy a ticket on the bus, if you need to.) After visiting the Arc, take a bus (probably 73) to l'Orangerie.

Return to hotel. Dinner.

Day 5—(*Do not plan this day for a Monday or Tuesday.*) Walk to Louvre (or take bus from the Latin Quarter, probably bus 27). Get in fast-access line before the Louvre opens (entry included, closed Tuesdays). Inside, go immediately to the Mona Lisa (gets *very* crowded later). Break for lunch or snack. Walk across the river to Orsay Museum (entry included, closed Mondays). Break for coffee/snack/meal. Return to hotel. Rest. Dinner.

Day 6—(*Do not plan this day for a Monday or Tuesday.*) Last day of 4-day Museum Pass. Buy a *carnet* of public transportation tickets or single-use tickets, if not already done. Take bus to the Cluny Museum (from the Louvre area, probably bus 27 or 21; from the Latin Quarter, probably walk). (Museum entry included with Museum Pass, closed Tuesdays.) Take bus to Rodin Museum (probably bus 87) (entry included, closed Mondays). Snack or lunch at Rodin Museum café.

Walk to nearby Musée de l'Armée. Visit Napoleon's Tomb under the gold dome (entry included). Visit the Army Museum, if interested. Ride the bus back to the hotel area (possibly bus 69 to the Louvre area or bus 63 to the Latin Quarter). Rest up. Dinner.

Day 7—Day trip: Fontainebleau and Vaux le Vicomte

Day 8—Day trip: D-Day Beaches in Normandy
Day 9—Free day in Paris
Day 10—Day trip: Loire Valley Chateaux and Wine Tasting
Day 11—Day trip: Giverny, Monet's Gardens (morning tour). Afternoon: final souvenir shopping.
Day 12—Return to U.S. Use prebooked shuttle bus ride (or other) to get to the airport.

Arrival

Almost all international traffic flies into Charles de Gaulle Airport (CDG) (easycdg.com/), 16 miles northeast of Paris. The busiest domestic airport, Orly Airport (ORY) (www.air port-orly.com), is about 8 miles south of the city, but you are unlikely to land there. I'll discuss transportation options from Charles de Gaulle airport, but other than specifics, they apply to Orly, as well. You can find tourist information regarding both airports here: www.parisaeroport.fr/en.

To get from CDG to the city, you have your choice of train, bus, taxi, or private driver. The RER B **train** leaves every 10-20 minutes from Terminal 3. The ride takes about 50 minutes to central Paris and cost around €11.40 in late 2019. The most direct **bus** to the Paris-Opéra district in central Paris (11 rue Scribe) is the direct Roissybus, which can be found outside the Arrivals gates of terminals 1, 2, and 3. Tickets cost €15 in 2019, buses leave about every 20 minutes, and the ride takes about 60 minutes.

Taxis from Charles de Gaulle to the city have a flat fee of €50-€60 (depending on district) and take about 40-45 minutes to reach the center of the city. **Shuttle** services offer door-to-door transport from the airport to your hotel, with lower prices but longer times than taxis. Parishuttle (Paris Shuttle) (parishuttle. com/paris_airport_shuttle.php) charges from €16 to €25 per person, depending on number of people travelling together. Another company, Paris Airport Shuttle (www.paris-airportshuttle .com/cdg_shuttle.html), charges from €17 to €40, plus a €3 supplement in the morning and evening. Book shuttles at least 24 hours in advance.

Easy transportation options

Once in the city, your probable transportation choices are bus, métro, and taxi. The métro system (combined with the RER suburban train system) is excellent in and around Paris, but requires lots of walking (much of it underground) and often stairs. City buses can be easier to get to. Check the

Paris journey finder at www.ratp.fr/en to get help finding options for riding public transportation.

One easy way to get around to the sights is to ride a hop-on/hop-off (HOHO) tourist bus. You purchase a 1-day, 2-day, or 3-day ticket and then may hop on and hop off the buses (of the line you paid for) as much as you'd like in that time. Or you may decide that a HOHO *boat* is a preferable option, giving you 1 or 2 days of hop-on/hop-off access at main stops along the Seine.

You may choose to take the whole HOHO tour to get an overview and then, on the second time around, hop off to see sights up close. Buses and boats run year-round, though hours of operation and frequency may vary by season. Prices are listed below, but check each company's Web site for the latest information.

Taxis, of course, may offer the most convenient within-city transportation of all, but you'll pay for that convenience. Still, you are on vacation, and if riding taxis fits your budget and enhances your experience, that may be the right choice for you. Information about Paris taxis is provided below.

Hop-On/Hop-Off Tours

Big Bus Paris (www.bigbustours.com/en/paris/paris-bus-tours/) offers two Paris sightseeing routes on hop-on/hop-off double-decker buses with free WiFi on board.

The Classic (red) Route takes in the most iconic sights of central Paris, and the Montmartre (blue) Route swings around the Bohemian neighborhood by Sacre-Coeur Basilica. A full loop on the red route takes 2 hours 20 minutes, with buses leaving every 5-15 minutes for the 10 stops. Some red route buses have live guides. All other buses (both routes) have recorded commentary.

The earliest red route bus leaves from the Big Bus Information Centre at the Louvre-Pyramide stop at 9:15 a.m. The last bus leaves there at 6:30 p.m. (as of this writing). Stops on the red route are Eiffel Tower, Champ de Mars, Opéra Garnier, Louvre-Pyramide, Louvre-Pont des Arts, Notre Dame, Musée d'Orsay, Champs-Elysées, Grand Palais, and Trocadéro.

A full loop on the blue route takes 1 hour 15 minutes, with buses leaving approximately every 30 minutes. The blue route crosses the red route at Louvre-Pyramide and then stops only at Gard du Nord (train station). (You may hop off at a couple of other stops, but you can't board the bus there.) As of this writing, the first blue bus leaves the Big Bus Information Centre at Louvre-Pyramide at 9:30, and the last one at 6:40 p.m. From the Gare du Nord, the first bus leaves at 9:05 a.m. and the last one at 6:40

p.m. (as of this writing). (Note: More than one reviewer has said that the blue route is not worth the time it takes to ride it.)

Big Bus HOHO tickets include the following:

- Classic Ticket—1 day HOHO, adults from €35.10, children from €17.10
- Premium Ticket—2 day HOHO, adults from €38.70, children from €18.90.
- Deluxe Ticket—2 day HOHO, 1-hour Seine River cruise with Les Bateaux Parisiens, adults from €44.20, children from €22.10
- Classic Ticket + Night Tour—1 day HOHO, 2-hour panoramic night bus tour, adults from €50.40, children from €27
- Night Tour—pre-recorded commentary, adults from €27, children from €14
- Classic Ticket + River Cruise—1 day HOHO, adults from €43.20, children from €21.60
- Deluxe Ticket + Night Tour—2 day HOHO, 1-hour Seine River cruise with Les Bateaux Parisiens, 2-hour panoramic night bus tour, adults from €62.10, children from €34.20

Buy tickets online, download and print your ticket voucher from the link in your confirmation email. Show the printed ticket voucher at any of the stops or on the bus and you will be issued a receipt to use for hop-on/hop-off privileges during the validity period of your ticket.

Open Tour Paris (www.paris.opentour.com/en/) is a slightly less well reviewed company (but with broader range and more stops) that offers HOHO bus and boat routes.

Tickets for the 3-route HOHO **buses** are available for 1, 2, or 3 days. Double-decker buses offer free WiFi and recorded commentary. During peak season, buses leave every 5-15 minutes. In the off season, they leave every 20-30 minutes.

The blue line covers central Paris with 19 stops around the Louvre, d'Orsay, Eiffel Tower, and the Champs-Elysées; the red line runs farther north with 8 stops as far as Montmartre and Gare du Nord; the green line runs a 9-stop loop from Notre Dame farther south to Luxembourg Gardens and the Catacombs. Both the red and the green lines have a connecting stop with the blue line.

Some HOHO bus tickets include access to the Batobus river boat shuttle (not always available!—check under Batobus listings if not included under Open Tour listings). The **river boat shuttle service** stops at 8 or 9 points along the Seine on a HOHO boat. Bus ticket must be redeemed before the boat pass can be. Bring both passes to the Batobus Welcome Desk before boarding the boat. (See below for more information about Batobus.)

The HOHO bus passes can also be combined with a 1-hour **Bateaux Mouches cruise**. This round-trip boat ride departs from the Port de la Conférence-Pont de l'Alma, on the Rive Droite (Right Bank)–on the blue bus line. During peak season the cruise boats leave about every 30 minutes from 10 a.m. to 10:30 p.m., and in the off season, they leave approximately every 40 minutes from 11 a.m. to 9:20 p.m. (More on weekends.)

HOHO bus passes are also available with a 1½–hour **night tour**, again with free onboard WiFi and recorded commentary. Tours depart from 13 rue Auber (northwest of the Opéra Garnier), the Open Tour office. The night tour is also available on its own.

- 1-day HOHO bus pass + Night Tour, €49
- 2-day HOHO bus pass + Night Tour, €53
- 3-day HOHO bus pass + Night Tour, €57
- 1-, 2-, or 3-day HOHO bus pass, child 4-15, €21
- 2-day HOHO bus + Bateaux Mouches cruise, €44
- 1-day HOHO bus pass + Flyview virtual reality experience, €43

Order online and receive an e-ticket. Present the e-ticket on board a bus to redeem it. You must redeem the ticket on a bus or at the Open Tour agency (13 rue Auber) before using any boat shuttle portion.

Batobus HOHO river bus shuttles provide relaxed transportation up and down the Seine in central Paris (www.batobus.com/en/batobus-pass.html). Shuttles include free WiFi but are not guided tour boats. During peak season, boats leave every 20-30 minutes (10 a.m.–9:30 p.m.), and during the off season they stop every 25-45 minutes (10 a.m. to 5 or 7 p.m.).

The shuttle boat stops at the Eiffel Tower, Invalides, Musee d'Orsay, St-Germain-des-Pres, Notre Dame, Jardin des Plantes, Hotel-de-Ville, Louvre, Place de la Concorde. Service can (sometimes) be included as part of the Open Tour Paris HOHO tickets or (more reliably) purchased independently for just HOHO boat access. Ticket holders may ride the boat shuttle as much as they want during the period of their ticket's validity. Steps are required to get on and off the boats. Only the Eiffel Tower stop has wheelchair access. There are no customer toilets on board.

Tickets can be bought online as a voucher and redeemed at stops or bought directly at the boat stops.

- 1 day/24-hours, adult €17, child €8, senior €11
- 2 consecutive days, adult €19, child €10, senior €13
- 2 consecutive days, boat and Open Tour HOHO bus, adult €47, child €21
- 3 consecutive days, boat and Open Tour HOHO bus, adult €51, child €21

Bateaux Mouches boat cruises (www.bateaux-mouches.fr/en) offer straight boat rides (not necessarily as part of a HOHO ticket) and restaurant rides on the Seine. Cruises leave from the Pont de l'Alma every 30-40 minutes and last approximately 1 hour 10 minutes. Adults €14, children (4-11) €6. Other cruises include lunch, brunch, dinner, dinner show, and special evening (holiday) cruises for varying prices. Wheelchair access on main deck only, non-motorized wheelchairs only, no adapted restrooms available.

Taxis and ride services

If taking a **taxi** or arranging a private ride is your thing, you can certainly do so in Paris. You can check a taxi fare finder such as www.taxifarefinder.com (indicate Paris in the upper right corner) to get an estimate for how much a ride would cost. For example, taxi fare from Notre Dame Cathedral to the Eiffel Tower would range from €9.28 in low traffic to €68.11 in high traffic and would typically cost a little more than €20 for a trip of about 3 miles. A typical Uber fare for the same ride would be less. You can find a link to Uber and other ride-sharing service estimates on the taxi fare finder site.

You can easily locate cabs at taxi stands throughout the city. If you prefer to call for a cab, some Paris cab companies include the following:

- Taxi Paris, 01 83 58 36 00
- City Cab Paris, 01 82 53 23 51
- Taxi in Paris, 01 77 21 72 72
- Victor Cabs Paris, 01 59 83 73 18
- Alpha, 01 45 85 85 85
- Artaxi, 01 42 41 50 50
- Taxi, 01 47 39 47 39 (English: 01 41 27 66 99)

The all-purpose taxi call number is 01 45 30 30 30, but be aware that the meter runs from the time the taxi leaves on its drive to pick you up, so you may want to check with your hotel desk and order from the nearest company. (Taxi ranks with phone numbers are listed by district here: www.taxi-paris.net/page41.html.) Hailing taxis on the street is less successful in Paris than in other cities, so you may be better off just finding a taxi stand or calling for a ride. Also, it's important that you ride only in licensed cabs, which is another good reason to find a taxi stand. Be prepared to pay your fare in cash.

As of this writing, **Uber** is legal in Paris (although Uber Pop is not). Lyft is not available in Europe.

Other in-city transportation

Public transportation is excellent in Paris, particularly its well-known, well-regarded métro system, but the métro requires a fairly fit constitution to negotiate its many tunnels and stairs in a timely fashion. The transportation network covers all of Paris and its suburbs.

The **métro** is the crown jewel of the Paris transportation system, billed as the "cheapest, easiest and fastest way to get around Paris" (en.parisinfo.com/practical-paris/how-to-get-to-and-around-paris/public-transport). Trains start running around 6 a.m. and continue until after midnight. In late 2019, a single métro ticket valid for zones 1-2 cost €1.90. A group of 10 (called *un carnet*—"kahr-nay") cost €16.90. Tickets are for sale in machines at métro stations, at tobacconist shops, and online at parisinfo.com. Free métro maps are available at métro ticket stations.

The **RER** is the suburban train system, but for the portion that runs through Paris, it uses the métro stops and can be used along with the métro system. The RER has 5 color-coded lines. You need to use your ticket to *exit* the station after riding a stretch of the RER, as well as when you enter.

Paris has numerous city **bus** lines, as well, if you prefer to travel at street level. Bus 63 runs more or less alongside the Seine from the Pont d'Alama to beyond Notre Dame, if you want a route convenient for tourists. Routes 67 and 69 hit a lot of tourist spots, too. The bus number and direction are noted at the front of the bus. Hail it as it approaches the bus stop, so the bus driver knows you want that bus. Punch your ticket or validate your pass as you get on the bus. Push the red button when you want off at the next stop.

If you buy your ticket on the bus, a single ticket cost €2 in 2019 and can only be used for surface transportation (not the RER or the métro).

The t+ tickets are slightly less expensive (www.ratp.fr/en/titres-et-tarifs/t-tickets) and are good for buses, trams, métro and RER rides, but not transfers between all of them. You can buy them at vending machines or ticket offices, singly or in groups of 10.

The **Paris Visite Pass** allows unlimited transportation in Paris and its near suburbs (zones 1-3) or from Paris out to both airports, Disneyland and Versailles (zones 1-5) for either 1, 2, 3, or 5 consecutive days (www.ratp.fr/en/titres-et-tarifs/paris-visite-travel-pass). Paris Visite Passes cost as follows in 2019:

- Zones 1-3, 1-day, adult €12, child (4-11) €6
- Zones 1-3, 2-day, adult €19.50 child (4-11) €9.75
- Zones 1-3, 3-day, adult €26.65, child (4-11) €13.30
- Zones 1-3, 5-day, adult €38.35, child (4-11) €19.15
- Zones 1-5, 1-day, adult €25.25, child (4-11) €12.60
- Zones 1-5, 2-day, adult €38.35, child (4-11) €19.15
- Zones 1-5, 3-day, adult €53.75, child (4-11) €26.85
- Zones 1-5, 5-day, adult €65.80, child (4-11) €32.90

You can buy a Paris Visite Pass at transport ticket desks and vending machines at all Paris transport stations, including both airports. To use, write your name, start and end dates on the pass. The pass is validated the first time you use it. The pass has a magnetized strip, so keep it away from magnets in your bags. If the pass does become demagnetized, a transport ticket worker will replace it.

The **Paris Passlib** is a combined sightseeing and travel pass available in a Mini, 2-, 3-, or 5-day version. The Mini Passlib card includes a 1-hour boat cruise on Bateaux Parisiens and 1 day of the Open Tour sightseeing bus, but does not include the Museum Pass (covering entry to sights) or the Visite Pass (for public transportation). The Mini pass costs are: adult €45, youth (12-17) €40, child (4-11) €29.

The 2-, 3-, and 5-day Passlib cards all include everything the Mini Passlib does, plus unlimited travel on the Paris transportation system (with a **Visite Card**) for the chosen length of time and priority access to included sights (with a **Paris Museum Pass**—see below) for variable lengths of time. Costs are as follows:

- Passlib 2 days, adult €119, youth €70, child €39
- Passlib 3 days, adult €139, youth €79, child €45

- Passlib 5 days, adult €165, youth €95, child €49

Paris Passlib tickets can be purchased at Paris welcome centers (at the Hotel de Ville, Gare du Nord, and 29 Rue du Rivoli by the Louvre) or online (search on "buy Paris Passlib"), either with the pass delivered to you for a fee or picked up in Paris. All passes can be upgraded for €20 to include fast-track access to the second level of the Eiffel Tower.

Sightseeing pass

The **Paris Museum Pass** (en.parismuseumpass.com/) is a one-cost pass that allows free access to most of the major sights in and around Paris (except the Eiffel Tower), often with priority access. You buy a pass for 2, 4, or 6 consecutive days (not 24-hour periods), write on the back the day you want the pass to start, as well as your name, and then start visiting some of the world's best museums. Costs are as follows:

- 2 days, €48
- 4 days, €62
- 6 days, €74

You can buy passes at tourist information offices, including at both airports, as well as at museums in Paris.

Day trips

It's possible to see much of northern France (and beyond) without having to leave the convenience of your base hotel at night, because Paris has tourist companies that specialize in day trips.

As always, use the information here as a guide, but check each company's Web site for tour details and the most current price and schedule information. **Tour details—even which tours are offered—routinely change from season to season.** Whichever tours you decide on, look over cancellation policies, if your plans aren't completely firm.

Browsing through Web sites will also help you decide which company's tours seem a good fit for you. Be aware that some specific tours might have special requirements or recommendations, so you'll want to look descriptions over closely before you show up at the departure point.

Tour companies differ on which entry fees and meals they include in their prices, so check those specifics (and confirm online), if your selection comes down to price.

Also take into account where the tours depart from. Most of the Paris CityVision (Gray Line) tours depart from rue des Pyramides, across from the northwest end of the Louvre. France Tourisme Paris tours depart from the rue de l'Amiral de Coligny, just east of the Louvre. Other day tour companies will pick you up and drop you off at your hotel, so hotel location is less a concern. You may decide on tours according to which ones depart from near your hotel or will pick you up. Wherever you leave from, make sure you show up early for any tour so you are not considered a no-show and your seat sold to someone else!

If you want to save your walking energy for the tour itself but you select a tour with a departure point that is not close to your hotel, you may want to invest in a taxi ride to get there.

Paris CityVision (Gray Line)

Paris CityVision (Gray Line) (www.pariscityvision.com/en/daytripfrom paris) has TripAdvisor's Certificate of Excellence. The tour company says they offer 50 bus tours from Paris. A selection is listed below. (See the Web site for all currently available tours.) Register online and receive an emailed voucher. Turn the voucher in when meeting the company representative at the departure point. Large-group tours leave from the Paris City-Vision office at 2 rue des Pyramides, across from the Louvre. Many tours offer hotel pickup and drop-off options.

Guided Tour of the Loire Valley Châteaux and Wine Tasting, Lunch included—Tour highlights include a ride on an air-conditioned bus through the Loire Valley to Château de Chenonceau, lunch near the château, drive to Château de Chambord, priority access to the château, wine tasting in the château. Schedule, itinerary, and price vary by season. Depart near the Louvre at 7:15 a.m., return 8 p.m. From €159 (in winter) (or from €192.95 for pickup/drop-off from your Paris accommodation).

Audio Guided Tour of the Loire Valley Châteaux in a Small Group, Lunch included—Tour highlights include minibus transport to Château d'Amboise with audio commentary en route, the tomb of Leonardo da Vinci, Château d'Amboise gardens, Château de Chenonceau (built over the River Cher), its grounds and ornamental gardens, multi-course lunch in Chenonceaux (included), Château de Chambord (largest of the Loire Valley châteaux). Priority access and audio guides in 8 languages to all three châteaux included. Maximum 8 passengers. Hotel pickup early morning, hotel drop-off around 6:45 p.m. From €249. Private tour (1-4 people) from €1290.

Day Trip to Fontainebleau and Vaux le Vicomte—Tour highlights include a tour (with audio guide) of the château Vaux le Vicomte (admission included), free time in the gardens and grounds, time for lunch, drive to Fontainebleau for an audio guide tour of the famous château (admission included), followed by time to explore the grounds and gardens. Schedule varies by season. *May not be offered at all times.* Depart 9:15 a.m. near the Louvre, return around 6:15 p.m. From €79.

Guided Tour to Mont Saint-Michel, Lunch included—Tour highlights include a 4-hour drive through northern France each way in an air-conditioned coach, multi-course lunch featuring regional cuisine in Le Relais Saint Michel (included), shuttle transportation right up to the village of Mont-St-Michel, a guided walking tour up the Grand Rue to the top of the Mont (Note: *Ascent is difficult*), guided 1-hour tour of the abbey at the top (entry included), free time to wander the traffic-free village. Depart 7:15 near the Louvre, return approx. 9:15 p.m. From €169 (or from €209 for pickup/drop-off from your Paris accommodation).

Mont Saint-Michel—Tour highlights include the drive on an air-conditioned bus, lunch on the mainland across from Mont Saint-Michel (not included), free time in the medieval village, self-tour of the abbey at the top of the mont (entry included). (Note: *Ascent is difficult.*) Schedule varies by season. Depart from near the Louvre 7:15 a.m., return around 9:15 p.m. From €119.

Audio Guided Tour to Mont Saint-Michel—Similar to the previous tour (no lunch), but includes an audio guide for the day, available in 8 languages. Schedule varies by season. From €139.

Guided Tour of Bordeaux and Saint Emilion with Wine Tasting—Tour highlights include fast-speed train transport to/from Bordeaux, then travel in an air-conditioned minibus, guided 1-hour walking tour of the village of Saint Emilion, guided tour of a Grand Cru estate (wine) with a wine tasting, a 2-hour guided walking tour of the city of Bordeaux, free time to eat and stroll in Bordeaux. Limited availability. Schedule varies by season. *May not be offered at all times.* Depart 6:30 a.m. in Montparnasse Train Station at Raoul Dautry exit, return 8:42 p.m. From €389.

Guided Tour to Giverny Monet's Gardens and Palace of Versailles in a Small Group with Skip-the-Line Access, Lunch—Tour highlights include pickup/drop-off from Paris accommodations in air-conditioned minibus, 2 hours at Versailles palace and gardens (incl. priority access), multi-course lunch near Giverny featuring local food (included), the gardens and house of Claude Monet in Giverny (entry included), maximum 8 passengers. Schedule varies by season. *May not be offered at all times.* Hotel pickup 8 a.m., hotel drop-off 5:15 p.m. Small-group tour (up to 8) €239, private tour (1-4 people) €1090.

Audio Guided Tour of Giverny Monet's Gardens, Lunch included—Tour highlights include a leisurely exploration of Monet's house and gardens in Giverny (entry included), lunch at a restaurant across from Monet's house with traditional Norman cuisine from the days of Claude Monet (included), the Museum of Impressionisms (entry included), free time in the village of Giverny, a visit to an artisanal bakery (gourmet snack included) and Monet's tomb. Schedule varies by season. *May not be offered at all times.* Depart around 8:15 a.m. near the Louvre, return around 6:45 p.m. From €99.

Giverny Monet's Gardens (½-day excursion)—Tour highlights include transportation to Monet's Gardens on an air-conditioned coach, Monet's home (entry included), self tour of Monet's gardens (included). Schedule varies by season. *May not be offered at all times.* Depart 8:15 a.m. or 1:45 p.m. from near the Louvre, return approximately 5 hours later. From €49.

Guided Tour to Normandy D-Day Beaches, Lunch included—Tour highlights include a ride through Normandy on an air-conditioned coach, the Caen Memorial Museum (entry included), lunch at the Caen Memorial Museum (included), Pointe du Hoc (German fortified site stormed by American Rangers), American Cemetery above Omaha Beach, a stop at Arromanches or Juno Beach. Depart from near the Louvre around 7 a.m., return around 9 p.m. €179. With transfers to and from hotel: €219.

Guided Tour to Normandy D-Day Beaches in a Small Group, Lunch included—Tour highlights include pickup at hotel, 3-hour drive across Normandy with no more than 8 in a minibus, self-guided visit at Pointe du Hoc, free time at the Visitor Centre at Omaha Beach, a self-guided visit at the American Cemetery, multi-course lunch at a medieval manor house (included), Arromanches (where an artificial port was built for the D-Day landings). Schedule varies by season. *May not be offered at all times.* Hotel pickup around 6:30 a.m., hotel drop-off around 6:30 p.m. €259. Private tour (1-4 people) from €1290.

Skip-the-Line Full-Day Excursion to Versailles: Guided Tour of the Palace and the Trianon with Lunch at the Grand Canal—Tour highlights include an introduction to Versailles during the air-conditioned bus ride there, priority access and a guided tour of the palace, free time to explore the gardens, a multi-course lunch in the heart of the grounds near the Grand Canal, guided tour of the Large Trianon, the Small Trianon, and the Queen's Hamlet. All entries and lunch included. Depart at 8:45 a.m. from near the Louvre, return around 5:45 p.m. From €149.

Guided Tour of Versailles in a Small Group with Skip-the-Line Access, Lunch included—Tour highlights include priority access to the Palace of Versailles (included), individual exploration of the gardens at Versailles (included), multi-course lunch on the palace grounds near the Grand Canal (included), 1½-hour guided tour of the secondary residences (the Grand Trianon, the Small Trianon, the Queen's Hamlet) (included). Hotel pickup around 8 a.m., hotel drop-off around 4 p.m. From €212.

Skip-the-Line: Small Group Guided Tour to the Palace of Versailles (morning)—Tour highlights include priority access to the royal Palace of Versailles, guided tour of the palace, free time strolling the gardens (entry to all included). Maximum 8 in minibus. Schedule varies by season. *May not be offered at all times.* Pickup from hotel around 8 a.m., drop-off at hotel around noon. From €119. Private tour (1-4 people) from €590.

Guided Tour to the Reims Champagne Region—Tour highlights include a guided visit to the cellars of the Mumm Champagne House with tasting, guided tour of Reims gothic cathedral where French kings were crowned, free time for lunch (not included) and wandering in Reims city center, the Espace Georges Cartier Champagne House with a tasting. Schedule, itinerary, and price vary by season. *May not be offered at all times.* Depart from near the Louvre around 8 a.m., return around 6:30 p.m. From €149. With hotel pickup and drop-off €179.

Guided Tour to the Reims Champagne Region in a Small Group, Lunch included—Tour highlights include a photo stop over the vineyards on the mountain of Reims, visit to the gothic Notre Dame Cathedral in Reims, ride to Epernay, Moet et Chandon house with champagne tasting (included), multi-course lunch in Epernay (included), visit to a small wine-grower with champagne tasting (included). Maximum 8 in minibus. Hotel pickup around 7 a.m., hotel drop-off around 5:30. From €259.

Guided Tour of Bruges—Tour highlights include a guided 1½-hour walking tour through medieval Bruges, short cruise along canals (April to October only), free time for lunch (not included) and exploration of the city. *Must bring passport.* Depart near the Louvre at 7:15 a.m., return around 9 p.m. From €169. With hotel pickup and drop-off €205.

Day Trip to Bruges on Your Own—Tour highlights include an air-conditioned bus ride to Bruges, greeting by a hostess on arrival in the city, tickets for a canal cruise (summer only), information for a self-paced walk of the city. *Must bring passport.* Depart near the Louvre at 7:15, return around 9 p.m. From €109.

Audio Guided Tour of Bruges—Same as previous tour, but includes Bruges city center audio guide. From €129.

Disneyland Paris 1 Day 1 Park with Transport—Tour highlights include transportation in an air-conditioned coach, entry to either the Disneyland Park or Disneyland Studios, all day to explore. Schedule varies by season. *May not be offered at all times.* Depart near the Louvre around 8 a.m., return 8 p.m. From €99.

Disneyland Paris 1 Day 2 Parks: Pick up and Drop-off at Hotel—Same as above but includes transportation to and from hotel (times may vary) and entrance to both parks. Schedule varies by season. *May not be offered at all times.* From €155.

Paris Tours Service

Paris Tours Service (www.paris-tours-service.com) offers a number of tours within and around Paris, as well as excursions farther afield that leave from Paris. Their tours include hotel pickup and drop-off in their prices. Day trips from Paris have included the following. (Check the Web site for current offerings):

D-Day Tour Normandy and Landing Beaches—Tour highlights include free time at Pointe du Hoc (where American Rangers took over German fortifications), the American Cemetery, Omaha Beach, restaurant lunch (included), Arromanches' artificial harbor, drive along the Gold Coast, guided tour of Juno Beach. Hotel pickup around 6:45 a.m., hotel drop-off around 6:45 p.m. From €275.

Tour to Mont Saint-Michel—Tour highlights include a motor-coach drive across Normandy, stop in the picturesque village of Beuvron en

Auge, lunch (included), guided tour of the Abbey at Mont Saint-Michel (Note: *ascent is difficult.*), free time to explore the medieval village. Hotel pickup around 6:30 a.m., hotel drop-off around 9:30 p.m. From €220.

Loire Valley Castle Tour—Tour highlights include the Chambord Castle (the largest of Loire Valley castles), Amboise Castle overlooking the River Loire (site of da Vinci's tomb), Chenonceau Castle (built over the River Cher), all entrances included, audio guide tours included, lunch included. Hotel pickup around 6:30 a.m., hotel drop-off around 6:30 p.m. From €270.

Champagne Discovery Tour—Tour highlights include the gothic Reims Cathedral (no tour), Epernay Champagne cellar visit with tasting, local restaurant lunch featuring regional specialties, world-famous Champagne house "Moët and Chandon" with local expert explaining Champagne methods and processes. Hotel pickup around 7 a.m., hotel drop-off around 5 p.m. From €251.

Normandy D-Day Beaches Tour—Tour highlights include a drive across Normandy in a deluxe minivan (max. 8 people), Pointe du Hoc (where Army Rangers attacked and took over German fortifications), the American Cemetery overlooking Omaha Beach, Memorial Beach Museum in Caen, lunch not included. Hotel pickup around 6:15 a.m., hotel drop-off around 6:15 p.m. From €245.

Somme Battlefields—Tour highlights include the Great War Museum in Peronne, the "Lochnager Crater" largest WWI mine hole, the villages of Pozieres and Thiepval, the Beaumont-Hamel Newfoundland Memorial, the Australian Memorial of Villers Bretonneux. Lunch not included. Hotel pickup around 6:30 a.m., hotel drop-off around 5:30 p.m. From €198.

Fontainebleau—Tour highlights include round-trip transportation, entrance with audio-guide tour to Fontainebleau Palace, time to stroll through the gardens. Hotel pickup around 1:15 p.m., hotel drop-off around 5:45 p.m. From €94.

Giverny Tour—Tour highlights include round-trip transportation to Giverny, fast-track access to Monet's house and gardens. Hotel pickup around 1:15 p.m., hotel drop-off around 5:45 p.m. From €110.

Disneyland Paris—Tour highlights include round-trip transportation and entrance to either Disneyland Park or Walt Disney Studios. Hotel pickup around 7:15 a.m., hotel drop-off around 5:15 p.m. From €150.

Versailles—Many variations of day tours available to Versailles, with hotel pickup and drop-off. Prices range from €95 to €215, more in combinations with trip to Giverny (€240) and the Louvre (€240).

France Tourisme Paris

France Tourisme (www.francetourisme.fr/tour-day-tripfrance.html) offers many variations on its day trips out of Paris. A selection of popular tours is listed below, but visit the Web site for complete offerings. The agency office, where tours depart and return, is near the Louvre at 6 rue de l'Amiral de Coligny. Reviews indicate inconsistent satisfaction with this agency's tours.

Versailles at Your Leisure: Transport and Guided Visit of the Palace—Tour highlights include travel to and from the palace on an air-conditioned coach, entry to the palace, audio-guided tours. Free access to the gardens (except during musical fountain shows). Many optional upgrades available. Departures from near the Louvre at 8 a.m., 11 a.m., and 2 p.m., with returns at 1 p.m., 4 p.m., and 7 p.m. From €42 (basic tour with audio guide), from €52 (total priority access to the palace and a 1½-hour guided tour of the palace). Optional add-ons include lunch on the estate, packed lunch, tickets for the garden train, tickets to Marie-Antoinette's properties, and musical garden shows.

Versailles and Giverny—Tour highlights include transportation to Versailles and entry to the palace with an audio-guide tour, free access to the gardens, transfer to Giverny, access to Monet's house and gardens. April-October. Depart 8 a.m. from near the Louvre, return 6:30 p.m. From €95. Optional hotel pickup/drop-off additional €29 each way.

Loire Valley Castles Tour—Tour highlights include coach transportation to Chenonceau Castle over the River Cher, entry to the palace and gardens, free time for lunch (optional multi-course meal add-on), entry to Cheverny Castle and grounds (famous for their kennel of hunting dogs), entry to Chambord Castle, largest of the Loire Valley castles. "Prestige" version of this tour adds audio guides for all three castles, lunch time in Amboise, free entry to Clos Luce Castle (house of Leonardo da Vinci), and wine-tasting at Chambord Castle. Depart 7:15 a.m. from near the Louvre, return around 8:15 p.m. ("Prestige" tour return around 9:15 p.m.) From €99. "Prestige" tour from €160. Minibus option available for fee, hotel pickup and drop-off available for fee.

Mont Saint-Michel Tour—Tour highlights include coach transportation across Normandy to Mont Saint-Michel, entry and audio-guide tour of the abbey (Note: *Ascent is difficult*), free time on the mont. Optional sack lunch (€12). "Prestige" version of the tour adds small group designation (8 people max.), travel in a minibus, visit to the Mont Saint-Michel historic museum with audio guide, cider and Calvados tasting. Hotel pickup/drop-off available for either tour for a fee. Depart near the Louvre 7:15 a.m., return 9:15 p.m. From €99. "Prestige" version from €140.

Bruges Tour—Tour highlights include air-conditioned coach travel to Bruges (8-person minibus upgrade for €25), tickets for a canal cruise OR a city hall visit included, free time to explore the "Venice of the North." Optional multi-course restaurant lunch for fee. Depart near the Louvre at 7:15 a.m., return around 7:15 p.m. From €99.

Fontainebleau Castle Tour and Barbizon—Tour highlights include transportation to Fontainebleau Castle in an air-conditioned coach, entry and visio guide to Fontainebleau Castle, free time to stroll the estate gardens, short Barbizon village stop. Hotel pickup/drop-off for additional fee. Depart 1:30 p.m. from near Louvre, return around 7 p.m. From €59.

Disneyland Paris—Tour highlights include transportation from central Paris and priority access to one or two parks—the Disneyland Park and the Walt Disney Studios Park. Depart 8:45 a.m., return 8 p.m. (winter)/ 9 p.m. (summer). From €109.

Champagne Tour Rheims—Tour highlights include air-conditioned transport to Rheims, guided tour of the gothic Rheims Cathedral, visit to champagne producer with tasting, free time in Rheims, visit to a vineyard museum with a champagne tasting, stop in Hautvilliers (where Dom Perignon discovered the method to make champagne). Optional upgrades include minibus transportation (€25), lunch in Rheims, and hotel pickup/drop-off. Depart from near Louvre at 8 a.m., return around 7 p.m. From €115.

Normandy Landing Beaches Tour—Tour highlights include Pointe du Hoc (where American Rangers took over German fortifications), Omaha Beach, the American Cemetery, the city of Arromanches with its artificial harbor, free time for lunch, medieval city of Bayeux, free time to visit the Bayeux Cathedral or British Cemetery. Upgrades include minibus transportation, lunch in Arromanches, and hotel pickup/drop-off. Depart 7:15 a.m. by the Louvre, return 8:15 p.m. From €115.

Private tours

Paris Day Trip

Paris Day Trip (paris-day-trip.com) offers private tours to sights around Paris for a flat fee for 1-3 or 4-8 participants. Because they are private, tour itineraries are flexible. Custom tours are also available. Tours begin with hotel pickup and end with hotel drop-off. Some of their offerings include the following:

Versailles Palace and Gardens—Tour highlights include an introduction to Versailles on the private drive to the palace, no-wait access to the palace (entry included), official guide for a personalized tour, 30 minutes to stroll through the gardens. Hotel pickup around 9 a.m. or 2 p.m., hotel drop-off around 1 p.m. or 6 p.m. €550 (1-3 people), €632 (4-8 people).

Giverny and Versailles—Tour highlights include an introduction to Versailles on the private drive to the palace, no-wait access to the palace (entry included), guided 1.5-hour tour of palace, 30 minutes to stroll the gardens, lunch in Giverny (not included), Monet's house and gardens (entry included). Hotel pickup around 9 a.m., hotel drop-off around 6:30 p.m. €800 (1-3 people), €960 (4-8 people).

Versailles In Depth—Tour highlights include an introduction to Versailles on the private drive to the palace, no-wait access to the palace (entry included), guided tour of the palace, time to stroll through the gardens at Versailles, lunch in the gardens of Versailles (not included), drive to the Grand Trianon (entry included), Petit Trianon, Marie Antoinette's hamlet (entry included). Hotel pickup around 9 a.m., hotel drop-off around 5 p.m. €775 (1-3 people), €960 (4-8 people).

Versailles in Depth + Private Apartments—Tour highlights include an introduction to Versailles on the private drive to the palace, no-wait access to the palace (entry included), private guided tour of the palace, exclusive tour of private apartments of Kings Louis XV and Louis XVI, time to stroll through the gardens, lunch in the garden at Versailles (not included), drive to the Grand Trianon (entry included), the Petit Trianon and Marie Antoinette's hamlet (entry included). *Limited access tour. Must reserve at least 15 days in advance.* Hotel pickup around 9 a.m., hotel drop-off around 6:30 p.m. €1125 (1-3 people), €1280 (4-8 people).

Champagne Tour—Tour highlights include an introduction to Champagne country during the 1-hour private drive there, the historic city of Reims with its gothic cathedral, village of Hautvilliers (where Dom Perignon perfected the art of making champagne), break for lunch in Epernay (not included), visit a Champagne house, tour the cellars, be educated on the Champagne-making process, Champagne tasting, visit a smaller producer and sample their Champagne (entry to Champagne house and tasting fees not included). Hotel pickup around 7:30 a.m., hotel drop-off around 5:30-6:30 p.m. €800 (1-3 people), €960 (4-8 people).

Chablis Tour—Tour highlights include an introduction to the Chablis area during the 2.5-to-3-hour drive, coffee stop en route, Basilica Vézelay (UNESCO World Heritage Site), lunch in the town of Chablis (not included), visit to a working vineyard, introduction to wine production, Chablis sampling, visit to another vineyard with more wine tasting, lookout point over the valley (tasting fees not included). Hotel pickup around 7:30 a.m., hotel drop-off around 7:30-8:30 p.m. €900 (1-3 people), €1120 (4-8 people).

Fontainebleau + Vaux-le-Vicomte—Tour highlights include an introduction to Fontainebleau Palace during the 1-hour private drive, no-wait access to Fontainebleau Palace (entry included), private guided tour of the palace, lunch in the town of Barbizon (not included), no-wait access to Vaux-le-Vicomte Palace (entry included), 1-hour personalized guided tour of the palace, including the Bell Tower. Hotel pickup around 9 a.m., hotel drop-off around 6 p.m. €850 (1-3 people), €1000 (4-8 people).

Giverny—Tour highlights include an introduction to Monet's home and gardens during the private drive, visit to Monet's house, the Flower Garden, the Water Garden (entry included). Hotel pickup around 9 a.m. or 2 p.m., hotel drop-off around 2 p.m. or 7 p.m. €500 (1-3 people), €600 (4-8 people).

Giverny + Auvers sur Oise—Tour highlights include an introduction to Van Gogh's time during 1-hour drive to Auvers sur Oise, visit to the Van Gogh house (entry included), visit to graves of Vincent Van Gogh and his brother, lunch break in village of Giverny (not included), Monet's house, Flower Garden, and Water Garden (entry included). Hotel pickup around 9 a.m., drop-off around 6:30 p.m. €800 (1-3 people), €960 (4-8 people).

Loire Valley Castles—Tour highlights include an introduction to the Loire Valley during the private 3-hour drive to Amboise, Amboise Castle, Leonardo da Vinci's grave (entry included), lunch in a Loire Valley restaurant (not included), personal guided tour of Chambord Castle (largest of the Loire Valley castles) (entry included), personal guided tour of Chenonceau Castle (built over the River Cher) (entry included). Hotel pickup around 9 a.m., drop-off around 9-10 p.m. €1020 (1-3 people), €1240 (4-8 people).

Normandy Landing Beaches—Tour highlights include an introduction to Normandy during the drive, coffee stop, Pointe du Hoc (where American Rangers overtook German fortifications), guided walk along Omaha beach, 1-hour private walking tour of the American Cemetery, visitors' center/museum at the American Cemetery, lunch stop in Arromanches (not included), Arromanches lookout (for views over the coast), Juno Beach stop. Hotel pickup around 7 a.m., hotel drop-off around 7 p.m. €900 (1-3 people), €1120 (4-8 people).

Mont Saint-Michel—Tour highlights include an introduction to the island of Mont Saint-Michel during the 3.5-hour private drive there, coffee break en route, time to wander the ancient village, lunch on the main street (not included), personal guided tour of the abbey, Romanesque Church visit. *"There are a lot of stairs and the abbey is not accessible by wheelchair."* Hotel pickup around 7 a.m., hotel drop-off around 8 p.m. €1000 (1-3 people), €1200 (4-8 people).

My Private Paris

My Private Paris (myprivateparis.com) offers private tours in and around Paris. The company has TripAdvisor's Certificate of Excellence. Pickup and drop-off are from your hotel or other desired meeting place. Prices vary according to number of guests. Possible excursions from Paris include the following:

Versailles—Tour highlights include private transportation in an air-conditioned vehicle, no-wait access, a private 5-hour tour of Versailles palace and gardens, optional 3-hour extension for an exclusive tour of Marie Antionette Trianon sites. Times and pickup/drop-off locations flexible. 5 hours. From €108 to €499 per person.

Monet's House and Garden in Giverny—Tour highlights include private transportation in an air-conditioned vehicle, private 5-hour tour of Monet's gardens, skip-the-line access, optional 4-hour Versailles extension. Times and pickup/drop-off locations flexible. 5 hours. From €150 to €649 per person.

Loire Valley Castles—Tour highlights include a guided tour with visits to the castles of Chambord (skip-the-line access), Chenonceau (skip-the-line access), and Amboise. *Tour not always available.* 12 hours. Max. 6 people. From €333 to €1599 per person.

Normandy D-Day Beaches—Tour highlights include a private van ride to the Normandy beaches, Omaha Beach, Pointe du Hoc, German bunkers and artillery sites, American cemetery and museum, Norman countryside and food. Max. 6 people. 12 hours. From €333 to €1499 per person.

Independent travel—GetByBus

If you prefer to travel to these day-trip sites on your own, the blog GetByBus gives helpful information on how to do that: getbybus.com/en/blog/best-day-trips-from-paris/.

Lodging

Paris is one of the world's top tourist cities, with a wealth of lodging possibilities. That doesn't mean that all tourists are delighted with their stays there, though. Just keep one thing in mind, and you'll be much happier with your lodging—expect rooms, elevators, and bathrooms to be small. Perhaps tiny. There's also a good chance they will be noisy, mostly from street noise, but possibly from within the hotel itself. That's the tradeoff for staying in the center of one of the most beautiful, historic, romantic cities in the world. Most hotel rooms are small. Most bathrooms are small. Most elevators (if the building even *has* one) are tiny. If you end up with a room, a bathroom, and an elevator that *aren't* miniscule, that's a bonus, and you get to count yourself lucky.

Hotels on this list are based on location, good reviews, and general accessibility, including access to easy transportation. It favors buildings with elevators, but that doesn't mean the elevator will be larger than a phone booth. You may need to make several trips to get your luggage to upper floors. This section isn't the last word on acceptable accommodation, but it makes a good starting point to narrow down your search. Just check online to make sure that information is still accurate, both on TripAdvisor and on the hotel's own Web site.

You may find a wonderful deal on what looks like a good choice in a convenient location. By all means—grab it! Same with charming B&Bs, which aren't covered here because they tend to have a limited number of available rooms and generally don't have elevators. If you can nab one in a favorable location that gets good reviews, has a great breakfast, decent accessibility, and a workable price, do it!

I have included lodging possibilities for two areas in central Paris: around the Louvre and in the Latin Quarter (south of Notre Dame). The Latin Quarter is easy to reach from the airport via public transportation—just take an RER B train to the St. Michel stop. Getting to the Louvre area via the RER B train requires a transfer to a métro line. It's easier to get to the Louvre area either by taking the Roissybus from the airport to its destination near the Opéra Garnier or, *much* easier, arranging a shuttle transfer from the airport to your hotel before traveling to France.

When deciding where to lodge, keep in mind whether you will take commercial day trips and where those depart from.

- Paris CityVision (Gray Line) tours depart from near the Louvre. Their office is at 2 rue des Pyramides, just north of the NW corner of the Louvre, just north of the rue de Rivoli.
- France Tourisme Paris tours also depart from near the Louvre. Their office is across the street from the NE corner of the Louvre, just south of the Rue de Rivoli, at 6 rue de l'Amiral de Coligny.
- Paris Tours Service small-group tours offer hotel pickup and drop-off as part of their fee.
- Private tours include hotel pickup and drop-off.

Hotel price ranges are based on late 2019 TripAdvisor averages. Your own quotes may be higher or lower.

Louvre area

If you plan to take day trips from either Paris CityVision (Gray Line) or France Tourisme Paris, you would do well to lodge around the Louvre. Today the world's largest and most famous art museum, the Louvre used to be a royal palace. (Louis XIV lived there until he moved to Versailles.) On the right bank (the north side) of the Seine, it is "higher class" than the sometimes rowdy Latin Quarter that is recommended below.

The Big Bus Hop-On/Hop-Off Tours stop on the south side of the Louvre, by the Pont des Arts (bridge) and also at the Big Bus Information Centre at 11 Avenue de l'Opera (a few streets north of the Place du Carrousel). The Open Tour Hop-On/Hop-Off buses stop in the Louvre courtyard, by the Place du Carrousel. Open Tour also stops at the Place de la Concorde (at the other end of the Tuileries), and *both* bus companies have stops across the river near the Musée d'Orsay.

Hotels in the area include the following:

Grand Hotel du Palais Royal—4 rue de Valois (www.grandhoteldu palaisroyal.com). TripAdvisor's Traveler's Choice Award (top 1% in category) and Certificate of Excellence. Location: about 2 street north of the Louvre. Pros: free WiFi, good breakfast buffet, air conditioning, non-smoking hotel, restaurant, room service, bar/lounge, wheelchair access, facilities for disabled guests, airport shuttle available, fitness center, twin/triple/quad rooms. Cons: price, no singles, no price break for singles, breakfast overpriced according to reviewers. (TripAdvisor price range for standard room: $408-$849.)

Distances: Council of State (0 miles), Louvre (.2 miles), Palais Royal Métro (.2 miles), Opéra Garnier (.7 miles), Notre Dame (.9 miles), Arc de Triomphe (2.1 miles)

Hotel Relais du Louvre—19 rue des Pretres St-Germain l'Auxerrois (www.relaisdulouvre.com/?lang=en). TripAdvisor's Certificate of Excellence. Location: just east of the Louvre. Pros: free WiFi, air conditioning, non-smoking hotel, airport shuttle available, good breakfast, room service, elevator, single/twin/triple/quad rooms available, facilities for disabled guests. Cons: small rooms, small elevator, small bathrooms, limited views, limited number of rooms. (TripAdvisor price range for standard room: $174-$443.)

Distances: Saint-Germain l'Auxerrois Church (0 miles), Pont Neuf Métro Station (.1 miles), Pont Neuf (.1 miles), Rue de Rivoli (.2 miles), Louvre (.2 miles), Notre Dame (.6 miles), Opéra Garnier (1 mile), Arc de Triomphe (2.3 miles)

La Clef Louvre—8 rue Richelieu. TripAdvisor's Traveler's Choice Award (top 1% of category) and Certificate of Excellence. Location: north of the Pyramide du Louvre opposite the Comedie Francaise. Pros: free WiFi, breakfast buffet, air conditioning, non-smoking hotel, room service, bar/lounge, airport shuttle available, fitness center, microwave, refrigerator, wheelchair access, facilities for disabled guests, elevator. Cons: price, only doubles and triples available, no price break for singles. (TripAdvisor price range for standard room: $376-$685.)

Distances: Comedie Francaise (.1 miles), Pyramides Métro Station (.2 miles), Palais Royal Métro (.2 miles), Louvre (.2 miles), Opéra Garnier (.6 miles), Notre Dame (1 mile), Arc de Triomphe (2 miles)

Hotel Brighton—Esprit de France—218 rue de Rivoli. Trip Advisor's Certificate of Excellence. Location: across the street from the Louvre gardens (Tuileries). Pros: free WiFi, good breakfast buffet, air conditioning, non-smoking hotel, room service, bar/lounge, suites available, wheelchair access, facilities for disabled guests, airport shuttle available, single/twin/triple/quad rooms available. Cons: air conditioning can be weak, small breakfast room, some décor quite worn, small lift can be slow, outside noise from Tuileries and street, no restaurant, limited bar. (TripAdvisor price range for standard room: $222-$547.)

Distances: Tuileries Métro Station (.1 miles), Tuileries Garden (.1 miles), Musée de l'Orangerie (.2 miles), Louvre (.5 miles), Opéra Garnier (1 mile), Notre Dame Cathedral (1.2 miles), Arc de Triomphe (1.7 miles)

Best Western Premier Ducs de Bourgogne—19 rue de Pont Neuf. TripAdvisor Certificate of Excellence. Location: east of the Louvre, north of Pont Neuf. Pros: breakfast buffet, air conditioning, non-smoking hotel, free WiFi, room service, airport shuttle available, elevator, facilities for disabled guests. Cons: no single/triple/quad rooms, no price break for singles, high pillows, hotel sign hard to see, small rooms. (TripAdvisor price range for standard room: $201-$550.)

Distances: Rue de Rivoli (.1 miles), Pont Neuf Métro Station (.1 miles), Pont Neuf (.2 miles), Louvre (.3 miles), Notre Dame (.5 miles), Opéra Garnier (1 mile), Arc de Triomphe (2.4 miles)

Hotel Le Pradey—5 rue Saint Roch (www.lepradey.com/en/). TripAdvisor's Certificate of Excellence. Location: north of the Tuileries near the Place du Carrousel. Pros: free WiFi, good breakfast buffet, air conditioning, non-smoking hotel, room service, airport shuttle available, wheelchair access, elevator, family rooms available. Cons: no single rooms, no price break for singles, expensive breakfast. (TripAdvisor price range for standard room: $210-$573.)

Distances: Tuileries Métro Station (.1 miles), Musée de l'Orangerie (.1 miles), Pyramides Métro Station (.2 miles), Louvre (.4 miles), Opéra Garnier (.5 miles), Notre Dame (1.1 miles), Arc de Triomphe (1.8 miles)

Hotel Therese—5 rue Therese (www.hoteltherese.com/). TripAdvisor's Certificate of Excellence. Location: north of Place du Carrousel by the Louvre. Pros: free WiFi, good breakfast buffet, air conditioning, non-smoking hotel, bar/lounge, room service, facilities for disabled guests, elevator, airport shuttle available, twin beds available. Cons: no single/triple/quad rooms, no price break for singles, small rooms, small bathrooms, expensive breakfast. (TripAdvisor price range for standard room: $186-$456.)

Distances: Palais Royal Theatre (.1 miles), Pyramides Métro Station (.1 miles), Palais Royal Métro (.1 miles), Louvre (.4 miles), Opéra Garnier (.5 miles), Notre Dame (1.1 miles), Arc de Triomphe (1.9 miles)

Hotel Crayon Rouge by Elegancia—42 rue Croix des PetitsChamps (hotelcrayonrouge.com/en/). TripAdvisor's Certificate of Excellence.

Location: 3 streets north of the Louvre. Pros: free WiFi, good breakfast buffet, air conditioning, non-smoking hotel, bar/lounge, airport shuttle available, wheelchair access, facilities for disabled guests, single/twin/adjacent rooms available. Cons: small rooms, small number of rooms. (TripAdvisor' price range for standard room: $154-$428.)

Distances: Bank of France (.1 miles), Place des Victoires (.1 miles), Palais Royal Métro (.1 miles), Louvre (.3 miles), Opéra Garnier (.7 miles), Notre Dame (.9 mile), Arc de Triomphe (2.2 miles)

Hotel de la Place du Louvre—Esprit de France—21 rue des Pretres St Germain l'Auxerrois (www.paris-hotel-place-du-louvre.com). Trip Advisor's Certificate of Excellence. Location: just east of the Louvre. Pros: free WiFi, good breakfast buffet, air conditioning, non-smoking hotel, wheelchair access, elevator, twins available. Cons: no single/triple/quad rooms, no price break for singles, no restaurant, non-refundable rooms on 3rd-person sites, small number of rooms. (Trip Advisor price range for standard room: $176-$322.)

Distances: Pont Neuf Métro Station (.1 miles), Pont Neuf (.1 miles), Rue de Rivoli (.2 miles), Louvre (.2 miles), Seine River (.1 miles), Notre Dame (.6 miles), Opéra Garnier (1 mile), Arc de Triomphe (2.3 miles)

Hotel Odyssey by Elegancia—19 rue Herold (hotelodysseyparis.com/en/). TripAdvisor's Certificate of Excellence. Location: north of the Louvre and east of the Banque de France. Pros: free WiFi, good breakfast buffet, air conditioning, non-smoking hotel, bar/lounge, airport shuttle available, elevator, adjacent rooms available. Cons: no single rooms, no real price break for singles, small rooms, adjacent rooms not interconnecting, small bathrooms. (TripAdvisor price range for standard room: $137-$316.)

Distances: Place des Victoires (.1 miles), Palais Royal Métro (.2 miles), Louvre (.4 miles), Opéra Garnier (.7 miles), Notre Dame (.9 miles), Arc de Triomphe (2.2 miles)

Hotel Louvre Sainte Anne—32 rue Sainte Anne. TripAdvisor's Certificate of Excellence. Location: .4 miles north of the Louvre. Pros: free WiFi, parking, breakfast buffet, air conditioning, non-smoking hotel, wheelchair access, facilities for disabled guests, airport shuttle available Cons: no restaurant, no bar/lounge, small number of rooms. (TripAdvisor price range for standard room: $164-$226.)

Distances: Pyramides Métro Station (.1 miles), Monoprix supermarket (.1 miles), Louvre (.4 miles), Opéra Garnier (.4 miles), Notre Dame (1.1 miles), Arc de Triomphe (1.9 miles)

Hotel Crayon by Elegancia—25 rue du Bouloi (hotelcrayon.com). Trip Advisor's Certificate of Excellence. Location: .3 miles north of the Louvre. Pros: free WiFi, buffet breakfast, air conditioning, non-smoking hotel, airport shuttle available, bar/lounge, single/triple/quads available (as adjacent rooms), elevator. Cons: small rooms, no real price break for singles, elevator doesn't reach all floors, common to have poor lighting/lights not working, some reviewers question cleanliness, meager breakfast, limited number of rooms. (Trip Advisor price range for standard room: $125-$401.)

Distances: Place des Victoires (.2 miles), Rue de Rivoli (.2 miles), Palais Royal Métro (.2 miles), Chatelet-Les Halles RER station (.2 miles), Louvre (.3 miles), Opéra Garnier (.7 miles), Notre Dame (.8 miles), Arc de Triomphe (2.2 miles)

L'Empire Paris—48 rue de l'Arbe Sec (www.lempire-paris.com/en/). TripAdvisor's Certificate of Excellence. Location: just east of the Louvre. Pros: free WiFi, breakfast buffet, air conditioning, non-smoking hotel, restaurant, bar, room service, wheelchair access, facilities for disabled guests, airport shuttle available, spa, twin/king/triple/quad rooms available. Cons: no singles, no price break for singles. (TripAdvisor price range for standard room: $213-$567.)

Distances: Rue de Rivoli (.1 miles), Saint-Germain l'Auxer-rois Church (.1 miles), Pont Neuf Métro Station (.1 miles), Chatelet-Les Halles RER Station (.2 miles), Pont Neuf (.2 miles), Louvre (.2 miles), Notre Dame (.6 miles), Opéra Garnier (.9 miles), Arc de Triomphe (2.3 miles)

Best Western Premier Louvre Saint Honore—141 rue St Honore (bestwesternpremier-louvresainthonore.com). Location: just northeast of the Louvre. Pros: breakfast buffet, air conditioning, non-smoking hotel, free WiFi, room service, bar/lounge, wheelchair access, facilities for disabled guests, refrigerator, airport shuttle available, twins available, up to quad on fold-out available. Cons: no singles, no real price break for singles, standard rooms very small, small elevator, no restaurant, some upkeep wanting. (TripAdvisor price range for standard room: $168-$368.)

Distances: Oratoire du Louvre Protestant Church (0 miles), Rue de Rivoli (.1 miles), Saint-Germain l'Auxerrois Church (.2 miles), Louvre (.2 miles), Notre Dame (.7 miles), Opéra Garnier (.8 miles), Arc de Trimphe (2.2 miles)

Latin Quarter

Just south of the Isle de la Cité—where the city of Paris was born in the middle of the Seine River—is the Latin Quarter. Long populated by students (from the days when Latin was the language of scholarship, thus the name "Latin Quarter"), today there are still lots of students and other young people in the area, making it vibrant and lively, but sometimes raucous and noisy. The Latin Quarter bursts with bistros and nightlife, and some quieter districts in the city can seem stodgy in comparison.

This area does not have the easy access to day trip departures that the area around the Louvre does, but it has excellent connections on the métro and RER systems. One easy way to reach the neighborhood from either Charles de Gaulle airport or Orly airport is to take the Blue RER train straight to the St. Michel stop. It could hardly be easier. Just be prepared to carry or pull your luggage from the underground station to your hotel, which could be a bit of a hike.

For day trips, you could choose ones that include hotel pickup and drop-off, or you may prefer to take public transportation to the departure point. Bus lines 27 and 21, for example, may get you to the Louvre in short order.

Hotels in the area include the following:

Hotel Parc St. Severin-Esprit de France—22 rue de la Parcheminerie (www.paris-hotel-parcsaintseverin.com/en). TripAdvisor's Certificate of Excellence. Location: around the corner from St. Severin Church, SW of Notre Dame. Pros: free WiFi, breakfast buffet, air conditioning, non-smoking hotel, room service, elevator. Cons: elevator very small, small rooms, some street noise, WiFi is inconsistent, small number of rooms. (TripAdvisor price range for standard room: $185-$307.)

Distances: Cluny Museum (.2 miles), Cluny-La Sorbonne Métro Station (.2 miles), Notre Dame (.3 miles), Sorbonne University (.3 miles), Ste-Chapelle (.3 miles), Saint-Michel – Notre-Dame RER Station (.15 miles), Opéra Garnier (1.8 miles), Arc de Triomphe (3 miles)

Hotel Albe Saint Michel—1 rue de la Harpe (www.hotelalbestmichel.com/en/). TripAdvisor's Certificate of Excellence. Location: Place Saint-Michel. Pros: free WiFi, breakfast buffet, air conditioning, non-smoking hotel, elevator, facilities for disabled guests, single/twin/triple rooms available. Cons: small rooms, street noise, narrow corridors. (TripAdvisor price range for standard room: $159-$282.)

Distances: Saint-Michel Place (0 miles), Saint-Michel – Notre-Dame RER Station (0 miles), Saint-Michel Métro Station (.1 miles), Cluny-La

Sorbonne Métro Station (.1 miles), Seine River (.1 miles), Sainte Chapelle (.2 miles), Cite Métro Station (.2 miles), Cluny Museum (.2 miles), Conciergerie (.2 miles), Notre Dame (.2 miles), Louvre (.6 miles), Arc de Triomphe (2.7 miles)

Hotel du College de France—7 rue Thenard (www.hotel-collegedefrance.com/en/). TripAdvisor's Certificate of Excellence. Location: just north of the Sorbonne. Pros: breakfast buffet, non-smoking hotel, free WiFi, private balcony available, elevator, twin rooms available, airport shuttle available. Cons: no single/triple/quad rooms, no price break for singles, no air conditioning, a little farther away from Notre Dame than other hotels listed here, small number of rooms. (TripAdvisor price range for standard room: $128-$216.)

Distances: Sorbonne University (.1 miles), Maubert-Mutualité Métro Station (.1 miles), Cluny Museum (.1 miles), Saint-Michel–Notre-Dame RER Station (.3 miles), Saint-Michel Place (.3 miles), Notre Dame (.3 miles), Louvre (.8 miles), Opéra Garnier (1.7 miles), Arc de Triomphe (2.8 miles)

Hotel du Levant—18 rue de la Harpe (www.hoteldulevant.com/en/). TripAdvisor's Certificate of Excellence. Location: southwest of Notre Dame, between Place St. Michel and Cluny-Sorbonne métro stop. Pros: free WiFi, good breakfast included, air conditioning, facilities for disabled guests, elevator, single/twin/triple/quad/adjoining rooms available. Cons: small elevator, some street noise, small rooms, not a non-smoking hotel. (TripAdvisor price range for standard room: $187-$362.)

Distances: Saint-Michel Place (.1 miles), Cluny-La Sorbonne Métro Station (.1 miles), Saint-Michel – Notre-Dame RER Station (.1 miles), Saint-Michel Métro Station (.1 miles), Cluny Museum (.1 miles), Sorbonne University (.2 miles), Sainte Chapelle (.2 miles), Notre Dame (.2 miles), Louvre (.7 miles), Opéra Garnier (1.5 miles), Arc de Triomphe (2.7 miles)

Hotel Europe Saint Severin—38 rue Saint Severin (www.hoteleurope.net/en/). TripAdvisor's Certificate of Excellence. Location: SW of Notre Dame, between Place St-Michel and Saint Severin church. Pros: free WiFi, good breakfast buffet, air conditioning, non-smoking hotel, restaurant, bar/lounge, elevator, refrigerator, airport shuttle available, single/double/triple rooms available. Cons: small rooms, small bathrooms, street noise. (TripAdvisor price range for standard room: $132-$453.)

Distances: Saint-Michel Place (.1 miles), Saint-Michel Métro Station (.1 miles), Saint-Michel – Notre-Dame RER Station (.1 miles), Seine River (.1 miles), Cluny Museum (.2 miles), Odeon Métro Station (.2 miles), Saint Chapelle (.2 miles), Sorbonne University (.2 miles), Cité Métro Station (.2

miles), Notre Dame (.2 miles), Louvre (.6 miles), Arc de Triomphe (2.7 miles)

Hotel Henri IV Rive Gauche—9 rue Saint Jacques (/henri-paris-hotel.com/en/). TripAdvisor's Certificate of Excellence. Location: SW of Notre Dame, across from St. Severin Church. Pros: free WiFi, breakfast buffet, air conditioning, non-smoking hotel, room service, elevator, some rooms with handicapped and wheelchair access, many decent-sized rooms for central Paris, airport shuttle available, single/twin/triple rooms available. Cons: street noise, no bar/lounge, small number of rooms. (TripAdvisor price range for standard room: $177-$293.)

Distances: Cluny-La Sorbonne Métro Station (.1 miles), Saint-Michel – Notre-Dame RER Station (.1 miles), Maubert-Mutualité Métro Station (.1 miles), Saint-Michel Place (.1 miles), Cluny Museum (.2 miles), Notre Dame Cathedral (.2 miles), Sorbonne University (.2 miles), Cité Métro Station (.2 miles), Seine River (.1 miles), Louvre (.7 miles), Opéra Garnier (1.6 miles), Arc de Triomphe (2.9 miles)

Hotel le Notre Dame—1 quai Saint-Michel (hotelnotredameparis.com/en/). TripAdvisor's Certificate of Excellence. Location: across the Seine from Notre Dame Cathedral. Pros: free WiFi, air conditioning, non-smoking hotel, bar/lounge, breakfast available, airport shuttle available, elevator. Cons: some stairs at entrance of the property, only doubles, no price break for singles, small number of rooms. (TripAdvisor price range for standard room: $185-$316.)

Distances: Saint-Michel/Notre-Dame RER Station (0 miles), Saint-Michel Place (.1 miles), Saint-Michel Métro Station (.1 miles), Notre Dame (.1 miles), Cité Métro Station (.1 miles), Sainte Chapelle (.2 miles), Conciergerie (.2 miles), Seine River (0 miles), Louvre (.7 miles), Arc de Triomphe (2.7 miles)

Best Western Jardin de Cluny—9 rue du Sommerard. TripAdvisor's Certificate of Excellence. Location: just north of the Sorbonne. Pros: free WiFi, good breakfast buffet, air conditioning, non-smoking hotel, elevator, king/twin rooms available, airport shuttle available. Cons: no single/triple/quad rooms, little price break for singles, some hotel noise, a little farther away from Notre Dame than other hotels listed here. (TripAdvisor price range for standard room: $149-$321.)

Distances: Sorbonne University (.1 miles), Maubert-Mutualité Métro Station (.1 miles), Cluny-La Sorbonne Métro Station (.1 miles), Cluny Museum (.1 miles), Saint-Michel – Notre-Dame RER Station (.3 miles), Notre Dame (.3 miles), Saint-Michel Place (.3 miles), Seine River (.3

miles), Louvre (.9 miles), Opéra Garnier (1.7 miles), Arc de Triomphe (2.9 miles)

Les Rives de Notre Dame—15 quai Saint Michel (www.rivesdenotre dame.com/). TripAdvisor's Certificate of Excellence. Location: along Seine River across from Notre Dame. Pros: free WiFi, breakfast buffet, air conditioning, non-smoking hotel, room service, airport shuttle available, twin/triple rooms available. Cons: no real price break for singles, small elevator, only 10 rooms, street noise. (TripAdvisor price range for standard room: $230-$549.)

Distance: Seine River (0 miles), Saint-Michel – Notre-Dame RER Station (0 miles), Saint-Michel Place (.1 miles), Saint-Michel Métro Station (.1 miles), Cité Métro Station (.1 miles), Sainte Chapelle (.2 miles), Cluny-La Sorbonne Métro Station (.2 miles), Notre Dame Cathedral (.2 miles), Conciergerie (.2 miles), Cluny Museum (.2 miles), Louvre (.6 miles), Opéra Garnier (1.5 miles), Arc de Triomphe (2.7 miles)

Melia Paris Notre-Dame—7 rue de l'Hotel Colbert. TripAdvisor's Certificate of Excellence. Location: south of Notre Dame, close to river. Pros: free WiFi, good breakfast buffet, air conditioning, non-smoking hotel, room service, bar/lounge, elevator, twin/triple/quad rooms available. Cons: no single rooms, no real price break for singles, worn rooms/décor, problems with AC, some street noise. (TripAdvisor price range for standard room: $199-$473.)

Distances: Notre Dame (.1 miles), Seine River (.1 miles), Maubert-Mutualité Métro Station (.1 miles), Saint-Michel – Notre-Dame RER Station (.2 miles), Cluny-La Sorbonne Métro Station (.2 miles), Cluny Museum (.2 miles), Sorbonne University (.2 miles), Saint-Michel Place (.2 miles), Louvre (.8 miles), Opéra Garnier (1.6 miles), Arc de Triomphe (2.9 miles)

Hotel Royal Saint Michel—3 boulevard Saint Michel. TripAdvisor's Certificate of Excellence. Location: Place St-Michel. Pros: free WiFi, breakfast buffet, air conditioning, non-smoking hotel, elevator, single/twin/triple rooms available, airport shuttle available. Cons: small elevator, some rooms very small, limited breakfast for price. (TripAdvisor price range for standard room: $171-$339.)

Distances: Saint-Michel Place (0 miles), Saint-Michel Métro Station (.1 miles), Cluny-La Sorbonne Métro Station (.1 miles), Odéon Métro Station (.2 miles), Cluny Museum (.2 miles), Saint Chapelle (.2 miles), Cité Métro Station (.2 miles), Sorbonne University (.2 miles), Notre Dame (.3 miles), Louvre (.6 miles), Opéra Garnier (1.4 miles), Arc de Triomphe (2.7 miles)

Other base cities in France

France is a large country, and it's not really possible to see most of it from Paris. If you want to base in other areas, the city of Toulouse, in southwest France, has a hop-on/hop-off minibus and bus tour companies that lead excursions into the countryside. Additionally, Marseille and Nice along the Mediterranean in the southeast of the country, Bordeaux in the west, as well as Lyon in the southeast, also offer hop-on/hop-off bus tours and some day trip possibilities.

Madrid

Overview

Madrid is the capital and largest city of Spain, up on the central plateau of the country. It has the highest elevation of any European capital and is surrounded by arid but fertile land, including the fabled *la Mancha*, as in "Man of." With a population of 3.3 million, in Europe only London and Berlin have more people. Spain is a constitutional monarchy (as England is), and its government and monarchy are based in Madrid. The current monarch is King Felipe VI, in a mostly ceremonial position.

After occupation by various prehistoric tribes, the first recorded settlers of Madrid were Muslims. Christians conquered the city in 1085, after which Muslims, Christians, and Jews lived together and all contributed to the culture. Moorish influences are still seen in architecture, food, and language throughout Spain. (Look for horseshoe-shaped arches, for example.)

Today's Madrid celebrates two world-class soccer teams, Real Madrid and Atlético de Madrid. In the city, you can find many instances of traditional Spanish culture—flamenco, paella, Iberian ham, tapas, wine, bullfighting, and world-class art, including that housed in the Prado, one of the most important museums in the world.

Winters in Madrid are somewhat cold (January and December highs are around 50 degrees with lows around 37 degrees) and summers are hot, typically in the upper 80s, but highs can break 100 degrees Fahrenheit. Precipitation is low throughout the year.

The official Madrid tourism site is www.esmadrid.com/en and can be a good resource as you plan your trip.

Possible plan for Madrid (What I'd do)

If I were traveling to Madrid with my mother, this is what I would plan for us to do. Obviously, you may prefer to do something different, but you may find this itinerary handy as a starting point, changing it as much as you'd like. (And it will make more sense as you work your way through the chapter. Having a city map at hand will help, too.) **Please double check any details before relying on them, as specifics may have changed since I wrote these pages.**

Be aware that many sights in Madrid are closed on Mondays or Tuesdays. Arriving in Madrid on a Monday, Tuesday or Wednesday allows for the use of this sample itinerary with minimal or no modification. If you change the order of days, keep these points in mind:

- Keep the 2 days of HOHO bus access consecutive.
- Do not plan to visit Madrid sights (whether included on this itinerary or not) without checking to see whether they are closed any days during the week.

As for day trips, you probably don't want to plan for more than two consecutive out-of-town excursions at a time, to avoid bus fatigue.

This plan assumes lodging near the palace complex but could easily be modified for the Prado area or elsewhere.

Day 1—Depart U.S.

Day 2—Arrive Madrid. Find an ATM and withdraw euros, if needed. Take a pre-ordered private shuttle to the hotel. Check in or store luggage until check-in time. Rest and freshen up, if room is available. Scout out the neighborhood offerings. Find a local grocery store. If you are up to it, take an old-city walking tour, stopping as desired. Check out Plaza Mayor. Visit Tourist Information there. (Buy HOHO bus ticket?) Pick up any pre-ordered tickets. Stop for coffee and a snack. If you have time and energy, tour the Royal Palace (open daily until 8 p.m. in the high season). Rest before dinner, then go out to eat. (Or eat in.)

Day 3—(*Do not plan this day for a Monday.*) Start a 48-hour HOHO bus ticket (can be bought on the bus, online ahead of time—must print out voucher—or at tourist information offices). Take Route 1 bus (from, for example, the Teatro Real stop) and ride to the Museo Thyssen stop. Pick up a pre-ordered museum pass (Paseo del Arte) at the Thyssen-Bornemisza Museum at Paseo del Prado 8 or at the Prado (depending on where ordered). Visit the Prado Museum (fast-track entry with Paseo del Arte, open 10-7 or -8 daily). Grab lunch or snack. Visit Museo Thyssen-Bornemisza (fast-track entry, open 10-7/later in summer, closed Mondays).

If enough time, energy and interest, walk to the Parque del Buen Retiro and wander around. To return to hotel area after the

Thyssen-Bornemisza Museum, return to HOHO stop at Museo Thyssen. To return to hotel area after the park, walk to the Puerta de Alcalá stop on Route 1. (High-season HOHO hours: 9 a.m.-10 p.m.) Return to hotel. Relax in room. Dinner out or pick up food at a grocery store or take-out stand.

Day 4—(*Do not plan this day for a Monday or Tuesday.*) Take the HOHO bus Route 1 (possibly from Teatro Real stop) and ride to the Museo Reina Sofía stop. Fast-track entry to Reina Sofía (10-9, -7 on Sundays, closed Tuesdays). Visit the botanical garden at Atocha train station. Snack break at museum or train station.

Take HOHO bus from Reina Sofía to the Prado stop (or walk there). Switch to Route 2 at Plaza de Neptuno. Ride HOHO bus on Route 2 to Museo Arqueológico to visit (9:30-8, Sundays 9:30-3, closed Mondays).

If time, if interested, and if didn't do before, visit Parque del Buen Retiro (HOHO Route 2 to Puerta de Alcalá—or just walk). To finish Route 2 tour/commentary, ride to Plaza de Neptuno stop and switch to Route 1 to return back to hotel area. Return to hotel. Dinner.

Day 5—(*Do not plan this day for a Monday.*) Day trip: Toledo full day. **Comfort upgrade** (if within budget): semi-private or private tour.

Day 6—(*Do not plan this day for a Monday.*) Visit Royal Palace early in morning to beat crowds, if not already visited on arrival day (daily 10-8). Visit Monasterio de las Descalzas Reales (book in advance to ensure access) (10-2, 4-6:30; Sundays 10-3; closed Mondays).

Visit Madrid's huge department store, El Corte Inglés by the Puerta del Sol (Mon.-Sat. 10-22, Sun. 11-21). Special evening event: a flamenco show and dinner, e.g., Tablao Flamenco las Carboneras or Corral de la Morería (prebook).

Day 7—Day trip: El Escorial, Valley of the Fallen. **Comfort upgrade** (if within budget): private tour.

Day 8—Day trip: Avila and Segovia. **Comfort upgrade** (if within budget): semi-private or private tour.

Day 9—Return to U.S. Use prebooked private airport transfer (or other) to get to the airport.

Arrival

Barajas Airport (MAD) is the main airport serving Madrid, 7½ miles northeast of the city center (www.aeropuertomadridbarajas.com/eng/

home.html). To get from MAD to the city, you have your choice of airport transfer (specialized taxi service), Airport Express bus, metro, taxi, or a chauffeur service.

Airport transfers (a specialized taxi service) are available for airport pickup for up to four passengers. An English-speaking driver will take you to your destination in an air-conditioned sedan for a flat fee of €35, which includes all taxes, tolls, and gratuity. The GoMadrid city visitor Web site recommends this option over regular taxis and for all arrivals except those on a shoestring budget. Reservations can be made at www.gomadrid.com/aerocity/. A somewhat pricier service offered through the airport Web site lets you choose round-trip ("Return") transfers or separate private transfers "from" and "to" the airport at www.aeropuerto madrid-barajas.com/transportation/transfers-madrid-airport.htm.

The **Exprés Aeropuerto (Airport Express) bus** runs 24-hours and has three city stops after its three airport stops (Terminals 1, 2, and 4)—O'Donnell (east of Parque del Buen Retiro), Plaza de Cibeles (west of Parque del Buen Retiro at Paseo del Prado), and Atocha railway station (just southwest of Parque del Buen Retiro). The ride into the city takes about 40 minutes and costs €5 (tickets may be bought on board). Buses leave approximately every 15 minutes during the day and every 35 minutes at night (www.gomadrid.com/transport/Airport-Express.png).

The **metro** system has stops in Terminals 2 and 4 at the airport, giving access to line 8, which in about 12 minutes runs to the Nuevos Ministerios metro station, where connections to lines 6 and 10 are available. (Access to lines 4 and 9 is available en route.) Metro rides to or from the airport cost €5 and include an extra airport charge. (If you buy a Metro Tourist Travel Pass—www.gomadrid.com/transport/travel-pass.html—it includes all fees to and from the airport.) Trains depart every 5 minutes from 6 a.m. to 2 a.m. Be aware that you are likely to have to switch metro trains a couple of times to get near your lodging in Madrid.

Traditional **taxis** from the airport to Madrid are available (although less recommended than the airport transfer taxis above). Walk outside the terminal to find official traffic ranks. (The drivers inside the terminal who offer rides are likely illegal and will probably rip you off.) Rates to central Madrid are fixed at €30. You can *prebook* a taxi to the city center and be met by a driver with your name on a sign for €35 (includes reservation fee) at this link: gomadrid.rgi.ticketbar.eu/en/ticketbar-madrid/taxi-madrid-airport---hotel-/. Most taxis can carry up to three passengers. Suitcases and bags are included in fees. You should request a receipt for the ride when it is complete, in case there is any problem with the fare.

If your budget allows it, you may choose to look at a luxury **chauffeur service**, Ares Mobils, where a driver will greet you at the airport and transport you in the greatest comfort to your destination (www.gomadrid.com /aerocity/mobile.html). Airport transfers start at €68 for the smallest car. Listed prices do not include the VAT tax. You may also arrange personal tours or transfers elsewhere with this company.

If you buy a **Madrid City Pass** (see under Sightseeing passes), one of the benefits is private transfer from the airport to the city (along with skip-the-line access to the Prado Museum, 24-hour access to a hop-on/ hop-off bus, and 20% off many tourist attractions). Learn more about the City Pass here: gomadrid.rgi.ticketbar.eu/en/ticketbar-madrid/madrid-city-pass/.

Easy transportation options

Once in the city, your probable transportation choices are metro, bus, and taxi. The metro system is extensive in and around Madrid (it connects with the suburban train service), but requires lots of walking (much of it underground), possibly stairs, and can be very hot. City buses can be easier to get to. Check Madrid travel information at www.esmadrid.com/en/ getting-around-madrid for help finding options riding public or private transportation.

One easy way to get around to the sights is to ride a hop-on/hop-off (HOHO) tourist bus. You purchase a 1-day or 2-day ticket and then may hop on and hop off the buses as much as you'd like in that time.

You may choose to take the whole HOHO tour to get an overview and then, on the second time around, hop off to see sights up close. Buses run year-round, though hours of operation and frequency vary by season. Prices are listed below, but check the company's Web site for the latest information.

Taxis, of course, may offer the most convenient within-city transportation of all, but you'll pay for that convenience. Still, you are on vacation, and if riding taxis fits your budget and enhances your experience, that may be the right choice for you. Information about Madrid taxis is provided below.

Hop-On/Hop-Off Tours

Madrid City Tour Bus (madrid.city-tour.com/en/tourist-bus-routes-madrid) offers two Madrid sightseeing routes on hop-on/hop-off double-decker buses with audio commentary and free WiFi on board. Buses are adapted for people with reduced mobility and can accommodate a wheelchair. As with other HOHO bus companies, many tourists have a wonderful experience sightseeing in this way, while others complain about over-full buses and disrupted schedules (often because of roadworks). Transfers between routes are possible at several places, such as the Puerta del Sol (south side), across from the Prado by the Starbucks, at Plaza de Cibeles, and at Puerta de Alcalá.

Route 1 covers Historical Madrid, departing from the Prado Museum, and lasts about 80 minutes for a full loop. Two versions of the route, the regular one and an extended one, run through central Madrid with 21-28 stops. The regular route covers the area from the Royal Palace to along Retiro Park, with the extended route reaching farther to the northwest, the west and the southwest. Route 1 runs from 9 a.m. to 10 p.m. in high season (March through October) and from 10 a.m. to 6 p.m. in low season (November through February). Buses leave approximately every 8-14 minutes, depending on season. The extended tour route runs once in the morning and once in the afternoon.

Route 2 covers Modern Madrid over 16-24 stops, starting at the Plaza de Neptuno near the Prado and stretching north to Santiago Bernabéu, and lasts about 60 minutes for the basic loop. The extended route runs to Plaza de Castilla in the north and to Casón del Buen Retiro in the south. Route 2 runs from 9 a.m. to 10 p.m. in high season (March through October) and from 10 a.m. to 6 p.m. in low season (November through February). Buses leave approximately every 9-15 minutes. The extended tour route runs once in the morning and once in the afternoon.

Madrid City Tour Bus also sells passes to tourist attractions, with entrance to 3 or 5 attractions. Buy your choice online and pick it up at Julia Travel office at 15 San Nicolas Street. (Take your receipt for pickup, and allow at least 24 hours for processing.) Supplementary fees may be required for some tours. Sightseeing cards are good for 7 calendar days after activation.

Bus tickets are valid on both routes for as much use as you want during the 1 or 2 days of a ticket's validity. Costs are as follows:

- 1 day, adult (16-64), €19.80-€22
- 1 day, junior (7-15)/seniors (65+), €9-€10
- 1 day, child (0-6), €0
- 1 day, family (2 adults, 2 juniors), €49.50-€55
- 2 days, adult, €23.40-€26
- 2 days, junior/senior, €11.70-€13

- 2 days, child, €0
- 3-attractions tourist pass, adult (14+), €74-€78
- 3-attractions tourist pass, junior (4-13), €55-€58
- 5-attractions tourist pass, adult, €122-€128
- 5-attractions tourist pass, junior, €95-€100

Bus tickets can be bought at the company information center at Felipe IV (between the Prado Museum and the Ritz Hotel), through the Web site, at tourist information offices, through a company app, or, most easily, on the bus itself. If you pre-purchase a ticket, make sure you print out your voucher to turn in.

Taxis and ride services

If taking a taxi or arranging a private ride is your thing, you can certainly do so in Madrid. You can check a taxi fare finder such as www.taxifarefinder.com to get an estimate for how much a ride would cost. For example, taxi fare from the Royal Palace to the Prado Museum would range from €6.49 in low traffic to €31.79 in high traffic and would typically cost about €11.20, for a trip of about 2.4 miles. A typical Uber X fare for the same ride would be about €10. You can search on "Madrid taxi farefinder uber x" for one place to get Uber X fare estimates.

Taxis in Madrid are white with a diagonal red stripe on the front door. Cabs with a green light on top are available, and you raise your hand to hail one. You can also easily locate cabs at taxi ranks throughout the city—look for a blue sign with a white T on it. Taxi payment is generally in cash.

If you prefer to call for a cab, some Madrid cab calling services include the following:

- Radio Taxi de Madrid, +34 915 478 200
- Tele Taxi, +34 902 501 130

Be aware that the taxi meter starts running as soon as a cab leaves to pick you up. Your hotel desk may be able to provide useful information on the best taxi service for your area. To learn more about taxis in Madrid, look at a site such as www.esmadrid.com/en/madrid-taxi.

As of this writing, Uber X is legal in Madrid, but not the rest of Spain. Uber X drivers are licensed, so costs are comparable to taxi fares. Lyft is not available in most of Europe.

Other in-city transportation

Public transportation is excellent in Madrid, with bus, metro, and light rail (tram) systems across the city. Tram lines are in the outer neighborhoods, but tourists can easily avail themselves of the bus and metro systems.

The **metro** consists of 12 color-coded lines that stop at over 300 stations and run 6 a.m.-1:30 a.m. Line 8 connects to the airport and is particularly useful for visitors. (Find the metro map for tourists here: www.esmadrid.com/en/madrid-metro-tourist-map-pdf.)

Metro tickets cost €1.50-€2 for zones A and ML1, with rides to and from the airport costing €4.50-€5. Single-ride tickets can be purchased at vending machines. (Note that a single-ride ticket is available only for the day it is purchased on.) Run your ticket through the turnstile to enter the metro area, picking it up when it shoots back out. A 10-trip ticket that covers metro Zone A, EMT bus, and metrobus (zone ML1) costs €12.20. Metro fare can be loaded on a **Tarjeta Multi card** (a reloadable transit card that originally costs €2.50 at all metro and tram stations—make sure you select a machine that displays a red sticker stating, "Tarjeta MULTI disponible AQUI"). Metro fare can also be loaded on a Tourist Travel Pass/Tourist Ticket (see below). Make sure that you select "English" if you buy a ticket from a machine (unless you speak Spanish, in which case, good for you!). Many metro stations have lifts. The official metro map indicates stations that are accessible (www.esmadrid.com/en/madrid-metro-map).

Madrid's municipal **bus** company (EMT) offers more than 200 bus lines and over 2,000 buses that run on them. Most buses run 6 a.m.-11:30 p.m. during the week and 7 a.m.-11 p.m. on weekends and holidays. After regular service hours, night buses (called *búhos*—owls) run through the late night with line numbers preceded by an N. When riding a bus, you must request the stop you want by pressing one of the red "stop" buttons after you leave the previous stop. If you are waiting to ride a bus, you need to indicate to the approaching driver that you want to take that bus by waving or raising your hand. Buses have disabled access, heating, air conditioning, and WiFi access.

Bus tickets can be purchased on the bus, with a single ticket costing €1.50 in 2019. A 10-trip Bonobus (or Metrobus) ticket costs €12.20 and can be bought at many Bankia ATMs, tobacco shops, other retail points, and transportation interchange stations (Plaza de Castilla, Avenida de América, Plaza Elíptica, Príncipe Pío, and Moncloa). You can find an interactive bus map for Madrid here: www.esmadrid.com/en/bus-map-interactive (select English in the drop-down menu upper right). Even more useful (easier to use) is the Madrid tourist route map at www.esmadrid.com/en/madrid-bus-map. Between regular bus routes and night bus routes, buses run 24 hours a day.

A **Tourist Travel Pass** or **Tourist Ticket** allows unlimited travel on public transportation in the Region of Madrid. Passes may be purchased for 1, 2, 3, 4, 5, or 7 days of travel, with two choices for zone coverage (www.esmadrid.com/en/madrid-tourist-travel-pass).

Passes for Zone A cover the metro in the City of Madrid, blue EMT city buses (not the yellow airport express shuttle), metro light rail ML1, and Renfe Cercanías commuter trains covering zones 0 and A.

Passes for Zone T cover the entire Metro network, all blue city buses and the green intercity buses in the Region of Madrid (including to Toledo and Guadalajara, but not the airport express shuttle), all 8 zones (from A to E2), all Renfe Cercanias commuter trains covering zones 0, A, B1, B2, B3, C1, C2, and light rail lines ML1, ML2, ML3, and ML4. Zone T is recommended for people planning day trips to El Escorial, Aranjuez, or Alcalá de Henares.

Passes can be purchased most easily at metro stations (including at the airport) from ticket machines that display a red "Tarjeta MULTI Disponible AQUÍ" sticker, from light rail stations, and from tobacco shops and other authorized retailers.

Ticket prices are as follows (late 2019):

- Zone A, 1 day, adult, €8.40
- Zone A, 2 days, adult, €14.20
- Zone A, 3 days, adult, €18.40
- Zone A, 4 days, adult, €22.60
- Zone A, 5 days, adult, €26.80
- Zone A, 7 days, adult, €35.40
- Zone T, 1 day, adult, €17.00
- Zone T, 2 days, adult, €28.40
- Zone T, 3 days, adult, €35.40
- Zone T, 4 days, adult, €43
- Zone T, 5 days, adult, €50.80
- Zone T, 7 days, adult, €70.80

Children 11 and under have a 50% discount. Under 4s travel for free. Tickets are valid for calendar days from their first use, through 5 a.m. of the following morning.

When the Tourist Travel Pass expires, the card can be used to top up for use as a regular **Tarjeta Multi pass**. (Or you could buy a Tarjeta Multi card from the start for €2.50 and add money for transportation.)

Sightseeing passes

If you plan on sightseeing a lot in Madrid, you might want to consider some sort of sightseeing pass. As with any sightseeing pass, compare the costs of what you would actually see with the cost of the pass. It doesn't do much good to pay for access to 20 sights if you only have time to see 3. Available options include the following:

The simple **Art Walk Pass/Paseo del Arte ticket** allows access to three great (and very close) art museums: the Prado, the Reina Sofia Museum, and the Thyssen-Bornemisza Museum (www.esmadrid.com/en/tourist-passes). Passes are good for one year. Order online from any of the museums and then pick the pass up at that museum (e.g., at www.museodelprado.es/en/visit-the-museum, select "Buy your ticket" under "Tickets"). If you order elsewhere online, the Web site will tell you where to retrieve your ticket. The pass allows no-wait access to the three museums at a 20% discount over regular ticket price. The 2019 price was €30.40.

The **Madrid City Pass** offers 20% reduced museum entry, free fast-track entrance to the Prado, free fast-track entrance to the Royal Palace, 1-day access to a hop-on/hop-off tour bus, optional add-on transfer by private taxi from the airport to your hotel (a €30 value) *and* 3-day Tourist Travel Card for use on public transportation (citypasses.rgi.ticketbar.eu/en/ticketbar-madrid/madrid-city-pass/). Order online and your ticket will be emailed to you. (It's important to get your ticket before you need to travel from the airport to your hotel, since a taxi ride is included.) Be aware that the 20% discount code can only be used online. In late 2019, tickets without an airport transfer or the 3-day Tourist Travel Card cost €55.50 (€19 for child 5-17), with the travel options adding €49.50 (€15 for child). Passes are good for one year, so the longer you will be in Madrid, the more likely the Madrid City Pass will make sense financially.

Another option is a **City Pass**, also known as an **iVenture Card**, briefly mentioned in the hop-on/hop-off bus section above (madrid.citytour.com/en/iventure-card). As with other cards of this kind, you pay an amount up front for free or reduced-price access (save up to 40%) to 3 or 5 sights from a list of more than 20 attractions in and near Madrid. (A number of sights or experiences do require a supplement that is paid when you buy your pass and select your sights. See Web site for information about that.) The card is validated the first time it is used and is good for seven consecutive days.

Order your pass in advance and pick it up at the Julia Travel office at 15 San Nicolas Street (east of the royal palace complex). Allow at least 24 hours to process orders, and bring your receipt to get your pass. Some sights require advance booking; check the Web site to see which attractions that applies to. The passes allow at least some skip-the-line access. Prices are as follows (late 2019 costs):

- 3 sights, adult (14+) from €78, child (4-13) from €58
- 5 sights, adult (14+) from €128, child (4-13) from €100
- unlimited sights, adult from €255, child from €180

If you look over the sights and experiences covered by these passes, realize that they do not include everything you might want to see in Madrid (e.g., Reina Sofia Museum), that numerous items require supplementary payments, and you must pre-register for a number of activities. The pass may be just what you want to see Madrid and its surroundings at a reduced price, but you need to compare with individual entrance fees to determine that, and also weigh whether the additional complication is worth the cost savings.

Madrid Card—*As of this writing, the* **Madrid Card** *discussed next is "out of operation." The longer-term cards look like a reasonable option for seeing the sights in Madrid, however, so do check into its availability before moving on. Consider asking about them at tourist offices, if you haven't pre-ordered anything.*

The **Madrid Card** offers free access to more than 50 of the city's museums and monuments (including the Prado, the Royal Palace, the Reina Sofia Museum, and Thyssen-Bornemisza Museum).

- 24 hours, adult €47, child €34
- 48 hours, adult €60, child €42
- 72 hours, adult €67, child €44
- 120 hours, adult €77, child €47

When available, **Madrid Cards** can be bought online or in **tourist offices in the airport or Madrid.** The card is activated at first use.

Day trips

It's possible to see much of central Spain without having to leave the convenience of your base hotel at night, because Madrid has tourist companies that specialize in day trips.

As always, use the information here as a guide, but check each company's Web site for tour details and the most current price and schedule information. **Tour details—even which tours are offered—routinely change from season to season.** There is a lot of turnover in the Madrid day trip offerings. What I wrote about in May 2019 was no longer the same (or even existent) in November. These listings reflect those changes, but they may well change drastically again by the time you read this. If specific listings below seem to be off, you may want to check out a consolidator, such as one of the following, for current offerings:

- Viator—www.viator.com/Madrid-tours/Day-Trips-and-Excursions/d566-g5
- Gray Line—www.grayline.com/things-to-do/spain/madrid/)
- Get Your Guide—www.getyourguide.com/madrid-l46/day-trips-tc172/

Whichever tours you decide on, look over cancellation policies, if your plans aren't completely firm.

Browsing through Web sites will also help you decide which company's tours seem a good fit for you. Be aware that some specific tours might have special requirements or recommendations, so you'll want to look descriptions over closely before you show up at the departure point. Also be aware that the popular day-trip destination of Toledo is very hilly. That doesn't mean it can't be done, but realize that a visit there will be more tiring than a flat location and getting around will take more time. You may want to investigate tourist trains or buses in the plaza by the train station.

Tour companies differ on which entry fees and meals they include in their prices, so check those specifics (and confirm online), if your selection comes down to price.

Also take into account where the tours depart from. The current City Tour Madrid tours depart from the Plaza de Ramales (just east of the palace complex). Tours return to Plaza de Oriente (just east of the palace complex) or Plaza de España (north of the palace complex). The Yellow Tours leave from Plaza de España but may offer other options closer to your hotel. Ibe tours leave from Plaza las Ventas and the Neptune Fountain by the Prada. Amigo Tours leave from Plaza las Ventas (northeast of the Parque del Buen Retiro on metro lines 2 and 5).

Private and semi-private tours include hotel pickup and drop-off.

If you want to save your walking energy for the tour itself but you select a tour with a departure point that is not close to your hotel, you may want to invest in a taxi ride to get there.

City Tour Madrid

Although most familiar for providing the red hop-on/hop-off buses, City Tour Madrid offers a limited number of day trips out of Madrid (madrid.city-tour.com/en). The company appears to be a local Gray Line affiliate, with tours leaving from the Julia Travel Office at 15 San Nicolas Str. (at the corner of Plaza Ramales—east of the palace complex), and buses return to Plaza de España (north of the palace complex) or Plaza de Oriente (east of the palace complex). Print your voucher and give it to your guide at the start of the tour. Tours from City Tour Madrid include the following:

Avila and Segovia—Tour highlights include the Walls of Avila (entrance included), Convent of Santa Teresa (entrance included), the Roman aquaduct in Segovia, Cathedral of Segovia (entrance included), Alcazar of Segovia (entrance included). Depart 9 a.m. from Julia Travel office, return around 6 p.m. to Plaza de España. Adults €89 (16-66), children (6-15) €67, seniors (65+) €80.

Monastery of El Escorial and the Valley of the Fallen (Half Day)—Tour highlights include world heritage site the Royal Monastery of San Lorenzo El Real (entrance included), Valley of the Fallen Basilica excavated in the side of a mountain (entrance included). Depart 8:45 from Julia Travel office, return to Plaza de Oriente level -2 around 1:45. Adults (16-65) €58, children (6-15) €43, seniors (65+) €52.

Toledo City Tour (Full Day)—Full-day tour highlights include the 13th-century Toledo Cathedral (entrance included), the Santa Maria La Blanca Synagogue (entrance included), Saint Tome Church (entrance included), Monastery San Juan of the Kings (entrance included). Depart 9 a.m. from Julia Travel office. Duration: 8 hours. Return to Plaza de España (north of the palace complex). Adults (16-65) €77, children €58 (6-15), seniors €69 (65+).

Toledo City Tour (Half Day)—Half-day tour highlights include panoramic views over the city, varying city sites that include some of the following: Monastery San Juan of the Kings (afternoon), Mosque of El Cristo de la Luz (afternoon), home/museum of El Greco or Hospital Tavera Museum (morning), Convent of Santo Domingo el Antiguo (morning). Depart 8:45 a.m. for morning tour, 3 p.m. for afternoon tour from Julia Travel office. Duration: half day, 5 hours. Morning return to Plaza de Oriente level -2 (east of the palace complex); afternoon return to Plaza de España (north of the palace complex). Half-day adults €58, children (6-15) €43, seniors (65+) €52.

The Yellow Tours

The Yellow Tours (www.busvision.net/en/tour/toledo-the-tour-2/) offer highly rated 1.5-hour tours around Madrid in their double-decker yellow buses, as well as various excursions to Toledo, El Escorial, and Segovia. (10% discount for early purchase.) They also offer tickets to a Madrid flamenco show. Their day trips from Madrid include the following:

Toledo "The Tour"—Tour highlights include transportation, panoramic stops in Toledo, 1.5-hour guided walking tour of Toledo, Toledo Cathedral, Monastery San Juan of the Kings, the church of Santo Tomé or the Alcazar (entrance included), free time, free sangria. Daily. Depart 9 a.m. or 12 p.m. from Plaza de España (north of the palace complex), return up to 8 hours later. Adult €26.50, senior €25 (more than 65), child (7-15) €25.

Toledo Experience—Tour highlights include transportation, an expert local guide in Toledo (1.5-hour walking tour), stops at major monuments, Cathedral of Toledo, Jewish Quarter, free time for sightseeing, shopping, and eating, panoramic city tour for views. Daily. Depart Plaza de España (and possibly elsewhere) 9 a.m., 12 p.m. and 3 p.m., return up to 8 hours later. Adult €27, senior €25 (more than 65), child (7-15) €25.

Toledo Full-Day All-Inclusive Tour—Tour is basically the same as above, but including lunch and entrances to Cathedral of Toledo, Church of Santo Tome (tomb of the Count Orgaz), Synagogue of Santa María La Blanca, and Monastery of San Juan de Los Reyes. Daily. Departs 9 a.m. from Plaza de España, return up to 8 hours later. Adult €89, senior €80 (more than 65), child (7-15) €80.

Toledo Segovia Tour—Tour highlights include transportation, a guided walk around Toledo, walk along the wall with views of Tajo River, panoramic tour with best views of the city, guided tour of Segovia, Roman aqueduct, historic center, main square, Cathedral of Santa Maria, Jewish

Quarter, Alcazar de Segovia (entrance included). Daily. Departs 9 a.m. from Plaza de España, returns up to 10 hours later. Adult €62, senior €56 (more than 65), child (7-15) €56.

El Escorial and the Valley of the Fallen—Tour highlights include a ride to the Sierra de Guadarrama, the Valley of the Fallen Spanish Civil War monument (entrance included), free time for lunch (not included) at Escorial Monastery, palace, basilica, Pantheon of the Kings and Pantheon of the Infantes, Royal Library and Cloister of the Four Evangelists. Not Monday. Departs 11 a.m. from Plaza de España, returns up to 6 hours later. Adult €57, senior €52 (more than 65), child (7-15) €52.

Avila and Segovia Tour—Tour highlights include transportation, 1.5-hour walking tour of medieval Avila, free time in Avila, guided walking tour of Segovia, Roman aqueduct, Cathedral of Santa Maria, Alcazar de Segovia, free time. Daily. Departs 9 a.m. from Plaza de España, returns up to 10 hours later. Adult €49, senior €44.29 (more than 65), child (7-15) €44.29.

Segovia on Your Own—Tour highlights include transportation to and from Segovia, 1.5-hour guided walking tour of the city, then the rest of the time to explore on your own. Daily. Departs 9 a.m. from Plaza de España, returns up to 10 hours later. Adult €39, senior €35 (more than 65), child (7-15) €35.

Ibe Tours

Ibe Tours (www.ibetours.com) is based in Madrid and offers generally well-reviewed tours. Most tours depart from the Plaza Las Ventas, outside the Ventas metro station (metro lines 2 and 5 connect the central tourist area with here) and also from near the Neptune Fountain by the Prado. Ibe Tours also offers many in-Madrid experiences. Here are some of their excursions from Madrid. (Check online listings for variations on these tours.)

Toledo Express—Tour highlights include private bus transport to and from Toledo, self-guided exploration in Toledo (at your own speed). Not Sun/Tues/Wed. Depart 9 a.m. from Plaza las Ventas/9:30 from Neptune Fountain by the Prado. 9 hours. Adult €25, child €21.

Toledo Tour: 7 Monuments & Cathedral Tour—Tour highlights include travel to and from Toledo, entrance to 7 different buildings and monuments in the city (3 guided, 4 on own), exclusive guided tour of Toledo Cathedral, Church of Santo Tomé. Not Sun/Tues/Wed. Depart 9 a.m. from Plaza las Ventas/9:30 from Neptune Fountain by the Prado. 9 hours. Adult €58, child €46.

Toledo Tour: Wine and Tapas Tasting—Tour highlights include transportation to and from Toledo, free time to explore Toledo independently, wine and tapas tasting in Toledo. Not Sun/Tues/Wed. Depart 9 a.m. from Plaza las Ventas/9:30 from Neptune Fountain by the Prado. 9 hours. Adult €49, child €39.

Segovia and Toledo—Tour highlights include transportation, Segovia's historic old town, Roman aqueduct, Alcazar of Segovia (entry included), ancient Toledo, Cathedral of Toledo (entry included). Daily. Depart 7:30 a.m. from Plaza las Ventas/8 from Neptune Fountain by the Prado. 12 hours. Adult €70, child €59.

El Escorial in the Felipe II Train—Various tour options available. Depart 10:20 a.m. from Príncipe Pío Train Station, return on 6:24 p.m. train from El Escorial. Adult prices €25.30-€39.10.

Soria Guided Tour with Monuments—Tour highlights include transportation, exploration of the city of Soria with expert guide, lunch with Torrezno de Soria/coffee/pastries (included), guided tour inside the Archeological Site of Numancia, free time in Soria, Hermitage of San Saturio. Depart 8 a.m. from the Santiago Bernabeu Stadium. 12.5 hours. Adult (7-99) €69, child (3-6) €63.

Soria Guided Tour with Footbal Match—Tour highlights include transportation, exploration of the city of Soria with expert guide, lunch with Torrezno de Soria/coffee/pastries (included), guided tour inside the Archeological Site of Numancia, free time in Soria, football match at the Pajaritos stadium. Departure time varies depending on time of football match, from the Santiago Bernabeu Stadium. 12.5 hours. Adult (7-99) €95, child (3-6) €89.

Amigo Tours

Amigo Tours (amigotours.com.es/madrid/) is a well-reviewed tour company that has TripAdvisor's Certificate of Excellence. They have offices in several Spanish cities. Their day trips from Madrid leave from the Plaza las Ventas (northeast of Parque del Buen Retiro on metro lines 2 and 5) and include the following:

Full-Day Tour to Toledo and Segovia—Tour highlights include transportation, the Cathedral of Toledo, the Mirador del Valle, the Monastery of San Juan de los Reyes, the Bridge of San Martin, Segovia aqueduct, Alcazar of Sevogia (entrance included), Cathedral of Segovia, Azoguejo Square. Daily. Depart 7:45 from Plaza las Ventas, return 6:45 p.m. Adult €69, child €62.

Avila, Segovia and El Escorial—Tour highlights include transportation, Cathedral of Avila, Cathedral of Segovia, Segovia Aqueduct, Alcazar of Segovia, Monastery of El Escorial (entrance included). Tue/Fri. Depart 7:30 a.m. from Plaza las Ventas, return 6:30 p.m. Adult €86, child €77.

Full-Day Tour to Avila and Salamanca—Tour highlights include transportation, the Salamanca Cathedral (entrance included), free time in Salamanca, walls of Avila, Sanctum of San Vicente, Avila Cathedral (entrance included), free time in Avila. Wed/Sat. Depart 7:45 a.m. from Plaza las Ventas, return 6:45 p.m. Adult €79, child €71.

Toledo and El Greco Guided Tour with Optional Cathedral and Lunch—This tour is available in 4 versions. 1) Transport only, with independent exploration of Toledo. Adult (12+) €34, child (3-11) €30.60. 2) Transport and guided tour of Toledo. Adult €49, child €44.10. 3) Transport, guided tour, and tickets to 3 main monuments: Cathedral, Synogogue of Santa Maria la Blanca, Church of Santo Tome. Adult €69, child €62.10. 4) Transport, guided tour, tickets, and a traditional lunch. Adult €83, child €74.70. Wed/Fri. Depart 7:45. Duration: 7 hours.

Pepe Tours

Pepe Tours (pepetours.com/en/day-trip-excursions/day-trips-excursions-from-madrid) offers day trips from numerous cities in Spain, including Madrid. Not many reviews of the company are available, and the ones that are aren't consistent. Still, here is a list of tours they offer (as of November 2019), should you want to check them out:

Toledo Half-Day Trip—Daily. Depart 8:45 a.m. and 3 p.m. Adult €55, child (3-12) €41.

Toledo Full-Day Trip—Daily. Depart 9 a.m. Adult €72, child (3-12) €54.

Monastery El Escorial and the Valley of the Fallen—Half-day. Not Monday. Depart 8:45. Adult €69, child (3-12) €31.

Avila & Segovia—Daily. Depart 9 a.m. Adult €80, child (3-12) €60.

Aranuez—Half-day. Tue/Thu/Sat. Depart 3 p.m. Adult €47, child (3-12) €24.

Private and semi-private tours

Spain Day Tours

Spain Day Tours (www.spaindaytours.com/madrid_tours/) is based in Seville but offers a limited number of small tours in minibuses out of Madrid. Its tours garner sterling reviews, earning it TripAdvisor's Certificate of Excellence. Spain Day Tours offers hotel pickup and drop-off and an English-speaking guide. (They also offer a 4-hour tour of Madrid.) Prices are not listed on the Web site but must be requested along with availability for a particular date. Prices listed below are from late May 2019.

Toledo Tour (half day or full day)—Tour highlights include the viewpoint over the city of Toledo, the famous Cathedral, Church of St Tomé (with its famous masterpiece by El Greco); the Synagogue of Santa María la Blanca; the Museum of Victorio Macho; the Monastery of San Juan de los Reyes, and much more. Toledo is sometimes referred to as an "open-air museum" because it is such a wonderful city to explore. Cost for a private chauffeured 5-hour tour is €149 per person; for an 8-hour tour is €189 per person. Adding a dedicated expert guide in Toledo adds €550 per 5-hour tour and €750 per 8-hour tour. Semi-private 5-hour tours for 4-6 people cost €69 per person.

El Escorial and Valley of the Fallen—Tour highlights include Royal Monastery of San Lorenzo El Real built by King Philip the 2nd, the Valle de Los Caidos (Valley of the Fallen), the grand monument for Spain's civil war casualties, the inside of the basilica, and a spectacular valley landscape around this massive monument. Cost for a 5-hour private chauffeured tour is €129 per person. Adding a dedicated expert guide costs €595 per tour.

Avila and Segovia—Tour highlights include the hilltop panoramic viewpoint of Los Cuatro Postes (the four posts) to admire the spectacular view outside the walled city of Avila; Avila's 88 towers, 9 gates, Romanesque-style churches, gothic palaces, and one fortified cathedral; Segovia's aqueduct, a relic of the Roman Empire; the Alcazar, a stunning 11th-century medieval castle set on a rocky outcrop, a favoured royal residence for many Spanish kings. An 8-9-hour private chauffeured tour costs €249 per person. Adding a dedicated expert guide costs an additional €950 per tour. Semi-private tours for 4-6 people cost €115 per person.

Tours by Locals

Tours by Locals (www.toursbylocals.com/find_tour&area=155) offers highly-rated private tours in and around Madrid. Tours are for a set price and private groups of 4-10 people. They offer a wide range of suggested tours (including experiences such as skiing/snow boarding or cooking classes) but can customize tours, as well. Users can filter tour offerings by selecting desired activity level. A small sample of available tours outside Madrid includes the following:

Toledo (with train)—Private, guided 8-hour tour from Madrid via high-speed train. Meet at hotel or train station. Tour duration 8 hours. Activity level, light. Child friendly. Wheelchair friendly. €360 for group up to 10 people. (Train tickets, meals, entrance fees extra.)

Toledo (with van)—Private, guided 8-hour tour in a Mercedes van. Hotel pickup and drop-off. Activity level, moderate. Child and wheelchair friendly. Entrance fees and lunch extra. €875 for up to 6 people.

Medieval Castles—Private, guided 9-hour tour that visits 4 medieval castles and a cathedral. Activity level, light. Not child or wheelchair friendly. Hotel pickup and drop-off. Full lunch at Parador de Sigüenza castle, entrance fees, tips, coffee breaks, car rental included. 9 hours. €850 for up to 5 people.

Segovia Top Monuments—Private, guided 8-hour tour in a Mercedes van. Activity level, light. Child friendly. Wheelchair friendly (though not wheelchair accessible). Hotel pickup and drop-off. Lunch and entrance tickets extra. €770 for up to 6 people.

A Wine Lover's Day—Private, guided 10-hour trip to the Duero Valley in a rental car (included) with visits to two bodegas, including wine tastings. Hotel pickup and drop-off. Lunch costs extra. Activity level, light. Child friendly. Not wheelchair friendly. €600 for 4 people.

Lodging

Madrid, like other top tourist cities, offers a wealth of lodging possibilities. Hotels on this list are based on location, good reviews, and general accessibility, including access to easy transportation. It favors buildings with elevators, but that doesn't mean the elevator will be larger than a phone booth. You may need to make multiple trips to get your luggage to upper floors. This section isn't the last word on acceptable accommodation, but it makes a good starting point to narrow down your search. Just check online to make sure that information is still accurate, both on TripAdvisor and on the hotel's own Web site.

You may find a wonderful deal on what looks like a good choice in a convenient location. By all means—grab it! Same with charming B&Bs, which aren't covered here because they tend to have a limited number of available rooms and generally don't have elevators. If you can nab one in a favorable location that gets good reviews, has a great breakfast, decent accessibility, and a workable price, do it!

I have included lodging possibilities for two areas in central Madrid: near the palace complex and around the Prado.

Both areas can be reached from the airport via the metro system, but only with transfers, which can be difficult to negotiate with luggage. It's much easier to arrange an airport (car) transfer in advance. The area near the Prado can be reached easily by using the Airport Express, at considerably less cost than an airport transfer, if you're OK walking a bit from the stops at Plaza de Cibeles or the Atocha train station. Both areas are amply served by the hop-on/hop-off buses.

When deciding where to lodge, keep in mind whether you will take commercial day trips and where those depart from.

- City Tour Madrid tours depart from the Plaza de Ramales (just east of the palace complex). Tours return to Plaza de Oriente (just east of the palace complex or Plaza de España (north of the palace complex).
- Yellow Tours leave from Plaza de España but may offer other options closer to your hotel.
- Ibe tours leave from Plaza las Ventas (northeast of the Parque del Buen Retiro on metro lines 2 and 5) and the Neptune Fountain by the Prada.
- Amigo Tours leave from Plaza las Ventas (northeast of the Parque del Buen Retiro on metro lines 2 and 5).
- Private and semi-private tours include hotel pickup and drop-off.

Hotel price ranges are based on late 2019 TripAdvisor averages. Your own quotes may be higher or lower.

Near the Royal Palace

If you plan to take day trips from either City Tour Madrid or Yellow Tours, you would do well to lodge north or east of the palace complex.

Hotels in the area include the following:

Barcelo Torre de Madrid—Plaza de España 18. TripAdvisor's Certificate of Excellence. Location: off northern corner of Plaza de España. Pros: free WiFi, excellent breakfast buffet, air conditioning, pool, non-smoking hotel, restaurant, room service, bar/lounge, wheelchair access, facilities for disabled guests, elevator, airport shuttle, fitness center, sauna, twins/triples available. Cons: no price break for singles, swimming pool does not open until 11. (TripAdvisor price range for standard room: $175-$493.)

Distances: Plaza de España Metro Station (.1 miles), Plaza de España Jardines de Ferraz (.1 miles), Ventura Rodriguez Metro Station (.2 miles), Lope de Vega Theatre (.2 miles), Noviciado Metro Station (.2 miles), Museo de Arte Contemporaneo (.2 miles), Santo Domingo Metro Station (.3 miles), Templo of Debod (.5 miles), Plaza Mayor (.6 miles), Puerta del Sol (.7 miles), Prado Museum (1.3 miles), Atocha Train Station (1.5 miles), Retiro Park (1.6 miles)

Gran Melia Palacio de Los Duques—Cuesta Santo Domingo 5 (www.lhw.com/hotel/Gran-Melia-Palacio-de-los-Duques-Madrid-Spain). TripAdvisor's Traveler's Choice Award (top 1% in category). Location: one street west of Plaza Santo Domingo. Pros: free WiFi, parking, excellent breakfast buffet, pool, air conditioning, non-smoking hotel, restaurant, excellent customer service, room service, bar/lounge, facilities for disabled guests, elevator, fitness center, spa, single/twin/ triple/quads/2-3-bedroom suites available, airport transportation, concierge, hot tub. Cons: price. (TripAdvisor price range for standard room: $283-$625.)

Distances: Ópera Metro Station (.1 miles), Teatro Real (.1 miles), Santo Domingo Metro Station (.1 miles), Plaza de Oriente (.2 miles), Callao Metro Station (.2 miles), Monasterio de las Descalzas Reales (.2 miles), Plaza Mayor (.3 miles), Gran Via (.3 miles), Puerta de Sol (.4 miles), Temple of Debod (.8 miles), Prado Museum (1 mile), Atocha Train Station (1.2 miles), Retiro Park (1.4 miles)

ApartoSuites Jardines de Sabatini—Cuesta de San Vicente 16 (www.jardinesdesabatini.com/en/). TripAdvisor's Certificate of Excellence. Location: just north of the Royal Palace complex. Pros: free WiFi, parking, breakfast buffet, air conditioning, non-smoking hotel, suites, wheelchair access, elevator, microwave, refrigerator, views of palace, airport shuttle, singles/twins/triples/family rooms available. Cons: very little price break for singles. (TripAdvisor price range for standard room: $117-$332.)

Distances: El Senado (.1 miles), Plaza de España Jardines de Ferraz (.2 miles), Plaza de Oriente (.2 miles), Príncipe Pío Metro Station (.3 miles), Plaza de España Metro Station (.3 miles), Royal Palace (.3 miles), Ópera Metro Station (.3 miles), Plaza Mayor (.5 miles), Temple of Debod (.6 miles), Puerta del Sol (.7 miles), Prado Museum (1.3 miles), Atocha Train Station (1.5 miles), Retiro Park (1.7 miles)

Room Mate Laura—Travesia Trujillos 3, Plaza de las Descalzas (room-matehotels.com/en/laura/). TripAdvisor's Certificate of Excellence. Location: between Teatro Real and Monasterio de las Descalzas. Pros: free WiFi, breakfast buffet, air conditioning, non-smoking hotel, suites available, kitchenette, room service, facilities for disabled guests, very good breakfast, singles/twins/quads available. Cons: can be noisy. (TripAdvisor price range for standard room: $116-$315.)

Distances: Monasterio de las Descalzas Reales (.1 miles), Callao Metro Station (.1 miles), Ópera Metro Station (.1 miles), Teatro Real (.1 miles), Plaza Mayor (.2 miles), Santo Domingo Metro Station (.2 miles), Sol Metro Station (.2 miles), Gran Via (.2 miles), Puerta del Sol (.2 miles), Thyssen-Bornemisza Museum (.7 miles), Prado Museum (.9 miles), Temple of Debod (1 mile), Atocha Train Station (1.1 miles), Retiro Park (1.2 miles)

Hotel Atlantico—Gran via 38 (www.hotelatlantico.es). TripAdvisor's Certificate of Excellence. Location: on Gran Via one street east of Plaza de Callao. Pros: free WiFi, breakfast buffet, air conditioning, non-smoking hotel, rooftop bar, concierge, wheelchair access, elevator, facilities for disabled guests, refrigerator, singles/twins available. Cons: some street noise. (TripAdvisor price range for standard room: $155-$280.)

Distances: Gran Via Station Metro Station (0 miles), Gran Via (.1 miles), Callao Metro Station (.1 miles), Monasterio de las Descalzas Reales (.2 miles), Santo Domingo Metro Station (.2 miles), Puerta del Sol (.3 miles), Plaza Mayor (.3 miles), Thyssen-Bornemisza Museum (.6 miles), Prado Museum (.8 miles), Temple of Debod (1 mile), Atocha Train Station (1.1 miles), Retiro Park (1.1 miles)

Hotel Preciados—Preciados 37 (us.preciadoshotel.com/en/). TripAdvisor's Certificate of Excellence. Location: between Plaza Santo Domingo and Plaza Callao. Pros: free WiFi, very good breakfast buffet, air conditioning, non-smoking hotel, wheelchair access, facilities for disabled guests, elevator, restaurant, room service, bar/lounge, suites, refrigerator, airport shuttle, single/twin rooms available. Cons: lack of bathroom privacy, interior noise. (TripAdvisor price range for standard room: $128-$305.)

Distance: Callao Metro Station (.1 miles), Santo Domingo Metro Station (.1 miles), Monasterio de las Descalzas Reales (.1 miles), Ópera Metro Station (.1 miles), Teatro Real (.1 miles), Gran Via Station Metro Station (.2 miles), Plaza Mayor (.3 miles), Puerta del Sol (.3 miles), Prado Museum (.9 miles), Temple of Debod (.9 miles), Atocha Train Station (1.1 miles), Retiro Park (1.3 miles)

Suites Viena Plaza de España—Calle Juan Alvarez Mendizabal 17 (www.suitesviena.com/en/). Location: east of Templo de Debod near Plaza de España. TripAdvisor's Certificate of Excellence. Pros: free WiFi, parking, very good breakfast buffet, air conditioning, non-smoking hotel, room service, suites available, microwave, refrigerator, room service, wheelchair access, facilities for disabled guests, elevator, spacious rooms, quiet side street, airport shuttle, singles/twins/triples available. Cons: some school noise from across street. (TripAdvisor price range for standard room: $83-$251.)

Distances: Plaza de España Jardines de Ferraz (.1 miles), Ventura Rodriguez Metro Station (.1 miles), Plaza de España Metro Station (.2 miles), Museo de Arte Contemporaneo (.3 miles), Príncipe Pío Metro Station (.4 miles), Temple of Debod (.4 miles), Plaza Mayor (.7 miles), Puerta del Sol (.8 miles), Prado Museum (1.4 miles), Atocha Train Station (1.7 miles), Retiro Park (1.7 miles)

Hyatt Centric Gran Via Madrid—Calle Gran Via 31. Location: on Gran Via east of Plaza de Callao. Pros: free WiFi, very good breakfast buffet, air conditioning, non-smoking hotel, restaurant, room service, bar/lounge, wheelchair access, facilities for disabled guests, elevator, fitness center, airport shuttle, singles/twins/suites available. Cons: price. (TripAdvisor price range for standard rooms: $230-$579.)

Distances: Gran Via Station Metro Station (0 miles), Principe Gran Via Theatre (.1 miles), Callao Metro Station (.1 miles), Monasterio de las Descalzas Reales (.2 miles), Sol Metro Station (.2 miles), Puerta del Sol (.2 miles), Plaza Mayor (.3 miles), Thyssen-Bornemisza Museum (.6 miles), Prado Museum (.7 miles), Atocha Train Station (1 mile), Retiro Park (1.1 miles), Temple of Debod (1.1 miles)

Dear Hotel Madrid—Calle Gran Via 80 (www.dearhotelmadrid.com/en/). TripAdvisor's Certificate of Excellence. Location: by eastern corner of Plaza de España. Pros: free WiFi, very good buffet breakfast, air conditioning, pool, non-smoking hotel, restaurant, bar/lounge, room service, refrigerator, wheelchair access, facilities for disabled guests, elevator, airport shuttle, singles/twins/triples/quads available. Cons: staff service is uneven. (TripAdvisor price range for standard room: $126-$293.)

Distances: Plaza de España Metro Station (0 miles), Lope de Vega Theatre (.1 miles), Plaza de España Jardines de Ferraz (.1 miles), Santo Domingo Metro Station (.2 miles), Santo Domingo Metro Station (.2 miles), Rialto Theater (.2 miles), Plaza Mayor (.5 miles), Puerta del Sol (.6 miles), Temple of Debod (.6 miles), Prado Museum (1.2 miles), Atocha Train Station (1.4 miles), Retiro Park (1.5 miles)

Room Mate Mario—Calle Campomanes 4 (room-matehotels.com/en/mario/). TripAdvisor's Certificate of Excellence. Location: between Teatro Real and Plaza Santo Domingo. Pros: free WiFi, excellent breakfast buffet, air conditioning, non-smoking hotel, suites, wheelchair access, elevator, singles/twins available. Cons: some problems with air conditioning, showers, noise (internal and external), no triples/quads. (TripAdvisor price range for standard room: $94-$257.)

Distances: Ópera Metro Station (.1 miles), Teatro Real (.1 miles), Plaza de Oriente (.2 miles), Monasterio de las Descalzas Reales (.2 miles), Santo Domingo Metro Station (.2 miles), Callao Metro Station (.2 miles), El Senado (.2 miles), Sabatini Gardens (.2 miles), Plaza Mayor (.2 miles), Puerta del Sol (.3 miles), Temple of Debod (.9 miles), Prado Museum (1 mile), Atocha Train Station (1.2 miles), Retiro Park (1.3 miles)

Hotel Europa—Calle Carmen 4 (www.hoteleuropa.eu/en/). TripAdvisor's Certificate of Excellence. Location: north side of Puerta del Sol. Pros: free WiFi, air conditioning, non-smoking hotel, restaurant, room service, bar, wheelchair access, facilities for disabled guests, elevator, airport shuttle, twins/triples/quads available. Cons: no price break for singles, some water pipe noise in mornings. (TripAdvisor price range for standard room: $107-$428.)

Distances: Sol Metro Station (.1 miles), Puerta del Sol (.1 miles), Monasterio de las Descalzas Reales (.1 miles), Gran Via Station Metro Station (.2 miles), Callao Metro Station (.2 miles), Plaza Mayor (.2 miles), Thyssen-Bornemisza Museum (.5 miles), Prado Museum (.6 miles), Atocha Train Station (.9 miles), Retiro Park (1 mile), Temple of Debod (1.2 miles)

Hotel Francisco 1—Calle Arenal 15. TripAdvisor's Certificate of Excellence. Location: between Puerta del Sol and Teatro Real. Pros: free WiFi, breakfast buffet, air conditioning, non-smoking hotel, suites, accessible rooms, facilities for disabled guests, elevator, family rooms, very good breakfast, singles/twins/triples/quads available. Cons: some complaints of noise, lack of privacy in bathroom. (TripAdvisor price range for standard room: $94-$236.)

Distances: Monasterio de las Descalzas Reales (.1 miles), Plaza Mayor (.1 miles), Teatro Real (.1 miles), Ópera Metro Station (.1 miles), Mercado San Miguel (.1 miles), Sol Metro Station (.2 miles), Callao Metro Station (.2 miles), Preciados Street (.2 miles), Puerta del Sol (.2 miles), Gran Via (.3 miles), Thyssen-Bornemisza Museum (.7 miles), Prado Museum (.8 miles), Temple of Debod (1 mile), Atocha Train Station (1 mile), Retiro Park (1.2 miles)

Hostal Oriente—Calle Arenal 23 (hostaloriente.es/?lang= en). TripAdvisor's Certificate of Excellence. Location: by Teatro Real and Ópera Metro Station. Pros: free WiFi, air conditioning, non-smoking hotel, elevator, private balcony, private bathrooms, singles/twins available. Cons: street noise at night, noise from neighboring rooms, small elevator, no triples/quads. (TripAdvisor price range for standard room: $66-$143.)

Distances: Teatro Real (.1 miles), Ópera Metro Station (.1 miles), Monasterio de las Descalzas Reales (.1 miles), Plaza Mayor (.2 miles), Casa de la Villa (.2 miles), Plaza de Oriente (.2 miles), Callao Metro Station (.2 miles), Sabatini Gardens (.2 miles), Puerta del Sol (.3 miles), Thyssen-Bornemisza Museum (.8 miles), Prado Museum (.9 miles), Temple of Debod (1 mile), Atocha Train Station (1.1 miles), Retiro Park (1.3 miles)

Hotel Indigo Madrid-Gran Via—Calle Silva 6 (www.indigomadrid.com/en/). TripAdvisor's Certificate of Excellence. Location: 1 street northwest of Plaza de Callao. Pros: free WiFi, parking, very good buffet breakfast, air conditioning, pool, non-smoking hotel, restaurant, bar, room service, refrigerator, wheelchair access, facilities for disabled guests, elevator, fitness center, airport shuttle. Cons: small rooms, lack of natural light, some noise, no price break for singles, no twins/triples/quads. (TripAdvisor price range for standard room: $144-$293.)

Distances: Rialto Theater (0 miles), Santo Domingo Metro Station (.1 miles), Callao Metro Station (.1 miles), Gran Via Station Metro Station (.2 miles), Monasterio de las Descalzas Reales (.2 miles), Gran Via (.2 miles), Ópera Metro Station (.2 miles), Plaza Mayor (.3 miles), Puerta del Sol (.3 miles), Thyssen-Bornemisza Museum (.8 miles), Temple of Debod (.9 mile), Prado Museum (.9 miles), Atocha Train Station (1.2 miles), Retiro Park (1.3 miles)

Principe Pio Hotel—Cuesta San Vicente 14 (www.hotelprincipepio.com/). TripAdvisor's Certificate of Excellence. Location: north of the Royal Palace complex. Pros: free WiFi, good breakfast buffet, air conditioning, non-smoking hotel, room service, suites, wheelchair access, facilities for disabled guests, elevator, twins/triples/quads available. Cons:

noise (inside and out), no price break for singles, no restaurant, no bar, small elevator, dated hotel. (TripAdvisor price range for standard room: $98-$278.)

Distances: El Senado (.1 miles), Plaza de España Jardines de Ferraz (.2 miles), Plaza de Oriente (.2 miles), Sabatini Gardens (.2 miles), Plaza de España Metro Station (.3 miles), Príncipe Pío Metro Station (.3 miles), Royal Palace (.3 miles), Plaza Mayor (.5 miles), Temple of Debod (.6 miles), Puerta del Sol (.7 miles), Prado Museum (1.3 miles), Atocha Train Station (1.5 miles), Retiro Park (1.6 miles)

Emperador Hotel Madrid—Calle Gran Via 53 (www.emperadorhotel.com/en/). Location: 2 streets northwest of Plaza de Callao. Pros: free Internet, parking, good breakfast buffet, air conditioning, pool, non-smoking hotel, bar/lounge, room service, wheelchair access, elevator, fitness center, singles/twins/triples available. Cons: construction noise, room-to-room noise, no restaurant. (TripAdvisor price range for standard room: $118-$283.)

Distances: Santo Domingo Metro Station (0 miles), Arlequin Theatre (0 miles), Rialto Theater (0 miles), Callao Metro Station (.1 miles), Gran Via Station Metro Station (.2 miles), Plaza de España Metro Station (.2 miles), Ópera Metro Station (.2 miles), Plaza Mayor (.4 miles), Puerta del Sol (.4 miles), Temple of Debod (.8 miles), Prado Museum (1 mile), Atocha Train Station (1.2 miles), Retiro Park (1.3 miles)

Near the Prado Museum

If you plan to take day trips from Ibe Tours or are planning to travel to tour departure sites (or take tours with hotel pickup), you would do well to lodge around the Prado. Both hop-on/hop-off bus routes (historical Route 1 and modern Route 2) have stops in this area. Hotels in the area include the following:

Gran Hotel Ingles—Calle Echegaray 8 (www.granhotelingles.com). Location: about 4 streets west of Neptune Fountain. Pros: top-ranked Madrid hotel, free WiFi, excellent breakfast buffet, air conditioning, non-smoking rooms, hot tub, restaurant, room service, bar/lounge, wheelchair access, elevator, facilities for disabled guests, fitness center, airport shuttle, triples/quads/2-6-person suites available. Cons: price, some street noise. (TripAdvisor price range for standard room: $333-$1,064.)

Distances: Plaza de Santa Ana (.1 miles), Sevilla Metro Station (.2 miles), Puerta del Sol (.2 miles), Preciados Street (.2 miles), Thyssen-Bornemisza Museum (.3 miles), Plaza Mayor (.4 miles), Parado Museum (.4 miles), Atocha Train Station (.7 miles), Retiro Park (.8 miles), Temple of Debod (1.4 miles)

The Principal Madrid—Calle Marques de Valdeiglesias 1 Esq. Gran Via (www.theprincipalmadridhotel.com). TripAdvisor's Certificate of Excellence. Location: 2 streets west of the Fountain of Cibeles at the start of Gran Via. Pros: free WiFi, very good breakfast buffet, air conditioning, non-smoking, restaurant, room service, bar/lounge, airport shuttle, wheelchair access, facilities for disabled guests, elevator, fitness center, twins/suites available. Cons: price, slow/strange elevator, confusing hotel layout, reception on floor 6, expensive breakfast, no singles. (TripAdvisor price range for standard room: $234-$446.)

Distances: Metropolis Building (0 miles), Bellas Artes Theatre (.1 miles), Sevilla Metro Station (.1 miles), Banco de Espana Metro Station (.1 miles), Cibeles Fountain (.2 miles), Puerta del Sol (.4 miles), Prado Museum (.5 miles), Plaza Mayor (.6 miles), Retiro Park (.7 miles), Atocha Train Station (.8 miles), Temple of Debod (1.4 miles)

Catalonia Las Cortes—Calle del Prado 6 (en.catalonialascortes.com). TripAdvisor's Certificate of Excellence. Location: 1 street east of Plaza Santa Ana. Pros: free WiFi, parking, excellent breakfast buffet, air conditioning, non-smoking hotel, room service, bar/lounge, suites, wheelchair access, facilities for disabled guests, elevator, singles/twins/triples available. Cons: smells from smoking area in hotel, uneven service. (TripAdvisor price range for standard room: $148-$446.)

Distances: Plaza de Santa Ana (.1 miles), Anton Martin Metro Station (.2 miles), Sevilla Metro Station (.2 miles), Thyssen-Bornemisza Museum (.2 miles), Puerta del Sol (.3 miles), Prado Museum (.4 miles), Plaza Mayor (.4 miles), Atocha Train Station (.6 miles), Retiro Park (.8 miles), Temple of Debod (1.5 miles)

Vincci The Mint—Calle Gran Via 10 (en.vinccithemint.com). TripAdvisor Certificate of Excellence. Location: on Gran Via north of Sevilla Metro Station. Pros: free WiFi, parking, excellent breakfast available, non-smoking hotel, restaurant, room service, bar/lounge, wheelchair access, facilities for disabled guests, elevator, twins/triples/suites available. Cons: no price break for singles. (TripAdvisor price range for standard room: $162-$430.)

Distances: Sevilla Metro Station (.1 miles), Bellas Artes Theatre (.2 miles), Chueca Metro Station (.2 miles), Puerta del Sol (.3 miles), Plaza

Mayor (.5 miles), Prado Museum (.5 miles), Retiro Park (.8 miles), Atocha Train Station (.9 miles), Templo of Debod (1.3 miles)

Hotel Urban—Carrera de San Jeronimo (www.hotelurban.com). TripAdvisor's Certificate of Excellence. Location: about 4 streets west of Neptune Fountain. Pros: free WiFi, very good breakfast buffet, air conditioning, pool, non-smoking hotel, restaurant, bar/lounge, room service, wheelchair access, fitness center, elevator, airport shuttle, refrigerator, airport shuttle. Cons: interior and exterior noise, only twins/doubles available. (TripAdvisor price range for standard room: $186-$492.)

Distances: Sevilla Metro Station (.1 miles), Plaza de Santa Ana (.2 miles), Bellas Artes Theatre (.2 miles), Thyssen-Bornemisza Museum (.2 miles), Puerta del Sol (.2 miles), Prado Museum (.4 miles), Plaza Mayor (.4 miles), Atocha Train Station (.7 miles), Retiro Park (.8 miles), Temple of Debod (1.4 miles)

Hotel Room Mate Alicia—Calle Prado 2 (room-matehotels.com/en/alicia/). TripAdvisor's Certificate of Excellence. Location: by Plaza de Santa Ana. Pros: free WiFi, good breakfast buffet, air conditioning, non-smoking hotel, refrigerator, wheelchair access, elevator, singles available. Cons: some dark rooms/corridors, some small rooms. (TripAdvisor price range for standard room: $126-$402.)

Distances: Plaza de Santa Ana (0 miles), Anton Martin Metro Station (.2 miles), Puerta del Sol (.2 miles), Thyssen-Bornemisza Museum (.3 miles), Plaza Mayor (.4 miles), Prado Museum (.4 miles), Atocha Train Station (.6 miles), Retiro Park (.8 miles), Temple of Debod (1.5 miles)

Hotel Villa Real—Plaza de las Cortes 10 (www.hotelvillareal.com/en/). TripAdvisor's Certificate of Excellence. Location: 2 streets west of Neptune Fountain. Pros: free WiFi, good breakfast buffet, air conditioning, non-smoking hotel, restaurant, room service, bar/lounge, wheelchair access, elevator, suites, fitness center, pool, airport shuttle, twins/quads available. Cons: some shower problems, hotel noise, expensive breakfast. (TripAdvisor price range for standard room: $132-$337.)

Distances: Congreso de los Diputados (0 miles), Teatro de la Zarzuela (.1 miles), Thyssen-Bornemisza Museum (.1 miles), Neptune Fountain (.2 miles), Sevilla Metro Station (.2 miles), Pardo Museum (.3 miles), Puerta del Sol (.3 miles), Plaza Mayor (.5 miles), Atocha Train Station (.6 miles), Retiro Park (.7 miles), Temple of Debod (1.5 miles)

Iberostar Las Letras Gran Via—Calle Gran Via 11 (hoteldelasletras.iberostar.com/en). TripAdvisor's Certificate of Excellence. Location: east of the Gran Via Metro Station. Pros: free WiFi, very good breakfast buffet, air conditioning, non-smoking hotel, wheelchair access, facilities for disabled guests, lift, restaurant, room service, bar/lounge, fitness center. airport shuttle, twins/triples available. Cons: street noise, no price break for singles. (TripAdvisor price range for standard room: $146-$335.)

Distances: Sevilla Metro Station (.1 miles), Bellas Artes Theatre (.2 miles), Chueca Metro Station (.2 miles), Puerta del Sol (.3 miles), Thyssen-Bornemisza Museum (.4 miles), Plaza Mayor (.5 miles), Prado Museum (.5 miles), Retiro Park (.8 miles), Atocha Train Station (.9 miles), Temple of Debod (1.3 miles)

Petit Palace Lealtad Plaza—Calle Antonio Maura 5 (en.petitpalace-lealtadmadrid.com). TripAdvisor's Certificate of Excellence. Location: just east of the Plaza de la Lealtad. Pros: free WiFi, excellent breakfast buffet, air conditioning, non-smoking hotel, room service, suites, bar/lounge, wheelchair access, facilities for disabled guests, elevator, twins/triples/quads/apt. available. Cons: lack of bathroom privacy, not many businesses around, expensive breakfast, no price break for singles. (TripAdvisor price range for standard room: $118-$280.)

Distances: Neptune Fountain (.2 miles), Cibeles Fountain (.2 miles), Museo Postal y Telegráfico (.2 miles), Thyssen-Bornemisza Museum (.2 miles), Prado Museum (.2 miles), Retiro Park (.4 miles), Atocha Train Station (.6 miles), Puerta del Sol (.7 miles), Plaza Mayor (.9 miles), Temple of Debod (1.8 miles)

The Westin Palace Madrid—Plaza de las Cortes 7 (www.marriott.com/hotels/travel/madwi-the-westin-palace-madrid/). Has TripAdvisor's Certificate of Excellence. Location: just west of Neptune Fountain. Pros: WiFi (free in public areas), parking, very good breakfast buffet, air conditioning, non-smoking hotel, restaurant, room service, bar/lounge, wheelchair access, facilities for disabled guests, elevator, fitness center, refrigerator, airport shuttle, ATM on site, twins available. Cons: price, some night noise, fee for in-room WiFi, very expensive breakfast, no price break for singles. (TripAdvisor price range for standard room: $290-$757.)

Distances: Thyssen-Bornemisza Museum (.1 miles), Neptune Fountain (.1 miles), Sevilla Metro Station (.2 miles), Prado Museum (.2 miles), Puerta de Sol (.4 miles), Atocha Train Station (.5 miles), Plaza Mayor (.6 miles), Retiro Park (.6 miles), Temple of Debod (1.6 miles)

Catalonia Atocha—Calle Atocha 81 (www.cataloniahotels.com/en/hotel/catalonia-atocha). TripAdvisor's Certificate of Excellence. Location: west of Prado area by Anton Martin Metro Station. Pros: free WiFi, very good breakfast buffet, air conditioning, hot tub, non-smoking hotel, restaurant, room service, bar/lounge, wheelchair access, facilities for disabled guests, elevator, twins/triples available. Cons: noisy street construction at the time of this writing, some rooms small, some need more lighting. (TripAdvisor price range for standard room: $128-$311.)

Distances: Anton Martin Metro Station (.1 miles), Museo Nacional Centro de Arte Reina Sofia (.1 miles), Plaza de Santa Ana (.2 miles), Lavapiés Metro Station (.3 miles), Prado Museum (.3 miles), Atocha Train Station (.4 miles), Puerta del Sol (.4 miles), Plaza Mayor (.6 miles), Retiro Park (.8 miles), Temple of Debod (1.7 miles)

Vincci Soho—Calle Prado 18 (en.vinccisoho.com). TripAdvisor's Certificate of Excellence. Location: about 3 streets west of Neptune Fountain. Pros: free WiFi, parking, very good breakfast buffet, air conditioning, non-smoking hotel, restaurant, room service, bar, refrigerator, wheelchair access, facilities for disabled guests, elevator, singles/twins/triples available. Cons: insufficient lighting in rooms, hotel noise in morning. (TripAdvisor price range for standard room: $134-$437.)

Distances: Congreso de los Diputados (.1 miles), Plaza de Santa Ana (.1 miles), Anton Martin Metro Station (.2 miles), Thyssen-Bornemisza Museum (.2 miles), Neptune Fountain (.2 miles), Puerta del Sol (.3 miles), Prado Museum (.3 miles), Plaza Mayor (.5 miles), Atocha Train Station (.6 miles), Retiro Park (.6 miles), Temple of Debod (1.5 miles)

Hotel Regina—Calle de Alcala 19. TripAdvisor Certificate of Excellence. Location: west of Sevilla Metro Station. Pros: free WiFi, very good breakfast buffet, air conditioning, non-smoking hotel, restaurant, room service, bar/lounge, refrigerator, wheelchair access, facilities for disabled guests, airport shuttle, singles/twins/triples available. Cons: street construction outside as of this writing, noise, lack of privacy in bathroom. (TripAdvisor price range for standard room: $116-$356.)

Distances: Sevilla Metro Station (.1 miles), Puerta del Sol (.2 miles), Bellas Artes Theatre (.2 miles), Thyssen-Bornemisza Museum (.3 miles), Plaza Mayor (.4 miles), Prado Museum (.5 miles), Atocha Train Station (.8 miles), Retiro Park (.8 miles), Temple of Debod (1.3 miles)

Other base cities in Spain

Spain is a large country, and it's not really possible to see most of it from Madrid. If you want to base in other areas, the city of Barcelona, on the Mediterranean coast of northeast Spain, has a hop-on/hop-off bus tour and companies that lead excursions into the countryside. So do Seville, Granada, and Malagá in southern Spain and Bilboa and San Sebastián in northern Spain's Basque country.

Rome

Overview

Rome (or Roma, as the locals would say) is one of the world's great cities. It's ancient, home of important history, architecture, art, and religious significance. It bursts with sights and people and passion. Tourists typically love Rome, because there is so much to see and do, so much that's familiar to us but also new.

But there are some challenges involved with a visit to Rome, as well. It is old, crowded, loud, disorderly, and often confusing. It is inherently chaotic, down to its pre-Christian bones. If you have a northern-European preference for order, reset your expectations for Rome. Expect the chaos. Appreciate the chaos, if you can. *Embrace* the chaos, if that's your thing. Because you can count on Rome being gloriously out of control when compared to other cities, and it's much simpler to go with the flow and expect frustrations and confusions than to try to fight them at every step. Remind yourself that it's all part of experiencing the city.

Rome has a Mediterrean climate, with mild and rainy winters and summers that are hot and sunny. Temperatures range from lows in the 30s and highs in the 50s in winter to an average high of 88 degrees Fahrenheit in July and August. Spring and fall are considered the best times to visit because the summers are so hot. Fall brings the most rain, but showers are common in winter and spring, as well. The sun shines almost all the time in summer.

The official Rome tourism site is www.romeinformation.it/en/and can be a good resource as you plan your trip.

Possible plan for Rome (What I'd do)

If I were traveling to Rome with my mother, this is what I would plan for us to do. It's a fairly short itinerary—just 8 days total, so it could fit if you wanted to fly to and from on Saturdays, for example, and just take a week off of work. Obviously, you may prefer to do something different, or add a bunch, but you may find this itinerary handy as a starting point, changing it as much as you'd like. (And it will make more sense as you work your way through the chapter. Having a city map at hand will help, too.) **Please double check any details before relying on them, as specifics may have changed since I wrote these pages.** This plan assumes lodging near the Plaza della Repubblica/Termini but could easily be modified for the Piazza Barberini or elsewhere.

Be aware that many sights in Rome are closed on Mondays (and some on Sundays or Saturdays). Order these days in such a way as to avoid Monday for some Rome sightseeing. I've noted places that are closed on certain days, but check with the latest information before setting any itinerary in stone.

Also be aware that visiting Rome requires *walking*. We can minimize the walking, but only to a certain extent. Expect to rely on leg power for much of the day and night. Probably the most practical plan for making Rome workable for those with walking difficulties is to deliberately take things slowly. Plan to rest when it's possible—at cafés, on benches, on buses. Build rest time into your day. Anywhere you can take a load off, *do*. As for day trips, you probably don't want to plan for more than two consecutive out-of-town excursions at a time, to avoid bus fatigue.

Day 1—Depart U.S.

Day 2—Arrive Rome. Find an ATM (*bancomat*) and withdraw euros, if needed. Look for the tourist information office at the airport. Get any tourist information you may want, including maps. Buy a ticket for the Leonardo Express to get into the city. Follow signs to the trains (*Stazione Ferroviaria*). Buy a ticket at a green ticket machine or—even easier—from a newsstand/tobacconist with a "Tickets" sign. Validate your ticket in a machine on or near the platform *before* boarding the train. Look for the train labeled "Leonardo Express" and enter at any door. (You may need to press the round button next to the door to get it to open.) Keep your ticket handy for the conductor to check. The train will take you to the back of the Termini Station. Work your way to the front to exit the station and make your way to your hotel.

Comfort upgrade: Prebook a private car with a driver who will meet you at the airport and take you directly to your hotel. (Honestly, given how much walking is required in airports and knowing that I want to walk around Rome later this day and that we'll be tired after the flight, I would probably book a private car for my mom and me.)

At the hotel, go to room and rest, if possible. If too early for that, leave luggage and start exploring. Line up cell phone service, if needed. Locate a handy grocery store. If interested (see Comfort upgrade below), buy a 3-day HOHO ticket (or pre-order online—printing voucher) and ride around (Big Bus, Red Line) for an introdution to Rome.

Get out at Piazza Barberini (near the end of the circuit). Visit the Capuchin Crypt at Santa Maria della Concezione (if interested in the macabre) (open daily). View the Piazza Barberini. Walk to Trevi Fountain. Take a break and get some ice cream or coffee. Walk to the Spanish Steps. Take another break. (Maybe check out the ritzy McDonald's to the right of the Spanish Steps.) Get to the top of the hill. (If you don't feel like scaling the 138 steps, there is an elevator by the Metro entrance that will take you up.) Walk to the HOHO stop on Via Ludovisi and ride back to Termini. (Pay attention to when the HOHO bus stops running for the day.) Rest before dinner, then go out to eat. (Or eat in. Or just go to bed.)

Comfort upgrade: You may choose to ride a taxi to and from the daily areas of exploration, possibly at not much extra expense, rather than take HOHO buses. The HOHO buses do provide a chance to see the city and get commentary each time you ride, but are less efficient and may require walks, waits, and dealing with crowded buses. If you take taxis, just keep in mind the warnings to avoid unlicensed cabs and ensure that the meter is running when starting a ride. If you ordered the cab, the meter should already be running when it picks you up.

Super comfort upgrade: If traveling around Rome by golf-cart tour fits into your budget, that sounds like a delightful (if pricey) way to see the city.

Day 3—(*Works on any day.*) Take the Red Line HOHO bus (or also the Purple one, if lodging near the Termini) (or a taxi) to the Colosseum. Enter on a *pre-ordered timed ticket*. (Make sure the timing works with the HOHO bus schedule, if that will be your transportation.) Allow time to get through security. Next visit the Forum and Palatine Hill, both included in your Colosseum ticket. If time, take the Purple Line HOHO bus from the Colosseum and ride around the southern loop, listening to the commentary, and returning to the Termini. Otherwise, take the Red Line HOHO bus (or a taxi) back to the Termini. (If your flight was delayed and you didn't have a chance for yesterday's sightseeing, now would be a time to visit the Spanish Steps and Trevi Fountain.)

Day 4—*(Don't do on Monday.)* Take the Red Line HOHO bus to the "Vatican" stop, across from the Castel Sant'Angelo. Cross the river on Angel Bridge and visit Castel Sant'Angelo (Hadrian's Tomb) (closed Mondays). Order timed ticket online for skip-the-line access.

Walk to Piazza Navona and find somewhere to eat or snack around there. Walk to the Pantheon, and then wander the historic streets before returning to the "Vatican" HOHO stop to return to the hotel area.

If using the Big Bus 3-day pass, eat a snack or lunch, then meet at 2 p.m. at Stop #6 for the included 1-hour walking tour of the Pantheon and Piazza Navona. Enjoy the area before returning to the hotel, resting, and having dinner.

Day 5—*(Do not plan this day for a Sunday.)* Take bus #64 to the Vatican City, "San Pietro." (Bus #40 is faster, but doesn't get as close to the Vatican.) (*Beware of pickpockets anyplace crowded, but especially on buses.*) The bus will take you to the opposite side of Saint Peter's Square from where the Vatican Museums are. Buy a ticket (and one for the return) at a tobacconist's shop at €1.50 each. You can't buy a ticket on the bus. Validate your ticket in the machine when you get on the bus. If taking the bus, walk around to the Vatican Museums. (Taxis can drop you off closer.) Use a *pre-ordered timed ticket* to enter the Vatican Museums (closed Sundays). Eat lunch. Visit St. Peter's Basilica (closed some Wednesday mornings) and St. Peter's Square. Visit some of the scads of tourist shops in the area. Return to the bus stop or to a taxi stand to ride back to the hotel. Rest a bit. Dinner.

Day 6—Day trip: Pompeii and the Amalfi Coast

Day 7—Day trip: Tuscan Hilltowns (Be careful if choosing a Florence walking tour—make sure that it does not require too much walking.)

Day 8—Return to U.S. Buy a ticket for the Leonardo Express going *to* Fiumicino Aeroporto from a vending machine, a newsstand, or a travel agency. Follow signs to the airport, to tracks 23-24. Validate your ticket in a machine before boarding the train. (Very important!) When you exit the train at Fiumicino Airport, you will see displays showing departing planes and indicating which terminal you need to go to to check in. (Know the time of your flight, your destination, and your flight number.)

Comfort upgrade: Arrange a private transfer ahead of time and be picked up at your hotel and delivered to the correct terminal at the airport.

Arrival

Almost all international traffic flies into Fiumicino Airport (FCO) (www.adr.it/en/web/aeroporti-di-roma-en-/pax-fco-travel-information), 18 miles southwest of Rome.

To get from FCO to the city, you have your choice of train, bus, hotel shuttle, taxi, or private driver. The "Leonardo Express" **non-stop train** is the most popular mode of transportation into the city (www.trenitalia.com/en/services/fiumicino_airport.html). It costs €14 in 2019 and takes 32 minutes to reach Termini Station in Rome. Buy tickets from salespeople or from self-service machines. Make sure you validate your ticket before departure (look for a green/white machine on/near the platform and put the QR code in the slot), or you could be fined.

Several **bus** lines run shuttle buses between the Termini and the airport (www.adr.it/en/web/aeroporti-di-roma-en-/pax-fco-bus). Buses cost less than the train (say, €6 one-way) but take longer (around an hour in normal traffic, longer in heavy traffic). You may want to buy a bus ticket when you need one rather than booking online ahead of time, in case your arrival is off-schedule. Follow the "Bus Station" signs to find bus bays. The most popular line is Terravision (www.terravision.eu), which is a little surprising, because it has loads of bad reviews. SIT bus (www.sitbusshuttle.com/en/) gets better reviews. See an overview of bus options here: www.rometoolkit.com/airport/fiumicino_airport_bus.htm.

Hotel shuttle vans offer door-to-door van service to selected hotels for a fee. (Well, as close as the van can get to the hotel. Not all streets are accessible.) Passengers are limited to 1 suitcase and 1 carry-on bag with extra fees for excessive luggage. Shuttle cost as of this writing are as low as €16.33 per person and can be booked online. You will receive a voucher to present to the shuttle driver. Some users report problems meeting up with their drivers, as well as problems with billing, so check reviews to see whether you want to do this.

Airport Shuttle Express gets decent reviews overall, but some users have had bad experiences (www.airportshuttlexpress.com/). For additional information, see www.rometoolkit.com/airport/fiumicino_airport_hotel_shuttle.htm.

Taxis from Fuimicino Airport to the center of the city (within the former walls) have a flat fee of €48. You must be alert to several things if taking a taxi into the city, however. First, make sure you use only a registered (official) city taxi (a white car with a "TAXI" sign on top and a number on the door). Get a cab from the official taxi rank and do not go with one that is *not* in that rank. Any suspicious cab is probably an imposter and the driver will rip you off. Second, be aware that taxis are usually small cars in Rome (e.g., a Toyota Prius) and luggage space will be limited. Third, if your hotel is *outside* the old Aurelian Walls (roughly encompassing the Vatican to the west, the Villa Borghese to the north, National Library to the east—a bit past the Termini—and the Basilica di San Giovanni in Laterno to the south), the flat fee doesn't apply to your trip, the meter will run, and you could easily face a higher cost than you expected.

All in all, if you normally take a taxi from the airport, it may make more sense to line up a **private car** in this case. The driver will track your plane, meet you when you come out of the baggage hall, escort you to the car, accommodate all your luggage (tell them when booking if you have excessive amounts), and make all arrangements in advance, so you don't need to worry about them after your flight. Rates are comparable with those for a taxi. For example, a one-way transfer for 1-2 people with luggage costs around €48 as of this writing. Larger vehicles are also available for larger groups.

More information and links for reservations (to or from the airport) are here (Select "Transfers" in the menu.):

- www.romeairporttransportation.com
- www.romecabs.com
- rome4.us
- www.rometoolkit.com/airport/fiumicino_airport_taxi.htm (is a secondary vendor, but collects information in one place for an overview)

Easy transportation options

Once in the city, your usual transportation choices are metro, bus, and taxi. The metro system in Rome is more limited than in other major cities, though. (The city is built on millennia of archeological sites, impeding tunnel construction.) Subway trains are typically overcrowded (to the point of being unridable), and, as in most other cities, riding the metro can require considerable walking and often the use of stairs. (Only a handful of metro stops are wheelchair accessible.)

City buses can be easier to get to, but they, too, are often overfull and have limited accessibility. Check the Rome journey finder at www.atac.roma.it to get help finding options for riding public transportation. (Select English in the upper right corner on the first page but not the second one—selecting English after you've requested a route seems to erase the search information. You may need to enter street or Italian piazza names or addresses, not just sight names, and not in English. "Cerca" means "search.")

One easier way to get around to the sights is to ride a **hop-on/hop-off (HOHO) tourist bus**. You purchase a 1-day, 2-day, or 3-day ticket (or as little as 5 hours) and then may hop on and hop off the buses (of the line you paid for) as much as you'd like in that time.

As with so many things in Rome, though, the HOHO buses are not the same easy solution to transportation that they are in other cities. First, the HOHO companies get spottier reviews than in other cities (mostly based on frequency of buses and poor customer service), and second, the HOHO buses run primarily around the periphery of the old city center. Well, much of it, anyway. Rome is sprawling and old. Buses simply don't have easy access to many areas. You can get a nice drop-off for the Colosseum and the Forum, but if you want to visit, say, the Pantheon or Piazza Navona, you will still need to walk a bunch. Same with the Vatican sights (a must-see visit for any tourist)—the "Vatican" stop is a 10-15-minute walk down the street from St. Peter's Square, and the walk to the Vatican Museums (Sistine Chapel) is another 10 minutes from there. Certainly it's doable to visit Rome using the HOHO buses, but you need to factor in more walking than you would for other cities.

Taxis, of course, may offer the most convenient within-city transportation of all, but you'll pay for that convenience. Still, Rome's transportation challenges may justify taxi use more than in other cities. If riding taxis fits your budget and enhances your experience, that may be just the right choice for you. Information about Rome taxis is provided below.

A special transportation option in Rome is handicapped-accessible **golf-cart tours**, which are recommended for slow walkers, as well. These tours cost more than HOHO tours, of course, but include a private guide and bring customers within easy reach of sights. They can allow for an efficient and comfortable overview of hard-to-reach sites. Carts stop at sights to allow better viewing and photography. It may make sense to combine a golf-cart tour to reach hardest-to-reach places with other transportation to get to easier-to-reach places.

HOHO bus options, golf-cart tours, taxis, and public transportation are discussed below.

Hop-On/Hop-Off Tours

Big Bus Rome (www.bigbustours.com/en/rome/rome-bus-tours/) offers two HOHO day routes and a non-HOHO night route through central Rome and beyond. Their double-decker buses offer audio commentary and free WiFi on board. Most buses are wheelchair accessible. Each ticket includes access to 4 free walking tours. Some Big Bus Rome tickets can be purchased with fast-track access to popular sights. As with other HOHO bus companies, tourists have variable experiences with this company, with some singing its praises and others complaining of disorganization, long wait times, and rude staff. *Re-check times of operation before riding, because those details change periodically.*

The Red route starts at the Termini train station and circles central Rome clockwise with the following 7 stops: Basilica Santa Maria Maggiore, the Colosseum, Circo Massimo, Piazza Venezia, Vatican, Ludovisi/Spanish Steps, and Piazza Barberini /Spanish Steps. Be aware that the Vatican stop is near Castel Sant'Angelo, a substantial walk from Vatican City. Red buses start running at 8:30 or 9:00 (depending on season) with buses every 20 minutes or so and the last bus departing around 6 or 7 p.m. (depending on season). Riding the route straight through takes approximately 1 hour and 40 minutes.

The Purple route overlaps some with the red route, but then dips to the south to cover major sites outside the city center. This route also starts at the Termini station and stops at Basilica Santa Maria Maggiore and the Colosseum, then dives south to Porta San Sebastiano, Catacombs and Church of San Sebastiano, before turning back north to stop at Caffarella Park, Domine Quo Vadis, and Terme di Carracalla. The Purple bus then stops at Circo Massimo and Piazza Venezia on the way back to the Termini stop. The first Purple bus leaves the Termini around 9 a.m. Buses run every 60 minutes or so, with the last bus departing around 5 p.m. Riding the route straight through takes approximately 1 hour and 30 minutes.

Big Bus Rome also offers a straight-through night tour (no hopping on or off) that follows the Red route with commentary and reveals the sights when lit up. The bus departs around 7:30 p.m. and the route takes about 1 hour.

Tickets may be purchased online, from Big Bus salespeople near the stops, from a kiosk in the Termini station or at the Colosseum, and some merchants that sell tourist services. Tickets purchased on the Web site are valid for 6 months. While e-vouchers are supposed to be valid, some customers have had trouble redeeming them on the bus. You are safer printing a paper copy if ordering online.

Bus tickets are valid on the HOHO routes you choose for as much use as you want during the 1, 2, or 3 days of a ticket's validity. (The Night Tour requires a separate ticket unless specifically included in a package and may be used just once.)

One-day tickets include the Red HOHO bus and the 4 walking tours. Premium tickets include the Red HOHO bus, the 4 walking tours, and the Purple HOHO bus for 2 days. Deluxe tickets include 3 days on both HOHO routes, the 4 walking tours, and the Night Tour. Costs (as of late 2019) are as follows:

- Classic, 1 day, adult, €28.80 (online), €32 (on-street)
- Classic, 1 day, child (5-15), €18.90 (online), €21 (on-street)
- 1 day, family (2 adults, 2 children), €85 (online)
- Premium, 2 days, adult, €35.10 (online), €39 (on-street)
- Premium, 2 days, child (5-15), €25 (online), €25 (on-street)
- Premium, 2 days, family (2 adults, 2 children), €103 (online)
- Deluxe, 3 days, adult, €43.20 (online), €48 (on-street)
- Deluxe, 3 days, child (5-15), €29.70 (online), €33 (on-street)
- Deluxe 3 days, family (2 adults, 2 children), €129 (online)
- Panaramic Night Tour, adult or child, €16 (online)

I Love Rome/Gray Line Tours (graylinerome.com/tours/rome/ilove-rome-hop-on-hop-off-panoramic-tour-9888_142/) runs easy-to-spot pink double-decker buses on a single HOHO route through central Rome. Buses have free WiFi and audio commentary. The single HOHO route has 9 stops, following much the same route as the Red route with Big Bus: Termini, Santa Maria Maggiore, Colosseum, Circo Massimo, Piazza Venezia, Vatican City & Castel Sant'Angelo, Spanish Steps, Piazza Barberini. As with Big Bus, the Vatican stop is by Castel Sant'Angelo, a good walk from the Vatican itself.

Tour buses leave approximately every 10-15 minutes from the Termini station starting at 8:30, with the final bus departing around 6:40 p.m. (around 5:40 Nov. 1-March 31), but you may get on or off the bus at any stop. Tour options include 24-, 48-, or 72-hour access, a daily ticket, a 5-hour ticket, and a single ride ticket. Bring your voucher to show bus attendants. Online costs (late 2019) are as follows:

- Panoramic Tour Single Ride after 1:15 p.m., adult (13-99) €20, youth (6-12) €14, child (0-5) €0

- Panoramic Tour Single Ride after 3 p.m., adult (13-99) €14, youth (6-12) €10, child (0-5) €0
- Panaromic Tour, 24 hours, adult (13-99) €20-€25, youth (6-12) €16, child (0-5) €0
- Panoramic Tour, 48 hours, adult (13-99) €25.60-€32, youth (6-12) €20, child (0-5) €0
- Panoramic Tour, 72 hours, adult (13-99) €39, youth (6-12) €27, child (0-5) €0
- Open Tour, 5 hours, adult (13-99) €18, youth (6-12) €13, child (0-5) €0

There are other HOHO companies available in Rome, but reviews are so uneven you should approach them with caution.

Golf-cart tours

Rolling Rome Tours (rollingrome.com/rome-by-golf-cart-tour/) has had TripAdvisor's Certificate of Excellence and offers half- and full-day tours of Rome in golf carts. Tours are customizable and offer hotel pick-up.

- Rome's Squares and Fountains (3 hours, daily 10-1, 3-6). 1-3 people, €250; 4 or more people €75 each.
- Hills of Ancient Rome (3 hours, daily 10-1, 3-6). 1-3 people, €250; 4 or more people €75 each.
- Rome Sunset Tour (3 hours, daily, 7-10). 1-3 people, €250; 4 or more people €75 each.
- Rome Food Tour (4 hours, Mon.-Sat., 9:30-1:30). 1-3 people, €400; 4 or more people €125 each.
- Rome in a Day (7 hours, daily, includes lunch). 1-3 people, €450; 4 or more people €150 each.
- Rome in a Day Vatican Museum & Sistine Chapel Plus City Center (6.5 hours, daily, includes lunch). 1-3 people, €750; 4 or more people €199 each.
- Rome in a Day Colosseum & Roman Forum Plus Hills of Ancient Rome (6.5 hours, daily, includes lunch). 1-3 people, €750; 4 or more people €199 each.

My Best Tour (golf-cart-tour-rome.com/golf-cart-tours-rome/) has TripAdvisor's Certificate of Excellence and offers private golf-cart tours of 4, 6, or 7 hours during the day and 2-hour night tours. Four-hour tours start at 9:30 or 2:30, and longer tours can be scheduled for whatever time you like. The company offers suggested tours, but you may choose your own itinerary, as you like. The company also offers wheelchair-accessible tours, including inside the Vatican.

Suggested itineraries are Fundamental Rome, Ancient Rome, Tucked-Away Rome, Angels & Demons, Present Roman Art & Architecture, All Rome in One Day, Full-Day Ancient Rome, and Rome by Night.

Tour pricing is as follows:

- 1-3 people—4-hour tour, €280; 6-hour tour, €410; 7-hour tour, €480, 2-hour night tour, €190
- 4 people—4-hour tour, €360; 6-hour tour, €470; 7-hour tour, €560, 2-hour night tour, €240
- 5-7 people—4-hour tour, €410; 6-hour tour, €540; 7-hour tour, €610; 2-hour night tour, €280
- 8+, per person—4-hour tour, €60; 6-hour tour, €85; 7-hour tour, €95; 2-hour night tour, €45

Golf Car Tours (golfcartours.com/en/) has stellar reviews and offers tailor-made English-speaking tours of Rome with hotel pickup. Select a 3- or 5-hour tour to cover your choice of sights. Guides include stops for coffee and gelato in their itineraries and take off-beat backstreet routes instead of busy thoroughfares.

- 3-hour tour—1-3 people, €249; 4 people, €349; 5 people, €395; 6 people, €465
- 5-hour tour—1-3 people, €389; 4 people, €450; 5 people, €530; 6 people, €590

Taxis and Uber

If taking a taxi or arranging a private ride is your thing, you can certainly do so in Rome. You can check a taxi fare finder such as www.taxifarefinder.com to get an estimate for how much a ride would cost. For example, taxi fare from the Piazza Navona to the Vatican Museums would range from €4.63 in low traffic to €16.86 in high traffic and would typically cost about €6.91, for a trip of about 1.8 miles.

Uber is banned in Rome. High-end Uber variants (Uber Black, Uber Lux, Uber Van) are available, but they cost considerably more than a regular taxi. An evening Uber Black fare for the same ride as above (Piazza Navona to Vatican Museums) would run about €19-€27.

It is not usual to hail a taxi on the street in Rome. You typically find a taxi at a taxi rank, located throughout the city, particularly at transportation hubs (like the train station) and outside major sights (although you may need to ask or search around the Vatican). The taxi rank is usually marked with an orange sign that says "TAXI" on it, and you'll generally see a line of taxis waiting there. You should go to the one at the front of the line. If it happens that all the taxis are out when you're looking for one, the orange sign tells you where to wait for one.

Official Roman taxis are white with a "Roma Capitale" sign on the door, along with a "Taxi" light on the roof and a taxi ID number on the door. These are the safest taxis to take, to avoid potential rip-offs.

If you prefer to call for a cab, that is also common in Rome. Taxis tend to show up within minutes after a call, so be prepared to leave right away. The cab will have an identity name/number written on its side, and you will be given that identifier to make sure that you take the correct cab. Your hotel concierge or workers in restaurants and bars are usually happy to call a taxi for you. If you have phone service and want to call yourself, try +39 063570. Be aware that the taxi meter starts running as soon as a cab leaves to pick you up and will arrive with some charge on it.

However you get your taxi, if the meter *isn't* running when you start a journey, point that out and make sure it is turned on for your ride, so you are charged the correct amount. (If the driver claims the meter is "broken," get out and get a different cab.)

You are supposed to be able to pay for taxis in Rome with a credit card, but drivers often report (claim?) that their machines are out of order and require cash payment. It is not customary to tip drivers of the white, metered city cabs. If you feel you must tip, only round up to the closest euro. If the driver provides service other than driving you (such as loading/unloading luggage), you may want to tip an extra euro or two. The Rome city tourism site writes that you should always receive a receipt, and you should ask for one, if necessary.

To learn more about taxis in Rome, check out the city taxi information at www.turismoroma.it/en/node/18690.

Other in-city transportation

Public transportation is available in Rome but is often overcrowded. If you can avoid traveling during the morning or afternoon commutes, you are more likely to find room aboard a train or bus. The metro system and city bus system are both useful for tourists, if you are comfortable with the crowds, with probably standing during your ride, and possibly having to use stairs to get to or from the metro. If mobility, balance or endurance is a concern, you probably want to get around the city in an easier fashion.

The **metro** system in Rome is constrained by the many archeological remains beneath the modern city. Constructing new tunnels is very slow going, and as a result, the metro system is far less extensive than in most European cities. Two main lines are of interest to tourists—the orange A line and the blue B line. The orange line has stops near the Vatican Museums, St. Peter's Basilica, the Spanish Steps, and Trevi Fountain. The blue line stops near the Colosseum and the Roman Forum. The lines intersect at the main train station, Termini. The **metro** runs from 5:30 a.m. to 11:30 p.m. (to 1:30 a.m. Friday and Saturday). A nice metro map is available at www.atac.roma.it/files/doc. asp?r=4.

Rome's municipal **bus** lines can be useful to tourists and easier to access than the metro. Bus route #64, for example, runs from the main train station to near the Forum, near the Pantheon, near the Piazza Navona, and near St. Peter's Basilica. (Bus #40 is an express version of this route.) *Beware of pickpockets* on all of the public transportation, but particularly routes that are popular with tourists. (I personally know people—plural—who have had a wallet lifted while riding bus #64.) For more information about the Roman bus system, including a high-resolution map, check out www.rometoolkit.com/transport/rome_bus.htm.

The same ticket applies for all forms of public transportion in Rome and must be purchased before boarding the transportation or entering the metro train area. Make sure you validate your ticket the first time you use it by sticking it into the validating machine (or running it through the metro entrance turnstile), or you will be riding illegally and could face a fine if caught.

Tickets and longer passes for Rome can be purchased at vending machines in metro stations, at some bus stops, at convenience stores, and at tobacconists' shops. Ticket options are as follows:

- A one-way ticket (BIT) costs €1.50 and is good for 100 minutes, covering transfers between metro and buses. (Leaving the metro system and returning later on the same ticket is not allowed, even

within the time limit. Metro transfers must be at the Termini stop.)
- A 24-hour ticket is available for €7 and allows unlimited travel on public transportation from the time of validation until 24 hours later.
- The Roma 48-hour ticket is available for €12.50 and allows unlimited travel on public transportation from the time of validation until 48 hours later.
- The Roma 72-hour ticket is available for €18 and allows unlimited travel on public transportation from the time of validation until 72 hours later.
- The week-long CIS ticket is available for €24 and allows unlimited travel on public transportation from the time of validation until midnight of the seventh day.
- The Roma Pass is a tourist ticket that offers unlimited travel on public transportation for either 48 or 72 hours in addition to reduced cost to enter tourist sights (see below). Cost is €28 for 48 hours and €38.50 for 72 hours.

Sightseeing passes

If you plan on sightseeing a lot in Rome, you might want to consider some sort of sightseeing pass. As with any sightseeing pass, compare the costs of what you would actually see with the cost of the pass. (A number of sights, such as the Pantheon, are free to enter.)

The **Roma Pass** (www.romapass.it) includes access to public transportation for either 48 (€28) or 72 hours (€38.50), as well as free entry to the first one (with the 48-hour ticket) or two (with the 72-hour ticket) tourist sights and reduced entrance fees (of 15%-50%) to additional sights and fast-track entry to Castel Sant'Angelo and Musei Capitolini. (For comparison, a combined ticket to the Colosseum/Forum/Palatine cost at least €12 on-site, more for fast-track entry. A full-price on-site ticket to Castel Sant'Angelo costs €10.50. Add to the prices of bus passes above to see whether this is a good deal for you. Remember, fast-track entry is worth something on its own.) This pass provides discounts on various tourists tours: see www.romapass.it/en/tourist-services/sightseeing-tours/. You can order online or buy the pass at museums and at tourist information points.

The **Omnia Vatican and Rome Card** (www.romeandvaticanpass.com) includes a 3-day Roma Pass (see above) in addition to the Omnia Vatican and Rome Card for Vatican sights and tours and unlimited use of the (not-highly-reviewed) Roma Cristian HOHO bus. The Roma Pass inclusions are listed above (free entry to 2 Rome sights, some fast-track entry, free public transportation for 3 days).

The Omnia Vatican portion includes free entry to the Vatican Museums (and Sistine Chapel), "jump-the-line" entry to St. Peter's Basilica (the basilica is free to enter; must still go through security line), and fast-track entry to the Colosseum. Price for 3 consecutive days is €113 for adults and €85 for children (aged 6-9). You can order the cards online for pickup in Rome or just buy directly in Rome at one of the following places: O.R.P. - Piazza Pio XII, 9 (St. Peter's Basilica); O.R.P. - Piazza di Porta S.Giovanni, 6 (St. John in the Lateran); or O.R.P. - Largo Argentina, Via dei Cestari 21 (Pantheon).

The **Rome City Pass-Turbo Pass** (www.turbopass.com/rome-city-pass) is available for 1, 2, 3, 4, 5, or 7 days. It includes public transportation for the length of time chosen (optional), unlimited rides on the (poorly-reviewed) City Roma HOHO bus, free fast-track entry to the Vatican Museums and Sistine Chapel, free entry to the Colosseum/Forum/Palatine, and many other free entries. Costs are as follows (add €12 for airport transfer).

- 1 day, adult €71.90, teen (10-17) €36.90, child (6-9) €26.90 (add €7.70 for public transportation)
- 2 days, adult €86.90, teen (10-17) €41.90, child (6-9) €31.90 (add €17 for public transportation)
- 3 days, adult €96.90, teen (10-17) €46.90, child (6-9) €36.90 (add €19.80 for public transportation)
- 4 days, adult €106.90, teen (10-17) €51.90, child (6-9) €41.90 (add €26.40 for public transportation)
- 5 days, adult €116.90, teen (10-17) €56.90, child (6-9) €46.90 (add €26.40 for public transportation)
- 7 days, adult €126.90, teen (10-17) €61.90, child (6-9) €51.90 (add €26.40 for public transportation)

Order in advance and either have mailed to you or pick up in Rome or you can print out or download an e-ticket.

The **Rome Tourist Card** (rome.ticketbar.eu/en/discount-card/roma-city-pass-/) is transferred all electronically and does not require picking up an order in Rome. (Show tickets on your phone.) It does not limit access to a certain number of days. The card includes fast-track entry to St. Peter's Basilica (with audio guide), the Colosseum (with audio guide), the Forum/Palatine, and elsewhere. Other sights, including at the Vatican, are available as options or at a 20% discount. It does not include a public transportation pass, but does include 1 day's free access to a HOHO bus and a 20% discount for additional HOHO days. Metro passes are also available at 20% off if ordered along with the Tourist Card. Includes 1-way transfer into the city (via bus) from either of the airports. Late 2019 prices are as follows:

- Adult (no Vatican Museum), €69.50
- Child, 6-17 (no Vatican Museum), €52
- Child, 0-5 (no Vatican Museum), €5
- Adult (with Vatican Museum), €101.50
- Child, 6-17 (with Vatican Museum), €73
- Child, 0-5 (with Vatican Museum), €13.59

Check prices carefully to see whether the Rome Tourist Card (or any other sightseeing pass) makes sense for you. Realize that some sights (such as the Colosseum) require online, timed reservations, even if you have a pass that allows free entry. Also, bear in mind that fast-track entry is worth something because of the time it can save. If you order tickets individually instead of using a pass, you are advised to select fast-track options to avoid long lines (e.g., at the Vatican Museums and the Colosseum).

Day trips

It's possible to see much of central Italy (and beyond) without having to leave the convenience of your base hotel at night, because Rome has tourist companies that specialize in day trips.

As always, use the information here as a guide, but check each company's Web site for tour details and the most current price and schedule information. **Tour details—even which tours are offered—routinely change from season to season.** Whichever tours you decide on, look over cancellation policies, if your plans aren't completely firm.

Browsing through Web sites will also help you decide which company's tours seem a good fit for you. Be aware that some specific tours might have special requirements or recommendations, so you'll want to look descriptions over closely before you show up at the departure point.

Tour companies differ on which entry fees and meals they include in their prices, so check those specifics (and confirm online), if your selection comes down to price.

Also take into account where the tours depart from. Walks of Italy tours depart from around the Piazza della Repubblica or the Termini train station. City Wonders leaves from multiple places, including Piazza del Popolo, Termini, and Piazza Cinquecento (next to Termini). Tours of Italy offers hotel pickup and drop-off. Gray Line picks up from selected central hotels or from a meeting point at Piazza della Repubblica or Termini. Destination Italia departs primarily from next to Termini at Via Amendola.

Private and semi-private day tour companies will pick you up and drop you off at your hotel, so hotel location is less a concern. You may decide on tours according to which ones depart from near your hotel or will pick you up. Wherever you leave from, make sure you show up early for any tour so you are not considered a no-show and your seat sold to someone else!

If you want to save your walking energy for the tour itself but you select a tour with a departure point that is not close to your hotel, you may want to invest in a taxi ride to get there.

Walks of Italy

Walks of Italy (www.walksofitaly.com/rome-tours/) is a TripAdvisor Certificate of Excellence Hall of Fame awardee. The company offers not only guided tours and experiences within Rome (see Web site), but also day trips out of Rome and other Italian cites. Tours are "all-inclusive," meaning that all costs—transportation, guide, entrance fees—are covered, except any tip you choose to give. Some locations require extensive walking—read details closely, if this is a concern.

Some tours fill up months or weeks in advance, so don't delay, if you want to register for one. After booking, the company strongly recommends that you print out the confirmation letter so all tour details are at hand. Their day-trip excursions include the following:

Pompeii Tour from Rome with Amalfi Coast Drive—Tour highlights include guided tour of the ruins of Pompeii with an archeologist who may have excavated at the site, scenic drive down the spectacular Amalfi Coast, stopping in the cliffside town of Positano (or Sorrento in winter) for free time to explore and lunch (not included). Includes round-trip air-conditioned bus transportation, guide, and entrance tickets in a small group of 18 or fewer. Depart 7:15 a.m., return around 8:15 p.m., both around Piazza della Repubblica. Adults from €189, children (2-14) from €169, students from €184.

Tuscan Hilltowns, Castles, and Vineyards—Tour highlights include the Tuscan town of Pienza for artisan food, wine, and other local specialities, a local farm for a Tuscan lunch feast, extended access to Montalcino Castle and its views over Tuscany, and a visit to an award-winning vineyard with wine tasting. Private bus transportation with no more than 18 people, food, drink, guide, and entrances all included. Mon/Thur/Sat (in season). Depart 7:15 a.m., return around 8:15 p.m., both around Piazza della Repubblica. Adults from €159, children (2-14) from €149, students from €159.

Boat-Hopping on the Amalfi Coast—Tour highlights include scenic overlooks for photos, the cliffside town of Positano for time to explore and eat (lunch not included), a boat ride to Amalfi Town, a visit to a lemon farm with provided drinks and snacks, free time, then a boat ride to Salerno. Includes round-trip high-speed train ride to Naples and back, private bus to the Amalfi Coast, boat rides between towns, private limoncello tasting, tour guide, maximum 18 people. Not in winter. Depart 7:15 a.m., return around 8:45 p.m., both from the Rome Termini train station. Adults from €198, children (2-14) from €188, students from €198.

Pope's Palace, Castel Gandolfo and Gardens—Tour highlights include interiors of the pope's summer residence (the apostolic palace), Barberini Garden, free time and lunch (not included) in the hill town of Castel Gandolfo. Includes train transportation to and from Rome, entrances to the palace and gardens, and official Vatican audio guides. Fridays only (as of this writing). Depart 9 a.m., return around 3:30 p.m. *Current dates/prices not available at press time.* From €45.

Rome in a Day—Tour highlights include the Vatican Museums, the Sistine Chapel, the Colosseum, the Pantheon, Trevi Fountain, Piazza Navona, and a self-guided tour of St. Peter's Basilica. Includes private transfer from historic city center to the Vatican, skip-the-line entries, groups no larger than 18, free homemade gelato, a tour guide, and a walking tour of the historic city center. (Considerable walking required!)

Days vary by season. Depart 8:45, return 4:15 p.m. Adults from €134, children (2-14) from €124, students from €134.

City Wonders Tours

City Wonders (citywonders.com/rome-tours) offers tours both in and out of Rome. The company has had TripAdvisor's Certificate of Excellence for at least five years running (is a Hall of Fame awardee), and in 2019 was awarded TripAdvisor's Travelers' Choice Award (representing the top 1% of a category). The company at one time claimed that its tour of the Vatican Museums, Sistine Chapel, and St. Peter's Basilica was the "Number 1 Booked Tour in the World." Out-of-town tours can leave from Piazza del Popolo (on the metro, between the Park Villa Borghese and the Tiber River), from the Termini station, from Piazza dei Cinquecento (just NW of the Termini station), Piazza dei Re Roma (on the metro, southeast of the Colosseum), and elsewhere, so play close attention to the listed meeting point. Their day-trip excursions include the following:

Pompeii and Mount Vesuvius Volcano—Tour highlights include round-trip, air-conditioned bus transportation to Pompeii, skip-the-line entrance to the ruins, an expert archeologist guide, authentic pizza lunch in Naples (included), drive to the top of Mount Vesuvius Volcano for the view, small groups (maximum 25), audio headsets, and a dedicated English-speaking guide. All entrance fees included. Daily. Depart 7:30 a.m. from Piazza del Popolo, return around 7:30 p.m. Adults from €139, children (2-14) from €129.

Tuscany from Rome with 3-Course Lunch and Wine Pairing—Tour highlights include round-trip transportation on an air-conditioned coach to the Tuscan Hills with an English-speaking guide, a walking tour of the hilltop town of Montepulciano, Sant'Antimo Abbey, a 3-course gourmet lunch in Montalcino at a winery, time to explore the UNESCO World Heritage village of Pienza, audio headsets through the day. Not Sundays. Depart 7:30 a.m. from Piazza del Popolo, return around 7:30 p.m. Adults from €129, children (2-14) from €119.

VIP Amalfi Coast Tour by High-Speed Train—Tour highlights include a guided tour of the Amalfi Coast by private coach, free time in the cliffside towns of Positano and Amalfi, cheese tasting, round-trip high-speed train between Rome and Naples, an expert local guide, small group limited to 18. Schedule varies by season. Depart 7:15 a.m. from the Termini Station, return around 8:45 p.m. Adults from €199, children (2-14) from €189.

VIP Pompeii and Sorrento Small Group Tour—Tour highlights include round-trip fast-speed train to Naples, a two-hour guided tour with skip-the-line access at Pompeii, coffee break and shopping, exploration time in Sorrento overlooking the Bay of Naples, limoncello tasting, local English-speaking guide, size limited to 15 people, audioguides provided throughout. Schedule varies by season. Depart 7:15 a.m., return around 7:15 p.m., from the Termini Station. Adults from €229, children (2-14) from €219.

Pompeii Express Tour from Rome via High-Speed Train—Tour highlights include train ride to Pompeii, skip-the-line access to Pompeii ruins, 2-hour tour with English-speaking guide, maximum group size 25, audio headsets available if desired. Not Sun/Wed. Depart 7:15 a.m. from Termini Station, return 1:45 p.m. Adults from €199, children (2-14) from €189.

Venice Day Trip from Rome by High-Speed Train—Tour highlights include a panoramic cruise of Venice, the Grand Canal, the Rialto Bridge, skip-the-line access to St. Mark's Basilica, special access to Basilica terraces, 2-hour guided city tour on foot, free time in Venice. Maximum 20 people. Head-phones provided if needed. Mon/Thur/Sat. Depart 6:30 a.m. from Piazza dei Cinquecento, return 9:15 p.m. Adults from €285, children (2-14) from €275.

Florence Day Trip from Rome by High-Speed Train—Tour highlights include skip-the-line access to the Accademia to view the original David statue, high-speed round-trip train to Florence, Florence Duomo and Baptistry, Ponte Vecchio, 3-hour guided tour of Florence with expert English-speaking guide, 4 hours of free time to explore Florence, audio headsets. Maximum group size of 25. Wed/Fri/Sat. Depart 7:05 a.m. from Piazza dei Cinquecento, return 5:50 p.m. Adults from €175, children (2-14) from €165.

Rome Countryside Vineyard Half-Day Tour with Frascati Wine Tasting—Tour highlights include a visit to Frascati vineyard and olive grove, professionally guided wine tour, round-trip air-conditioned coach transportation, English-speaking coordinator for the day, maximum group size of 25. Seasonal, Mon/Thur/Sat. Depart 3 p.m. from Piazza Re di Roma, return 6:30 p.m. Adults from €59, children (2-14) from €54.

Ostia Antica Half-Day Tour: An Ancient Roman City Frozen in Time—Tour highlights include round-trip transportation to ancient port remains with flexible open return, expert guide, audio headsets. Maximum group size of 25. Sun/Tue/Thur/Sat. Depart 8:40 a.m. from Café Piramide, return 12:40 p.m. Adults from €55, children (2-14) from €50.

Pompeii Skip-the-Line Tickets and Round-Trip Transportation from Rome—Tour highlights include round-trip air-conditioned coach transportation, skip-the-line entrance to archeological site, 3 hours free time at site for independent exploration, English-speaking coordinator for day. Sun/Thur/ Sat. Depart 7:15 a.m. from Piazza del Popolo, return 5:15 p.m. Adults from €79, children (2-14) from €69.

Tours Italy—Avventure Bellissime Rome

Avventure Bellissime Rome (www.tours-italy.com) offers multi-day, daylong, and partial-day tours in and around Rome. The company has had TripAdvisor's Certificate of Excellence for at least five years running (is a Hall of Fame awardee). Their day-trip excursions include the following:

Semi-Private Pompeii, Positano & Amalfi Coast with Lunch Included—Tour highlights include hotel pickup and drop-off, maximum tour size 7 or 8, skip-the-line tickets to Pompeii archeological site, 2-hour tour of Pompeii site with expert guide, 1½ hour free time in the hillside town of Positano, light pasta lunch in family restaurant. Schedule varies by season. Depart around 6:45-7:15 a.m. (hotel pickup), return (hotel drop-off). 12 hours. From €219 per person.

Other day tours available include Grand Day Tour of Venice, Doges Palace, Walking tour and Grand Canal boat tour (5 hours, €114 per person, meets in Venice); Venice in 1 Day Tour (3 hours, from €67, meets in Venice); Grand Day Tour of Rome in 2 Days: Vatican, Colosseum, Piazzas, Fountains, and Trastevere (9 hours over 2 days, €249).

Gray Line—I Love Rome

Gray Line—I Love Rome Tours (graylinerome.com) lacks the consistently stellar ratings of smaller tour companies but offers more affordable day trips both in and out of Rome and pickup at central Rome hotels. It does have TripAdvisor's Certificate of Excellence for 2019. Their out-of-town excursions include the following full-day trips:

Pompeii and its Ruins—Tour highlights include pickup at selected central Rome hotels, round-trip transportation, panoramic tour of Naples, skip-the-line entrance to Pompeii, professional guided tour of the ruins, audio headset, authentic pizza lunch. Depart around 7:30 a.m. (either hotel pickup starting at 6:30 a.m. or meet around Piazza della Repubblica, NW of Termini, by 7:15 a.m.). 12 hours. Adults from €140, children (3-7) €112.

Other tours offered by Gray Line include Rome in 1 Day: Vatican and Colosseum Skip the Line (9 hours, from €92 (from €49 in off-season)); Semi-Private Vatican Tour (3 hours, from €65); UNESCO Jewels: Venice Day Trip from Rome (13 hours, from €200); Vatican Museums, Sistine Chapel, and St. Peter's Basilica Skip-the-Line Morning Tour (3.5 hours from €64).

Destination Italia/Gartour Experiences Rome

Destination Italia (www.gartourprograms.net/worldwide/excursions-rome.html) has TripAdvisor's Certificate of Excellence and offers tours both in and out of Rome. Departures are from Via Amendola (just NW of the train station) or Piazza del Popolo. The first two tours are available English-only; others are multi-lingual.

Best in Tuscany in 1 Day—Tour highlights include round-trip transport in air-conditioned coach, English-speaking tour assistant, historic hill-owns of Multepulciano, Pienza, and vineyards of Montalcino, gourmet 3-course lunch and wine-tasting at a Tuscan farm (included), Sant'Antimo Abbey. Maximum group size 25. Headsets available. Not Sunday. Depart around 7:30 a.m. from Piazza del Popolo, return around 7:30-8:30 p.m. Adults €129, children (2-14) €119.

Prestige Full-Day Tour Pompeii and Vesuvius—Tour highlights include round-trip transport in air-conditioned coach, English-speaking tour assistant, entry to Pompeii archeological site with a guided tour, entry to Mount Vesusius (in season), headsets in Pompeii. Maximum tour size 25. Tues/Thur/Sat/Sun. Depart 8:40 a.m. from Café Piramide, return around 8:40 p.m. Adults €134, children (2-14) €124.

Taste of Italy—Tour highlights include round-trip transportation in an air-conditioned coach, Tuscan village of Cortona (featured in *Under the Tuscan Sun*), drive along lake Trasimeno, lunch in a countryside restaurant (included), drive through the Chianti region, stop in Montepulciano, visit a wine cellar, local guide, multi-lingual. Tues/Sun. Depart 7:30 a.m. from Via Giovanni Amendola (near the Termini), return to vicinity of your hotel around 7-8 p.m. Adults €125, children (3-7) €117.20.

Full-Day Tour Assisi and Orvieto—Tour highlights include round-trip transportation with air-conditioned coach, a 14th-century cathedral in the Etruscan town of Orvieto, drive along the Tiber Valley, a guided walking tour in Assisi including St. Francis' birthplace and his childhood home, St. Francis' Basilica, restaurant lunch (included), earphones, multi-lingual. Mon/Thur/Sat. Depart 7:30 a.m. from Via Giovanni Amendola (near the Termini), return around 8 p.m with drop-off near hotel. Adults €118, children (3-7) €94.40.

Full-Day Tour Capri—Tour highlights include round-trip coach transportation to Naples, hydrofoil transportation to Isle of Capri, minibus panoramic drive to clifftop town of Anacapri, lunch (included), free time after lunch, optional tour of the Blue Grotto (additional €28), multi-lingual. Depart 7:30 a.m. from Via Giovanni Amendola (near the Termini), return around 8:30 p.m. with drop-off near hotel. Adult €156, children (3-7) €124.80.

Half-Day Tour of Ancient Ostia—Tour highlights include round-trip air-conditioned coach transportation, a guided tour in Ostia. Fri/Sun. Depart 8 a.m. from Via Giovanni Amendola (near the Termini), return around 12 p.m. Adults €65, children (3-7) €60.

Roman Castles Tour—Tour highlights include round-trip coach transportation, driving by the ruins of the Baths of Caracalla, the Appian Way, Castelgandolfo, Rocca di Papa, with a stop at Frascati for food and drink at a tavern, earphones. Bus tour. Multi-lingual tour. Mon/Sat. Depart 2:30 p.m. from Via Giovanni Amendola (near the Termini), return around 6:30 p.m. with drop-off near hotel. Adults €60, children (3-7) €48.

Tivoli, Villa Adriana & Villa D'Este Tour—Tour highlights include round-trip transportation, Villa Adriana (entry included), Villa D'Este (entry included) with fountains and gardens, local guide, earphones, multi-lingual tour. Tues/Thur/Sun. Depart 8 a.m. or 2:30 p.m. from Via Giovanni Amendola (near the Termini), return around 4 hours later to vicinity of your hotel. Adults €73, children (3-7) €63.73.

Private and semi-private tours

Welcome Italy

Welcome Italy (www.welcome-italy.it) offers numerous small-group tours in and around Rome. Day-trip excursions include the following:

Assisi and Orvieto Cathedral—Tour highlights include pickup and drop-off at your hotel, travel in air-conditioned minivan, 2-hour guided tour of Assisi, St. Francis Basilica, Convent of Santa Chiara, Orvieto walking tour, Orvieto cathedral, English-speaking tour assistant. Mon/Wed/Fri/Sat. Depart 8 a.m. Adults €496 (for a single-person reservation), €248 (for minimum two people), child (4-8) €178 (with minimum two paying adults), infant (0-3) €60. Private tours also available.

Tuscany Wine Tour, Siena, and San Gimignano—Tour highlights include travel in air-conditioned minivan, maximum 6 people, hotel pickup and drop-off, drive through the Chianti hills, hilltown of San Gimignano ("The City of the Hundred Towers"), wine tasting (included), 10 different kinds of wine and oil, lunch on the estate (included), Siena, Piazza del Campo, coffee break, English-speaking tour assistant. Sun/Mon/Wed/Fri. Depart 7 or 8 a.m., leave Siena 5 p.m. Adults per person €248, children (4-8 years) €178. Private tours also available.

Florence, Cradle of the Renaissance, and Pisa—Tour highlights include transportation in air-conditioned minivan, drive through Tiber River Valley, by Chianti vineyards to Pisa, Leaning Tower, Baptistery and Duomo, lunch break (not included), 2-hour walking tour of Florence, David statue (entry included), Duomo, Baptistry and Bell Tower, panoramic view from Piazzale Michelangelo over Florence, English-speaking assistant. Not Mon. Depart 7 a.m., leave Florence 4:30 p.m. Adult (single person reservation) €496, adult (per person minimum 2) €248, child (4-8 years) €178, infant (0-3) €60. Private tours also available.

Amalfi Coast and Pompeii—Tour highlights include round-trip transportation in air-conditioned minivan, English-speaking tour assistant, maximum 6 people on tour, Pompeii archeological site, 2-hour guided tour through ruins, Positano on Amalfi Coast, lunch (not included), free time in Positano. Daily. Depart 7 a.m. Return to Rome at end of day. Adult (single person reservation) €496, adult (per person minimum 2) €248, child (4-8 years) €178, infant (0-3) €60. Private tours also available.

Pompeii and Naples, Tasting Local Products—Tour highlights include round-trip transportation in air-conditioned minivan, English-speaking tour assistant, maximum 6 people on tour, Pompeii archeological site, 2-hour guided tour through ruins, lunch of local foods (included), Bay of Naples, walk in Naples, Neopalitan coffee. Mon/Wed/Fri/Sat. Depart 7 a.m., return to Rome at end of day. Adult (single person reservation) from €456, adult (per person minimum 2) €228, child (4-8 years) €148, infant (0-3) €60. Private tours also available.

Roman Countryside, Food, and Wine Tasting—Tour highlights include half-day tour with food and wine included, hotel pickup and drop-off, the Via Appia Antica, summer residence of the Pope, wine tasting at a local cellar, food and drink at restaurant, air-conditioned minivan (max 6 people). Not Tue/Thur. Pickup from 10-10:30 a.m., return approximately 6-7 hours later. Adults (minimum 2 people) €189, child (4-8 years) €159. Private tours also available.

Relive Ancient Ostia, the other Pompeii—(Private tour option) Tour highlights include pickup and drop-off at hotel, the archeological site of Ostia, 3 hours with professional local guide, round-trip transportation in air-conditioned minivan. (Ostia entrance fee not included.) Not Sunday. Depart 9 a.m. or 11 a.m., return (drop-off) 5 hours later. Group 1-6 people €420; group 7-12 people €460; Ostia entrance adult €20, child (4-8 years) €15.

Tivoli, The Best of Hadrian, Villa and Villa D'Este—(Private tour option) Tour highlights include skip-the-line private half-day tour, transportation in air-conditioned minivan, Hadrian's Villa, Villa D'Este, famous fountains, walk the historic town of Tivoli. Not Sun/Mon. Depart 9, 11, 1:30 from hotel, drop-off 5 hours later. Group 1-6 people €420, group 7-12 people €460; tickets for villas adult €30, child (4-8 years) €20.

See the Welcome Italy Web site for **additional tour options** in and out of Rome, including cooking lessons.

LivItaly Tours

LivItaly Tours (www.livitaly.com) offers small-group and private tours from Rome. The company is a TripAdvisor Hall of Fame awardee, with at least five consecutive years with a Certificate of Excellence.

Pompeii Day from Rome, small group—Tour highlights include transportation in a Mercedes, Naples, Gulf of Naples, lunch in Naples, skip-the-line access to the archeological ruins of Pompeii with an expert guide,

2½-hour guided tour of Pompeii, maximum 6 people in group. All tickets and reservations included. Tue/Fri/Sun. Depart 8 a.m. from Palazzo Venezia. Full day. Adults €299. Other prices on Web site.

Other tours from Rome include Ostia Antica Half-Day Tour (base price €218 for 2 adults); VIP Pompeii, Capri & Amalfi Helicopter Tour (base price €13,900 for up to 5 passengers).

Lodging

Rome is chock-full of wonderful neighborhoods to lodge in. The city presents a problem, though, when it comes to finding that magic mix of easy access and charm. Hands-down the best area for access to hop-on/hop-off buses, city transportation, trains, and day trips is near the Termini Station and Piazza della Repubblica, but the Termini area, in particular, is notably lacking in historical interest and attractive atmosphere, when compared to other Roman neighborhoods. The Piazza del Popolo (by the Villa Borghese) is convenient for some day-trip excursions and has bus and metro access, but the HOHO buses do not stop there.

The most historic and appealing area is probably the historical center, around the Piazza Navona and the Pantheon, but its very age, resulting in narrow and winding streets, makes it inaccessible to buses, and its ancient foundations render it inaccessible by metro. The nearest HOHO stop is so-called "Vatican," by the Castel Sant'Angelo, but city buses do run along Corso Vittorio Emanuele. The Vatican area is accessible by city bus and the metro but is not near most day-trip departures, and the HOHO stop is not particularly close (by Castel Sant'Angelo).

If you want to wander a pleasant neighborhood and don't mind working harder (or paying more) to get around, the historic city center is probably for you. If you plan to focus your visit on the Vatican, that is clearly a rich lodging possibility for you.

Because this book prioritizes ease and accessibility, I will discuss lodging in two areas—the super-convenient Termini/Piazza della Repubblica area (which also tends to have lower room rates) and the area from around the Spanish Steps to Piazza Barberini, which offers considerably more in atmosphere but is also reasonably accessible (compared to the rest of the city).

When deciding where to lodge, keep in mind whether you will take commercial day trips and where those depart from.

- Walks of Italy tours depart from around the Piazza della Repubblica or the Termini train station.
- City Wonders leaves from multiple places, including Piazza del Popolo, Termini, and Piazza Cinquecento (next to Termini).
- Tours of Italy offers hotel pickup and drop-off.
- Gray Line picks up from selected central hotels or from a meeting point at Piazza della Repubblica or Termini.
- Destination Italia departs primarily from next to Termini at Via Amendola.

Realize that if you plan to tour Rome on one of the golf-cart or private tours and if you plan to take excursions that offer hotel pickup and drop-off, you can conveniently lodge *anywhere* in Rome and should choose the area that most appeals to you.

Wherever you stay, be aware that hotel air conditioning is usually nonfunctional outside the summer months, however warm the off-season weather may be. Many tourists find the heat of their hotel room quite uncomfortable during late winter and spring. If you know that could be the case for you, you may want to contact the hotel ahead of time and see whether you can arrange to have a fan in your room.

Hotels on this list are based on location, good reviews, and general accessibility, including access to easy transportation. It favors buildings with elevators, but that doesn't mean the elevator will be larger than a phone booth. You may need to make several trips to get your luggage to upper floors. This section isn't the last word on acceptable accommodation, but it makes a good starting point to narrow down your search. Just check online to make sure that information is still accurate, on TripAdvisor, on Booking.com, or on the hotel's own Web site.

You may find a wonderful deal on what looks like a good choice in a convenient location. By all means—grab it! Same with charming B&Bs, which aren't covered here because they tend to have a limited number of available rooms and generally don't have elevators. If you can nab one in a favorable location that gets good reviews, has a great breakfast, decent accessibility, and a workable price, do it!

Hotel price ranges are based on late 2019 TripAdvisor averages. Averages can vary considerably throughout the year. Your own quotes may be higher or lower.

Termini/Piazza della Repubblica

If you plan to take day trips from Walks of Italy, City Wonders, Gray Line, or Destination Italia, you would do well to lodge around the Termini/Piazza della Repubblica. All the Hop-On/Hop-Off bus tours stop at or near the Termini, walking distance from Piazza della Repubblica, and the area also provides excellent access to city buses, the metro, trains, and airport shuttles.

Hotels in the area include the following:

Hotel Artemide—Via Nazionale 22 (www.hotelartemide.it/en/). TripAdvisor's Traveler's Choice Award (top 1% of category). Location: SW of Piazza della Repubblica. Pros: free WiFi, non-smoking hotel, air conditioning, excellent breakfast, restaurant, bar/lounge, room service, fitness center, airport shuttle, facilities for disabled guests, elevator, twins/triples/quads available. Cons: price, no price break for singles, some hotel noise. (TripAdvisor price range for standard room: $168-$444.)

Distances: Piazza della Repubblica (.2 miles), National Museum of Rome (.3 miles), Termini (.3 miles), Piazza Barberini (.3 miles), Santa Maria Maggiore (.4 miles), Trevi Fountain (.5 miles), Forum (.7 miles), Spanish Steps (.7 miles), Piazza Navona (1.1 miles), Castel Sant'Angelo (1.4 miles), St. Peter's Basilica (2 miles)

iQ Hotel Roma—Via Firenze 8 (www.iqhotelroma.it/en/). TripAdvisor Certificate of Excellence. Location: west of Termini. Pros: free WiFi, non-smoking rooms, air conditioning, refrigerator, bar/lounge, fitness center, airport shuttle, restaurant, wonderful breakfast, elevator, twin/triple rooms available, ATM on property. Cons: no singles, no price break for singles. (TripAdvisor price range for standard room: $127-$303.)

Distances: Piazza della Repubblica (.2 miles), National Museum of Rome (.2 miles), Termini (.3 miles), Santa Maria Maggiore (.3 miles), Termini Metro Station (.3 miles), Trevi Fountain (.6 miles), Forum (.7 miles), Colosseum (.7 miles), Spanish Steps (.8 miles), Piazza Navona (1.1 miles), Castel Sant'Angelo (1.5 miles), St. Peter's Basilica (2.1 miles)

The Independent Hotel—Via Volturno 48 (www.maghotels.it/eng/the-independent-hotel/index.html). TripAdvisor's Certificate of Excellence. Location: north of Termini. Pros: non-smoking hotel, air conditioning, free WiFi, refrigerator, good breakfast included, bar/lounge, room service, airport shuttle, wheelchair access, elevator, fitness center, twin/triple/quad rooms available. Cons: some rooms small, small lift, very firm beds, street noise, rooms can be warm in off-season, no singles, no price break for singles. (TripAdvisor price range for standard room: $152-$393.)

Distances: Termini (.2 miles), National Museum of Rome (.2 miles), Piazza della Repubblica (.2 miles), Trevi Fountain (.9 miles), Piazza di Spagna (1 mile), Colosseum (1 mile), Forum (1.1 miles), Piazza Navona (1.5 miles), Castel Sant'Angelo (1.8 miles), St. Peter's Basilica (2.3 miles)

Hotel Diocleziano—Via Gaeta 71 (www.hoteldiocleziano.it/en/). TripAdvisor's Certificate of Excellence. Location: north of Termini. Pros: non-smoking rooms, air conditioning, very good breakfast included, free WiFi, airport shuttle, bar/lounge, wheelchair access, facilities for disabled guests, elevator, fitness center, twin/triple rooms. Cons: small showers, some rooms small, no price break for singles. (TripAdvisor price range for standard room: $99-$228.)

Distances: Termini (.1 miles), National Museum of Rome (.2 miles), Piazza della Repubblica (.2 miles), Termini Metro Station (.2 miles), Trevi Fountain (.9 miles), Spanish Steps (.9 miles), Colosseum (1 mile), Forum (1 mile), Piazza Navona (1.4 miles), Castel Sant'Angelo (1.7 miles), St. Peter's Basilica (2.3 miles)

Dharma Luxury Hotel—Via Torino 122 (www.dharmagroup.it/en/hotel/dharma-luxury/). TripAdvisor's Certificate of Excellence. Location: south next to Piazza della Repubblica. Pros: non-smoking hotel, air conditioning, good breakfast included, restaurant, room service, free WiFi, airport shuttle, ATM on site, elevator, single/twin/triple/quad/quint rooms available. Cons: no price break for singles, street noise. (TripAdvisor price range for standard room: $130-$339.)

Distances: Piazza della Repubblica (.1 miles), National Museum of Rome (.2 miles), Termini (.2 miles), Termini Metro Station (.3 miles), Santa Maria Maggiore (.3 miles), Piazza Barberini (.4 miles), Trevi Fountain (.6 miles), Spanish Steps (.7 miles), Forum (.8 miles), Colosseum (.8 miles), Piazza Navona (1.2 miles), Castel Sant'Angelo (1.5 miles), St. Peter's Basilica (2.1 miles)

Hotel Raffaello—Via Urbana 3 (www.hotelraffaello.it/it/). TripAdvisor's Certificate of Excellence. Location: west of Termini Station. Pros: very good breakfast sometimes included, free WiFi, elevator, non-smoking hotel, singles/twins/triples/quads available. Cons: very firm beds, small lift. (TripAdvisor price range for standard room: $71-$256.)

Distances: Santa Maria Maggiore (.2 miles), Cavour Metro Station (.2 miles), National Museum of Rome (.3 miles), Piazza della Repubblica (.3 miles), Termini (.4 miles), Colosseum (.6 miles), Forum (.6 miles), Trevi Fountain (.7 miles), Spanish Steps (.9 miles), Piazza Navona (1.2 miles), Castel Sant'Angelo (1.5 miles), St. Peter's Basilica (2.1 miles)

Gioberti Art Hotel—Via Gioberti 23. TripAdvisor's Certificate of Excellence. Location: near SW side of Termini. Pros: non-smoking hotel, free WiFi, room service, very good breakfast included, wheelchair access, accessible rooms, air-conditioning, elevator, twins/suites/triples available, slight price break for singles. Cons: some street noise at night, crowded sidewalks, warm rooms in off-season, some find neighborhood sketchy at night, bad WiFi. (TripAdvisor price range for standard room: $121-$236.)

Distances: Termini Metro Station (.1 miles), Termini (.2 miles), National Museum of Rome (.2 miles), Santa Maria Maggiore (.2 miles), Piazza della Repubblica (.3 miles), Vittorio Emanuele Metro Station (.4 miles), Colosseum (.8 miles), Forum (.9 miles), Trevi Fountain (.9 miles), Spanish Steps (1.1 miles), Piazza Navona (1.4 miles), Castel Sant'Angelo (1.8 miles), St. Peter's Basilica (2.4 miles)

UNAHotels Deco Roma—Via Giovanni Amendola 57 (www.gruppouna.it/en/unahotels/unahotels-deco-roma). TripAdvisor's Certificate of Excellence. Location: west of Termini. Pros: non-smoking rooms, very good breakfast included, free WiFi, bar/lounge, restaurant, room service, elevator, facilities for disabled guests, single/triple/family rooms available. Cons: street noise at night, some rooms dark, rooms can be too warm in off-season. (TripAdvisor price range for standard room: $137-$278.)

Distances: National Museum of Rome (.1 miles), Termini Metro Station (.1 mile), Santa Maria Maggiore (.2 miles), Piazza della Repubblica (.3 miles), Colosseum (.8 miles), Trevi Fountain (.8 miles), Forum (.9 miles), Spanish Steps (1 mile), Piazza Navona (1.4 miles), Castel Sant'Angelo (1.7 miles), St. Peter's Basilica (2.3 miles)

Hotel Sweet Home—Via Principe Amedeo 47 (www.hotelsweethome.it/index_en.html). TripAdvisor's Certificate of Excellence. Location: near SW side of Termini. Pros: air conditioning, free WiFi, airport shuttle, non-smoking hotel, elevator, single/twin/triple/quad/quint/family rooms available, high security doors. Cons: only 13 rooms. (TripAdvisor price range for standard room: $61-$165.)

Distances: Santa Maria Maggiore (.1 miles), National Museum of Rome (.2 miles), Termini Metro Station (.2 miles), Termini (.2 miles), Piazza della Repubblica (.3 miles), Vittorio Emanuele (.4 miles), Colosseum (.7 miles), Forum (.8 miles), Trevi Fountain (.9 miles), Spanish Steps (1 mile), Piazza Navona (1.4 miles), Castel Sant'Angelo (1.7 miles), St. Peter's Basilica (2.3 miles)

The Britannia Hotel—Via Napoli 64. TripAdvisor's Certificate of Excellence. Location: west of Termini. Pros: free WiFi, non-smoking hotel, air conditioning, very good breakfast included, bar/lounge, room service, elevator, twin/triple rooms. Cons: hard beds, some rooms very small, no singles, virtually no price break for singles. (TripAdvisor price range for standard room: $125-$308.)

Distances: Piazza della Repubblica (.2 miles), National Museum of Rome (.3 miles), Termini (.3 miles), Barberini Metro Station (.3 miles), Piazza Barberini (.3 miles), Trevi Fountain (.5 miles), Forum (.7 miles), Spanish Steps (.7 miles), Colosseum (.8 miles), Piazza Navona (1.1 miles), Castel Sant'Angelo (1.4 miles), St. Peter's Basilica (2 miles)

Hotel Morgana—Via Filippo Turati 33/37 (www.hotelmorgana.com/en/). TripAdvisor's Certificate of Excellence. Location: near SW side of Termini. Pros: free WiFi, non-smoking hotel, very good breakfast available, air conditioning, refrigerator, elevator, accessible rooms, airport shuttle, bar, room service, single/twin/triple/quad rooms available. Cons: street noise at night, some find neighborhood a bit sketchy at night, small rooms, small lift, single can cost more than double. (TripAdvisor price range for standard room: $118-$281.)

Distances: Vittorio Emanuele Metro Station (.2 miles), Santa Maria Maggiore (.3 miles), Termini Metro Station (.3 miles), Termini Station (.4 miles), National Museum of Rome (.4 miles), Colosseum (.8 miles), Forum (1 mile), Trevi Fountain (1.1 miles), Spanish Steps (1.3 miles), Piazza Navona (1.6 miles), Castel Sant'Angelo (2 miles), St. Peter's Basilica (2.6 miles)

Ariston Hotel—Via Filippo Turati 16 (www.hotelariston.it/en/). Has TripAdvisor's Certificate of Excellence. Location: near SW side of Termini. Pros: bar/lounge, very good breakfast included, free WiFi, air conditioning, refrigerator, non-smoking hotel, elevator, accessible rooms, room service, single/twin/triple/quad rooms available. Cons: street noise, thin walls, warm rooms in off-season, not the most attractive neighborhood. (TripAdvisor price range for standard room: $101-$278.)

Distances: Termini Metro Station (.2 miles), Santa Maria Maggiore (.2 miles), Termini Station (.2 miles), National Museum of Rome (.2 miles), Vittorio Emanuale Metro Station (.3 miles), Piazza della Repubblica (.4 miles), Colosseum (.8 miles), Forum (.9 miles), Trevi Fountain (.9 miles), Spanish Steps (1.1 miles), Piazza Navona (1.4 miles), Castel Sant'Angelo (1.8 miles), St. Peter's Basilica (2.4 miles)

Starhotels Metropole—Via Principe Amedeo 3 (www.starhotels.com/en/our-hotels/metropole-rome/). TripAdvisor's Certificate of Excellence. Location: west of Termini. Pros: non-smoking rooms, free WiFi, good breakfast included, non-smoking rooms, air conditioning, refrigerator, restaurant, bar/lounge, room service, fitness center, accessible rooms, facilities for disabled guests, airport shuttle, single/twin/triple/quad rooms available. Cons: can be too warm in off-season. (TripAdvisor price range for standard room: $152-$367.)

Distances: National Museum of Rome (.1 miles), Piazza della Repubblica (.2 miles), Termini (.2 miles), Termini Metro Station (.2 miles), Santa Maria Maggiore (.2 miles), Trevi Fountain (.7 miles), Colosseum (.8 miles), Forum (.8 miles), Spanish Steps (.9 miles), Piazza Navona (1.2 miles), Castel Sant'Angelo (1.6 miles), St. Peter's Basilica (2.2 miles)

Best Western Premier Hotel Royal Santina—Via Marsala 22 (www.hotelroyalsantina.com). TripAdvisor's Certificate of Excellence. Location: north of Termini. Pros: non-smoking hotel, air conditioning, free WiFi, good breakfast, restaurant, bar, room service, wheelchair access, accessible rooms, fitness center, twin/triple rooms, ATM on site. Cons: some small rooms, small bathrooms, slow WiFi, rooms can be warm in off-season, shower problems, no singles, very small price break for singles. (TripAdvisor price range for standard room: $104-$309.)

Distances: Termini (.1 miles), National Museum of Rome (.2 miles), Piazza della Repubblica (.3 miles), Trevi Fountain (1 mile), Colosseum (1 mile), Piazza de Spagna (1 mile), Forum (1.1 miles), Piazza Navona (1.5 miles), Castel Sant'Angelo (1.8 miles), St. Peter's Basilica (2.4 miles)

Best Western Plus Hotel Universo—Via Principe Amedeo 5/B (www.hoteluniverso.com/en/home-page.aspx). TripAdvisor's Certificate of Excellence. Location: west of Termini. Pros: non-smoking hotel, free Internet, airport shuttle, restaurant, bar/lounge, room service, very good breakfast available, fitness center, elevator, wheelchair access, facilities for disabled guests, single/triple/suite/family rooms available. Cons: some hotel noise, rooms can be too warm in off-season, some rooms smaller than expected. (TripAdvisor price range for standard room: $91-$340.)

Distances: National Museum of Rome (.1 miles), Termini (.2 miles), Piazza della Repubblica (.2 miles), Termini Metro Station (.2 miles), Santa Maria Maggiore (.2 miles), Trevi Fountain (.7 miles), Colosseum (.8 miles), Forum (.8 miles), Spanish Steps (.9 miles), Piazza Navona (1.3 miles), Castel Sant'Angelo (1.6 miles), St. Peter's Basilica (2.2 miles)

Augusta Lucilla Palace—Via Massimo d'Azeglio (www.augustalucillapalace.com). TripAdvisor's Certificate of Excellence. Location: west of Termini. Pros: non-smoking rooms, very good breakfast included, bar/lounge, room service, WiFi, elevator, facilities for disabled guests, airport shuttle, air conditioning, single/twin/triple/quad rooms available. Cons: single can cost as much as double, décor needs updating, breakfast lacks vegetarian options, small rooms. (TripAdvisor price range for standard room: $88-$258.)

Distances: National Museum of Rome (.1 miles), Termini (.2 miles), Termini Metro Station (.2 miles), Piazza della Repubblica (.2 miles), Santa Maria Maggiore (.2 miles), Colosseum (.7 miles), Trevi Fountain (.7 miles), Forum (.8 miles), Spanish Steps (.9 miles), Piazza Navona (1.3 miles), Castel Sant'Angelo (1.6 miles), St. Peter's Basilica (2.2 miles)

Quirinale Hotel—Via Nazionale 7 (www.hotelquirinale.it/en/). TripAdvisor's Certificate of Excellence. Location: NW of Termini near Piazza della Repubblica. Pros: non-smoking hotel, air conditioning, free WiFi, good breakfast included, airport shuttle, restaurant, bar/lounge, room service, refrigerator, fitness center, wheelchair access, facilities for disabled guests, single/twin/triple/quad rooms. Cons: rooms can be warm in off-season, basic breakfast, hard beds and pillows, weak showers, street noise, no price break for singles. (TripAdvisor price range for standard room: $112-$295.)

Distances: Piazza della Repubblica (.1 miles), National Museum of Rome (.2 miles), Termini (.3 miles), Termini Metro Station (.3 miles), Barberini Metro Station (.3 miles), Piazza Barberini (.4 miles), Santa Maria Maggiore (.4 miles), Trevi Fountain (.6 miles), Spanish Steps (.7 miles), Forum (.7 miles), Colosseum (.8 miles), Piazza Navona (1.1 miles), Castel Sant'Angelo (1.5 miles), St. Peter's Basilica (2 miles)

Hotel Nord Nuova Roma—Via Giovanni Amendola 3 (www.hotelnordnuovaroma.it/en/). TripAdvisor's Certificate of Excellence. Location: NW of Termini. Pros: non-smoking rooms, free WiFi, air conditioning, refrigerator, elevator, good breakfast included, bar/lounge, room service, airport shuttle, fitness center, single/twin/triple rooms available. Cons: small rooms, some showers bad. (TripAdvisor price range for standard room: $93-$269.)

Distances: National Museum of Rome (.1 miles), Termini (.1 miles), Piazza della Repubblica (.1 miles), Termini Metro Station (.2 miles), Santa Maria Maggiore (.3 miles), Trevi Fountain (.7 miles), Colosseum (.8 miles), Forum (.8 miles), Spanish Steps (.9 miles), Piazza Navona (1.3 miles), Castel Sant'Angelo (1.6 miles), St. Peter's Basilica (2.2 miles)

Near Spanish Steps/Piazza Barberini

This area does not have the fantastic connections of the Termini/Piazza Repubblica area, but is, in general, a more appealing quarter and still has good connections. There are metro stops at Spagna (near the Spanish Steps) and Piazza Barberini (leading to Termini Station in one direction—with a stop at Piazza della Repubblica on the way—and Piazza del Popolo in the other), HOHO bus stops there as well, and city bus access. Be aware that this area borders a drop down to the Tiber River basin—the Spanish Steps are there because there's a severe difference in elevation. The hotels I list here are on the "upper" level, where the HOHO bus stops are. As in other parts of Rome, there are many wonderful, charming hotels that do not include elevators and, as such, are not listed here.

Barocco Hotel—Via della Purificazione 4 (www.hotelbarocco.com). TripAdvisor's Certificate of Excellence. Location: Piazza Barberini. Pros: non-smoking hotel, free WiFi, air conditioning, wonderful breakfast included, bar/lounge, room service, elevator, airport shuttle, single/twin rooms. Cons: slow WiFi. (TripAdvisor price range for standard room: $187-$384.)

Distances: Piazza Barberini (0 miles), Trevi Fountain (.3 miles), U.S. Embassy (.3 miles), Spanish Steps (.3 miles), Termini (.6 miles), Forum (.7 miles), Piazza Navona (.8 miles), Colosseum (1 mile), Castel Sant'Angelo (1.1 miles), St. Peter's Basilica (1.7 miles)

Hotel Hassler—Piazza della Trinita dei Monti 6 (www.hotelhassler roma.com). TripAdvisor's Certificate of Excellence. Location: top of Spanish Steps. Pros: non-smoking hotel, air conditioning, free WiFi, restaurant, bar/lounge, room service, fitness center, wheelchair access, elevator, good breakfast, airport shuttle. Cons: price, only doubles. (TripAdvisor price range for standard room: $579-$1,347.)

Distances: Spanish Steps (.1 miles), Piazza Barberini (.3 miles), Trevi Fountain (.3 miles), Piazza Navona (.7 miles), Termini (.9 miles), Forum (.9 miles), Castel Sant'Angelo (.9 miles), Colosseum (1.2 miles), St. Peter's Basilica (1.5 miles)

Hotel Splendide Royal—Via di Porta Pinciana 14 (www.splendide royal.com). TripAdvisor's Certificate of Excellence. Location: NE Spanish Steps by south end of Borghese park. Pros: very good breakfast included, non-smoking rooms, air conditioning, free WiFi, restaurant, bar/lounge, room service, fitness center, wheelchair access, elevator, facilities for disabled guests, airport shuttle, twin/triple rooms available. Cons: bar is part of restaurant, price, no single rooms. (TripAdvisor price range for standard room: $290-$589.)

Distances: U.S. Embassy (.2 miles), Spagna Metro Station (.2 miles), Spanish Steps (.3 miles), Barberini Metro Station (.3 miles), Villa Borghese (.3 miles), Trevi Fountain (.5 miles), Termini (.8 miles), Piazza Navona (.9 miles), Forum (1 mile), Castel Sant'Angelo (1.1 miles), Colosseum (1.3 miles), St. Peter's Basilica (1.7 miles)

Sofitel Rome Villa Borghese—Via Lombardia 47 (sofitel.accor.com/hotel/1312/index.en.shtml). TripAdvisor's Certificate of Excellence. Location: NE Spanish Steps by Villa Borghese. Pros: free Internet, non-smoking hotel, restaurant, bar/lounge, room service, very good breakfast, elevator, airport shuttle. Cons: price, paid WiFi, needs updating, some rooms very small, no single/twin/triple rooms, no price break for singles. (TripAdvisor price range for standard room: $290-$585.)

Distances: U.S. Embassy (.2 miles), Spagna Metro Station (.2 miles), Spanish Steps (.2 miles), Barberini Metro Station (.3 miles), Villa Borghese (.4 miles), Trevi Fountain (.5 miles), Termini (.8 miles), Piazza Navona (.9 miles), Forum (1 mile), Castel Sant'Angelo (1.1 miles), Colosseum (1.2 miles), St. Peter's Basilica (1.7 miles)

Hotel Modigliani—Via della Purificazione 42 (www.hotelmodigliani.com/en/). TripAdvisor's Certificate of Excellence. Location: NW of Termini. Pros: free WiFi, non-smoking rooms, air conditioning, refrigerator, elevator, good breakfast included, bar/lounge, room service, airport shuttle, fitness center, single/twin/triple rooms available. Cons: small rooms, some showers bad, only 24 rooms. (TripAdvisor price range for standard room: $95-$212.)

Distances: Piazza Barberini (.1 miles), U.S. Embassy (.2 miles), Spanish Steps (.2 miles), Trevi Fountain (.3 miles), Termini (.7 miles), Forum (.8 miles), Piazza Navona (.8 miles), Colosseum (1.1 miles), Castel Sant' Angelo (1.1 miles), St. Peter's Basilica (1.7 miles)

Hotel Majestic Roma—Via Vittoria Veneto 50 (hotelmajestic.com). TripAdvisor's Certificate of Excellence. Location: east of the Spanish Steps. Pros: non-smoking hotel, air conditioning, good breakfast, restaurant, bar/lounge, room service, lift, fitness center, single/triple rooms. Cons: poor WiFi, noise, slow elevator (sometimes out of service). (TripAdvisor price range for standard room: $208-$808.)

Distances: Barberini Metro Station (.1 miles), U.S. Embassy (.2 miles), Spanish Steps (.3 miles), Trevi Fountain (.4 miles), Termini (.7 miles), Forum (.9 miles), Piazza Navona (.9 miles), Colosseum (1.1 miles), Castel Sant'Angelo (1.1 miles), St. Peter's Basilica (1.7 miles)

Hotel Savoy Rome—Via Ludovisi 15 (www.savoy.it/). TripAdvisor's Certificate of Excellence. Location: east of Spanish Steps. Pros: free WiFi, non-smoking hotel, air conditioning, good breakfast included, restaurant, bar/lounge, room service, wheelchair access, accessible rooms, facilities for disabled guests, airport shuttle, single/twin/triple rooms. Cons: small rooms, hard pillows and beds, street noise, hotel noise, breakfast may be overpriced. (TripAdvisor price range for standard room: $150-$346.)

Distances: U.S. Embassy (.1 miles), Piazza Barberini (.2 miles), Spanish Steps (.3 miles), Trevi Fountain (.5 miles), Termini (.7 miles), Forum (1 mile), Piazza Navona (1 mile), Colosseum (1.2 miles), Castel Sant'Angelo (1.2 miles), St. Peter's Basilica (1.8 miles)

Hotel Alexandra—Via Vittoria Veneto 18 (www.hotelalexandraroma.com). TripAdvisor's Certificate of Excellence. Location: by Piazza Barberini, Capuchin Church. Pros: non-smoking hotel, breakfast included, air conditioning, elevator, restaurant, free WiFi, airport shuttle, single/twin/triple/quad rooms. Cons: small rooms, shower and hot water problems, needs renovation, some stairs. (TripAdvisor price range for standard room: $86-$446.)

Distances: Piazza Barberini (.1 miles), U.S. Embassy (.2 miles), Spanish Steps (.3 miles), Trevi Fountain (.4 miles), Termini (.7 miles), Forum (.8 miles), Piazza Navona (.9 miles), Colosseum (1 mile), Castel Sant'Angelo (1.1 miles), St. Peter's Basilica (1.7 miles)

Berg Luxury Hotel—Via Aurora 29 (bergluxuryhotel.com). TripAdvisor's Certificate of Excellence. Location: NE of Spanish Steps by Villa Borghese. Pros: non-smoking hotel, air conditioning, free WiFi, bar/lounge, room service, wheelchair access, elevator, facilities for disabled guests, airport shuttle. Cons: so-so breakfast, hotel noise, only doubles available. (TripAdvisor price range for standard room: $124-$289.)

Distances: U.S. Embassy (.1 miles), Barberini Metro Station (.2 miles), Spanish Steps (.3 miles), Trevi Fountain (.5 miles), Termini (.7 miles), Piazza Navona (.9 miles), Forum (1 mile), Castel Sant'Angelo (1.1 miles), Colosseum (1.2 miles), St Peter's Basilica (1.7 miles)

La Residenza—Via Emilia 22-24 (www.laresidenzaroma.com/en/). TripAdvisor's Certificate of Excellence. Location: east of Spanish Steps. Pros: non-smoking hotel, air conditioning, refrigerator, good breakfast included, restaurant, bar/lounge, room service, elevator, facilities for disabled guests, airport shuttle, twin/triple/quad rooms. Cons: paid WiFi, hard beds, no singles, no price break for singles, only 29 rooms. (TripAdvisor price range for standard room: $118-$351.)

Distances: U.S. Embassy (.1 miles), Barberini Metro Station (.2 miles), Spanish Steps (.3 miles), Trevi Fountain (.5 miles), Termini (.7 miles), Piazza Navona (1 mile), Forum (1 mile), Castel Sant'Angelo (1.2 miles), Colosseum (1.2 miles), St Peter's Basilica (1.8 miles)

Hotel Ludovisi Palace—Via Ludovisi 43 (www.ludovisipalacehotel.com/en/). Location: east of Spanish Steps. Pros: non-smoking hotel, air conditioning, good breakfast included, free WiFi, bar/lounge, accessible rooms, elevator, facilities for disabled guests, airport shuttle, twin/triple/

quad rooms, some price break for singles. Cons: uneven staff friendliness, hard beds, weak WiFi. (TripAdvisor price range for standard room: $129-$328.)

Distances: U.S. Embassy (.1 miles), Barberini Metro Station (.2 miles), Spanish Steps (.3 miles), Trevi Fountain (.5 miles), Termini (.7 miles), Piazza Navona (1 mile), Forum (1 mile), Castel Sant'Angelo (1.2 miles), Colosseum (1.2 miles), St Peter's Basilica (1.7 miles)

Opera Suites—Via di Porta Pinciana 4 (opera-suites.tophotelsrome.com/en/). TripAdvisor's Certificate of Excellence. Location: NE of Spanish Steps by Villa Borghese. Pros: good breakfast included, non-smoking hotel, air conditioning, refrigerator, free WiFi, elevator, room service, airport shuttle, twin/triple/suite rooms. Cons: thin walls, no singles, very little price break for singles, only 9 rooms. (TripAdvisor price range for standard room: $81-$196.)

Distances: U.S. Embassy (.2 miles), Spagna Metro Station (.2 miles), Spanish Steps (.2 miles), Barberini Metro Station (.3 miles), Trevi Fountain (.4 miles), Termini (.8 miles), Piazza Navona (.9 miles), Castel Sant' Angelo (1.1 miles), Colosseum (1.2 miles), St. Peter's Basilica (1.6 miles)

Other base cities in Italy

Italy is a long country, and it's not really practical to see much of it from Rome. If you want to base in other areas, Naples, Florence, Milan, Bologna, and Verona have hop-on/hop-off buses and tour companies that lead excursions into the countryside and to other towns. Venice has a hop-on/hop-off cruise and also day trips into the surrounding area.

Vienna

Overview

Vienna (Wien to German speakers, pronounced VEEN) is a world capital, from when the Habsburg Dynasty ruled the vast and sprawling Austro-Hungarian Empire. While the empire is dissolved and Vienna is now the capital of a rather small country, many of the city's glories remain. Vienna is distinguished not just by its history, artwork, and Baroque architecture, but by its rich and easygoing way of life. The Viennese know how to enjoy the many delights that abound in their city. In 2018 and 2019, Vienna was named the most livable city in the world because of its excellent and affordable transportation, healthcare, and cultural offerings.

Historically, Vienna has been known for its music (Strauss, Beethoven, Mozart), Sigmund Freud, turn-of-the-century intellectualism, its coffeehouse culture, and the beautiful "blue" Danube. (Don't expect to see much of the famous river unless you head out of town, though. The Danube is a bit of an afterthought in the city, which based its most important activities and buildings some distance from the river banks.)

The main historical and tourists sights are clustered in the middle of the city, within and along the Ring Straße (Ring Street), a broad boulevard where the old city walls used to encircle the city center. The Ring is loaded with imposing buildings and lush city parks, and most sights are a fairly easy walk away. While there are hills (wine-producing hills!) outside Vienna, the city center itself is quite flat.

Viennese summers are warm, with July running an average high of 81 degrees Fahrenheit. (June and August aren't far behind.) Summers have grown hotter recently (record temperatures topped 100 degrees), which makes hotel air conditioning a welcome amenity. Winters in Vienna are typically cold and windy, with January the coldest month, posting an average high of 36-39 degrees Fahrenheit. Winter lows are typically around freezing.

The official Vienna tourism site is www.wien.info/en and can be a good resource as you plan your trip. Under the "Hotels in Vienna and Travel Info" tab, there is a section on accessibility, if that is a concern.

Possible plan for Vienna (What I'd do)

If I were traveling to Vienna with my mother, this is what I would plan for us to do. It's a fairly short itinerary—just 9 days total, so it could fit if you wanted to fly to Vienna on a Saturday and return on a Sunday, for example. Obviously, you may prefer to do something different than I would, or add a bunch, but you may find this itinerary handy as a starting point, changing it as much as you'd like. (And it will make more sense as you work your way through the chapter. Having a city map at hand will help, too.) **Please double check any details before relying on them, as specifics may have changed since I wrote these pages.** This plan assumes lodging near the the State Opera, where most of the sightseeing I include can be done on foot, but lodging elsewhere and using the convenient public transportation system to get around would also work.

Be aware that many sights in Vienna are closed on Mondays or Tuesdays (and occasionally other days). In my suggested itinerary, I've noted places that are closed on certain days, but check with the latest information before setting any itinerary in stone. If you use this itinerary and arrive in Vienna on a Sunday, Monday, or Tuesday, the order listed below works. If you'll arrive on a different day and want to follow this plan, you'll need to shuffle some things around.

Although central Vienna is fairly compact and flat, walking between sights and then walking *through* sights (e.g., palaces and museums) is still tiring. Remember to take things slowly, if mobility is an issue for you. Plan to rest when it's possible—at cafés, on benches, back in your hotel. Build rest time into your day. Anywhere you can take a load off, *do*. As for day trips, you probably don't want to plan for more than two consecutive out-of-town excursions at a time, to avoid bus fatigue.

Day 1—Depart U.S.

Day 2—Arrive Vienna. Find an ATM (*Bankomat*) and withdraw euros, if needed. Meet private transfer driver for ride to hotel (arranged in advance). Check into hotel, if possible. Take a short rest, if possible and desired. If not, leave luggage and start exploring the city.

    Walk to main tourist office on Albertinaplatz, immediately northwest of the Opera. Get a city map (if needed) and a copy of *Wien-Programm* for a list of concerts during your stay. Consider buying the *Vienna from A to Z* sightseeing guide at the tourist information office.

    Go out for lunch or coffee and cake, perhaps at the nearby (and famous) Hotel Sacher. (Sachertorte, anyone?) Take a self-guided tour of the Opera/Ring area. Line up cell phone service, if needed. Locate a handy grocery store and possible cafés or restaurants to visit. Rest in one of the city's many parks when the opportunity arises. Go out for dinner or get picnic supplies from a grocery store. Plan for an early night.

Day 3—(*Don't do on a Sunday.*) Stroll down Kärntnerstraße to St. Stephen's Cathedral. Catch the guided English tour at 10:30 a.m. (Monday-Saturday only; rely on audioguide for Sunday, 1-4:30, or at other times, if you want to tour more slowly than the guide). Break for lunch or coffee. Walk to the Opera for an afternoon tour. (Tour times vary throughout the year. Check online in advance.) Free time until dinner.

Take the one-hour Vienna Night Tour around the Ring offered by Vienna Sightseeing (in front of the State Opera, 8 p.m. in summer, 7:30 p.m. in winter). Return to hotel.

Day 4—Day trip: Hallstatt

Day 5—(*Do not plan this day for a Monday or Tuesday.*) Walk to the Hofburg on the Ring. Tour the royal palace. Break for lunch or snack. Tour the Treasury in the afternoon (closed Monday and Tuesday). (Consider buying a "Treasures of the Habsburgs" combination ticket.) Rest a bit. Dinner and an evening out, possibly a musical performance. If too far to walk comfortably in the evening, check public transportation options or take a taxi. Return to hotel.

Day 6—Day trip: Budapest

Day 7—(First option: *Not a Monday, Tuesday, or Wednesday*; Second option: *Not a Monday*) Walk along the Ring to the Kunsthistorisches Museum (10-6, closed Mondays) and visit it. If not a Sunday, then stroll to the Naschmarkt (outdoor market) for a late lunch and other shopping. (Get lunch supplies elsewhere if on a Sunday.) If the weather is good, visit the Resselpark by Karlsplatz (possibly eat lunch there).

Visit the Karlskirche (St. Charles Church—some steps are required to enter), or just view it from the outside. Continue to the Wien Museum Karlsplatz (Historical Museum of the City of Vienna, open 2-10 p.m., not Monday, Tuesday or Wednesday, free). (*Note*: The Wien Museum Karlsplatz is scheduled for renovations starting late 2019. *Alternate plan if the museum is unavailable*: After visiting Karlskirche, return to the hotel to take a break, then have another night out.)

Day 8—(*Not a Tuesday.*) Walk along the Ring to the Natural History Museum. (9-6:30, until 9 p.m. on Wednesday, not open Tuesday). After the museum, break for lunch.

For a hearty Viennese dinner, take tram 49 from a stop on the west side of the museum across the street, in the direction of Breitensee, three or four stops to Neubaugasse, then walk to Neubaugasse 52 for a lunch at Schnitzelwirt restaurant (11-9:30, closed Sunday). Buy tickets from a machine or on the tram. Consider buying a day ticket for €5.80 to ride public transportation as much as desired until 1 a.m. of the next day. If day tickets are not available, a 24-hour ticket costs €8. (U-Bahn stations and most tobacconists sell tickets.) Whatever kind of ticket you get, you *must* validate it by putting it into one of the stamping machines, or you will be riding illegally and could be fined.

After eating, finish any shopping you have to do. Later in the afternoon, take things slowly and enjoy a typical Viennese outing, to a traditional wine tavern. Experience the new wine and an order-at-the-counter cafeteria snack or meal (I'm partial to the Liptauer cheese spread) at a *Heuriger* (HOY-rig-uh). The easiest *Heurigen* to get to are in Nussdorf. (Grinzing is the better known *Heurigen* suburb, but it is slightly harder to get to on public transportation, is highly touristed and—fair or not—locals look down on visiting there.)

Take Tram D from Opera/Karlsplatz (or from the Ring/Volkstheater stop, if coming from Schnitzelwirt or otherwise from around the Natural History Museum). Ride to the end of the line in the suburb of Nussdorf (Nußdorf/Beethovengang). (If you bought and used a day ticket earlier, it's good for the rest of the day. If you don't have a ticket yet, two single tickets will cost you a little less and will cover your ride out and back. Make sure you validate tickets in the stamping machine, though, at the time you use them.) After arriving in Nussdorf, you could look for Heuriger Kierlinger at Kahlenberger Strasse 20 or Schübel-Auer Heuriger at Kahlenberger Strasse 22.

You would be wise to conduct an Internet search on "Nussdorf Vienna Heurigen" in advance, to check which businesses are open when you want to go, because they are usually not open every day. If you prefer to wander around and find one that catches your fancy, look for branches of evergreen hung above the outside door to announce which ones are in season. *Heurigen* are typically open from 3:30 or 4 p.m. to midnight. Be aware that Tram D stops running before midnight.

After wine and simple food in a *Heuriger*, take Tram D back to the Oper/Karlsplatz stop and return to the hotel to prepare for the next day's departure. (A single-use ticket will need to be validated. A day ticket will still be good from its first validation.)

Day 9—Private transfer from hotel to airport (arranged ahead of time). Return home.

Arrival

The Vienna airport (VIE) is known as Wien-Schwechat and is located 11 miles southeast of Vienna in the town of Schwechat. To get from VIE to the city, you have your choice of train, bus, hotel shuttle, taxi, or private driver.

There are actually several options for train travel to and from the city. The **City-Airport-Train (CAT)** whisks you from the airport to the Wien Mitte terminal (just outside the Ring, east of St. Stephen's Cathedral) in 16 minutes, leaving every 30 minutes. At the Wien Mitte station, travelers can connect with subway lines U3 and U4. A single trip costs €12, and round-trip (good for six months from purchase date) costs €21. (When returning *to* the airport, it's possible to check in for your flight at the City Air Terminal in Wien Mitte, depending on airline.) Children under 15 years ride for free; wheelchair users receive a discount; slight discounts for online purchases (www.cityairporttrain.com/en/home).

Austrian Federal Railways (ÖBB)(www.oebb.at) runs a non-stop **Railjet train** service between the airport and Wien Hauptbahnhof (south of Belvedere Garden) (15 minutes) and Wien Meidling (southwest of city center) (half an hour) stations. Adult tickets cost €4.20, ages 6-14 cost €2.10 each, and 5 and under ride free. The ride to and from the airport is included in the Vienna City Card Transfer (www.wien.info/en/travel-info/to-and-around/airport-to-center/vienna-citycard-transfer). If using a Vienna City Card, make sure to validate it first. Tickets are available at www.oebb.at (select English at upper right), at the ÖBB counter in the airport, or from ticket machines.

Express Train (S-Bahn) S7 leaves the airport every 30 minutes and stops at Wien Mitte (central Vienna, east of St. Stephen's) (25 minutes) and Vienna Praterstern (north of the Danube) (half an hour). Also run by Austrian Federal Railways (ÖBB) (www.oebb.at), Express Train tickets cost the same and are available in the same places as Railjet tickets.

As for **buses**, **Vienna Airport Lines (VAL)** provides three bus lines for getting into the city. VAL 1 runs from the airport to the main train station (Hauptbahnhof, connections with U1) and West train station (connections with U3 and U6) in 40 minutes, leaving every half hour. VAL 2 delivers riders to Morzinplatz/Schwedenplatz (in Central Vienna along the Danube Canal) (connections with U1 and U4) in 22 minutes. VAL 3 takes passengers to Donauzentrum (northeast of the central part of the city) (connections with U1) in 39 minutes.

Single tickets are €8 for adults and €4 for children 6-14.

Round-trip tickets are €13 for adults and €8 for children 6-14. Discounts with Vienna City Card. Tickets may be purchased from www.viennaairportlines.at or from the bus driver (cash only) or from Vienna Airport Lines ticket machines at the airport or the Westbahnhof (West Train Station).

Another bus transfer option is **Air-Liner (Blaguss)**. With one line running from bus terminal 3, bus platform 9 at the airport via VIB (Vienna International Bus Terminal) Erdberg (east of the city center, south of the Prater, connection with U3) to the Main Station (Hauptbahnhof, south of Belvedere Garden, connection with U1). Single-ride tickets are €5 for adults and €9 for round-trip. Children 6-11 ride half price. Tickets are for sale online at www.air-liner.at or from the bus driver.

Hotel shuttle vans offer door-to-door van service to selected hotels for a fee. If your hotel description lists an airport shuttle service, search the hotel Web site or contact the hotel to learn more.

Private transfers to and from the airport can be arranged online ahead of time. The drive to the city center typically takes about 20 minutes. **Vienna Airport Cab** (www.vienna-airport-cab.at/index.php/en/) is a private **taxi** service that receives excellent reviews. A sample ride from the airport to the Opera costs €27. **Wientransfer** (wientransfer.com/en/) is another recommended company. A sample private taxi ride for up to 4 people from the airport to central Vienna costs €38, at this writing. **Airport Transfer Agency Vienna (ATAV)** (www.atav.at/airporttransfer/flughafen-taxi-airport-transfer) receives rave reviews, although you may have to make your way through German listings and easy-to-understand pictures to get to an English order form.

Other highly reviewed options include the following:

- Austria Transfers (austriatransfers.at)
- Vienna Airport Taxi (www.viennadriver.com/en/)

- Trinitas Airport Transfer (www.tapt.at/en/)
- Silverline (www.silverline.wien/en)

The private transfer price often includes meeting you at the airport and all taxes, fees, and gratuities. All transfer services limit how much luggage you can take, so make sure to check restrictions before registering for a pickup. In the airport, after you leave baggage claim, go left into the Arrivals hall to the City Transfer counter (unless your transfer company gives you other instructions on where to meet up).

Another option for getting into the city, of course, is to find your way to the **taxi** ranks when you arrive and take a cab. Exit the Arrivals hall on the right to get to the taxi stand most directly. The average price for a taxi from the airport to the city center is €36 and the ride takes about 20 minutes.

Easy transportation options

Once in the city, your usual transportation choices are metro, bus, tram, and taxi. Vienna has a wonderful public transportation system, wide-ranging and very accessible for people with disabilities. A city route planner is available at anachb.vor.at/, if you want help finding your way around.

Another way to get around to the sights is to ride a **hop-on/hop-off (HOHO) tourist bus**. You purchase a 1-day, 2-day, or 3-day ticket and then may hop on and hop off the buses (of the line you paid for) as much as you'd like in that time. (To be honest, though, the public transportation system is so nice, it may make sense to ride trams and buses and just get a one-time sightseeing bus ticket for a city overview—see below.)

Taxis, of course, may offer the most convenient within-city transportation of all, but you'll pay for that convenience. Nonetheless, if riding taxis fits your budget and enhances your experience, then that may be the right choice for you.

HOHO bus options, public transportation, and taxis are discussed below.

Hop-On/Hop-Off Tours

Big Bus Vienna (www.bigbustours.com/en/vienna/vienna-bus-tours/) offers two main HOHO routes and a limited auxiliary route for certain tickets. Their double-decker buses provide digital audio commentary and free WiFi on board. Most buses are wheelchair accessible. Two- and three-day tickets include a free 90-minute guided walking tour in English and German (starting at 11:30 and also on weekends at 1:30 in summer). Three-day tickets also include an "Old-Time" tram ride in the evening. As with other HOHO bus companies, tourists have variable experiences with this service, but in general reviews are postive. Re-check times of operaion before riding, because schedules change according to season.

The Vienna Red Route circles central Vienna and has 16 stops, two of which overlap with the Blue Route (stops 2 and 4). The stops are as follows: 1) Opera, 2) House of Music, 3) Museumsquartier/Mariahilferstraße, 4) Museums/Hofburg, 5) City Hall, 6) Votive Church, 7) Augarten, 8) Prater, 9) Pier 3, 10) Blue Danube/Cruises Pier 8, 11) Danube Tower, 12) Old Danube, 13) UNO City/DC Tower, 14) Danube Island, 15) Schwedenplatz/Danube Canal (River Cruise), 16) Stadtpark. Tours leave Stop 1 from 9:30 a.m. to 4-6 p.m., departing every 15-20 minutes. The full circuit takes about 1 hour 45 minutes.

The Schönbrunn Blue Route swings farther afield over 9 stops, with crossovers to the Red Route at stops 1, 8, and 9. The Blue stops are as follows: 1) Museums/Hofburg, 2) Haus des Meeres/Aqua Terra Zoo, 3) Mariahilferstraße/Ibis Hotel, 4) Schönbrunn Palace, 5) Main Train Station/Hauptbahnhof, 6) Upper Belvedere, 7) Lower Belvedere, 8) House of Music, 9) Museumsquartier/Mariahilferstraße. A complete circuit of the Blue Route takes about 1 hour 25 minutes. Buses leave Stop 1 from 9:30 a.m. to 6 p.m.

The Green Route (Hundertwasser Tour) is limited to 2- and 3-day passes and is a special minibus to the Hundertwasserhaus and back. Tours depart every hour between 10 a.m. and 3 p.m. from near Stop 1 of the Red Route and take 20 minutes each way. An "Old-Time" tram night tour is included in the Premium 3-day HOHO ticket or can be purchased separatedly. The tour starts at 7 p.m.

Tickets may be purchased at a discount online or from representatives near bus stops. E-tickets are valid for 6 months after purchase. While e-vouchers are supposed to be valid, you are safer printing a paper copy if ordering online. Bus tickets are valid for as much use as you want during the 1, 2, or 3 days of a ticket's validity. The night-time tram tour requires a separate ticket unless specifically included in a package and may be used just once.

- Classic ticket, 1 day, Red Route and Blue Route—adult €27 online (€30 on-street); child 5-15 years €21.60 online (€24 on-street); family, 2 adults and 2 children, €96

- Premium ticket, 2 days, Red and Blue Routes, guided walking tour, Hundertwasser tour (Green Route)—adult €31.50 online (€35 on-street); child 5-15 years €25.20 online (€28 on-street); family €112
- Deluxe ticket, 3 days, Red and Blue Routes, guided walking tour, Hundertwasser tour (Green Route), Live-guided old-timer tram night tour—adult €49.50 online (€55 on-street); child 5-15 years €39.60 online (on-street €44); family €176
- Live-Guided "Old-Timer" Tram Night Tour—adults €25; child €20
- Vienna and Budapest Tour Package, 2 days HOHO bus in Vienna + 2 days HOHO bus in Budapest, with walking tour in each city—adult €54 online (€60 on-street); child 5-15 years €43.20 online (€48 on-street); family €191

Vienna Sightseeing (www.viennasightseeing.at/hop-on-hop-off) is associated with Gray Line Tours and offers more HOHO routes and stops than Big Bus, but with slightly lower customer satisfaction, on average. Vienna Sightseeing has six routes and 50 stops. Double-decker yellow buses have free WiFi and include audio guides, as well as an extra children's channel in German and English. All tickets include a guided walking tour, and HOHO tickets can be combined with a cruise on the Danube River or Danube Canal, the Vienna Ring Tram, a night tour, or a transfer to the Vienna airport.

The Red Line has 14 stops that circle the Ring Straße. The first bus leaves around 9:20 and the last bus leaves at 4:30-7 p.m., depending on season. Stops also vary by season and construction. Regular summer stops are at 1) Staatsoper, 2) Kunsthistorisches Museum, 3) Mariahilfer Straße/Museumquartier, 5) Burgtheater/Rathaus, 6) Liebenberg Denkmal, 7) Liechtensteinstraße, 8) Augarten, 9) Taborstraße, 10) Schwedenbrücke, 11) Morzinplatz, 12) Schwedenplatz, 13) MAK/Wien-Mitte, 14) Hotel Hilton/Stadtpark, 15) Kursalon. Buses leave every 6-15 minutes (15-25 in winter), and a full circuit takes around 60 minutes.

The Yellow Line has 10 stops and swings out to both Schönbrunn and Belvedere Palaces. The first bus leaves at 9:15 a.m. from the Staatsoper or 9:00 from the West Train Station (a bit later in winter), and the last bus leaves at 4:30-6 p.m., depending on season. Stops are at 1) Staatsoper, 2) Kunsthistorisches Museum, 27) Naschmarkt/Theater an der Wien, 29)

Westbahnhof/Mariahilfer Straße, 30) Schloss Schönbrunn, 31) Hauptbahnhof/Sonnwendgasse, 32) Heeresgeschlichtliches Museum, 33) Belvedere 21, 34) Schloss Belvedere, 35) Schwarzenberg Platz (may vary slightly in the off season). Buses leave every 15-22 minutes (22-30 in winter), and a full circuit takes around 90 minutes.

The Blue Line has 9 stops and visits the Hundertwasser House, the Danube Tower, and the Prater amusement park, home of the giant Ferris wheel (the Riesenrad). The first bus leaves at 9:30 a.m. from Wien-Mitte (9:15 from the train station by the Prater) and the last leaves at 6:30 p.m. (condensed schedule in winter). Stops are at 13) MAK/Wien-Mitte, 17) Kunst Haus, 18) Prater, 20) DDSG (Pier 6), 21) Donauturm, 22) Alte Donau, 23) UNO City, 24) Reichsbrücke/Donauinsel, and 25) Praterstern. Buses leave every 18-25 minutes (26-35 in winter), and a full circuit takes around 75 minutes.

The Green Line has 12 stops and goes farther afield to include nature and wine—the wine village of Grinzing and Kahlenberg Hill, with hiking and views over Vienna. The first bus leaves at 10:30 from the Votivkirche (later in winter) and the last bus departs at 6 p.m. (as early as 2:30 in the off season). Stops are at 47) Votivkirche, 48) Friedrich-Schmidt-Platz, 5) Burgtheater/Rathaus, 6) Liebenberg Denkmal, 7) Liechtensteinstraße, 36) Palais Liechtenstein, 37) Grinzing/Sandgasse, 38) Grinzing/Cobenzlgasse, 39) Kahlenberg, 40) Grinzing/Himmelstraße, 45) Schlumberger/Spittalau, 46) Rossauer Lände. Buses leave every 30-45 minutes, and a full circuit takes about 90 minutes.

The guided walking tour starts and ends in front of the Vienna State Opera and is included in every Vienna Sightseeing HOHO ticket. Three boat rides are available as an option with the 3-day Imperial ticket (choose one route, if you opt to take a boat tour). Look over itineraries and times closely to decide what would work best for you. Some people inadvertently take the Danube Canal cruise and end up disappointed. You can also combine a HOHO ticket with a bus or train transfer from the Vienna airport.

Tickets may be purchased online with a 10% discount or from representatives near bus stops. E-ticket vouchers are good for 12 months after purchase. Bus tickets are valid for as much use as you want during the 24, 48, or 72 hours of a ticket's validity. Special inclusions (e.g., boat ride) are valid for one use.

- Classic Ticket, 24 hours, HOHO buses and walking tour—adult (17+) €30; child (6-16) €20; family (2 adults + 2 children) €90

- Royal Ticket, 48 hours, HOHO buses, walking tour, and night tour *or* Vienna tram—adult €36; child €23; family €105
- Imperial Ticket, 72 hours, HOHO buses, walking tour, night tour, and Vienna Ring tram *or* boat ride—adult €54; child €33; family €160
- One-hour night tour from in front of the State Opera (*not* HOHO), 8 p.m. summer (7:30 p.m. winter)—adult €15; child €10

Private tours

Vienna is quite easy to get around in on public transportation or in taxis, if needed, but here are a couple of private options, if you want to indulge in something different.

Wienguide Tours (www.wienguide.net) has TripAdvisor's Certificate of Excellence and excellent reviews and rankings. In addition to walking tours, it offers motorized private tours, including the following for within Vienna:

- Classic City Tour of Vienna by Mini-Van or Limousine—view the main sights in central Vienna, the Ring, the Riesenrad, the blue Danube, Belvedere Palace, Hundertwasser House. 7-hour tour, up to 7 people, €790; 4-hour tour, up to 7 people, €500; 3-hour tour, up to 7 people, €400

Vienna Food Walk (viennafoodwalk.at/) has TripAdvisor's Certificate of Excellence and excellent reviews. The tour takes 3-4 hours in the oldest part of the city, but most of that time is spent sitting and eating, with 5 food stops. Food, beer, wine, and schnaps included. Walking narrow and uneven cobblestone paths may be difficult for some, but distances are short, a total of around 1.2 miles. Vegetarian and alcohol-free options available. Register online, pay via PayPal. Max. 8 people. €100 per person.

Taxis and Uber

If taking a taxi or arranging a private ride is your thing, you can certainly do so in Vienna. You can check a taxi fare finder such as www.taxifarefinder.com to get an estimate for how much a ride would cost. For example, taxi fare from the State Opera House to the Votivkirche (Votive Church) would range from €5.74 in low traffic to €13.08 in high traffic and would typically cost about €7.10, for a trip of about 1.2 miles. Taxis in Vienna are generally considered safe, reliable, and reasonably priced.

It is not typical for taxis to cruise around looking for fares. You usually find a taxi at a taxi rank, located throughout the city, particularly at transportation hubs (like a train station), shopping areas, and outside major sites. The car will have a taxi sign on the top, and the license plate should end in TX. Do not get into a cab that does not have a meter.

If you prefer to call for a cab, that is also common in Vienna. Your hotel concierge or workers in restaurants and bars are usually happy to call a taxi for you. If you have phone service and want to call yourself, try this number: +43140100.

It is common to tip drivers in Vienna, generally by rounding up to a convenient number. Ten percent or so would be a good amount, if you are satisfied with the service.

UberX is available in Vienna, as are high-end Uber variants (Uber Black, Uber Van). Check www.uber.com/cities/vienna/ for fare information.

Other in-city transportation

Public transportation is readily available and easy to use in Vienna. A flat-fare ticket will get you access to bus, streetcar, subway (U-Bahn) and suburban train (S-Bahn) networks and is good for one ride with transfers. Tickets can be bought most easily in machines in subway stations or at tobacconist shops (a *Tabaktrafik*). Tickets *must* be validated before riding any public transportation in Vienna. Failure to do so could result in a hefty fine, if an undercover transportation agent catches you riding illegally, even if it's unintentional. There are validating machines located at the entrances to the subway and on buses and trams. Stick your ticket into the slot to stamp it with the date and time. Tickets costs are as follows:

- single transportation ticket, €2.40 (children €1.20)
- 24-hour ticket, €8
- 48-hour ticket, €14.10
- 72-hour ticket, €17.10
- weekly ticket (Mon. 9 a.m.-Mon. 9 a.m.), €17.10
- single ticket bought on tram, €2.60 (children €1.40)

You can find very useful maps of the various transportation networks (and a tourist map) here: viennamap360.com. If you want to know how to get from Point A to Point B, use a journey planner, such as the one at anachb.vor.at/. ("Suchen" means "search.") Two tram lines that you'll want to know are Tram #1 and Tram #2, which circle around the Ring in opposite directions.

The **subway** system in Vienna is called the **U-Bahn** (OO-bahn). (The trains that extend out into the suburbs are part of the **S-Bahn** system, which connects up with the U-Bahn system.) The U-Bahn comprises 5 lines—U1, U2, U3, U4, and U6—with 109 stations and over 50 miles of track. U-Bahn entrances are marked with a big white U on a blue cube, like a giant die. As in any other city, subterranean walks and possible climbs are normally part of using the subway system, but Vienna has excellent handicapped accessibility, with wheelchair access at all stops, via ramps or elevators. (Elevators are occasionally out of service. If that is vital information for you, check for shut-downs at www.wienerlinien.at/aufzugsinfo—the word for elevator is "Aufzug." The status indicator of a red circle with a white bar across it means that an elevator at that stop is not working.)

U-Bahn trains typically run from around 5 a.m. to midnight, but run through the night on Fridays and Saturdays. You can find a map of the subway system here: www.wienerlinien.at/media/files/2018/svp_281610.pdf.

Vienna runs an equally good (and easily accessible) **bus and tram** system. The city has 28 tram lines that cover 137 miles of track, making it the sixth-largest tram system in the world. Vienna also runs 128 bus lines. Buses and trams have more limited hours of use than the U-Bahn does, but some bus routes do run through the night, just with less frequency.

Sightseeing passes

If you plan on sightseeing a lot in Vienna, you might want to consider some sort of sightseeing pass. As with any sightseeing pass, compare the costs of what you would actually see with the cost of the pass.

The **Vienna Pass** (www.viennapass.com) is a flat-rate pass that offers free entrance to more than 60 sights in and around Vienna, many with fast-track entry. Passes include unlimited use of the Vienna Sightseeing Tours HOHO buses during the duration of the pass. Determined tourists can definitely save money—but some say the price makes it hard to recoup your investment, and tourists who aim to see as many sights as possible are advised against relying on the HOHO buses for their transportation, because of schedule creep.

Passes may be purchased for 1, 2, 3, or 6 consecutive days. Passes are good for 12 months after purchase and are activated on first use. If ordering online, you can choose to have instant delivery to your smartphone or visit the customer service center in Vienna to pick up a pass (print your email voucher to trade for a pass). The customer service center is at Opernpassage, Top 3 (in the metro station Karlsplatz, go towards exit Opera/Opernpassage). You can also buy a pass on the spot in the Opernpassage office in Vienna, if you did not pre-order one. Or you can collect a pass at the airport at the Airport Driver's desk in the Arrivals hall. Or, instead, you could choose to have a pass sent to you in the U.S. for an €11 shipping fee and 15-20 working days until it arrives. Prices are as follows (possible discount for online purchases):

- 1-day Vienna Pass—adult €70; child (6-18) €35
- 2-day Vienna Pass—adult €95 (€85 online); child €47.50 (€42.75 online)
- 3-day Vienna Pass—adult €125 (€112.50 online); child €62.50 (€56.25 online)
- 6-day Vienna Pass—adult €155 (€139.50 online); child €77.50 (€69.75 online)

You can compare the gate price of sights you want to visit with the cost (and convenience) of the pass here: www.viennapass.com/vienna-attractions/.

The **Vienna City Card** (www.wien.info/en/travel-info/vienna-city-card) provides discounts on tourist sights and experiences, restaurants, shopping, and transportation, often just a euro or two but sometimes much more, and it includes free access to public transportation. Optional add-ons are the Big Bus HOHO tour (see above) or an airport transfer. Covered benefits can be found here: www.wien.info/en/travel-info/vienna-city-card/vienna-city-card-benefits. It gets a little confusing, because different aspects of the card and options are valid for different time periods. See discussion here: www.visitingvienna.com/transport/vienna-card/.

You can buy a Vienna City Card online (www.viennacitycard.at/index.php?lang=EN), at tourist information centers in Vienna, in many hotels, and in outlets of the Vienna transportation system. If you order online, you may choose a voucher that you can redeem for a card at any tourist information office in Vienna or you can print out your card at home (But be aware that you will need to choose an activation date! Entering the wrong date *cannot* be fixed.), or you can order and activate a card immediately using the Vienna Card app. If you don't know exactly when you will want to start using the card, it may be safer to buy one in Vienna (perhaps at the airport), even if that takes a bit longer.

There is only one price level for cards. Each card allows for one child up to age 15 to ride along on the transportation portion and the HOHO bus. (Two are allowed through age 14 on the airport transfer.) No discounts are given for seniors, students, or groups, but there is a slight discount for ordering online. Prices are as follows:

- Vienna Card, includes public transportation—24 hours €17 (€15.70 online); 48 hours €25 (€22.50 online); 72 hours €29 (€26.10 online)
- Vienna Card, includes public transportation and 24-hour Big Bus HOHO tour—24 hours €43 (€38.70); 48 hours €51 (€45.90 online); 72 hours €55 (€49.50 online)
- Vienna Card, includes public transportation and airport transfer—24 hours €34 (€30.60 online); 48 hours €42 (€37.80 online); 72 hours €46 (€41.40 online)
- Vienna Card, includes public transportation and 24-hour Big Bus HOHO tour AND airport transfer—24 hours €60 (€54 online); 48 hours €68 (€61.20 online); 72 hours €72 (€64.80 online)

The **Vienna Sightseeing Flexi-Pass** (www.viennasightseeing.at/flexi-pass) offers a choice of 3, 4, or 5 sights over 30 days after the pass is activated. (Write the start date on the back of the pass.) You may choose to include some of these sights or activities (among others): 24-hour HOHO on Vienna Sightseeing bus, Vienna Ring Tram, Wiener Riesenrad (giant Ferris wheel), Imperial Treasury of Vienna, Imperial Burial Vault, Schönbrunn Zoo, Spanish Riding School, Klosterneuburg Monastery, Albertina Museum, Jewish Museum, Kunsthistorisches Museum, Upper Belvedere, Beethoven Museum, Madame Tussauds. Flexi-Pass holders also receive a 15% discount on excursions and guided tours offered through Vienna Sightseeing.

Children ages 6-18 receive a junior Flexi-Pass at a 50% reduction. Children under age 6 are admitted free with a paying adult. (Or one with a pass.) Prices are as follows:

- 3 attractions—adult €40.50 online, youth €20.25 online
- 4 attractions—adult €49.50 online, youth €24.75 online
- 5 attractions—adult €58.50 online, youth €29.25 online

If you order a ticket online, you will receive an emailed booking confirmation. Print the confirmation and show it at the Vienna Sightseeing Tours office in the underground passage by the State Opera to receive your pass.

Day trips

It's possible to see much of Austria (and beyond) without having to leave the convenience of your base hotel at night, because Vienna has tourist companies that specialize in day trips.

As always, use the information here as a guide, but check each company's Web site for tour details and the most current price and schedule information. **Tour details—even which tours are offered—routinely change from season to season.** Whichever tours you decide on, look over cancellation policies, if your plans aren't completely firm.

Browsing through Web sites will also help you decide which company's tours seem a good fit for you. Be aware that some specific tours might have special requirements or recommendations, so you'll want to look descriptions over closely before you show up at the departure point.

Tour companies differ on which entry fees and meals they include in their prices, so check those specifics (and confirm online), if your selection comes down to price.

Most day trips leave from around the State Opera or provide hotel pickup and drop-off. Make sure you show up early for any tour or pickup so you are not considered a no-show and your seat sold to someone else!

If you want to save your walking energy for the tour itself but you select a tour with a departure point that is not close to your hotel, you may want to invest in a taxi ride to get there.

White Alligator Tours

White Alligator Tours (whitealligatortours.com) has TripAdvisor's Certificate of Excellence and excellent reviews and rankings. It offers small-group and private tours in minivans, including the following day trips:

Small-Group Day Trip to Hallstatt—Tour highlights include the Vienna Woods, several stops in the Salzkammergut region (famous from *The Sound of Music*), Hallstatt tour with local guide, free time in Hallstatt. Hotel pickup around 7 a.m., hotel drop-off around 7-8 p.m. From €145 per person, minimum of 5 required. Private small-group tour also available.

Small-Group Day Trip to Salzburg—Tour highlights include a drive through the ViennaWoods, stops in the Salzkammergut mountain lake district, walking tour in Salzburg with local guide, Mirabell Garden, Mozart's birth house, Salzburg Cathedral, St. Peter's Abbey, and free time in Salzburg. Hotel pickup around 7 a.m.; hotel drop-off 7-8 p.m. From €135 per person, minimum 5 required for tour. Private small-group tour also available.

Small-Group Day Trip to Budapest—Tour highlights include the view from Gellért Hill, the Castle District, Matthias Church, Fisherman's Bastion, Hungarian Parliament, St. Stephen's Basilica, and free time in Budapest. Hotel pickup around 7 a.m., drop-off around 7 p.m. From €135 per person, minimum 5 required for tour. Private tour also available.

Small-Group Day Trip to Cesky Krumlov—Tour highlights include a drive through the Forest Quarter of Lower Austria, a stop in Weitra on the way to the Czech Republic, walking tour with local guide in Cesky Krumlov, Vltava River, medieval castle, historic buildings, free time in Cesky Krumlov. Hotel pickup around 7 a.m., hotel drop-off around 7 p.m. From €155 per person. Private small-group tour also available.

Wine-Tasting Tour in the Wachau Valley—Tour highlights include private transportation through the Wachau Valley with live commentary, sightseeing and free time in Dürnstein, wine-tasting and guided tour in local vineyard, sightseeing and free time in Melk. Hotel pickup at 7, 7:30, or 8; hotel drop-off 6 hours later. Private group up to 8 people, €670.

Also available: private day trip to Prague (€1050 for up to 8 people); private half-day trip to Bratislava (€599 for up to 8 people); small-group Christmas trip to Hallstatt (€155); small-group Christmas trip to Salzburg (€155).

Vienna Sightseeing Tours/Gray Line

Vienna Sightseeing Tours (www.viennasightseeing.at/tours) is part of the same company that offers the more extensive HOHO bus tours of Vienna. Associated with Gray Line Tours, they are a larger company with larger buses. They offer numerous city and half-day trips (see Web site), in addition to the following day trips:

Daytrip to the Danube Valley—Tour highlights include transportation to the Wachau Danube Valley, guided tour of Melk Abbey (included), lunch and walking tour in Krems or Dürnstein (winter months only, included), boat tour (mid-April to late October only, included). Tour may be in any combination of English, German, and Spanish. Depart 9 a.m. from Vienna State Opera, return 5:45 to Vienna State Opera. Adult (13-99) €79, child (3-12) €35.

Vienna Woods and Mayerling Half-Day Tour—Tour highlights include a bus tour through the Vienna Woods, guided tour of the memorial chapel at Mayerling (included), guided tour of Heiligenkreuz Abbey (included), coffee and cake in Heiligenkreuz (included), guided walking tour through Baden. Tour may be conducted in any combination of English, German, and Spanish. Tues/Wed/Fri/Sun. Depart 9:15 a.m. from the Vienna State Opera; return 2 p.m. to the Vienna State Opera. Adult (13-99) €57, child (2-12) €21.

Day Trip to Salzburg—Tour highlights include bus ride through the beautiful Salzkammergut resort region, photo stop at Wolfgangsee, walking tour through the historic center of Salzburg, including many *Sound of Music* sights, Mirabell Palace and Garden, the Getreidegasse, Mozart's birth house, University Church, St. Peter's Abbey, Salzburg Cathedral, Festival Hall, free time to eat lunch, shop, and see sights. Tour in English and Spanish. Free hotel pickup possible. Tues/Thur/Sat/Sun. Depart from the Vienna State Opera 7 a.m.; return 8:15 p.m. to the Vienna State Opera. Adult (13-99) from €107.10, child (2-12) from €43.20.

Budapest Day Trip from Vienna—Tour highlights include bus travel to Budapest, a bus tour through the district of Pest, a guided walking tour through Buda district, the Royal Palace, Fishermen's Bastion, Matthias Church, Margaret Island, free time for eating, sightseeing, and shopping. Tour may be conducted in any combination of English, Spanish, and Japanese. Must bring passport. Free hotel pickup possible. Not Wed/Sat. Depart 7:15 a.m. from Vienna State Opera; return 7:30-8 p.m. to Vienna State Opera. Adult (13-99) €119, child (3-12) €48.

Prague Day Trip from Vienna—Tour highlights include bus transportation through Moravia to Prague, coffee break at Czech border (not included), Prague Castle, guided city walk, Riding School, Gothic cathedral of St. Vitus, Charles Bridge, Old City Hall with clock tower, National Museum, Wenceslas Square, free time for lunch, sightseeing, and shopping. Tour may be in English and Spanish. Must bring passport. Free hotel pickup possible. Wed/Sat. Depart 7:15 a.m. from Vienna State Opera; return 8 p.m. to Vienna State Opera. Adult (13-99) €119, child (3-12) €48.

Bratislava: Day Trip from Vienna by Bus and Boat—Tour highlights include bus trip to Bratislava (1 hour), guided walk though Bratislava, Plague Column, National Theater, Michael's Gate, City Hall, Maximilian's Fountain, St. Martin's Cathedral, free time to eat, explore, and shop, return trip on high-speed catamaran on the Danube. Tour in German and English. Bring passport. Free hotel pickup possible. Daily in summer, reduced schedule in off-season. Depart Vienna State Opera 8:30 a.m.; return Schwedenplatz 8 p.m. Adult (13-99) €72, child (3-12) €38.

Hallstatt Day Trip from Vienna—Tour highlights include bus ride to the Salzkammergut region, photo stop at Orth Castle in Gmunden, city walk of 7000-year-old Hallstatt, ossuary (bone house with decorated skulls), 20-minute boat tour on the lake (included), free time for lunch and sightseeing, funicular ride to the Skywalk viewing platform above the town (included). Free hotel pickup possible. Tues/Wed/Fri/Sat. Depart 7:15 a.m. from Vienna State Opera; return 8 p.m. Adult (13-99) €119, child (3-12) €48.

Royal Tours

Royal Tours (www.royaltours.at/tours/) offers small-group tours to Salzburg, Budapest, and Prague with hotel pickup and drop-off. The company's Web site is not particularly informative, but this family business has been leading tours since 1978 and reviews are solid. All tours require a minimum of 4 participants to run.

Budapest—Tour highlights include a drive through the Austrian state of Burgenland to Hungary, Castle Hill, the Danube River, Matthias Church, Fisherman's Bastion, House of Parliament, St. Stephen's Cathedral, Chain Bridge, Royal Palace, free time for lunch and shopping. Available daily. Pickup and return to hotel. Adult €119, child (up to 12) €54.

Salzburg—Tour highlights include views of Melk Abbey, Hohensalzburg Fortress, Mirabell Gardens, Mozart's birth place, Salzburg Cathedral, St. Peter's cemetery, free time in Salzburg for lunch and shopping. Available daily. Pickup and return to hotel. Adult €119, child (up to 12) €54.

Prague—Tour highlights include a drive through Moravia and Bohemia, Wenceslas Square in Prague, the Charles Bridge, St. Nicholas Church, astronomical clock, imperial palace, free time for lunch and shopping in Prague. Not available Fri/Mon. Pickup and return to hotel. Adult €119, child (up to 12) €54.

Viator

Given the relative sparcity of group day-trip companies out of Vienna, you may want to turn to the consolidator Viator (www.viator.com/Vienna/d454-ttd) to get a fuller overview of possibilities. Select "Day Trips & Excursions" on the left side, and you'll find possibilities from Salzburg, Budapest, and Hallstatt to Mauthausen concentration camp, Prague, and Bratislava.

Private and semi-private tours

Wienguide Tours (www.wienguide.net–you can select English) has TripAdvisor's Certificate of Excellence and excellent reviews and rankings. In addition to walking tours and private Vienna tours, it offers the following day trips:

Day Trip from Vienna to Budapest—Tour highlights include a two-hour drive through the Hungarian lowlands in a private minivan or limousine, introduction to the main sights in Buda and in Pest with a licensed guide, the castle district, Matthias Church, the Fisherman's Bastion, Buda Castle, Chain Bridge, St. Stephen's Cathedral, and more. Includes free time for lunch (not included) and afternoon exploration or shopping. Tours can be customized. Entrance fees not included. Hotel pickup and drop-off, duration 10 hours. €880 for private group up to 7 people.

Day Trip from Vienna to Salzburg—Tour highlights include the Vienna Woods, Melk Abbey, the Salzkammergut mountain lakes region, guided tour in Salzburg, Mirabell Palace and Gardens, Hohensalzburg

Fortress, St. Peter's Monastery. Hotel pickup and drop-off, duration 12 hours. €990 for private group up to 7 people.

Other **private day trips for small groups** (1-7) include: Half-Day Trip to the Vienna Woods (4 hours, €500); Day Trip to Burgenland (10 hours, €750); Day Trip to Hallstatt and Salzburg (12 hours, €1090); Day Trip to Graz (12 hours, €960); Day Trip to Danube Valley (8 hours, €750).

Discover Vienna Tours

Discover Vienna tours (discoverviennatours.com) offers the following private day trips from Vienna. All include hotel pickup and drop-off and transportation in a luxury Mercedes Benz vehicle.

Private day trip to Salzburg—includes 2-hour walking tour of Salzburg with guide (St. Peter's Abbey, the Cathedral, Mozart's birth house, Getreidegasse, Mirabell Gardens, other *Sound of Music* sites), then free time to explore the city at your leisure, return trip through the Salzkammergut region (Lake District). Depart 8 a.m., return 7 p.m. €779 for 1-7 people.

Private day trip to Budapest—includes 2-hour walking tour of Budapest with guide (Royal Castle, Fishermen's Bastion, St. Stephen's Basilica, Opera House, Buda Castle, Parliament, Heroes Square, Matthias Church, Danube River, central Pest), free time to explore on your own. Depart 8 a.m., return 7 p.m. €115 per person.

Private day trip to Prague—includes 2-hour guided walking tour of Prague (Prague Castle, Charles Bridge, Old Town Square, Wenceslas Square, old Jewish quarter), free time to explore on your own. Depart 7 a.m., return 7 p.m. €789 for 1-7 people.

Private ½-day tour to Bratislava—includes 2-hour tour of Bratislava with guide (WWII defensive bunker, Parliament, Bratislava Castle, Michael's Gate, National Theater, Old Town Hall, Cathedral of St. Martin, Palffy Palace, de Pauli's Palace), free time to have lunch on your own. 5 hours. Flexible departure. €550 for 1-7 people.

Private day trip to Cesky Krumlov—includes 1-hour walking tour of Cesky Krumlov with guide (Vltava River, Krumlov Castle with bear moat, Old Town, town square, Plague Column and Fountain, Latran Street), free time to explore and eat lunch. Depart 8 a.m., return 7 p.m. €115 per person.

Private day trip to Krakow—includes 2-hour walking tour of Krakow with guide (Old Town, Market Square, Dragon Wavel Old City Walls and main gate, old Jewish quarter, ghetto, Oscar Schindler's factory, Vistula River), free time to explore at leisure. Depart 6:45 a.m., return 7:45 p.m. €142 per person.

Discover Vienna Tours **also offers** the following: Private Wachau Tours (including a 5-hour Danube cruise and a Wine & Danube cruise); Winery Bike Tour; Private Wine Tours; Vienna Evening Walk; Private Vienna Tours; Private Walking Tour; Segway Tours.

Vienna Explorer

Vienna Explorer (www.viennaexplorer.com) is a highly rated "adventure" company that has TripAdvisor's Certificate of Excellence. It is based along the Danube Canal, which is less convenient for most tourists than departures around the Opera, but the area is easy enough to reach on public transportation or with a taxi. Vienna Explorer offers numerous bike and walking tours, in addition to the following day-trip bus tours:

Hidden Wachau Valley—Tour highlights include touring by van between the Danube cities of Krems and Melk, known as the Wachau, UNESCO World Heritage site of Dürnstein, at least two Austrian wine tastings (included), river cruise on the Danube (May-October). Hotel pickup and drop-off for additional €30. Not Tues/Thurs. Depart 9 a.m. from Franz-Josefs-Kai 45, return 6 p.m. Adult €125, child (under 12) €89.

Salzburg Tour, Small Group—Tour highlights include Mercedes van transportation through the Vienna Woods and Austrian Lake District (*Sound of Music* locations), coffee-and-cake stop, photo stop at the Attersee Lake and the Wolfgangsee Lake in the the village of St. Gilgen, comprehensive walking tour of Salzburg's Old Town (1.5 hours), Mozart's birthplace, Mirabell Garden, cemetery of St. Peter's Abbey, Salzburg Cathedral, Archbishop's Palace, free time to explore and eat (2.5 hours). Fullday guided tour. Maximum 8 passengers. Tour transfer to morning departure point for max. €12 per person. Hotel drop-off included in Central Vienna. Sun/Wed/Fri. Depart 7:30 a.m., return 7:30 p.m. Adult from €179, child (less than 26 years) €119.

Lodging

Hotels on this list are based on location, good reviews, and general accessibility, including access to easy transportation. It favors buildings with elevators, but that doesn't mean the elevator will be larger than a phone booth. You may need to make several trips to get your luggage to upper floors. This section isn't the last word on acceptable accommodation, but it makes a good starting point to narrow down your search. Just check online to make sure that information is still accurate, on TripAdvisor, on Booking.com, or on the hotel's own Web site.

You may find a wonderful deal on what looks like a good choice in a convenient location. By all means—grab it! Same with charming B&Bs, which aren't covered here because they tend to have a limited number of available rooms and generally don't have elevators. If you can nab one in a favorable location that gets good reviews, has a great breakfast, decent accessibility, and a workable price, do it!

Hotel price ranges are based on late 2019 TripAdvisor averages. Averages can vary considerably throughout the year. Your own quotes may be higher or lower.

Vienna State Opera area

Pretty much all of the HOHO buses, day trips, and other tours of Vienna leave from near the State Opera house (or else offer hotel pickup and drop-off). There is easy public transportation here, as well. If a stop is listed as Oper or Karlsplatz, that will get you close to home, if you stay around here. Fortunately, this is also a highly desirable area in which to lodge, walking distance from much of Central Vienna (or all of it, if you are highly mobile).

This is not the most economical part of the city to lodge in, however. Numerous grand old hotels cluster here—the Sacher, the Bristol, the Grand Hotel Wien, the Imperial—remnants of Vienna's international glory during the waning days of the Austro-Hungarian Empire. If your budget is stretched tight and you can't get into the budget-friendly options on this list, you can easily choose a hotel elsewhere in the city and get to any day trip departures either by choosing a hotel pickup, taking a taxi, or riding the city's excellent public transportation system.

I will not list hotels in other areas of the city you may choose to lodge in, because none stands out as an obvious alternative. Just be aware that the area around a train station (Vienna has several) is typically tawdry but economical. Look at online reviews to see whether other visitors have recommended a particular hotel, if you are considering one in a possibly sketchy neighborhood. I have more than once stayed around the Westbahnhof (West Train Station), and while it wasn't a neighborhood I wanted to spend extra time in, it was fine for lodging. (I do not typically stay out late, for what that's worth. Night owls might have a different experience.) The Mariahilfer Strasse connects the Westbahnhof with central Vienna and may be a good compromise for those looking for less-expensive lodging.

Hotels around the State Opera include the following:

Hotel Das Tyrol—Mariahilferstrasse 15 (www.das-tyrol.at/en/). TripAdvisor's Travelers' Choice Award 2019 (top 1% in category). Location: outside the Ring, south of the Museum Quarter. Pros: non-smoking hotel, air conditioning, soundproof rooms, elevator, free WiFi, excellent breakfast buffet, bar, airport shuttle available, private parking available, ATM on site, twin/studio rooms available. Cons: small rooms, tiny lift, no restaurant, no singles, no price break for singles. (TripAdvisor price range for standard room: $168-$328.)

Distances: Leopold Museum (.1 miles), Museumquartier Metro Stop (.2 miles), Kunsthistorisches Museum (.2 miles), State Opera (.5 miles), Albertina Museum (.5 miles), Volksgarten (.5 miles), St. Stephen's Cathedral (.8 miles)

Hotel Kaiserhof Wien—Frankenberggasse 10 (wien.hotelkaiserhof.at/en). TripAdvisor's Traveler's Choice Award (top 1% of category) 2019. Location: outside the Ring, south of the State Opera. Pros: non-smoking hotel, air conditioning, exceptional free breakfast, elevator, bar/lounge, free WiFi, airport shuttle available, fitness center, singles/twins/allergy-free/triples/suites available. Cons: some complaints about A/C. (TripAdvisor price range for standard room: $160-$362.)

Distances: Karlskirche (.2 miles), Karlsplatz Metro Station (.3 miles), State Opera (.4 miles), Albertina Museum (.5 miles), St. Stephen's Cathedral (.8 miles)

The Guesthouse Vienna—Führichgasse 10 (theguesthouse.at/en). TripAdvisor's Travelers' Choice Award 2019. Location: two streets north of the Opera. Pros: non-smoking hotel, air conditioning, airport shuttle, soundproof rooms, free WiFi, facilities for disabled guests, lift, restaurant, breakfast available, room service, bar/lounge, coffeeshop, singles/triples available. Cons: no twin or quad rooms, some showers leak out door, some rooms a little small, pillows too soft for some. (TripAdvisor price range for standard room: $252-$727.)

Distances: Imperial Crypt (.1 miles), Albertina Museum (.1 miles), Vienna State Opera (.2 miles), Burggarten (.2 miles), St. Stephen's Cathedral (.3 miles), Volksgarten (.4 miles)

Living Hotel an der Oper—Kärntner Strasse 44 (www.livinghotels.com/hotel-an-der-oper-wien/en/). TripAdvisor's Certificate of Excellence. Location: south of the State Opera, one street south of the Ring. Pros: non-smoking hotel, air conditioning, free WiFi, elevator, very good breakfast buffet, refrigerator, microwave, airport shuttle, triple/quad rooms available. Cons: rooms are dated, small and slow elevator, some problems with air conditioning and showers. (TripAdvisor price range for standard room: $172-$362.)

Distances: Karlsplatz Metro Stop (0.0 miles), State Opera (.1 miles), Albertina Museum (.2 miles), Burggarten (.2 miles), Karlskirche (.3 miles), St. Stephen's Cathedral (.5 miles)

Hotel Sacher—Philharmonikerstrasse 4 (www.sacher.com/en/hotel-sacher-wien/). TripAdvisor's Traveler's Choice Award (top 1% of category) 2019. Location: across the street from the Opera next to Kärnterstrasse. Pros: non-smoking hotel, air conditioning, facilities for disabled guests, elevator, soundproof rooms, free WiFi, restaurant, room service, bar/lounge, wonderful breakfast buffet, fitness center, parking, airport shuttle available, twins/kings available. Cons: price, no singles, no price break for singles. (TripAdvisor price range for standard room: $502-$1,286.)

Distances: Albertina Museum (0.0 miles), State Opera (.1 miles), Karlsplatz Metro Station (.2 miles), St. Stephen's Cathedral (.4 miles), Karlskirche (.4 miles), Volksgarten (.5 miles)

Opera Suites—Kärnterstrasse 47 (www.operasuites.at/en/). Location: just north of Opera. Pros: no-smoking hotel, elevator, air conditioning, free WiFi, very good breakfast, sound-proof rooms, parking, ATM on site, single/twin/triple rooms. Cons: no restaurant/bar, some street noise, elevator very small, only 12 rooms. (TripAdvisor price range for standard room: $145-$378.)

Distances: Albertina Museum (.1 miles), State Opera (.1 miles), Karlsplatz Metro Station (.2 miles), St. Stephen's Cathedral (.4 miles), Karlskirche (.4 miles), Volksgarten (.5 miles)

Hotel Beethoven—Papagenogasse 6 (www.hotel-beethoven.at). TripAdvisor's Travelers' Choice Award 2019. Location: outside the Ring, southwest of the State Opera. Pros: free WiFi, non-smoking rooms, air conditioning, wonderful breakfast buffet, bar/lounge, elevator, facilities for disabled guests, refrigerator, airport shuttle available, twin rooms available. Cons: no singles/triples/quads, no price break for singles, some rooms rather small. (TripAdvisor price range for standard room: $148-$267.)

Distances: Naschmarkt (.1 miles), Karlsplatz Metro Station (.3 miles), Kunsthistorisches Museum (.3 miles), State Opera (.3 miles), Albertina Museum (.4 miles), Karlskirche (.4 miles), St. Stephen's Cathedral (.7 miles)

Hotel Imperial—Kärntner Ring 16. TripAdvisor's Travelers' Choice Award 2019. Location: just south of the Ring, three streets east of the State Opera. Pros: non-smoking hotel, air conditioning, free WiFi, facilities for disabled guests, elevator, private balcony, DVD/CD player, restaurant, room service, coffee shop, very good breakfast buffet, ATM on site, bar/lounge, fitness center, airport shuttle, twin rooms/suites available. Cons: price, no singles, no real price break for singles. (TripAdvisor price range for standard room: $343-$1,034.)

Distances: Karlsplatz Metro Station (.2 miles), State Opera (.2 miles), Karlskirche (.2 miles), Albertina Museum (.3 miles), St. Stephen's Cathdral (.3 miles)

The Ritz-Carlton—Schubertring 5-7. TripAdvisor's Traveler's Choice Award 2019. Location: east of the State Opera on the Schubertring. Pros: non-smoking hotel, air conditioning, free WiFi, facilities for disabled guests, elevator, restaurant, very good breakfast buffet, refrigerator, bar/lounge, fitness center, parking, airport shuttle available, ATM on site, swimming pool, twins/kings/suites/triples available. Cons: price, no real price break for singles. (TripAdvisor price range for standard room: $327-$1,015.)

Distances: Akademietheater (.2 miles), State Opera (.3 miles), Albertina Museum (.4 miles), Karlskirche (.4 miles), St. Stephen's Cathedral (.5 miles)

Hotel Bristol—Kärntner Ring 1. TripAdvisor's Traveler's Choice Award 2019. Location: east across Kärntner Street from the State Opera. Pros: non-smoking hotel, air conditioning, free WiFi, restaurant, room service, very good breakfast buffet, bar/lounge, private balcony, elevator, facilities for disabled guests, fitness center, on-site parking, ATM on site, airport shuttle available, singles/twins/kings/suites available. Cons: price, smoking in bar, high prices in bar. (TripAdvisor price range for standard room: $254-$1,165.)

Distances: State Opera (.1 miles), Karlsplatz Metro Station (.1 miles), Albertina Museum (.1 miles), Karlskirche (.3 miles), St. Stephen's Cathedral (.4 miles)

Schlosshotel Römischer Kaiser—Annagasse 16 (schlosshotelroem ischer-kaiser.hotelsinvienna.org/en/). TripAdvisor's Certificate of Exellence. Location: two streets north of the State Opera and a bit east. Pros: non-smoking hotel, air conditioning, free WiFi, facilities for disabled guests, elevator, soundproof rooms, excellent breakfast buffet, breakfast in room, airport shuttle, ATM on site, twins/triples available. Cons: no bar or restaurant, no singles, no price break for singles, old décor, beds and pillows too firm for some. (TripAdvisor price range for standard room: $171-$377.)

Distances: State Opera (.2 miles), Albertina Museum (.2 miles), Karlsplatz Metro Station (.2 miles), St. Stephen's Cathedral (.4 miles), Karlskirche (.4 miles), Volksgarten (.6 miles)

Grand Hotel Wien/Vienna—Kärntnerring 9 (www.grandhotelwien.com/en/). TripAdvisor's Traveler's Choice Award (top 1% in category) 2019. Location: southeast of the State Opera on the Ring. Pros: air conditioning, non-smoking hotel, restaurant, room service, excellent breakfast, buffet, bar/lounge, on-site parking, airport shuttle available, free WiFi, elevator, facilities for disabled guests, fitness center, sound-proof rooms, twin rooms available. Cons: no singles/triples/quads, no price break for singles, expensive breakfast, some smoking rooms. (TripAdvisor price range for standard room: $220-$1,938.)

Distances: Karlsplatz Metro Station (.1 miles), State Opera (.2 miles), Albertina Museum (.2 miles), Karlskirche (.3 miles), St. Stephen's Cathedral (.5 miles)

Motel One Wien—Staatsoper—Elizabethstrasse 5 (www.motel-one.com/en/hotels/vienna/hotel-vienna-staatsoper/). TripAdvisor's Certificate of Excellence. Location: south of the State Opera, one street past the Ring. Pros: non-smoking hotel, air conditioning, free WiFi, elevator, soundproof rooms, bar/lounge, good breakfast buffet, single rooms available. Cons: no twin/triple/quad rooms, rooms a bit small, no phone in room. (TripAdvisor price range for standard room: $90-$120.)

Distances: Karlplatz Metro Station (.1 miles), State Opera (.1 miles), Albertina Museum (.2 miles), Burggarten (.2 miles), Karlskirche (.3 miles), St. Stephen's Cathedral (.5 miles)

Hotel Pension Suzanne—Walfischgasse 4 (www.pensionsuzanne.at/en/). TripAdvisor's Certificate of Excellence. Location: 50 meters east of State Opera. Pros: non-smoking hotel, elevator, excellent breakfast buffet, free WiFi, some kitchenettes, single/triple/quad/quint/more rooms available. Cons: hotel starts at 3rd floor, lift is small and slow, some rooms very small, 3 steps up to access entrance and elevator, a bit dated, no restaurant/bar, only 25 rooms. (TripAdvisor price range for standard room: $118-$229.)

Distances: State Opera (.1 miles), Albertina Museum (.1 miles), Karlsplatz Metro Station (.2 miles), Karlskirche (.4 miles), St. Stephen's Cathedral (.4 miles), Volksgarten (.5 miles)

Le Meridien Vienna—Robert-Stolz-Platz 1. TripAdvisor's Certificate of Excellence. Location: almost two streets west of the State Opera, on the south side of the Ring. Pros: non-smoking hotel, air conditioning, free WiFi, facilities for disabled guests, elevator, restaurant, room service, very good breakfast buffet, bar/lounge, refrigerator, fitness center, airport shuttle. Cons: no single/triple/quad rooms, no price break for singles, problems with air conditioning, loud nightclub, expensive breakfast. (TripAdvisor price range for standard room: $189-$570.)

Distances: State Opera (.1 miles), Burggarten (.1 miles), Albertina Museum (.1 miles), Karlsplatz Metro Station (.2 miles), Museumquartier (.4 miles), St. Stephen's Cathedral (.5 miles)

The Ring Hotel—Relais & Chateau—Kärntnerring 8 (theringhotel.com/en/). TripAdvisor's Traveler's Choice 2018 (top 1% of category). Location: on the Ring southeast of the Opera. Pros: non-smoking hotel, air conditioning, free WiFi, facilities for disabled guests, elevator, fitness center, bar/lounge, room service, good breakfast, airport shuttle available, soundproof rooms, singles/twins/triples available. Cons: hotel "tired"/"worn," hotel and service not 5-star standard. (TripAdvisor price range for standard room: $193-$528.)

Distances: Karlsplatz Metro Station (.1 miles), State Opera (.1 miles), Albertina Museum (.2 miles), Karlskirche (.3 miles), St. Stephen's Cathedral (.5 miles)

Pension Aviano—Marco-d'Aviano-Gasse 1 (www.avianoboutiquehotel.com/en/). TripAdvisor's Certificate of Excellence. Location: three streets north of the State Opera. Pros: non-smoking hotel, free WiFi, elevator, good breakfast available, breakfast in room available, convenience store on site, airport shuttle, single and triple rooms available. Cons: no air conditioning, noise, limited number of rooms, some complaints about showers/hair dryers, no twin or quad rooms, no restaurant or bar, only 17 rooms. (TripAdvisor price range for standard room: $109-$253.)

Distances: Imperial Crypt (0.0 miles), Albertina Museum (.1 miles), State Opera (.2 miles), Stephansplatz Metro Station (.2 miles), St. Stephen's Cathedral (.3 miles), Volksgarten (.5 miles), Karlskirche (.5 miles)

Hotel am Konzerthaus Vienna—Am Heumarkt 35-37. TripAdvisor's Certificate of Excellence. Location: outside the Ring, southeast of the State Opera. Pros: non-smoking hotel, air conditioning, facilities for disabled guests, elevators, free WiFi, restaurant, room service, very good breakfast buffet, bar/lounge, private parking, twin rooms available. Cons: worn and dark rooms, no triples/quads, no real price break for singles, expensive breakfast. (TripAdvisor price range for standard room: $127-$260.)

Distances: Akademietheater (0.0 miles), Karlskirche (.3 miles), State Opera (.4 miles), Albertina Museum (.5 miles), St. Stephen's Cathedral (.7 miles)

Austria Trend Hotel Astoria—Kärntner Strassse 32-34 (www.austria-trend.at/en/hotels/astoria). Location: two streets north of the State Opera. Pros: non-smoking hotel, free WiFi, elevator, restaurant, room service, very good breakfast buffet, breakfast in room, bar/lounge, single/twin/suites available. Cons: no air conditioning in most rooms, small and slow lift. (TripAdvisor price range for standard room: $141-$328.)

Distances: Imperial Crypt (.1 miles), Albertina Museum (.1 miles), State Opera (.1 miles), St. Stephen's Cathdral (.3 miles), Volksgarten (.5 miles), Karlskirche (.5 miles)

Hotel Ambassador—Kärntner Strasse 22. Location: three streets north of the State Opera. Pros: non-smoking rooms, free WiFi, elevator, restaurant, room service, very good breakfast buffet, bar/lounge, airport shuttle. Cons: dated/worn, uneven desk service, lax cleaning, expensive breakfast, local construction noise in 2019. (TripAdvisor price range for standard room: $166-$398.)

Distances: Imperial Crypt (.1 miles), Stephansplatz Metro Station (.1 miles), Albertina Museum (.2 miles), St. Stephen's Cathdral (.2 miles), State Opera (.2 miles), Karlskirche (.5 miles)

Hotel zur Wiener Staatsoper—Krugerstrasse 11 (www.hotel-staatsoper.at/en/). TripAdvisor's Certificate of Excellence. Location: just northeast of State Opera. Pros: non-smoking hotel, free WiFi, elevator, free breakfast buffet, breakfast in room, ATM on site, single and triple rooms available. Cons: no air conditioning, small rooms and very small bathrooms, no bar/lounge, only 17 rooms. (TripAdvisor price range for standard room: $115-$183.)

Distances: Albertina Museum (.1 miles), State Opera (.2 miles), Karlsplatz Metro Station (.2 miles), St. Stephen's Cathedral (.3 miles), Karlskirche (.4 miles), Volksgarten (.6 miles)

Other base cities in Austria

Vienna is located way in the east of Austria, putting it closer to the other capital cities of Bratislava, Budapest, and Prague than to much of its own country to the west. It's not really practical to see all of Austria from Vienna. If you want to base in other areas, Graz (in southeast Austria) has electric bus tours of the city, Salzburg (to the west of Vienna, more in the center of the country) has HOHO buses and bus day-trip and half-day excursions, and Innsbruck (in the western panhandle) has a HOHO line.

Munich

Overview

Munich (or München—MYOON-chen—as the locals would say) is the capital of the large German state of Bavaria. When most people picture Germany, what they're thinking of is Bavaria, and Munich is right in the heart of it. Beer. Pretzels. Wurst. Oompah bands. Lederhosen. Oktoberfest. If those are your thing, visiting Munich will be a spiritual homecoming.

Munich is not all bratwurst and beer, however. It has a long royal history, impressive churches, art museums, the German version of the Smithsonian, and, not to be whitewashed, a dark association with the rise of Adolf Hitler and Nazism. The city's offerings are so rich that you can focus on whatever you want and have plenty to see and do without trying to fit everything in.

Munich is a wonderfully walkable city, flat, with a compact Old City inside the ring of streets that mark the former city walls. The city has excellent and affordable public transportation and goes out of its way to be handicapped accessible. It also has significant pedestrian zones, giving many opportunities for strolling.

Munich's climate is continental, with cold winters and mild to warm summers. Winter lows average about 27 degrees Fahrenheit with occasional cold snaps around zero, while summer highs tend to be in the 70s, though they can reach the mid-90s. Rain is heaviest in the summer, with afternoon thunderstorms fairly common.

The official Munich tourism site can be a good resource as you plan your trip: www.muenchen.de/int/en/.

Possible plan for Munich (What I'd do)

If I were traveling to Munich with my mother, this is what I would plan for us to do. It's a fairly short itinerary—just 9 days total, so it could fit if you wanted to fly to Germany on a Saturday and fly home on Sunday, for example, and just take a week off of work. Obviously, you may prefer to do something different, or add a bunch, but you may find this itinerary handy as a starting point, changing it as much as you'd like. (And it will make more sense as you work your way through the chapter. Having a city map at hand will help, too.) **Please double check any details here before relying on them, as specifics may have changed since I wrote these pages.** As for day trips, you probably don't want to plan for more than two consecutive out-of-town excursions at a time, so you can avoid bus fatigue.

This plan assumes lodging near the train station but could easily be modified for elsewhere.

Day 1—Depart U.S.

Day 2—(*Works on any day.*) Arrive Munich. Find an ATM (*Geldautomat*) and withdraw euros, if needed. Exit the terminal and look for the white Lufthansa Express Bus at bus stop (buy round-trip ticket online ahead of time). Ride bus to end stop, the main train station, and then find hotel. At the hotel, go to the room and rest, if possible. If too early for that, leave luggage and start exploring. Visit the Tourist Information Office at the train station. Get any tourist information you may want, including maps. Line up cell phone service, if needed. Locate a handy grocery store.

Check out the pedestrian zone between the train station and Marienplatz. Stop for lunch, snack, or coffee. Try to be in the Marienplatz at 5 p.m. to watch the Glockenspiel on the city hall (Rathaus). Work your way back to the hotel. Rest before dinner, then go out to eat. (Or eat in.)

Day 3—(*Don't do on Monday.*) Have a late breakfast. Buy 48-hour Grayline HOHO ticket. (Or buy online ahead of time.) Take the Grand Circle route to Nymphenburg Palace. Tour the main palace, the carriage house (Marstallmuseum), and wander the grounds as much as desired. Fortify self with coffee and a snack.

Take the HOHO bus the rest of the route back to the main train station. Switch to the Express Circle route and ride to the first stop ("Galleries and Exhibitions, Kunstareal"). Walk to the Alte Pinakothek art museum (*closed Monday*). Buy ticket and view old masters, using audioguide. Ride HOHO bus the rest of the route, returning to the main train station and then the hotel. Relax in evening. Go out to eat. (If not too far away, try the Augustinerkeller, NW of the train station.)

Day 4—(*Works on any day—can switch with Day 3 itinerary if Day 3 falls on a Monday.*) Day 2 of HOHO bus ticket. Ride to stop at Deutsches Museum. Spend several hours in the museum. Ride to HOHO stop Marienplatz/Tal. Walk to Hofbräuhaus for a late lunch. Walk to Residenz. Visit the Treasury/Schatzkammer. Ride HOHO bus back to main train station. Relax in room. Dinner in or out.

Day 5—(*On a Wed. or Sun, if taking Gray Line tour.*) Day trip: Romantic Road with Harburg.

Day 6—(*On a Tues. Thurs., or Sat., if taking Gray Line tour.*) Day trip: Salzburg and Lake District.

Day 7—Free day in Munich. Wander the Old City—St. Peter's, Viktualienmarkt (Biergarten for lunch, closed Sunday), possibly return to Deutsches Museum, Asam Church. Shop.

Day 8—Day trip: Neuschwanstein, Linderhof, and Oberammergau. Suggestion: possibly don't go inside Linderhof Palace. Explore exterior, gardens, and gift shop. At Neuschwanstein, reserve ticket in advance online (Wittelsbach ticket) for Hohenschwangau Castle and the Bavarian Kings Museum. Pick up at Reservation desk in ticket center. Take carriage ride up to Hohenschwangau. (Pay driver.) View Neuschwanstein Castle across the valley. Tour Hohenschwangau Castle. Ride carriage back down the hill and walk to the Bavarian Kings Museum (or replace activity with shopping and coffee—don't get combo ticket then, though).

Day 9—Return to U.S. Use return Lufthansa Express Bus ride from main train station to airport, purchased in advance.

Note: I would usually recommend a day trip to the memorial at Dachau, because of its historical importance. Visiting the site of the former concentration camp, however, requires a great deal of walking and standing, which is why I have omitted it from my sample itinerary. If you are fine with walking and standing for hours at a time, then you are fine including a trip to Dachau. Or, if you are *not* able to walk and stand for such a long time but have a collapsible stool to rest on, you can also manage a visit.

A lot of walking combined with a lack of seats to rest on is also why I don't include the Residenz on my itinerary. As a highly restricted royal palace (you must check all bags), I doubt authorities would allow a collapsible stool to be used inside. If you really want to go through the palace, though, it's worth asking to see whether a collapsible stool would be allowed as a medical concession. If you do that, make sure you allot plenty of time for the self-paced tour, because the palace is massive. (And then tell me that it's possible to take your own seat to rest on!)

Arrival

International traffic flies into Franz Josef Strauss Airport (MUC) (www.munich-airport.com), about 18 miles northeast of Munich. To get from MUC to the city, you have your choice of train, bus, hotel shuttle, taxi, or private driver.

S-Bahn train lines S-1 and S-8 both run between the airport and the city. Trains depart every 10-20 minutes for a 35-minute ride into the city. An Airport-City-Day Ticket (in German, a *Gesamtnetzkarte*) will meet all your public transportation needs for the day, both to (or from) the city and around in it. Tickets are valid until 6 a.m. the next day. All ticket machines at the airport and most S-Bahn stations sell the tickets. (First select "MVV Münchner Verkehrs- und Tarifverbund" on the screen, then choose "Airport-City-Day-Ticket.") A single day ticket costs €13, and a group day ticket (for up to 5 people) costs €24.30. You will find the S-Bahn trains in Terminal 1 of the Munich Airport Center (MAC). Follow the green "S" signs to get to the trains.

Lufthansa runs an **express bus** from the airport to the main station and back (www.airportbus-muenchen.de/en/). The bus stops four places in the airport—Terminal 2, Terminal 1 Area A, Munich Airport Center, and Terminal 1 Area D—in Munich North/Schwabing, and at the Hauptbahnhof (main train station). Look for the big white bus with yellow Lufthansa markings. The buses depart every 15 minutes and the ride from end to end lasts approximately 45 minutes. Adult single tickets cost €10.50, and round-trip tickets cost €17. Tickets may be purchased in advance online (for best prices) or from the bus driver for a slightly higher price of €11 (one-way) and €18 (round-trip). Board the bus directly in front of the terminals. Buses leave from the airport 6:30 a.m.-10:30 p.m. They leave from the main train station 5:15 a.m.-10:00 p.m.

You can arrange a **private shuttle**, including meeting you at the airport, if you want, through the Web site at www.airport shuttles.com/munich-hotel-shuttles.php. If you are a heavy packer, be aware of listed luggage restrictions. Some hotels offer **hotel shuttle** services. If your hotel lists this as an option, look over the hotel Web site or contact the hotel to get more information.

Taxis from the Munich airport are available in taxi ranks outside the arrival halls. Taxis rides to the city center take about 45 minutes and cost around €70. Most travelers choose other transfer options. (The S-Bahn train is most popular.) Most taxis in Munich accept credit cards, but ask before boarding, if you are relying on plastic.

Easy transportation options

Once in the city, your usual transportation choices are metro, tram, bus, and taxi/Uber. One easy way to get around to the sights is to ride a hop-on/hop-off (HOHO) tourist bus. You purchase a 1-day or 2-day pass and then may hop on and hop off the buses (of the line you paid for) as much as you'd like in that time.

Hop-On/Hop-Off Tours
Gray Line Sightseeing

Gray Line, the ubiquitous international tour bus company, has blue double-decker hop-on/hop-off buses in Munich (www.grayline.com/tours/munich/munich-24-hour-hop-on-hop-off-tour-5868_1_12130_16 /). In general, reviews are not as strong as for the Gray Line day tours, with complaints about customer service and inadequate commentary in English. Nonetheless, many users are quite pleased with their experiences.

There are two Gray Line HOHO routes—the 8-stop Express Circle (1 hour straight through) and the longer Grand Circle, which adds 4 more stops (and an additional 90 minutes).

The Express Circle starts at 1) Hauptbahnhof-Central Station and hits the following 7 stops before returning to the main train station: 2) Kunstareal (Galleries and Exhibitions); 3) Odeonsplatz (Hofgarten, Theatiner Church); 4) City Surfer/Icewave (Haus der Kunst, Nationalmuseum); 5) Deutsches Museum; 6) Marienplatz/Tal (City Hall/Rathaus, Frauenkirche); 7) Max-Joseph-Platz (Opera House, Residence, Treasury); 8) Karlsplatz–Stachus (shopping center), then back to the main train station. The Express Circle route starts at 9:40 a.m. March 17-Oct. 31 and ends at 5 p.m. (starting at 10 a.m. the rest of the year), with buses running approximately every 20 minutes (less frequently in winter, with reduced hours).

The extended Grand Circle route picks up at the Haupbahnhof (main train station) and continues to 9) Nymphenburg Palace; 10) BMW World & Museum; 11) Olympic grounds; 12) Schwabing/Siegestor/English Garden, return to Hauptbahnhof. The Grand Circle route starts at 10:40 a.m.

March 17-Oct. 31 with buses running approximately every 20 minutes (less frequently in winter, with reduced hours).

Routes include live commentary in German and recorded commentary in English and seven other languages. Riding both circuits back-to-back straight through takes 2.5 hours. Tickets are good for 24 or 48 hours. Prices are as follows:

- 24-hour HOHO—adult €21 online (€23 on-site); child (4-14) €11 online (€12 on-site); family €49 (2 adults and up to 4 children)
- 48-hour HOHO—adult €28; child (4-14) €15

Tickets may be purchased online (mobile or printed vouchers accepted) at a slight discount, on the buses, or at Stop 1 (Central Station, in front of the department store KARSTADT) or Stop 6 (Marienplatz/Tal). For the latest version of the HOHO bus routes, try this link: www.stadtrundfahrten-muenchen.de/_default_ upload_ bucket/tour-guide-02.png.

CitySightseeing Munich

CitySightseeing Munich (www.citysightseeing-munich.com) has red double-decker buses that circle the city center on three different 1-hour HOHO routes. Unfortunately, reviews of this company are even spottier than for Gray Line Sightseeing, above. (Perhaps because Munich didn't allow HOHO buses until recently, so they are all relatively new.) The three routes are the City Tour (city center), the Nymphenburg/Olympia Tour (palace and Olympic Park), and the Schwabing Tour (English Garden, Pinakotheken), all with commentary in 8 languages.

The City Tour (red) starts and ends at the main train station (Hauptbahnhof) with the following stops: H2) Odeonplatz, H3) Marienplatz, H4) Oper, H5) Haidhausen, H6) Deutsches Museum, and H7) Stachus (Karlsplatz). First departure is 10 a.m. and last departure is 5 p.m., with buses leaving every 15 to 30 minutes.

The Nymphenburg/Olympia Tour (purple) also starts and ends at the main train station (Hauptbahnhof) with the following stops: H8) Neuhausen, H9) Nymphenburg, H10) Olympiapark. First departure is 10 a.m. and last departure is 5 p.m. Buses run approximately every 60 minutes Monday-Friday and every 30 minutes on the weekend.

The Schwabing Tour (blue) starts and ends at the main train station, as well, and hits the following stops: H11) Englischer Garten, H12) Schwabing, H13) Pinakotheken. First departure is 10:30 a.m. and last departure is 4:30 p.m. Buses leave every 2 hours Monday-Friday and every 1 hour Saturday-Sunday.

Check here for the latest route map (Click on "Our Tour Map"): www.citysightseeing-munich.com/our-sightseeing-tours/#alltours1day.

Tickets may be purchased for a discount online up to one year in advance (print out a voucher to redeem in person) or at the bus. Costs are as follows:

- City Tour HOHO Ticket (valid for one time around route)—Adult online €15.90 (on-site €18); child (5-15) online €9.90 (on-site €11)
- 3-Tours Day HOHO Ticket—Adult online €20.90 (on-site €23); child (5-15) online €9.90 (on-site €11); family (2 adults and up to 3 children) online €46.90 (on-site €49)
- 3-Tours 2-Day HOHO Ticket—Adult online €24.90 (on-site €28); child (5-15) online €9.90 (on-site €11)

Taxis and Uber

If taking a taxi or arranging a private ride is your thing, you can certainly do so in Munich. You can check a taxi fare finder such as www.taxifarefinder.com to get an estimate for how much a ride would cost. For example, taxi fare from Marienplatz to the Alte Pinakothek gallery would range from €8.85 in low traffic to €18.27 in high traffic and would typically cost about €10.61, for a trip of about one and a half miles.

Uber is available in Munich, possibly at a lower rate than a taxi. Rates can contain a surge multiplier without warning, however, so don't assume that an Uber will always save you money compared to a taxi.

It is not usual to hail a taxi on the street in Munich. You typically find a taxi at a taxi stand, located throughout the city, particularly at transportation hubs (like the train station) and outside major sights. If you prefer to call for a cab, that is also common in Munich. You can order taxis through the following dispatchers:

- Taxi-München eG, +49 / (0)89/21 610 or +49 / (0)89/19 410
- IsarFunk, +49 / (0)89/450540

The two cab companies listed above both accept credit cards for payment. There is an additional 1 euro fee for ordering a taxi in the central zone of the city (Zone 1). Small tips (between 50 cents and 2 euros) are typical for taxi drivers, usually rounding up a fare to a convenient amount. For example, if you have a cab fare of €8.50 and you pay with a €10-euro bill, you could tell the driver "Nine euros, please" and would receive one euro back.

To learn more about taxis in Munich, you can check out the official city Web site at www.muenchen.de/int/en/traffic/taxi.html.

Other in-city transportation

Public transportation is so good in Munich that many people advise taking it instead of HOHO buses or taxis. Consider whether the extensive and affordable public transportation system can meet your needs.

The **U-Bahn** (subway) system in Munich is excellent and, connecting with the **S-Bahn** (suburban train system), far-reaching. Slick, modern **trams** gird the old city center and fling out into farther neighborhoods. Blue city **buses** are also available. Subway stations are marked with a white U on a blue background. S-Bahn stations are marked with a white S on a green background. Tram and bus stops are marked with a yellow H in a yellow circle on a green background. Major transportation stops include the main train station (Hauptbahnhof), Karlsplatz/Stachus, and Marienplatz.

PDF maps of Munich's transportation networks can be found at the following Web site: www.mvv-muenchen.de/en/maps-stations/maps/index.html.

The same ticket applies for all forms of public transportation in Munich. You can move from suburban train to subway train to tram to bus, as long as it's all the same trip. You can buy tickets from blue vending machines in U-Bahn and S-Bahn stations and at many bus and tram stops and Tourist Information offices. Many newspaper kiosks also sell them. Types of tickets include the following:

- Single ticket (*Einzelfahrkarte*)—good for one single trip in one direction, valid for 3 hours, €2.90 for within Munich

For tourists, day tickets are the easiest, least complicated, and usually the most economical option, especially if more than one person will be traveling. Day tickets allow unlimited travel on all U-Bahn, S-Bahn, trams, and buses from the time validated until 6 a.m. the following day.

- Single day ticket, inner zone (*Single Tageskarte Innenraum*)—unlimited use in the white zone, €6.70
- Single 3-day ticket, inner zone (*Single 3-Tageskarte Innenraum*)—unlimited use in the white zone, €16.80

- Single day ticket, XXL area (*Single Tageskarte XXL*)—unlimited use in the city enter (white zone on transport maps) and city outskirts (green zone on transport maps) €8.90
- Single day ticket, entire network (*Single Tageskarte Gesamtnetz*)—unlimited use, covers entire Munich transportation system, including transfers to and from the airport, €13

For group tickets, up to five adults can travel together. Two children aged 6-14 count as one adult.

- Group day ticket, inner zone (*Gruppe Tageskarte Innenraum*)—unlimited group use in the white zone, €12.80
- Group 3-day ticket, inner zone (*Gruppe 3-Tagekarte Innenraum*)—unlimited group use in the white zone, €29.60
- Group day ticket, XXL area (*Gruppe Tageskarte XXL*)—unlimited group use in the white and green zones, €16.10
- Group day ticket, entire network (*Gruppe Tageskarte Gesamtnetz*)—unlimited group use of the entire Munich transportation system, €24.30

Another option is the **City Tour Card**, which is also available as a single or group ticket (same restrictions as above), for a specific number of hours or days, covering all public transportation but also providing (usually small) discounts to more than 80 tourist attractions (www.mvv-muenchen.de/en/tickets-and-fares/tickets-daytickets/citytourcard/index.html). For example, the card provides €1 off entrance to Nymphenburg Castle, €10 off a Munich Segway Tour, and 25% off Gray Line sightseeing excursions. Look over the discount list carefully to see whether it's worth paying more than for the regular public transportation day tickets.

Prices for the City Tour Card are as follows:

- Single ticket, inner district—24 hours (€12.90); 48 hours (€18.90); 3 days (until 6 a.m. the following day) (€21.90); 4 days (€26.90); 5 days (€32.90); 6 days (€38.90)
- Single ticket, entire network—24 hours (€22.90); 48 hours (€33.90); 3 days (until 6 a.m. the following day) (€36.90); 4 days (€46.90); 5 days (€56.90); 6 days (€66.90)

- Group ticket, inner district—24 hours (€19.90); 48 hours (€29.90); 3 days (until 6 a.m. the following day) (€32.90); 4 days (€41.90); 5 days (€49.90); 6 days (€57.90)
- Group ticket, entire network—24 hours (€35.90); 48 hours (€54.90); 3 days (until 6 a.m. the following day) (€57.90); 4 days (€75.90); 5 days (€92.90); 6 days (€109.90)

City Tour Cards may be purchased as an online ticket, from ticket vending machines in U-Bahn and S-Bahn stations, or from MGV ticket offices and customer service centers.

Sightseeing pass

If you plan on sightseeing a lot in Munich, you might want to consider a sightseeing pass. There are slight discounts offered with the City Tour Card above (primarily a transportation card). Another option is the Munich City Pass, a more extensive sightseeing card that offers free entry and the same public transportation options as above. As with any sightseeing pass, compare the costs of what you would actually see with the cost of the pass.

The **Munich City Pass** (www.turbopass.com/munich-card-munich-city-pass/munich-city-pass.html) provides free entrance to 45 tourist attractions, free public transportation, and fast-track entrance to some sights, as well as discounts to other partners. The list of covered sights includes the Alte Pinakothek, the Deutsches Museum, Nymphenburg Palace and the park palaces, the Residence Museum and its treasury, HOHO bus Express Circle, and much more. (See here for complete list: www.turbopass.com/munich-card-munich-city-pass/attractions.html.)

Prices for the Munich City Pass are as follows:

- 1 Day, inner district (for transportation pass)—adult (18+) €39.90; teen (15-17) €29.90; child (6-14—always includes transportation for the whole network) €19.90
- 2 Days, inner district (for transportation pass)—adult (18+) €59.90; teen (15-17) €39.90; child (6-14—always includes transportation for the whole network) €24.90
- 3 Days, inner district (for transportation pass)—adult (18+) €79.90; teen (15-17) €49.90; child (6-14—always includes transportation for the whole network) €29.90

- 4 Days, inner district (for transportation pass)—adult (18+) €89.90; teen (15-17) €59.90; child (6-14—always includes transportation for the whole network) €34.90
- 5 Days, inner district (for transportation pass)—adult (18+) €99.90; teen (15-17) €69.90; child (6-14—always includes transportation for the whole network) €39.90
- 1 Day, entire network (for transportation pass)—adult (18+) €46.90; teen (15-17) €36.90; child (6-14—always includes transportation for the whole network) €19.90
- 2 Days, entire network (for transportation pass)—adult (18+) €74.90; teen (15-17) €54.90; child (6-14—always includes transportation for the whole network) €24.90
- 3 Days, entire network (for transportation pass)—adult (18+) €99.90; teen (15-17) €69.90; child (6-14—always includes transportation for the whole network) €29.90
- 4 Days, entire network (for transportation pass)—adult (18+) €114.90; teen (15-17) €84.90; child (6-14—always includes transportation for the whole network) €34.90
- 5 Days, entire network (for transportation pass)—adult (18+) €129.90; teen (15-17) €99.90; child (6-14—always includes transportation for the whole network) €39.90

You can buy a Munich City Pass online and on-site at various locations, including the Tourist Information Office at Marienplatz (in the town hall) and at the main train station in the Deutsche Bahn ticket office.

Bavarian Castle Pass

If you plan to visit more than a couple of castles in Bavaria (the largest German state, of which Munich is the capital), you should look into getting a Bavarian Castle Pass (*Mehrtagestickets der Bayerischen Schlösser Verwaltung*)(www.schloesser.bayern.de/deutsch/schloss/objekte/jahresk.htm). These passes provide free admission to over 40 palaces, castles, fortresses and more, including the most popular in and around Munich: the Residenz (regular entrance price €7), Treasury/Schatzkammer (€7), and Cuvillies-Theater (€3.50) (all in Munich), Nymphenburg Palace with the park palaces and museums (€11.50), Neuschwanstein Castle (€13—requires reserving ahead of time, then getting credit for pass at pickup counter), Linderhof Palace (€8.50), Herrenchiemsee Palace (€9-€11), and many more (but *not* Hohenschwangau Castle, because it's still privately owned).

A 14-day ticket can be purchased at the ticket office of any of the included sights (€26 for an individual). If you will be traveling with a family or a partner, you can save money with a *Familiekarte* or a *Partnerkarte* (€48).

Day trips

It's possible to see much of southern German (and beyond) without having to leave the convenience of your base hotel at night, because Munich has tourist companies that specialize in day trips.

As always, use the information here as a guide, but check each company's Web site for tour details and the most current price and schedule information. **Tour details—even which tours are offered—routinely change from season to season.** Whichever tours you decide on, look over cancellation policies, if your plans aren't completely firm.

Browsing through Web sites will also help you decide which company's tours seem a good fit for you. Be aware that some specific tours might have special requirements or recommendations, so you'll want to look descriptions over closely before you show up at the departure point.

Tour companies differ on which entry fees and meals they include in their prices, so check those specifics (and confirm online), if your selection comes down to price.

Also take into account where the tours depart from. Private day tour companies will pick you up and drop you off at your hotel, so hotel location is less of a concern. You may decide on tours according to which ones depart from near your hotel or will pick you up. Wherever you leave from, make sure you show up early for any tour so you are not considered a no-show and your seat sold to someone else!

If you want to save your walking energy for the tour itself but you select a tour with a departure point that is not close to your hotel, you may want to invest in a taxi ride to get there.

Neuschwanstein Warning

A note of warning is in order here. The standard day trip from Munich is to visit Neuschwanstein Castle in the Alpine foothills. Neuschwanstein is that iconic, romantic white castle at the top of a hill, reputed to have been the inspiration for Disney's *Sleeping Beauty* castle. Neuschwanstein ("New

Swan Stone") *is* beautiful and dramatic, but *it is not easy to visit!* Tour buses stop at the *base* of that huge hill. To get to the top, you either have to 1) climb up, 2) ride a shuttle bus, or 3) ride in a horse-drawn carriage. The considerations of each are as follows:

1) The climb is difficult because of the long, steep ascent and takes a good 30-40 minutes, longer if you have mobility issues. It is challenging for all but the fittest. The paved drive is 1.5 km long (almost 1 mile), all uphill.
2) The shuttle bus ride (€2.50 uphill, €1.50 downhill, buy ticket or pay cash to bus driver) can require a wait in line of more than an hour but does drop you off *above* the castle entrance, near the Marienbrücke (Mary's Bridge). This option requires you to descend a steady incline to get to the castle entrance. The distance from the stop to the castle is about 500 meters (more than 5 city blocks) down a gradient of 12%-19%.
3) The horse-drawn carriage is the most expensive option (€7 uphill, €3.50 downhill, pay the driver) and may also require a wait for availability, but it will deposit you above the worst of the climb, with a manageable walk to the castle entrance. But even that walk is not flat. It's about 450 meters—or 5 city blocks—up an incline of up to 15%. The carriage does not bring you near to Mary's Bridge, with its great views of the castle. Getting *there* requires a significant climb farther *up*.

A further challenge awaits once you arrive at the castle. If you take the tour of the interior, you must be able to climb and descend a lot of stairs—more than 300 steps—during a fairly short tour (about 35 minutes). It is possible to arrange a special tour that uses a lift between floors, but you *must* prearrange this.

So, what's a mobility-challenged tourist to do? That depends on your desire and determination to see this iconic landmark. In order of easiest to most challenging, this is what I would recommend:

1) If you only want to see Neuschwanstein because you think you're supposed to, I would give it a pass and use your day trip time to reach something more easily accessible.

2) If you want to be able to say you've seen the castle, take a day trip that gets you to Neuschwanstein but spend your time in the village at the base of the hill. Possibly visit Hohenschwangau Castle, which is easier to get to above the village than Neuschwanstein is, and it offers a view to the more famous castle. As a true medieval castle and the home where King Ludwig II grew up, Hohenschwangau is historically the more interesting and important of the two. There are still steps required if you tour inside (no elevator), but considerably fewer than in Neuschwanstein. You may just want to take a carriage ride up (€4.50 uphill, €2 downhill, pay the driver), take in the view *without* an interior tour, and then walk or ride back down. (Decide before you go up, though, because you have to buy your castle ticket in the valley.) Another option is to visit the Museum of the Bavarian Kings, in the village of Hohenschwangau, a 5-minute walk from the ticket office.

3) If you are set on visiting the castle regardless, to say you've seen it up close, then I would take the shuttle bus up and a carriage down, so walking is minimized and limited to downhill. (If you are at all unsteady walking down steep inclines, then take the carriage in both directions, to avoid the trail at the top of a steep dropoff.) I would skip the interior tour in this case, because the castle is most interesting from the outside, and the inside has so many stairs.

4) If you are commited to getting the whole Neuschwanstein experience, however, and definitely want to go inside, be prepared for the stairs or else make special arrangements for a "limited mobility" tour. (Fill out this advance reservation form: www.hohen schwangau.de/850.0.html. Unfortunately, I cannot find an English version of it. In the section marked "Mitteilung," indicate that you will need to use the lift. If you wanted to make sure there would be no misunderstanding, in German that would be, "Wir benötigen den Aufzug.") Make sure that you have enough time to get up and down the hill and through the interior tour.

If you decide to go, keep in mind that as Germany's most popular tourist sight, Neuschwanstein is often crowded, especially during the summer, *most* especially during August, and you are likely to have to fight crowds throughout your visit. Mary's Bridge can be so crowded that you may have to stand in line half an hour or more to get to it. The waiting area to get into the castle can have so many groups milling about that you may not be able to get one of the few benches to rest on.

Visiting Neuschwanstein Castle requires a commitment. Be aware of that as you weigh your options, and if you decide to visit Linderhof Palace or Herrenchiemsee Palace instead, you will still get a taste of King Ludwig II's grand vision but without so many physical difficulties. (See book excerpt pp. 322-329.)

Radius Tours

Radius Tours (www.radiustours.com/) is a local company that has TripAdvisor's Certificate of Excellence. Founded by a former British rugby player and his Bavarian wife, the company offers only Munich-based tours, specializing in high-quality, English-language excursions. (Many tours also available in Spanish.) Tours depart from the Radius Tours office in the Hauptbahnhof (main train station), across from platforms 32-34. Day trips include the following:

Neuschwanstein Castle Tour—Tour highlights include a two-hour bus or train ride (depending on season) to Neuschwanstein Castle, the Marienbrücke Bridge with view to the castle, a possible easy hike, possible visit at lake, castle tour (entrance fee not included). *Steep uphill walk of approximately 30 minutes to get to the castle.* Horse-drawn carriage or bus ride up the hill is possible. (Consider contacting company ahead of time, if mobility will be an issue.) *Castle tour requires stairs.* Guests may choose to omit the interior tour. Tour also available in Spanish. Daily. Depart 9:30 a.m. and 10:30 a.m. from the main train station, return 6:30 p.m. and 7:30 p.m. Adult (14+) €52, student (with ID) €50, child (6-13) €33, infant (5 and under) €9.

Dachau Concentration Camp Memorial Site Tour—Tour highlights include travel by bus and train 12 miles to the Dachau site, then a fully guided tour in English. Wear clothing and shoes for outdoor walking. Bring water. No food inside the memorial. Tour also available in Spanish. Depart 9:15 a.m., 10:15 a.m. (June/July only) and 12:15 p.m. (1 April-15 Oct. only) from the main train station. Considerable standing and walking. Return 5 hours later. No children under 14 years. Adult (14+) €29.50, student (with ID) €27.50.

Munich to Salzburg Day Trip and Tour—Tour highlights include a two-hour train ride to Salzburg (included), half-hour guided tour of Salzburg, Mozart's birthplace, filming sites for *The Sound of Music*, Mirabell Castle and Mirabell Garden, Salzburg Old Town, cathedral, Fortress Hohensalzburg, 3 hours free time. *Passports required.* Daily in summer. Tues/Thur/Sat/Sun Jan. 7-March 31. Depart 9:15 a.m. from the main train station. Return 6:45 p.m. No children under 6 years. Adult (14+) €52, student (with ID) €50, child (6-13) €33.

Oktoberfest—The World-Famous Party—Tour includes a guided tour of the grounds, ferris wheel ride, seats at private reserved table in the Hofbräu tent, 2 liters of beer, ½ roast chicken. Only during Oktoberfest time, late Sept to early Oct. Depart 10 a.m. from the main train station. Return 5 p.m. Ages 16+ only. Adult (16+) €160.

Munich Bavarian Beer Tour—Tour highlights include a beer-centric tour of Munich, Oktoberfest Museum, beer tasting, traditional Munich beer garden, and the famous Hofbräuhaus. *No stag parties.* Tues/Thur/Sat. Depart 6 p.m. from main train station. Return 9:30 p.m. Ages 16+ only. Adult (16+) €39, student (with ID) €37.

Munich to Nuremberg Day Trip and Tour—Tour highlights include train transport to Nuremberg (1.5 hours), guided tour of city, Imperial Castle, St. Sebald Church, marketplace, Christmas Market (Nov. 30-Dec. 23), Congress Hall of the Nazi Party, Party Rally Grounds, Old Town, free time. Days vary by season but always include Wed/Sat. Depart 8:40 a.m from main train station. Return 6:40 p.m. Ages 6+ only. Adult (14+) €52, student (with ID) €50, child (6-13) €33.

Day Trip and Tour from Munich to Regensburg—Tour highlights include a 1.5-hour train ride to Regensburg, medieval architecture, a guided walking tour of Old City, St. Peter's Cathedral, free time to explore the ancient Stone Bridge, Town Hall, and Sausage Kitchen. Mon/Sat. Depart 10:15 a.m. from main train station, return 7:15 p.m. Ages 6+ only. Adult (14+) €48, student (with ID) €46, child (6-13) €31.

Herrenchiemsee Castle Tour—Tour highlights include a 1-hour train journey to Herrenchiemsee, fully guided tours of both islands, an old-fashioned "lake train" and two boat trips, palace grounds and walkways, palace interior tour (optional, not included), Fraueninsel island and convent. Wed/Sun, May 20-Sept. 17 only. Depart 9:20 a.m. from main train station, return 6:50 p.m. Ages 6+ only. Adult (14+) €44, student (with ID) €42, child (6-13) €31. Additional fees paid at Radius Tour office: €9 optional palace entrance, €11 boat rides.

Sandeman's New Europe

Sandeman's New Europe tours (www.neweuropetours.eu/munich-walking-tours/) has TripAdvisor's Certificate of Excellence. All departures from the main train station (Hauptbahnhof) in front of Starbucks Coffee by Platform 11. In addition to a highly rated, tips-only walking tour of Munich, the company offers the following tours:

Munich Oktoberfest Experience—Tour highlights include a half-liter welcome beer, 1.5-hour walking tour of the Oktoberfest grounds, reserved seat in the Löwenbräu tent, two liters of beer, half a roasted chicken. Wheelchair accessible. *Note: bag size on the Oktoberfest grounds is limited to 20 cm x 15 cm x 10 cm.* Late Sept.-early Oct. only. Depart 10 a.m. from the main train station. Adult €115.

Day Trip to Neuschwanstein Castle—Tour highlights include a 2-hour train or bus ride through the Bavarian Alps, exploration of the village of Hohenschwangau with a local guide, Pöllat waterfall gorge, Marienbrücke Bridge, optional 35-minute tour inside castle (additional €13.50). (*Note: Castle is near top of steep mountain lane. If unable to climb for 30 minutes or more, consider alternate ways up. Inside castle tour requires considerable use of stairs.*) Tour also available in Spanish. Depart 9 a.m. from main train station, return 7 p.m. (6:30 p.m. in winter). Adult €48, student €45, child (3-12) €25.

Dachau Concentration Camp Memorial Tour—Tour highlights include 35-minute train ride and 5-minute bus ride to memorial in Dachau, guided tour of memorial, information about the founding of Dachau, the daily lives of prisoners, liberation and aftermath. Considerable walking and standing. Tour also available in Spanish. Wheelchair accessible. Must be 14+ years old. Depart 8:45 a.m. from main train station, return 1:45 p.m. Adult €28, student (with ID) €26.

Munich Beer Tasting Tour—Tour highlights include a walking tour with a local beer expert, samples of 3 local beers in beer gardens or beer halls, soft pretzel. Tour also available in Spanish. Wheelchair accessible. Must be 18+ (with ID) to sample beers. (Ages 4-17 receive 2 soft drinks and a pretzel.) Depart 6 p.m. from main train station, return 10 p.m. Adult €24, student (with ID) €22, child (4-17) €17.

Day Trip to Salzburg—Tour highlights include a 2-hour train ride through the Bavarian Alps to Salzburg in Austria, 2.5 hour walking tour of Old City, *Sound of Music* sites, Mirabell Palace and Garden, Salzburg Cathedral, Mozart's birth house, free time for sightseeing and eating. Tour also available in Spanish. Wheelchair accessible. *Must bring passport.* Sun/Tues/Thurs. Depart 9:15 a.m. from main train station, return 7 p.m. Adult €48, student (with ID) €45, child (3-12) €25.

Gray Line Munich

Gray Line Tours (www.grayline.com/things-to-do/germany/munich/) is a large international tour company that offers generally well received large-group tours on full-sized tourist buses, with some small-group tours also available. Departures are across from the main train station in front of the Karstadt department store in the Bahnhofplatz square. Their offerings include the following:

Neuschwanstein, Linderhof Royal Castle and Oberammergau—Tour highlights include air-conditioned coach travel (with bathroom and room for some luggage) 1.5 hours through the Bavarian Alps, 1 hour at Linderhof Castle (entrance not included), 30 minutes at Oberammergau village, 3.5 hours at Neuschwanstein Castle. Entrance to both castles an additional €27. (Purchase in cash on the bus. No-wait access to castles.) *(Note: Neuschwanstein Castle is near top of steep mountain lane. If unable to climb for 30 minutes or more, consider alternate ways up. Inside castle tour requires considerable use of stairs.)* Depart 8:30 a.m. from Bahnhofplatz, return 6:30 p.m. Adult (27+) €57, student/youth (15-26) €46, child (4-14) €29.

Neuschwanstein and Linderhof Premium Tour—Royal Selection—Tour highlights include a small-group tour on a luxury coach with bathroom, personal on-board service with a selection of snacks and drinks, castle fees included, free WiFi, 1.5 hour drive through the Bavarian Alps to Linderhof Castle, 40-minute visit in Oberammergau to view woodcarving, Neuschwanstein Castle and Marienbrücke bridge. *(Note: Neuschwanstein Castle is near top of steep mountain lane. If unable to climb for 30 minutes or more, consider alternate ways up. Inside castle tour requires considerable use of stairs.)* Daily. Depart 8:30 a.m from Bahnhofplatz, return 6:30 p.m. Adult €146, child €123.

Salzburg and Lake District Tour—Tour highlights include transportation in air-conditioned coach with a live guide through the Bavarian Alps to Salzburg, Austria, time for shopping and a walk through Salzburg, bus ride through the countryside seen in *The Sound of Music*, a cruise on Lake Wolfgangsee (additional fee €13) to the Whitehorse Inn and the Pilgrim Church, travel past Lake Mondsee. *Passport required.* Tues/Thur/Sat. Depart 8:30 a.m from Bahnhofplatz, return 7 p.m. Adult (27+) €54, student/youth (15-26) €43, child (4-14) €27.

Romantic Road: Rothenburg and Harburg Tour—Tour highlights include transportation in air-conditioned bus along the Romanic Road to Harburg Castle, live tour guide, travel through Dinkelsbühl, time to explore, eat, and shop in the medieval town of Rothenburg. Wed/Sun. Depart 8:30 a.m from Bahnhofplatz, return 7:30 p.m. Adult (27+) €54, student/youth (15-26) €43, child (4-14) €27.

Berchtesgaden and Eagle's Nest—Tour highlights include transportation in air-conditioned coach through a German Alpine road to Berchtesgaden, special bus and elevator to Hitler's Eagle's nest (extra fee €20), lunch in the Grafenhöhe Restaurant (not included), possible visit to the NS-Documentation Center (fee not included). *Note: In case of bad weather, visit to Berchtesgaden salt mine instead of Eagle's Nest.* Mon/Fri. Depart 8:30 a.m. from Bahnhofplatz, return 6:30 p.m. Adult (27+) €54, student/youth (15-26) €43, child (4-14) €27.

Königssee Lake and Berchtesgaden Salt Mines—Tour highlights include air-conditioned bus ride (with bathroom and room for some luggage) to Königssee Lake with live commentary, 35-minute boat ride to island of St. Bartholomä with guided tour and trumpet show, 1.5 hours on the island, 2 hours at 500-year-old salt mine, including guided tour. *Note: €29 for boat ride and salt mine extra and must be paid in cash on the bus. Note: Tour requires approx. 3 miles of walking through day. Note: Temperature inside mountain is 53F.* Wed. Depart 8:30 a.m. from Bahnhofplatz, return 6:30 p.m. Adult (27+) €54, student/youth (15-26) €43, child (4-14) €27.

Munich Beer Tour—Highlights include live guided city tour of top sites, guided tour of original Munich brewery, beer sampler at the brewery. Fri/Sat. Not in winter. Adults only. Depart 2:45, return 5:45. Adult €28.

Dachau Concentration Camp and Herbertshausen—Tour highlights include transportation on an air-conditioned bus, a guided tour through the camp's memorial sites, a 22-minute documentary film about life in the camp, free time at the memorial site for museum, bookstore, or lunch, 10-minute drive to visit to the former SS shooting range of Herbertshausen. *Note: Minimum walking distance 2 miles, including on unpaved paths.* Must be

14+. Mon/Thur/Sun. Depart 9 a.m. from Bahnhofplatz, return 3:30 p.m. Adult (27+) €29, student/youth €24.

Nuremberg Day Trip—Tour highlights include drive in air-conditioned coach, visit to Nuremberg Trials memorial (entrance fee €5), Nazi party rally ground, guided tour of historic town center. Thur, not in winter. Depart 8:30 a.m. from Bahnhofplatz, return 7 p.m. Adult (27+) €54, student/youth €43, child (4-14) €27.

Royal Castle of Herrenchiemsee—Tour highlights include transportation on air-conditioned coach, boat ride to Herreninsel, visit King Ludwig II's castle, boat ride to Fraueninsel, Benedictine church visit and walk on island. (Boat and castle fees €26 extra.) Mon, not in winter. Depart 8:30 a.m. from Bahnhofplatz, return 6:30 p.m. Adult (27+) €54, student/youth €43, child (4-14) €27.

Innsbruck and Swarovski's Crystal World—Tour highlights include an air-conditioned coach ride through Bavaria and the Karwendel Mountains, time to explore Innsbruck, Swarovski's "World of Crystal" (€20 fee). *Passport required.* Fri, not in winter. Depart 8:30 a.m. from Bahnhofplatz, return 6 p.m. Adult (27+) €54, student/youth €43, child (4-14) €27.

Other Tour Companies function as agents and offer registration for the Gray Line tours above. Should you for some reason prefer to buy a Gray Line excursion ticket indirectly, you can do so through these companies:

- **Veltra City Discover**—www.veltra.com/en/europe/germany/munich/ctg/162228:Full_Day_by_Coach/
- **Get Your Guide**—www.getyourguide.com/munich-l26/day-trips-tc172/

Private tours

You may prefer to pay for the convenience and generally suberb service of a private tour. Here are a few highly rated options to investigate.

InMunich Tours

InMunich Tours (www.inmunichtours.com) has TripAdvisor's Certificate of Excellence, but their tours are walking-based. Private tours can be fully customized, so contact them ahead of time to see whether you can maximize sitting/resting possibilities. They offer a daily 3-hour free city walking tour (tips only), a 6-hour Dachau tour, and the following private tours:

Private Munich Tour—up to 3 hours, €185.

Private Dachau Tour—5-6 hours total, 3-4 hours on site, €250 for 1-4 guests (on train—private car transport available, and larger group size available—for higher price)

Private Third Reich Tour—3 hours, €185.

German Resistance Tour—3 hours, €185

Big Hat Tours

Big Hat tours (www.bighattours.com) also has TripAdvisor's Certificate of Excellence and offers numerous tours in and out of Munich. Tours are highly rated, but walking-intensive. Contact the company to inquire about modifying intensity before registering.

The Munich City Tour and Third Reich Tour take 3.5 hours each; the Dachau tour takes 5 hours but includes train travel; the All-Day Munich Tour takes 7 hours. Day trips include the following:

Salzburg Tour—Train ride through Alpine lake country to Salzburg, then private, customized time in the city with personal guide. 10 hours. €295, plus train fare (e.g., €31 for two adults) and any optional entrance tickets and meals.

Nuremberg Tour—Train ride to Nuremberg, then private, customized walking tour through city. 10 hours. €295, plus train fare (e.g., €31 for two adults).

Neuschwanstein Castle Tour—Train ride with commentary, tour outside and optional inside the castle. 10 hours. €380, plus train fare (e.g., €31 for two adults) and optional castle entry (€13.80 per adult).

Neuschwanstein Castle and Hohenschwangau Castle—Neuschwanstein visit plus a visit to the nearby Hohenschwangau Castle. 10 hours. €390, plus train fare (e.g., €31 for two adults) and optional castle entry fees (€26.60 for both castles, per adult).

Herrenchiemsee Palace—Train ride, palace tour, steam engine, lake boat ride, Frauen Island. 8 hours. €295, plus train fare (e.g., €31 for two adults), castle entry (€8.50 per adult), steam train and boat (€8.80 per adult).

Munich Family Tour—Geared for teenagers and young children. 2 hours. €175.

Tours by Locals

Tours by Locals (www.toursbylocals.com/Munich-Tours) has TripAdvisor's Certificate of Excellence and advertises that they have 153 unique and customizable tours in Munich. You can search for types of tours ranging from Museums/Culture to Adventure/Active. Some topics of particular interest may be First Time Visitor, Food and Wine, Local Experience, and Religious Heritage. The standard day trips are available—Neuschwanstein and Linderhof Palaces, for example—but the list below includes only offerings that are marked as light-to-moderate activity and wheelchair-friendly, as an indication of generally easy accessibility.

These listings are only a sample of the many, many tours that you may choose from. You can filter by activity level, if desired. *Warning: At the time of this writing, the "Tours by Locals, Munich" Web site was flaky and would sometimes crash if the "Back" button was used. Be prepared to navigate by links rather than the "Back" button.*

Romantic Road and Rothenburg Private Tour— Tour highlights include hotel pickup and drop-off, dedicated guide/driver in an air-conditioned vehicle, Dinkelsbühl, snack time, St. George Cathedral, city tour of Rothenburg, free time for sightseeing, shopping, eating. 9 a.m.-6 p.m. €789 for up to 6 people.

Concentration Camp Memorial Site—Tour highlights include train and bus travel to the city of Dachau and then to the memorial (about 50 minutes), 3 hours at the camp, possible electric scooter for camp visit. 5 hours total. €245 for up to 7 people.

Munich to Nuremberg Day Tour—Tour highlights include hotel collection, guided train travel to Nuremberg (1 hour, 49 minutes), 2-hour city tour, bus to former Nazi Party rally grounds. Price range: €500 for 1 person-€580 for 9 people. (Note: Tour with private car transportation also available for €879 for up to 6 people.)

Salzburg—Austria's Charming Gem—Tour highlights include hotel collection, guided train travel to Salzburg (1.75 hours), 2-hour orientation of Salzburg, optional lunch in Europe's oldest restaurant, free time to explore and shop. 10 hours. Price range: €620 for 1 person-€710 for 10 people. (Note: Tour with private car transportation also available for €695 for up to 6 people.)

Eagle's Nest with Berchtesgaden—Tour highlights include hotel pickup and drop-off, visit to Kehlstein Mountain and Hitler's Eagle's Nest, lunch and shopping in village of Berchtesgaden. 9.5 hours. €789 for up to 6 people.

Herrenchiemsee Palace—Tour highlights include a guided 1-hour train ride, short steam train ride (on the world's oldest continuously operating steam train), ferry ride to the island of Herreninsel, visit to palace, boat ride to the island of Fraueninsel, snack and relaxed time. 9 hours. Price range: €559 for 1 person-€586 for 4 people.

Special Private Tours

Special Private Tours (www.specialprivatetours.com) can provide individually designed tours but also offers some set private tours. They include the following:

Neuschwanstein Castle and More Private Tour—Tour highlights include hotel pickup and drop-off, a dedicated guide/driver in an air-conditioned vehicle, shuttle ride to the Marienbrücke bridge, skip-the-line access for inside tour of Neuschwanstein Castle, horse carriage to Hohenschwangau village, free time in the Passion Play village of Oberammergau, Linderhof Palace. Everything included except meals and gratuities. *Note: Shuttle and carriage rides dispense with the most difficult climbing at Neuschwanstein, but castle tour includes many stairs.* Depart 8:30 a.m., return 6 p.m. Minimum 2 adults. Children up to 17, €59 each, adult price varies by number, from €350 per each of 2 adults to €129 per each of 7 adults.

Romantic Road: Rothenburg ob der Tauber and More Private Tour—Tour highlights include hotel pickup and drop-off, professional driver/guide in air-conditioned vehicle, medieval Harburg Castle, the medieval village of Dinkelbühl, the preserved medieval town of Rothenburg, St. James Church with revered Altar of the Holy Blood, free time in Rothenburg. All costs included except meals and gratuities. Depart 8:30 a.m., return 6 p.m. Minimum 2 adults. Children up to 17, €59 each, adult price varies by number, from €350 per each of 2 adults to €129 per each of 7 adults.

Eagle's Nest and Salt Mines—Tour highlights include hotel pickup and drop-off, a professional driver/guide in an air-conditioned vehicle, mountain bus ride and vintage mountain-shaft elevator ride to Hitler's Eagle's Nest, tour of Berchtesgaden's 500-year-old salt mine. All costs included except meals and gratuities. Depart 8:30 a.m., return 6 p.m. Minimum 2 adults. Children up to 17, €59 each, adult price varies by number, from €350 per each of 2 adults to €129 per each of 7 adults.

Salzburg and Salt Mines Private Tour—Tour highlights include hotel pickup and drop-off, professional driver/guide in air-conditioned vehicle, Salzburg Old City, Mirabell Castle and Garden, Mozart's birth house, possible visit to Hohensalzburg Fortress (not included), Domplatz, cathedral, drive to Berchtesgaden, visit to 500-year-old salt mine (included). *Bring passport.* Depart 8:30 a.m., return 6 p.m. Minimum 2 adults. Children up to 17, €59 each, adult price varies by number, from €350 per each of 2 adults to €129 per each of 7 adults.

Private Tour to Zugspitze and Garmisch-Partenkirchen—Tour highlights include hotel pickup and drop-off, professional driver/guide in air-conditioned vehicle to the highest mountain in Germany, the Zugspitze cable car, then Garmisch-Partenkirchen, Baroque church of St. Martin, free time for lunch and shopping, Olympic Stadium, Ludwig's Street with its house paintings. All costs included except meals and gratuities. Depart 9 a.m., return 6 p.m. Minimum 2 adults. Children up to 17, €59 each, adult price varies by number, from €375 per each of 2 adults to €157 per each of 7 adults.

Zugspitze and Innsbruck—Tour highlights include hotel pickup and drop-off, professional driver/guide in air-conditioned vehicle to the highest mountain in Germany, the Zugspitze cable car, into Austria to Innsbruck, the Golden Roof. All costs included except meals and gratuities. *Bring passport.* Depart 8:30 a.m., return 6 p.m. Minimum 2 adults. Children up to 17, €59 each, adult price varies by number, from €375 per each of 2 adults to €155 per each of 7 adults.

Innsbruck and Ambras Castle—Tour highlights include hotel pickup and drop-off, a professional driver/guide in an air-conditioned vehicle to Ambras Castle above Innsbruck in Tyrol, tour of castle and gardens, Innsbruck's Old Town, Golden Roof, Hofburg, Cathedral of St. James, time for shopping. All costs included except meals and gratuities. *Bring passport.* Depart 8:30 a.m., return 6 p.m. Minimum 2 adults. Children up to 17, €59 each, adult price varies by number, from €350 per each of 2 adults to €130 per each of 7 adults.

Innsbruck and Swarovski Crystal Worlds—Tour highlights include hotel pickup and drop-off, professional driver/guide in air-conditioned vehicle to Innsbruck, Innsbruck's Old Town, Golden Roof, Hofburg, Swarovski Crystal Worlds art museum in Watten. *Bring passport.* Depart 8:30 a.m., return 6 p.m. Minimum 2 adults. Children up to 17, €59 each, adult price varies by number, from €350 per each of 2 adults to €130 per each of 7 adults.

Lodging

Munich is known as a very safe city with excellent public transportation. As such, you can choose to lodge just about anywhere and can get to other areas of the city fairly easily. The most convenient location is, not surprisingly, around the main train station. Most day trips leave from there (unless a private tour includes hotel pickup and drop-off), and all the hop-on/hop-off buses cycle through there, as does much of the public transportation. Be aware that the area around the train station can be a little seedy—you might see beggars, drunks, sex shops—but it's not considered dangerous, especially during the day, and as long as you're sensible at night.

Hotels on this list are based on location, good reviews, and general accessibility, including access to easy transportation. It favors buildings with elevators, but that doesn't mean the elevator will be larger than a phone booth. You may need to make several trips to get your luggage to upper floors. This section isn't the last word on acceptable accommodation, but it makes a good starting point to narrow down your search. Just check online to make sure that information is still accurate, on TripAdvisor, on Booking.com, or on the hotel's own Web site.

You may find a wonderful deal on what looks like a good choice in a convenient location. By all means—grab it! Same with charming B&Bs, which aren't covered here because they tend to have a limited number of available rooms and generally don't have elevators. If you can nab one in a favorable location that gets good reviews, has a great breakfast, decent accessibility, and a workable price, do it!

Hotel price ranges are based on late 2019 TripAdvisor averages. Averages can vary considerably throughout the year—during major trade conventions and especially during Oktoberfest, rates can spike alarmingly. Your own quotes may be higher or lower than these.

Hauptbahnhof/Main Train Station

If you plan to take group day trips, ride the HOHO buses, or want excellent access to city buses, trams, trains, and airport shuttles, then the area around the train station will probably work well for you. It's a walkable distance to Old City sights, and room rates are generally reasonable. Should you choose to lodge farther away from the train station, handy access to a tram is valuable for getting around easily.

Hotels in the area include the following:

The Charles Hotel—Sophienstrasse 28 (www.roccofortehotels.com/hotels-and-resorts/the-charles-hotel/rooms-and-suites/). TripAdvisor's Traveler's Choice Award (top 1% of category). Location: 3 streets north of Bahnhofplatz. Pros: non-smoking rooms, air conditioning, free WiFi, restaurant, wonderful breakfast buffet, room service, bar/lounge, airport transportation, fitness center, facilities for disabled guests, elevator, refrigerator, smoking rooms available, twins/suites available. Cons: price, expensive breakfast, no single/triple/quad rooms, no price break for singles, smoking rooms available. (TripAdvisor price range for standard room: $410-$1,063.)

Distances: Königsplatz Metro Station (.1 miles), Central Station (.2 miles), Karlsplatz Metro Station (.3 miles), Frauenkirche (.6 miles), Marienplatz (.7 miles), Viktualienmarkt (.8 miles), Hofbräuhaus (.9 miles), Deutsches Museum (1.3 miles)

Euro Youth Hotel (Hostel)—Senefelderstr. 5 (www.euro-youth-hotel.de). TripAdvisor's Certificate of Excellence. Location: ½ block south of Main Train Station. Pros: non-smoking rooms, free WiFi, very good affordable breakfast, bar/lounge, elevator, single/twin/triple/quad rooms available. Cons: no air conditioning, bathrooms not always clean/supplied, can be loud, basic rooms, some rooms with shared baths/dormitories/bunks. (TripAdvisor price range for standard room: $24-$300.)

Distances: Central Train Station (.1 miles), Karlsplatz/Stachus (.3 miles), Frauenkirche (.6 miles), Marienplatz (.7 miles), Viktualienmarkt (.8 miles), Hobräuhaus (.9 miles)

Hotel Metropol—Mittererstrasse 7 (hotel-metropol-muenchen.hoteles-munich.com/en/). TripAdvisor's Certificate of Excellence. Location: ½ block south of the Main Train Station. Pros: non-smoking hotel, air conditioning, free WiFi, free wonderful breakfast buffet, bar/lounge, elevator, twins/suites available. Cons: small rooms, slow elevator, not all rooms easily accessible from elevator, no singles/triples/quads, very little price break for singles. (TripAdvisor price range for standard room: $86-$408.)

Distances: Hauptbahnhof Metro Station (.1 miles), Main Train Station (.2 miles), Karlsplatz/Stachus (.5 miles), Frauenkirche (.7 miles), Marienplatz (.8 miles), Viktualienmarkt (.9 miles), Hofbräuhaus (1 mile), Deutsches Museum (1.3 miles)

B&Bs Hotel Bayers—Bayerstr. 13 (hotel-bayers.hoteles-munich.com/en/). TripAdvisor's Certificate of Excellence. Location: 1 street east of Bahnhof Platz. Pros: non-smoking hotel, air conditioning, free WiFi, airport transportation, refrigerator, facilities for disabled guests, elevator, ATM on site, single/twin/triple/quad rooms available. Cons: street noise, no restaurant/bar, some air-conditioning problems. (TripAdvisor price range for standard room: $107-$317.)

Distances: Main Train Station (.1 miles), Hauptbahnhof Metro Station (.1 miles), Karlsplatz/Stachus (.2 miles), Asamkirche (.4 miles), Frauenkirche (.5 miles), Marienplatz (.6 miles), Viktualienmarkt (.7 miles), Hofbräuhaus (.8 miles)

Wombat's Munich (Hostel)—Senefelderstr. 1 (www.wombats-hostels.com/munich/). TripAdvisor's Certificate of Excellence. Location: across the street south of the Main Train Station. Pros: non-smoking hotel, free WiFi, very good affordable breakfast buffet, bar/lounge, twin and dormitory rooms available. Cons: noise, bare-bones, no air conditioning, steps to elevator, small elevator, no single rooms. (TripAdvisor price range for standard room: $19-$342.)

Distances: Hauptbahnhof Metro Station (0 miles), Main Train Station (.1 miles), Karlsplatz/Stachus (.3 miles), Frauenkirche (.6 miles), Marienplatz (.7 miles), Viktualienmarkt (.8 miles), Hofbräuhaus (.9 miles), Deutsches Museum (1.2 miles)

Schiller5 Hotel—Schillerstr. 5 (www.schiller5.com/en/home-en). TripAdvisor Certificate of Excellence. Location: just south of Bahnhofplatz. Pros: non-smoking rooms, air conditioning, free WiFi, bar/lounge, wonderful buffet breakfast, elevator, refrigerator, microwave, singles/suites available. Cons: strip clubs on street, compact bathrooms, no triples/quads. (TripAdvisor price range for standard room: $119-$371.)

Distances: Hauptbahnhof Metro Station (.1 miles), Main Train Station (.1 miles), Karlsplatz/Stachus (.3 miles), Frauenkirche (.5 miles), Marienplatz (.6 miles), Viktualienmarkt (.7 miles), Hofbräuhaus (.9 miles), Deutsches Museum (1.2 miles)

Marc Munchen—Senefelderstrasse 12 (www.hotel-marc.de/en/). TripAdvisor Travelers' Choice Award. Location: ½ block south of the

Main Train Station. Pros: non-smoking hotel, air conditioning, free WiFi, wonderful free breakfast, single/twin rooms available. Cons: no triples/quads. (TripAdvisor price range for standard room: $136-$460.)

Distances: Hauptbahnhof Metro Station (.1 miles), Main Train Station (.2 miles), Karlsplatz/Stachus (.3 miles), Frauenkirche (.6 miles), Marienplatz (.7 miles), Viktualienmarkt (.8 miles), Hofbräuhaus (.9 miles), Deutsches Museum (1.2 miles)

25Hours Hotel The Royal Bavarian—Bahnhofplatz 1 (www.25hours-hotels.com/en/hotels/munich/the-royal-bavarian). TripAdvisor Certificate of Excellence. Location: just east of the Main Train Station. Pros: non-smoking hotel, air conditioning, free WiFi, restaurant, excellent buffet breakfast, bar/lounge, fitness center, facilities for disabled guests, elevator, single rooms available. Cons: some small rooms, street noise, no door to shower (floor gets wet), dark interiors, no twins/triples/quads. (TripAdvisor price range for standard room: $132-$427.)

Distances: Main Train Station (.1 miles), Hauptbahnhof Metro Station (.1 miles), Karlsplatz/Stachus (.3 miles), Frauenkirche (.5 miles), Marienplatz (.6 miles), Viktualienmarkt (.8 miles), Hofbräuhaus (.9 miles), Deutsches Museum (1.2 miles)

Aloft Munich—Bayerstr. 37 (www.marriott.com/hotels/travel/mucal-aloft-munich/). TripAdvisor Certificate of Excellence. Location: south across the street from the train station. Pros: non-smoking hotel, air conditioning, free WiFi, telephone, breakfast buffet, bar/lounge, elevator, convenience store, fitness center, twin rooms available. Cons: no singles/triples/quads, virtually no price break for singles. (TripAdvisor price range for standard room: $139-$587.)

Distances: Hauptbahnhof Metro Station (0.0 miles), Karlsplatz/Stachus (.4 miles), Frauenkirche (.6 miles), Marienplatz (.7 miles), Viktualienmarkt (.8 miles), Hofbräuhaus (1 mile), Deutsches Museum (1.3 miles)

Jedermann Hotel—Bayerstr. 95 (jedermann.hoteles-munich.com/en/). TripAdvisor Certificate of Excellence. Location: south side of Main Train Station, 6 streets west of Bahnhofplatz. Pros: non-smoking hotel, air conditioning, free WiFi, excellent free breakfast buffet, bar/lounge, elevator, extra long beds, tram stop outside hotel, walking distance to Oktoberfest, single/twin/triple rooms available. Cons: not all rooms air-conditioned, some rooms with shared baths, some street noise. (TripAdvisor price range for standard room: $76-$212.)

Distances: Theresienwiese Metro Station (.2 miles), Augustiner Brewery (.3 miles), Main Train Station (.4 miles), Theresienwiese (site of Oktoberfest) (.6 miles), Karlsplatz/Stachus (.7 miles), Frauenkirche (1 mile),

Marienplatz (1.1 miles), Viktualienmarkt (1.2 miles), Hofbräuhaus (1.3 miles)

Hotel Cocoon Hauptbahnhof—Mittererstr. 9 (cocoon-hotels.de/en/cocoon-hauptbahnhof.html). TripAdvisor Certificate of Excellence. Location: 3 streets west of Bahnhofplatz, a little south of the Main Train Station. Pros: non-smoking hotel, air conditioning, free WiFi, breakfast buffet, bar/lounge, facilities for disabled guests, elevator, single/triple/quads available. Cons: small rooms, no phone in some rooms, staff not all friendly, some problems with check-in/getting rooms as reserved. (TripAdvisor price range for standard room: $101-$659.)

Distances: Main Train Station (.2 miles), Karlsplatz/Stachus (.4 miles), Theresienwiese (Oktoberfest site) (.6 miles), Frauenkirche (.7 miles), Marienplatz (.8 miles), Viktualienmarkt (.9 miles), Hofbräuhaus (1 mile), Deutsches Museum (1.3 miles)

Arthotel Munich—Paul-Heyse-Str. 10 (www.arthotelmunich.com/en/). TripAdvisor Certificate of Excellence. Location: 4 streets west of Bahnhofplatz, just south of Main Train Station. Pros: non-smoking hotel, air conditioning, free WiFi, excellent free breakfast buffet, bar/lounge, elevator, refrigerator, ATM on site, single/twin/triple/quads available. Cons: some rooms small, annex rooms may not have elevator access. (TripAdvisor price range for standard room: $86-$353.)

Distances: Hauptbahnhof Metro Station (.2 miles), Main Train Station (.3 miles), Karlsplatz/Stachus (.5 miles), Augustiner Brewery (.6 miles), Theresienwiese (Oktoberfest site) (.6 miles), Frauenkirche (.8 miles), Marienplatz (.9 miles), Vitualienmarkt (1 mile), Hofbräuhaus (1.1 miles), Deutsches Museum (1.4 miles)

Excelsior by Geisel—Schuetzenstr. 11 (www.excelsior-hotel.de/en). TripAdvisor Certificate of Excellence. Location: 1 street east of Bahnhofplatz. Pros: non-smoking hotel, air conditioning, free WiFi, very good breakfast buffet, restaurant, room service, bar/lounge, elevator, friendly staff, airport shuttle, single rooms available. Cons: not all rooms have air conditioning, no twin/triple/quad rooms. (TripAdvisor price range for standard room: $155-$505.)

Distances: Main Train Station (.1 miles), Karlsplatz/Stachus (.2 miles), Frauenkirche (.5 miles), Marienplatz (.6 miles), Viktualienmarkt (.7 miles), Theresienwiese (.8 miles), Hofbräuhaus (.8 miles), Deutsches Museum (1.2 miles)

Motel One Munich-Sendlinger Tor—Herzog-Wilhelm-Str. 28 (www.motel-one.com/en/hotels/munich/hotel-munich-sendlinger-tor/). TripAdvisor Certificate of Excellence. Location: north of Sendlingertorplatz, inside old walls. (*Note: This hotel is farther away from the train station, but I have stayed here and like it very much.*) Pros: non-smoking hotel, air conditioning, elevator, free WiFi, very good breakfast buffet, bar/lounge. Cons: small rooms, no phone in room, only doubles (may get price break for single). (TripAdvisor price range for standard room: $88-$105.)

Distances: Sendlinger Tor (.1 miles), Asamkirche (.1 miles), Karlsplatz/Stachus (.4 miles), Frauenkirche (.4 miles), St. Peter's Church (.4 miles), Marienplatz (.4 miles), Viktualienmarkt (.4 miles), Main Train Station (.5 miles), Hofbräuhaus (.6 miles), Theresienwiese (.8 miles), Deutsches Museum (.8 miles)

Sofitel Munich Bayerpost—Bayerstr. 12 (www.sofitel-munich.com). TripAdvisor Certificate of Excellence. Location: southwest corner of Main Train Station. Pros: non-smoking hotel, air conditioning, free WiFi, restaurant, room service, very good breakfast buffet, bar/lounge, fitness center, facilities for disabled guests, elevator, airport shuttle, twins/triples/suites available. Cons: price, weak/slow WiFi, slow service, lack of privacy in bathroom, very little price break for singles. (TripAdvisor price range for standard room: $250-$652.)

Distances: Main Train Station (.1 miles), Karlsplatz/Stachus (.4 miles), Frauenkirche (.7 miles), Marienplatz (.8 miles), Viktualienmarkt (.9 miles), Hofbräuhaus (1 miles)

King's Hotel First Class—Dachauer Str. 13 (www.kingshotels.de/en/first-class). TripAdvisor Certificate of Excellence. Location: 1 street north of the Main Train Station/Bahnhofplatz. Pros: non-smoking rooms, air conditioning, free WiFi, excellent breakfast buffet, bar/lounge, room service, elevator, refrigerator, single/twin rooms available. Cons: some street noise, some air conditioning complaints, small rooms, small bathrooms, expensive breakfast. (TripAdvisor price range for standard room: $99-$379.)

Distances: Königsplatz Metro Station (.2 miles), Main Train Station (.3 miles), Löwenbräukeller (.3 miles), Karlsplatz/Stachus (.4 miles), Frauenkirche (.7 miles), Marienplatz (.8 miles), Viktualienmarkt (.9 miles), Hofbräuhaus (1 mile)

Vi Vadi Hotel Bayer 89—Bayerstr. 89 (www.vivadihotels.com/de/hotels/bayer-89). TripAdvisor Certificate of Excellence. Location: west of the train station on the south side, almost to Hermann Lingg Str. Pros: non-smoking hotel, air conditioning, free WiFi, very good breakfast buffet, restaurant, room service, bar/lounge, elevator, tram stop, airport shuttle, twin/triple/quad rooms available. Cons: elevator small and slow, reception staff not always friendly, weak WiFi, small rooms, some street noise, no price break for singles. (TripAdvisor price range for standard room: $115-$424.)

Distances: Main Train Station (.4 miles), Augustiner Brewery (.4 miles), Theresienwiese (Oktoberfest site) (.6 miles), Frauenkirche (1 miles), Marienplatz (1.1 miles), Viktualienmarkt (1.2 miles), Hofbräuhaus (1.3 miles)

Mercure Hotel Muenchin City Center—Senefelderstr. 9. TripAdvisor Certificate of Excellence. Location: 1 street west of Bahnhofplatz, south of the Main Train Station. Pros: free WiFi, non-smoking hotel, air conditioning, restaurant, room service, very good breakfast buffet, bar/lounge, facilities for disabled guests, elevator, twins/triples available. Cons: sketchy area, questions about cleanliness, some shower drain problems. (TripAdvisor price range for standard room: $121-$494.)

Distances: Main Train Station (.1 miles), Karlsplatz/Stachus (.3 miles), Frauenkirche (.6 miles), Marienplatz (.7 miles), Viktualienmarkt (.8 miles), Hofbräuhaus (.9 miles)

Eden Hotel Wolff—Arnulfstr. 4 (www.eden-hotel-wolff.de/english). TripAdvisor Certificate of Excellence. Location: north side of the Main Train Station, across the street. Pros: free WiFi, non-smoking hotel, air conditioning, restaurant, room service, very good breakfast buffet, bar/lounge, fitness center, facilities for disabled guests, elevator, single/twin/triple rooms available. Cons: needs updating, some rooms too small. (TripAdvisor price range for standard room: $122-$281.)

Distances: Main Train Station (.1 miles), Karlsplatz/Stachus (.4 miles), Frauenkirche (.7 miles), Marienplatz (.8 miles), Viktualienmarkt (.9 miles), Hofbräuhaus (1 mile)

King's Hotel Center—Marsstr. 15 (www.kingshotels.de/en/). TripAdvisor Certificate of Excellence. Location: 2 streets north and 1½ streets west of Bahnhofplatz. Pros: non-smoking hotel, air conditioning, free Wi-Fi, iPod docking station, very good breakfast buffet, elevator. Cons: small bathrooms, some small rooms, some problems with air conditioning, no triples/quads, no bar or restaurant. (TripAdvisor price range for standard room: $86-$359.)

Distances: Main Train Station (.2 miles), Löwenbräukeller (.3 miles), Karlsplatz/Stachus (.4 miles), Frauenkirche (.7 miles), Marienplatz (.9 miles), Viktualienmarkt (1 miles), Hofbräuhaus (1.1 miles), Deutsches Museum (1.5 miles)

Anna Hotel by Geisel—Schuetzenstr. 1 (www.annahotel.de/en.html). TripAdvisor Certificate of Excellence. Location: 1 block east of Main Train Station. Pros: non-smoking hotel, air conditioning, free WiFi, restaurant, breakfast buffet, bar/lounge, elevator, airport shuttle, singles/triples/suites available. Cons: noise, small reception/no lobby, some small rooms, steps up to reception area, no twin/quad rooms. (TripAdvisor price range for standard room: $165-$439.)

Distances: Karlsplatz/Stachus (.1 miles), Main Train Station (.2 miles), Asamkirche (.4 miles), Frauenkirche (.4 miles), Marienplatz (.5 miles), Viktualienmarkt (.6 miles), Hofbräuhaus (.7 miles), Deutsches Museum (1.1 miles)

Hotel Europaischer Hof—Bayerstr. 31 (www.heh.de/en/). TripAdvisor Certificate of Excellence. Location: just over 1 street to the west of Hauptbahnhofplatz, across the street from the Main Train Station. Pros: smoke-free hotel, free WiFi, excellent free breakfast buffet, elevator, tram stop, single/twin/triple rooms available. Cons: no air conditioning, needs updating (especially bathrooms), street noise. (TripAdvisor price range for standard room: $91-$369.)

Distances: Main Train Station (.1 miles), Karlsplatz/Stachus (.3 miles), Frauenkirche (.6 miles), Marienplatz (.7 miles), Viktualienmarkt (.8 miles), Hofbräuhaus (.9 miles)

Eurostars Book Hotel—Schwanthalerstr. 44 (www.eurostarshotels.co.uk/eurostars-book-hotel.html). TripAdvisor's Certificate of Excellence. Location: 1 street south of the Main Train Station. Pros: non-smoking hotel, air conditioning, free WiFi, restaurant, snack bar, very good breakfast buffet, bar/lounge, room service, fitness center, elevator, allergy-free room, twins/triples available. Cons: WiFi problems, noise, some cleanliness complaints, seedy location, no singles/quads, no price break for singles. (TripAdvisor price range for standard room: $105-$485.)

Distances: Main Train Station (.2 miles), Karlsplatz/Stachus (.5 miles), Theresienwiese (.6 miles), Frauenkirche (.7 miles), Marienplatz (.8 miles), Viktualienmarkt (.9 miles), Hofbräuhaus (1 miles), Deutsches Museum (1.3 miles)

Hotel Meier City Munich—Schuetzenstr. 12 (hotel-meier-city-munchen.hoteles-munich.com/en/). TripAdvisor Certificate of Excellence. Location: just east of Hauptbahnhofplatz. Pros: non-smoking hotel, free WiFi, very good free breakfast buffet, telephone, ATM on site, pedestrian zone, airport shuttle, single/twin/triple rooms available. Cons: no air conditioning, outside noise when windows open, thin pillows, some rooms/bathrooms very small, small elevator. (TripAdvisor price range for standard rooms: $109-$379.)

Distances: Main Train Station (.1 miles), Karlsplatz/Stachus (.2 miles), Frauekirche (.5 miles), Marienplatz (.6 miles), Viktualienmarkt (.7 miles), Hofbräuhaus (.8 miles)

Alpen Hotel Munchen—Adolf-Kolpin-Str. 14 (www.alpen hotel-muenchen.de/?lang=en). TripAdvisor Certificate of Excellence. Location: 1 street south and 1 street east of Bahnhofplatz. Pros: non-smoking hotel, air conditioning, free WiFi, restaurant, excellent breakfast buffet, bar/lounge, telephone, single rooms available. Cons: noise, small lift, not all rooms with air conditioning, sketchy neighborhood, reception staff not always warm, street noise, slow/weak WiFi, no twin/triple/quad rooms. (TripAdvisor price range for standard room: $118-$355.)

Distances: Main Train Station (.2 miles), Karlsplatz/Stachus (.3 miles), Asamkirche (.4 miles), Frauenkirche (.5 miles), Marienplatz (.6 miles), Viktualienmarkt (.7 miles), Hofbräuhaus (.8 miles), Deutsches Museum (.8 miles)

Fleming's Hotel Munich-City—Bayerstr. 47 (www.flemings-hotels.com/hotel-muenchen-city). TripAdvisor Certificate of Excellence. Location: across street from SW corner of Main Train Station. Pros: air conditioning, non-smoking rooms, free WiFi, restaurant, room service, very good breakfast buffet, bar/lounge, fitness center, facilities for handicapped guests, elevator, twin rooms available. Cons: shower transparent to bedroom, restaurant not recommended, some cigarette odor, some problems with staff/service, no single/triple/quad rooms, no price break for singles. (TripAdvisor price range for standard room: $111-$550.)

Distances: Main Train Station (.2 miles), Karlsplatz/Stachus (.5 miles), Frauenkirche (.7 miles), Marienplatz (.8 miles), Viktualienmarkt (.9 miles), Hofbräuhaus (1.1 miles)

Other base cities in Germany

Germany is a large country for Europe, and it's not really practical to see most of it from Munich. If you want to base in other areas, Dresden (east central), Berlin (northeast), Hamburg (north), and Frankfurt (west central) have hop-on/hop-off buses and tour companies that lead excursions into the countryside and to other towns.

Acknowledgments

I never finish a book without debts to many people, and this one is no exception. I am grateful to have had lively and enjoyable travel companions on trips to many of these featured cities in my early days, long before mobility was ever an issue: namely, Judith Diers, Cindy Weckwerth, Lynn Olson, Jackie Dammann, Dave Zelle, Elaina Toenjes, Bruce Toenjes, John Toenjes, Rachel Toenjes Zander, Chris Harris, Natalie Reinemund, Gordon Hoffert, Beverly Moffitt, Linda Bingham, Karl George, Robert Wood, Ross Petra, and John Zelle. You folks will always be a treasured part of my youthful travel memories.

More recently, I've added trips with (and incurred gratitude toward) these companions, as well, including visits to the cities featured in this book: Olivia Dunn, Micki Reints, Paul Zelle, Jackie and Josi Kramer, Kim and Mila Smith, Debra Zelle, Carol, Spencer and Abby Luvert, Dave and Lynn Hickman, Trista and Levi Benning, Jim and Connie Mohn, Vanessa Anderson-Smith, Ryan Smith, Cheryl Anderson, Valerie Anderson, Todd and Sara Walter, Paul Andersen, Karen McCray, Matt and Sabrina Smith, Nathan and Mae Jean Zelle, and Emily Bingham.

A number of intrepid individuals helped me test these easy-walking concepts and itineraries in Amsterdam and Edinburgh. I thank them for their willing spirits, their good humor, and their insightful feedback: Linda Bingham, Emily Bingham, Paul Zelle, John Zelle, Micki Reints, Debra Zelle, Dave Zelle, Lucy Groth, John Meyer, Barbara Meyer, and Chrissy Meyer.

I will be forever grateful to the locals who took me into their homes or met up with me in cities covered in this book: Ellie and Reinhard Holzer, Christoph and Charlie Holzer, Dr. Jürgen Koppensteiner, and Dudley Parker. You are (or were) warm, generous, and welcoming people, the best representatives your countries could hope for.

I owe special thanks this time to five people at home. First, my mother, Linda Bingham, who was the catalyst for developing plans for easy-walking travel; second, Karen Thalacker, who saw that other people would be interested in this approach and urged me to write a book about it; third, Darla Grapp, an early reader who encouraged me to continue with this project; fourth, Peter Newell, who suggested a reordering of sections that makes each city's description more useful and engaging; and, fifth, my long-time friend Ann Dirksen, who has provided steady and uplifting encouragement through this entire process, from conception to printing.

As always, my deepest gratitude goes to my husband, John, who has endured, encouraged, and supported both my writing and my travels over many, many years. I couldn't do this without him, and I can't wait to experience more of these itineraries with him.

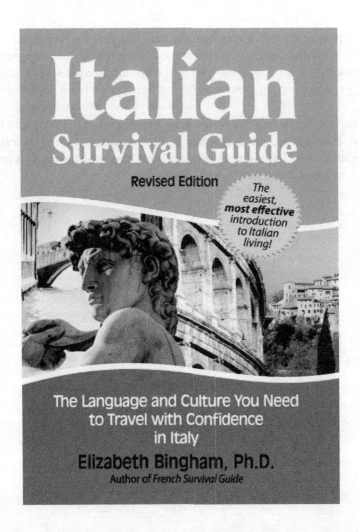

Italian Survival Guide: The Language and Culture You Need to Travel with Confidence in Italy

Italian Survival Guide is a down-to-earth, bare-bones introduction to Italian that aims to make a trip abroad as smooth and enjoyable as possible. This information-packed mini-course concentrates on preparing readers to travel in Italy in a limited time by focusing on what is most useful or interesting to travelers and cutting out unnecessary vocabulary and grammar.

This Survival Guide helps readers communicate in the Italian language and culture. It prepares travelers for what to expect and how to deal with it, what to say and when to say it. It's like three books in one—a phrase book (so you know what to say), a grammar book (so you know how to say it), and a culture book (so you understand daily social expectations)—all focused on a traveler's needs.

Learn how to greet people and introduce yourself in Italian, how to line up lodging, order food, and pay properly, how to shop and ask for directions in Italian, how to drive a car or take the train in Italy, how to get help in an emergency or talk about your family or discuss the weather, and much, much more!

Get key insights into Italian social conventions: how to talk to people, how to avoid taboo subjects, how not to look like a tourist, how to tip, how to have good table manners, how to be a gracious guest, how to discourage unwanted admirers, how to overcome poor customer service, how to avoid petty crime.

Discover the fine points of city buses, grocery stores, train stations and coffee shops. Read how to achieve *la bella figura*—the style and classiness Italians prize. Learn gestures and geography and how to pronounce Giorgio.

Italian Survival Guide is packed with culture notes, study tips, travel hints, and reality checks galore. It includes optional exercises for practicing material from the lessons, Italian-English and English-Italian dictionaries, and inside-the-cover Survival Summaries travelers can use on the spot. In addition, Italian pronunciations are written throughout the book, so users always have guidance on how to pronounce new words and phrases. Includes an extensive index to help readers find the topics they want, fast.

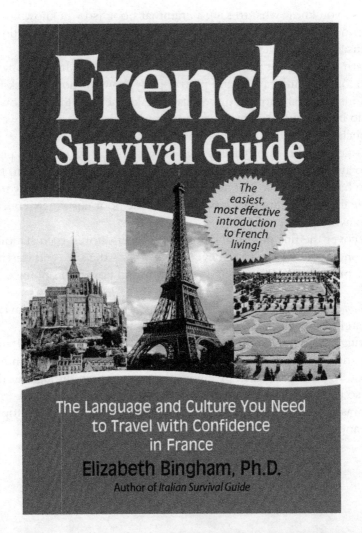

French Survival Guide: The Language and Culture You Need to Travel with Confidence in France

French Survival Guide is a down-to-earth, bare-bones introduction to French that aims to make a trip abroad as smooth and enjoyable as possible. This information-packed mini-course concentrates on preparing readers to travel in France in a limited time by focusing on what is most useful or interesting to travelers and cutting out unnecessary vocabulary and grammar.

This Survival Guide helps readers communicate in the French language and culture. It prepares travelers for what to expect and how to deal with it, what to say and when to say it. It's like three books in one—a phrase book (so you know what to say), a grammar book (so you know how to say it), and a culture book (so you understand daily social expectations)—all focused on a traveler's needs.

Learn how to greet people and introduce yourself in French, how to line up lodging, order food and pay properly, how to shop and ask for directions in French, how to drive a car or take the train in France, how to get help in an emergency or talk about your family or discuss the weather, and much, much more!

Get key insights into French social conventions: how to talk to people, how to avoid taboo subjects, how not to look like a tourist, how to tip, how to have good table manners, how to be a gracious guest, how not to invade the privacy of others, how to overcome poor customer service, how to avoid petty crime.

Discover the fine points of city buses, grocery stores, train stations and coffee shops. Learn how to eat and drink the French way, how to establish a relationship with your waiter, how to avoid signalling that you want to start a flirtation with strangers on the street.

French Survival Guide is packed with culture notes, study tips, travel hints, and reality checks galore. It includes optional exercises for practicing material from the lessons, French-English and English-French dictionaries, and inside-the-cover Survival Summaries travelers can use on the spot. In addition, French pronunciations are written throughout the book, so users always have guidance on how to pronounce new words and phrases. Includes an extensive index to help readers find the topics they want, fast. All this packed into one volume small enough to tuck into a bag and take along.

German Survival Guide:
The Language and Culture You Need to Travel with Confidence in Germany and Austria

German Survival Guide is a down-to-earth, bare-bones introduction to German that aims to make a trip abroad as smooth and enjoyable as possible. This information-packed mini-course concentrates on preparing readers to travel in Germany and Austria in a limited time by focusing on what is most useful or interesting to travelers and cutting out unnecessary vocabulary and grammar.

This Survival Guide helps readers communicate in the German language and culture. It prepares travelers for what to expect and how to deal with it, what to say and when to say it. It's like three books in one—a phrase book (so you know what to say), a grammar book (so you know how to say it), and a culture book (so you understand daily social expectations)—all focused on a traveler's needs.

Learn how to greet people and introduce yourself in German, how to line up lodging, order food and pay properly, how to shop and ask for directions in German, how to drive a car or take the train in Germany and Austria, how to get help in an emergency or talk about your family or discuss the weather, and much, much more!

Get key insights into German and Austrian social conventions: why not to use first names, how not to look like a tourist, how to tip, how to have good table manners, how to be a gracious guest, how to act on a nude beach.

Discover the fine points of ice cream parlors, grocery stores, train stations and the Autobahn. Read how to handle tricky room windows and grumpy bathroom attendants. Learn insider German words so commonly used that you will want to know them even though you don't have to.

This book is packed with culture notes, study tips, travel hints, and reality checks galore. It includes optional exercises for practicing material from the lessons, German-English and English-German dictionaries, and inside-the-cover Survival Summaries travelers can use on the spot. In addition, German pronunciations are written throughout the book, so users always have guidance on how to pronounce new words and phrases. Includes an extensive index to help readers find the topics they want, fast. All this packed into one volume small enough to tuck into a bag and take along.

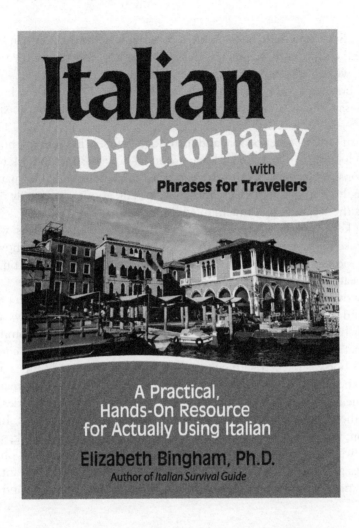

**Italian Dictionary with Phrases for Travelers:
A Practical, Hand-On Resource
for Actually Using Italian**

You can visit Italy and use the local language, without studying it for years. *Italian Dictionary with Phrases for Travelers* is an extensive tourist dictionary that breaks the rules to make it more useful. Start with key phrases and fill in with whatever words you need from the dictionary. Word entries are in easy-to-find alphabetical order and include pronunciations for virtually everything.

This dictionary offers:

- A pronunciation guide
- A grammar summary
- An English-Italian dictionary
- An Italian-English dictionary
- 4 pages of important vocabulary and language patterns, easy to find inside the covers
- Loads of help with genders, articles, plurals, and verb forms

Discover how easy it can be to speak, read, and write Italian!

French Twist:
A Refreshingly Frank Travel Memoir
by a Modern American Puritan

There's the fantasy of a visit to France, and then there's the reality. See what happens when in-the-cloud dreams collide with hard truths on the ground.

When two middle-aged women leave their families behind in rural Iowa for two weeks of exploring France, they are sure to find trouble. Join

Libby and Micki as they bumble their way through failing *métro* passes, irate policemen, continual language challenges, and endlessly baffling maps and road signs. They visit the magical sights, glimpse the brutal history, and are shocked by the sexual openness of France, all the while struggling to get things right in a country that seems to do everything backwards from what they are used to.

Ride along with these rollicking Sunday School teachers as they venture into the countryside, get lost repeatedly, discover Turkish toilets, and cause a minor international incident at an *autoroute* toll booth. France's glorious artwork, breathtaking palaces, somber D-Day sites, famous medieval island fortress—they're all here, along with the notorious French reserve, lack of English language use, exacting expectations for how people should act, and reasons why the typical American tourist doesn't stand a chance of fitting in.

Language and culture writer Elizabeth Bingham (*French Survival Guide: The Language and Culture You Need to Travel with Confidence in France*) divulges what happens behind the scenes when she investigates a new culture and tries out a new language so she can tell readers what to expect and how to handle it. In *French Twist*, she weaves together three trips to France—one with her elderly grandmother, one with her young daughter, and one with her same-age friend—to reveal the delights and pitfalls of visiting that country.

Excerpt from *French Twist* on pp. 330-334.

**German Shepherd: A Guided Tour
Through Germany and Austria
with a Faithful Companion**

Libby and Micki are back in Europe, this time touring Germany and Austria. Following the call of beer, pretzels, and *The Sound of Music*, they start off in Berlin, fly to Munich, and then brave the *Autobahn* through Bavaria and Austria.

They stay with Libby's beloved German "mother," hearing her vivid first-hand accounts of life as a child refugee after WWII and then as an adult in the police state of East Germany. Their stay—and their story—weave back and forth between East and West, between past and present, in a fascinating historical overview.

In Bavaria they delve into the life of King Ludwig II (the "crazy" king who might have been murdered) and battle the hordes at his fairy tale castle. In Austria they explore the glorious landscape celebrated in one of the most famous movies of all time. And through it all, despite wilting heat, incessant rain, their typical travel confusion, and recurring sleep deprivation, they get a rich taste of local life and a heaping helping of *Gemütlichkeit*.

German Shepherd excerpt on pp. 322-329.

Excerpt from

German Shepherd: A Guided Tour Through Germany and Austria with a Faithful Companion

We were heading to Neuschwanstein castle next, the incredibly popular tourist mecca of Germany, that white-turreted Romantic confection soaring so dramatically at the top of a hill. (Hill?? Hell! Climb up it and you'll give it mountain status!) I had been to Neuschwanstein at least twice before, but my last visit had been 25 years earlier, and the experience had changed considerably in that time, in a way I was unprepared for.

As the Bavarian government rightfully brags, "Today Neuschwanstein is one of the most popular of all the palaces and castles in Europe. Every year 1.4 million people visit 'the castle of the fairy-tale king.' In summer around 6,000 visitors a day stream through rooms that were intended for a single inhabitant" (www.neuschwanstein.de/de/englisch/palace/). Micki and I were heading to Neuschwanstein ("new swan stone") at the height of the August tourist rush. We had no idea what we were getting into.

Amazingly, we found the castle with no problems, but for some reason, traffic slowed to a standstill outside the nearby village of Füssen. Only as the line slowly inched forward did we eventually realize that this long snaking column of cars, whose front was far out of sight, was *the line to enter the castle parking area!*

People in other cars would give up on the wait and pull off to the side of the little road to park. That hardly seemed fair—the road was narrow enough as it was—and how far would those people then need to walk? A car behind us whipped past us to turn around in a little drive and then buzzed off, abandoning their attempt to enter. Although we had left very early from Linderhof to make sure we would get to Neuschwanstein in plenty of time, we were afraid we'd miss our pickup time for our pre-scheduled, pre-purchased tour tickets.

We'd been in the line more than an hour and started coming up with backup plans—I'd drop Micki off to walk up and claim our tickets, meeting up at point A or, as time continued to tick by, we could meet *after* she took the tour, at point B, or I could catch her on the way down from the castle, if I missed our tour. After all, I'd seen the castle multiple times before. She really needed to see it, though, this iconic symbol of Germany, this beloved tourist sight.

But we finally saw a yellow castle looming above us—Hohenschwangau! This was the smaller, more practical castle of Ludwig's parents, the one he grew up in, and it is on the hill next to Neuschwanstein. We were near!

We drove into the tiny village and to the first parking lot. It was closed. The gatekeeper at the closed chain barricade waved us on—along with everyone else creeping by. We rolled slowly by the second parking lot. Full. Closed.

We came to an intersection and turned right, ignoring the next potential parking lot to try our luck at the farthest one. We carefully nosed our way through packs of tourists and other vehicles to get to the fourth lot, at the foot of Hohenschwangau Castle. We inched up the hill, past hordes of pedestrians who couldn't care less that they had taken over the street. The whole place was overrun with visitors.

We advanced toward the lot under the hill with agonizing slowness and saw with excitement that the lot was open. *Oh, please*, we begged—*stay open until we get to the front of the line!* Wonder of wonders, it did, and we paid our 5 euros to enter. The worker indicated that our best luck for finding a free space was straight ahead and to the back, up against the cliff beneath the yellow castle, but Micki had spied a potential spot in the little lot section off at a hard right next to the entrance, pretty much behind us there at the gate.

I asked the guy whether that spot was too small for us, and he said to go ahead and try it. I cranked the steering wheel to pull a tight U-turn, and we approached the opening. It took about a 9-point turn to get in, and we upset the warning system in the car by getting too close on all sides, at one time or another, but we wedged ourselves into the spot! The car's safety system dinged, warning us that the hedge in front was too close, but I told it to be quiet, and we turned the car off to emerge victorious.

We walked down the hill to get our tickets, bypassing a couple hundred people waiting in *their* line to buy *their* tickets. It pays to order ahead. We breezed right to the front of the line at the window to pick up reserved tickets. I'm sure hundreds of people hated us on the spot. We had to wait behind the people who were standing at the window, but that was it. We were next. Then a couple of women entered at a side door and tried to horn in in front of us. We were not in the mood for that.

"Sind Sie zusammen?" I asked, ("Are you together?"), gesturing to the people in front of us being served.

"Nein."

"Wir warten hier," I said, ("We're waiting here."), indicating our line (of us). Fortunately, a worker headed off a confrontation by gesturing us to a side office where we were immediately waited on (so we could ignore the interlopers), and we left.

We looked for the bus next, to get a ride to the top, as we thought we would like to do based on travel guidebook advice. I knew from painful experience that the walk to the top was a real killer. But the line for bus tickets, zigzagging through cattle chutes, was long and packed, too. More than 100 people stood there, we quickly calculated. We didn't want to wait for that mess, so we started hiking up, up, up the curved drive that hugged the hillside, up to the castle.

Oh. My. God.

The paved drive just kept going up and onward, unrelentingly higher. Every once in a while, I stopped to take some pictures, to catch my breath, as much as anything. (What a charming little brook! I want a picture of that!) Micki kept charging ahead better than I did. When had I devolved into such poor shape?? I had thought we were better matched than that, but obviously not. Micki was coming off as a finely tuned athlete next to my gasps and wheezes. At times, we had to step aside to allow the teams of horses to pull their carriage loads past us. That was yet another way to ascend the mountain. We felt sorry for the beasts of burden, for the uphill work they had to do, not just hauling themselves up the mountainside—as we did—but pulling carriages and people, as well. We also had to keep our eyes open to dodge the significant droppings they had left on the road. (Micki had a bad history with manure.)

There were crowds of people, masses, heading up, all struggling to some degree. It took at least 30 minutes to climb up. A painful 30 minutes. I was *dying* when I got there. We, of course, visited the bathroom that awaited us at the top.

If we'd had time, we would have liked to visit the Marienbrücke before our tour. That's the slender-looking bridge that spans a deep gorge a short walk from the castle. But it was too late for that. We didn't want to have *any* risk of missing our tour after all the trouble we'd had getting here. So we delayed our visit to the bridge and hung around the castle, ate snacks, read tourist pamphlets, and watched the information board that listed which group was gathering now, which group was next, and which was the one after that. (Each group had a specific time and tour number.)

One of the benches along the courtyard where we were waiting opened up, so we plonked down to rest our weary legs. A British lady from Hampton sat down next to us and started chatting. She and her husband had been at Neuschwanstein since eight in the morning.

"Our hotel warned us to get here early, because it gets so busy."

She had taken the bus up to the bridge area (as Micki and I had wanted to), and then walked downhill from there to the castle.

"We had to wait an hour and fifteen minutes to get our bus tickets, and standing that long was murder on my bad knees! We're going to take a carriage ride back down the hill." After our lonely visit to France, where we couldn't get the dog catcher to talk with us, Micki and I were happily at home chatting with strangers in Germany.

Our tour number appeared at the top of the sign by the entrance, so we went to the turnstile and fed our tickets through. Our group soon gathered, and our guide, who looked like he was about fifteen years old and moved like a sloth, led us to the building. He did not speak loudly, often did not project to the audience, and was often hard to hear or understand. Basically, he wasn't a very good guide.

In the first room after we climbed some stairs, in a kind of welcoming hall, our guide started telling us about the castle, and a young Japanese boy had to be shushed because he was making too much noise. The same boy had to be reprimanded in the last room of the tour for pulling on the ropes that kept visitors from wandering to the wrong part of the room. There were a surprising number of instances on this trip of Japanese tourists being neither quiet nor polite, as I had thought was their traditional reputation.

The dramatic, soaring castle offered plentiful stairs for us. As if the haul up the hill hadn't been enough of a strain, we had quite the thigh workout inside, too. We went through the few rooms tourists are allowed in—the one I liked the most was Ludwig's bedroom, with the elaborately carved bed that reportedly took 14 woodcarvers four and a half years to complete. Unfortunately for Ludwig, he had very few opportunities to use that bed, because Neuschwanstein was not completed during his short life. He lived in it only 172 days.

While Linderhof Castle paid homage to the Sun King, Neuschwanstein celebrated the operas of Wagner, with walls decorated with scenes from *Lohengrin*, *Tristan and Isolde*, *Parsifal*, and others. Near the end of the tour, we reached the Singers' Hall. Here we learned that one of the main architectural influences on the design of Neuschwanstein had been the Wartburg Castle, where Martin Luther had found refuge from persecutors and first translated the New Testament into German. I had never been to that fortress, but I'd imagined it as plain and hardy—like Martin Luther—not gilded and gaudy. But the Singers' Hall, so bright and Byzantine, was consciously modeled on the Festival Hall at Wartburg, so clearly there was more pomp going on there than I had realized.

Finally, at the end of the tour, we went *down* stairs. We had to pass through two gift shops and the kitchen, loaded with copper objects, before we could exit the building. We did spend a little time in the second little gift shop, crammed with customers and merchandise, so Micki could buy a couple of books. Then we escaped the crowded castle and followed the signs to the Marienbrücke (the "Maria Bridge"). The trek was ungodly uphill again. At least we had to stop along the way to take pictures of the castle and across the valley to where Hohenschwangau and our car were. The trail was very crowded—Germany's top tourist attraction was pulling them in on this day!

We finally dragged ourselves up more of that mountain, past the bus drop-off area to the bridge, where we faced a mass of Japanese tourists sprinkled with Germans and others waiting to get out on the narrow span, where they could take unobstructed photos of the castle across the gorge. I stopped in my tracks. The bridge itself was wall to wall with people. When I'd been there 25 years before, we'd simply walked out on the bridge to get the view back to the castle at the top of the cliff. My expectation that we'd do so again was pure fantasy, as distant from the ugly reality before us as Ludwig's dream world had been.

From the back of the line, it looked like a tour group was waiting to gather together, as they do, so we forged ahead at the side of the pack. Near the front, I heard a German woman mutter something about why wait in line if others were just going to push ahead like that. Oh. . . . Well. . . . That changed the picture. I couldn't face being jammed in so tight on the bridge—especially if we'd jumped the queue—so I told Micki to go ahead without me, and I'd wait farther back.

It took her longer than we expected to get out onto the bridge, snap some pictures, and get back. She said it was crazy out there. Some of the wooden planks "gave" with the weight on them, and there were two German youth who thought it was great fun to jump on them. She was afraid the flooring was going to break, and it would be a long, long fall to the bottom of the gorge.

We left the bridge and started back on the paved path down the mountain toward the castle. While I may have labored on the way *up* the mountain, I did great when I had gravity on my side. From the bridge, we high-tailed it back down, through the crowds, dodging dawdlers left and right. We passed all those irritating people who shuffled along enjoying the view and who just got in our way. We had more driving to do!

We made it back down to the castle but soldiered on, trucking down the hill. The masses venturing up had thinned but still they came, even though it must have been 4:30 or close to 5:00 by then. From the castle down, only one person passed us, a young man walking so fast that he looked like a race walker. (Well, *he* looked ridiculous. Not cool like us.)

We got to our car—there were far fewer pedestrians to shove through at this time—and got ready to leave. A woman pulling into the lot rolled down her window and asked us whether we were leaving. (Even late in the day, new arrivals were desperate for parking spots. Or maybe she wasn't a new arrival. Maybe she'd been circling the parking lots for hours looking for an opening.) I confirmed that we were. So after about six or seven turns, routinely setting off the various alarms in our car by our proximity to other vehicles, we were out of there.

Of course, at the end of the workday, we had the horrible traffic backup in *reverse* from our arrival, along the street as we *left* the castle, the same street we'd had to wait on going in. We eventually made it through the line and onto the main road to the nearest town, Füssen. On the far side of Füssen (not that we thought we were heading out of town on the right road), we saw a gas station with a sign out front: "Buy a *Vignette*." I remembered then, *Oh, cripes, we need one of those,* and I quickly pulled in to take care of it, since we would need the toll sticker for our stay in Austria.

Then it was clear sailing on our road, wherever it might be leading us to, and when we got to a bridge crossing a river, we recognized it as the one we had crossed earlier and realized that we had inadvertently found the right road back out of town. It was an easy drive to Austria despite all the twists and turns, up and down, until we *finally* got to the *Autobahn*. (Good thing I was driving, or I would have gotten motion sick.) We were lucky not to have to deal with any rain since it had sprinkled on us when we left Linderhof. Once on the *Autobahn*, it was a short jaunt to Innsbruck.

We successfully followed our driving instructions into the city center, right to the street where we should find our hotel. The street where our hotel was located was a boulevard—trees in the middle, nice and broad, but unfortunately it was all torn up with construction. Sighing, we went down one side of the boulevard, but didn't see our hotel anywhere. It was the kind of nebulous situation we excelled at getting lost in. And we did have a few errant turns but eventually we parked in a garage and, walking, found the back entrance to our hotel and checked in. The nice young woman who was working at the desk asked whether we wanted a parking spot behind the hotel. It was only 10 euros instead of the 16 it would cost us in the parking ramp, so we took it. We jammed our luggage into the tiny hotel lift and went to the third floor to unload in our room. Then we ran and moved our car.

Now we were safely settled into Innsbruck and could finally relax. I'd wanted to come here so Micki could see its beautiful setting amid the snow-capped mountains of the high Alps. The city sits in a valley between peaks. It has been populated since the Stone Age, at the spot where an important trade route crossed the Inn River on a bridge—*Brücke*—which led to the name Innsbruck.

Just nineteen miles to the south is the vital Brenner Pass and access to Italy. Innsbruck is surrounded by peaks up to 8,900 feet, with enough snow and height and ski runs that it hosted the winter Olympics in 1964 and 1976. (I've stood at the top of the ski jump—in summer. Just beyond the landing area lies a cemetery, which I thought must be a sobering sight when getting ready to make a leap.) For sheer natural beauty, the area around Innsbruck is hard to beat.

When the sun is out.

The sun was not out when we were there. In fact, the skies hung low and threatened more rain. If we couldn't see the mountains around Innsbruck, we could at least view the city's greatest tourist attraction—the famous Golden Roof, or *Goldenes Dachl*.

This was a three-story balcony that was built in the late 1400s for Emperor Maximilian as a royal box, so he and his entourage could view the events that took place in the square below. The roof topping the balcony is covered with 2,657 gold-plated copper tiles (according to www.innsbruck. info). We joined the hordes of Japanese tourists gawking at it. With the leaden skies, the tiles did not gleam and shine as they normally might have, and Micki was underwhelmed. To be honest, even in the best weather, it's hard to believe that this roof is Innsbruck's biggest tourist attraction, Emperor Maximilian or not, even if it *is* 600 years old.

After eating, we took a quick turn down the main pedestrian drag, the broad arcaded Herzog-Friedrich-Strasse, and hurried back to our room as it started to sprinkle. In our room, we had good Internet, so I was able to catch up on Facebook, including posting a picture from Linderhof that morning:

Cloudy, but no rain! Wonderful visit at Linderhof castle. Neuschwanstein was an overcrowded nightmare, but we did manage to get in. My, how things change in 25 years! Hiked at least three miles straight up. We may not be able to move tomorrow.

I pulled out my surprise this evening, a one-pound bag of Twizzlers I'd brought for us. We both had several pieces. To our credit, the pack lasted us almost to the end of our trip, pretty good for a couple of Twizzler addicts.

Cleaning up for the night, we had to adjust to the glass-walled bathroom in the corner of our room. We were used to the all-glass showers we'd been using, but this was the first time the bathroom walls themselves were made of glass. It was mostly frosted glass, clear only in sections higher up than body height, so a person would have to deliberately invade another person's privacy, but it did take us aback at first.

I read through my Facebook news feed for the day while Micki showered. There were numerous comments and tributes to Robin Williams, and eventually it became clear that he had died, that he'd committed suicide. While Micki and I had been dipping in and out of King Ludwig's life of Romantic fantasy for the day, much of the world had been mourning the loss of a comic genius. In true Ludwigian fashion, we felt quite cut off from the rest of the world. And like Ludwig's tragic life, our fantasy day ended with a sudden death, this time clearly self-inflicted.

Excerpt from

French Twist: A Refreshingly Frank Travel Memoir by a Modern American Puritain

Cheap, trashy, touristy—that's how many see the Latin Quarter these days (and maybe always have), but I have a certain fondness for it. Maybe it's because students and immigrants congregate there, making it, on the one hand, one of the more vibrant sections of Paris, and, on the other, relatively affordable compared to the many swish districts in that posh city. In any case, when it was time to do large-scale souvenir shopping, we headed to the Latin Quarter, and it didn't disappoint. Same with the cheap eats. I was sad to observe that the area was noticeably dirty and littered when Micki and I were there, in a way I did not recall from when I had stayed there before with my grandmother, on my first trip to France.

I had been the unofficial travel agent for that earlier trip, scouting locations not just for the two of us, but for my sister and her family, who would need a room for four to house them. Thank God for online searches, where I was able to quickly rule out most Paris hotels right off the bat. (Old buildings. Small rooms. Few quads.) Further limited by considering only affordable hotels, and centrally-located ones, and, ideally, those with breakfast included, we soon ended up in the Latin Quarter, just minutes from Notre-Dame Cathedral and even closer to a couple of easy métro stops.

The hotel did not have an elevator, as so many don't, so I made sure to tell the manager in advance that I would be there with my elderly grandmother, who really was not in terrific shape, but probably not as decrepit as I made her sound. I suffered a pang or two of guilt later when we saw our fellow hotel guest, a shrunken and bent old woman in Indian-looking clothes, shuffling up and down the many stairs to her room on deformed and swollen feet. Nonetheless, I was well aware that climbing stairs multiple times a day would be an ordeal for my grandmother, so I was grateful to find that we had been placed in the one bedroom on ground level.

This was the hotel owned and run by Paul, the Frenchman who had nothing whatsoever to do with the Paul I would deliver to the world about nine months later. Sure, our room location just across a small hall from the reception desk would certainly allow my husband to speculate, should he choose to, and should he conveniently ignore the fact that I was with my grandmother the whole time and never exchanged more than a *bonjour* with the innkeeper. And if that weren't enough, I had my brother-in-law chaperoning me, as became clear later in the week.

We were served breakfast each day in this hotel, a continental fare of hot drink, orange juice, a partial baguette, butter, jam, and fruit cocktail. We also had full access to a compact ground-floor kitchen, where French families sometimes prepared their evening meals. The breakfast room also served as a gathering place or lounge, and our group frequently met up there to make plans, compare experiences, and eat our take-out or grocery-store suppers together.

A highlight of the breakfast room was the large row of windows that looked out to the street. We could watch the traffic and pedestrians, observe the students climbing the spiral staircase to enter the building across the street (I think it was an architectural school), and watch other tourists loaded with luggage bump their way down the sidewalk, looking down to consult their instructions and then looking up for building numbers. By far the most fun, though, was the time a parking spot opened up right before the large central window, providing ongoing entertainment during that particular breakfast room visit.

The car that had left must have been wedged into the spot, or else it was one of those tiny Smart micro-cars, because the open parking space was far too small to accommodate even a compact vehicle. But that didn't stop people from trying! Driver after driver screeched to a halt when they saw the opening, backed in, tried to swing the front in, to no avail. Some drivers realized after one attempt that physics would not allow their car to fit, but others were more determined. They would twist around in their seats, spin their steering wheels this way and that, but all for naught. Even with the accepted French practice of actually nudging the cars both fore and aft, they could not make their cars fit. Eventually, all roared off, with those who had tried the longest being the most visibly disgusted. No one succeeded on our watch. It was most amusing.

I had actually read about parking problems in Paris before we embarked on that first trip, along with the need for pedestrians to be on guard for drivers who would not respect crosswalks (which would be most of them). Much of my preparation, though, focused on learning about the countless social differences between Americans and French people. Different ways of eating, greeting, shopping, and interacting in general.

One of the differences that had impressed me most deeply was what American expatriate Polly Platt (author of *French or Foe*) called "The Look," a sexually charged, sweeping head-to-toe visual caress that is supposed to be a compliment to the woman receiving it. Coming from a fairly Puritan background (literally—the family genealogist says we go back to an indentured servant on the Mayflower, one George Soule), it all sounded too intense for my taste, but given my down-to-earth, completely Plain Jane looks, there was little chance I would have to deal with it. I had shared this French cultural information with my relatives before we left, and my grandmother and I, at least, were curious to see whether we'd see any evidence of the fabled French sexuality, any instances of The Look.

One morning, as we readied ourselves for the day, I rolled my hair up into a French twist and secured it with a large, curved, claw-like comb. This is a style that looks achingly glamorous on Audrey Hepburn when she is in Paris with Cary Grant in the movie *Charade*, but considerably less so on me. Sturdy, I could be called. Practical. But never glamorous. I well knew I could never be mistaken for a Frenchwoman by the way I dressed, moved, or acted, but I could at least go with an authentic hairstyle.

"You know, you can really see the gray at the sides when you wear your hair like that," my sister informed me, in that helpful way siblings have. I didn't care. I didn't have that much gray. My hair was out of the way, it was relatively neat looking, and, in my head, at least, the style lent me a wisp—a bare hint—of sophistication. We left the building to venture forth for the day.

My grandmother and I turned to the right outside the hotel, heading to the nearest métro stop. We chatted happily with each other, and when we met a Frenchman on the sidewalk, I saw him staring at me intently. Quickly, I dropped my eyes.

"Did you see that?!" my grandmother whispered urgently after he had passed. "That man gave you The Look!"

I blushed and thought, indeed, as Polly Platt had written, there was no mistaking the penetrating Look when it was directed at a person. I guess it just went to show that, as Platt noted, you didn't have to be young or gorgeous to merit a Look. Or, as we might put it where I'm from, it takes all kinds. It was the kind of look that would easily be considered rude back home—far too intrusive—but here I was supposed to consider it a compliment. It just flustered and bewildered me.

So many things in France were backwards from what we were used to. Social rules are all twisted, turned around from those in the United States and most other Western countries. White is black in France, and black is white. Don't smile unless there's a good reason to. Don't make eye contact. Don't say hello to people on the street. Don't invade their space at all, physically, visually, audibly. Don't chat with strangers. Don't talk about work, family, health, money. Don't mix social levels. Don't flaunt wealth or wear flashy items or brag. Do be cold and reserved. Do be rude and snub people if they're not following the rules—that's part of being polite in France.

The rules were as confusing and scrambled as the crazy, mixed-up picture pieces on my son's Rubic's cube—upside down, sideways, on the wrong side of my "social experience" cube altogether. Sure, it all made sense and snapped into place if you knew what you were doing, what was going on, but we didn't. We were Americans. Friendly, chatty, loud Americans. Worse yet, we were from Iowa, where it is bred into us to greet all we meet with a smile and a hello. Most of us love to talk with strangers. We happily discuss prices. I will say that we didn't flaunt wealth in Paris, but that could be because we didn't *have* wealth. So, yes, I knew about French reserve and privacy, I knew that eye contact and smiles should be avoided with people I didn't know (which was pretty much everyone in the country). It was just so hard not to react naturally!

My pre-trip reading had also informed me that love affairs were common in France, for men and women. Discreet affairs are routine and accepted. Sex is not a big deal or a dirty deed—it's just part of life. I remember reading about a respectable French businesswoman who wrote a book detailing her sexual encounters, often with anonymous strangers in public places, dozens of lovers, known and unknown. While (as I recall, at least) even the French were said to be taken aback by the number of casual sex partners this woman had had, she was not made a pariah. Sex, even extramarital sex or voluminous casual sex, is just another of life's physical appetites. This casual attitude toward sex and fidelity upended the beliefs I'd long been surrounded by and certainly contradicted my own practices. My morals were in conflict with French codes, a clanging, deafening dissonance, but fortunately the clash was purely abstract, at least at this point, and I could ignore it.

Later in our stay, after our sidewalk encounter with The Look, my grandmother and I went to a small supermarket on our way back to our hotel in the evening. After selecting our food and wine, we waited in a long line that stretched back into the last aisle of the store. Speaking quietly with her about the frozen seafood displayed next to us (tiny frozen octopi were visible in a clear bag), I realized that the man in line ahead of us was watching me intently, and we had eye contact (deep, searing, very personal) before I quickly looked away, blushing, I'm sure. That should have been the end of it. But in my discomfort, I occasionally slid a glance in his direction, just to see whether he was still watching. He was, as piercingly as before, his dark eyes locked on mine. My face warmed even more.

As our checkout line advanced past the narrow aisle that had been confining us, it split into two lines for two cashiers. The man went left. I, a practical American, realized that the left line was much shorter than the right, so I also went that way. I continued to talk quietly with my grandmother, studiously ignoring the Frenchman now. Soon he checked out and, to my relief, he left the store. My grandmother and I soon left, as well.

When we exited the building, though, there was the man, standing outside. As we walked down the sidewalk the few blocks to our hotel, the man shadowed us across the narrow street. We went inside our hotel, thinking that was the end of it. But no. From the window of the breakfast room where we met up with the others, I could see the man lounging against the building across the street, smoking a cigarette, waiting. And waiting. And, cigarette tip now glowing in the dusk, still waiting.

My grandmother and I couldn't go to our room, because I didn't want him to see us crossing the hall through the glass hotel entrance and then see our room light up right at the front of the hotel. It was no doubt paranoid of me, but I didn't want him to know we were right there in that street-level room, the one with all the windows across the front of the building. My brother-in-law, a take-charge and protective attorney, wanted to go out and send him on his way, but I asked him not to, because I was sure the man would leave. Eventually, he did, but only after he had waited almost an hour, time we had filled with talking, writing postcards, and calling home on the only phone we could use in the building. That was a lot of cigarettes for him, and a lot of false hope.

By American rules, his pursuit was ridiculous. I'd done nothing to encourage him. I was even out with my grandmother, for Pete's sake! But by French rules? Maybe things weren't so clear-cut. I had returned his look, however briefly, probably smiling a bit with discomfort and embarrassment. I was obviously very aware of him, snatching occasional peeks. I had even followed him into his checkout line, virtually shouting my interest. (At least, this is how I've pieced it together from his perspective.) So he followed me home and waited for me to join him. He was no doubt perplexed why I never did.

Social rules are, indeed, different in France, and I now believed what I had read: eye contact is powerful and can even be the first step to an affair. Maybe I'm flattering myself, but I'm quite sure that, had I wanted a quick affair with a lean brown-eyed Frenchman who chain smoked cigarettes and wore a leather sports-team jacket (white with red and blue), I could have had one.

We made it through the rest of our stay without any more noticeable Looks, which I might be offended about if I were vainer. As it was, I was relieved not to have those smoldering stares directed at me. My staid Midwestern frumpiness could not handle the heat. Instead, my grandmother and I simply enjoyed our visit and, after a week, headed back to real life, where the social rules made sense, where we could smile at people, say hello to strangers, chat to locals as we shopped, and no one locked eyes with the burning strength of a laser.

I must admit, however, that the whole time we were in Paris, I did not see women with gray hair, so maybe my sister was on to something. There were lots of unlikely apricot and auburn tints, but no gray, except on the oldest women and a number of men. I also saw only one other French twist while we were in Paris. It was at the airport and was on an American tourist.

Made in the USA
Monee, IL
24 October 2023